UNLOCKING HUMAN POTENTIAL

Chapter II - Bhagavad Gita (Sankhya Yoga)

Gita Odyssey Book 2

AVANTI KUNDALAIA,
RAJESH RABINDRANATH,
DR. VIKRANT SINGH TOMAR

ISBN 979-8-89673-773-5

With Gratitude to Pujya Swami Swaroopananda

Your gracious foreword blesses this sacred journey, offering guidance and inspiration to the Author Trio and the Project Self Team

With Heartfelt Gratitude to Our Sponsors

Your unwavering generosity and support illuminate this sacred journey, enabling us to share the timeless wisdom of the *Bhagavad Gita* with hearts and minds across the world

CONTENTS

ॐ

Foreword

The Bhagavad Gita is not merely an ancient scripture; it is a timeless manual for life. The Gita's wisdom and practical guidance speaks to every seeker, regardless of their station in life, presenting solutions to life's dilemmas with simplicity and clarity.

I commend the authors on bringing out the second volume of the Gita Odyssey Series. They have undertaken the task of illustrating how the Gita's teachings can be integrated into everyday life. By drawing upon their own lived experiences, they seek to show how the profound truths of the Gita illuminate the path to fulfilling our responsibilities and navigating life's challenges with strength and grace.

Systematic study, combined with practical application, is essential to bringing the Gita's teachings to life. Like Arjuna on the battlefield of Kurukshetra, each one faces moments of doubt and confusion. Like him, one must move beyond intellectual understanding to actively experiment with the teachings and realise their true import in one's life.

To those who turn these pages, may this book inspire you to delve deeper into the teachings of the Gita and, more importantly, to live the Gita. The Gita is not just a philosophy to be pondered over in solitude but a companion in every moment of our journey.

I invoke the blessings of God and Pujya Gurudev Swami Chinmayananda upon all who walk this sacred path of self-discovery and self-mastery. May the eternal light of the Gita guide you to the highest peace and fulfilment.

At His Feet,

Swami Swaroopananda
Global Head, Chinmaya Mission

2 January 2025

Central Chinmaya Mission Trust

Sandeepany Sadhanalaya, Saki Vihar Road, Powai, Mumbai 400 072
E ccmt@chinmayamission.com   W www.chinmayamission.com   T +91-22-2857 2367   F +91-22-2857 3065

Opening Remarks

In a world crammed with constant distractions, emotional turmoil, and an unending race for material success, it is easy to lose sight of what truly matters. Someone who begins to see through this mirage and realizes something glaringly amiss helplessly wonders: *"Is there a way to find clarity, purpose, and enduring peace while still engaging fully with life?"* The **Bhagavad Gita declares a decisive yes!** And here is where an ordinary human becomes a seeker.

Welcome to Project Self's second offering in the **Gita Odyssey series—Unlocking Human Potential.** This book takes you on an **immersive journey through Chapter II of the Bhagavad Gita,** exploring its teachings verse by verse and uncovering its profound wisdom in a contemporary context. Whether you are a **curious beginner,** a **seasoned seeker,** or someone **juggling a fast-paced life but yearning for meaning,** this book is designed to meet you where you are.

Chapter II-Sankhya Yoga: The Heart of the Bhagavad Gita

Chapter II, titled **Sankhya Yoga,** is often called the **'Index Chapter' of the Bhagavad Gita.** Just as an index offers a glimpse into the contents of a book, this chapter provides a **bird's-eye view of the entire Gita,** summarizing its key teachings while laying down the foundation for the journey ahead.

Two fundamental aspects of human life addressed in Chapter II:

1. **Elevating Our Goals:** Krishna urges us to aim higher, redefine success beyond fleeting material pursuits, and set our sights on the **ultimate human goal—Moksha (liberation)**.

2. **Empowered Action:** Knowing how to live and act aligned with those goals is equally important. Krishna introduces **Karma Yoga**—the art of **skillful action**—and **Jnana Yoga**—the path of **knowledge**—to help us navigate life's complexities without losing inner peace.

Through Krishna's **revolutionary dialogue with Arjuna**, this chapter dispels the myth that spirituality advocates an escape from the world. Instead, it **empowers us to fulfill our responsibilities with inner poise and efficiency**, teaching us how to **thrive in the world with wisdom, clarity, and resilience**

Connecting Arjuna's Story with Our Own

The chapter opens with a vulnerable Arjuna, paralyzed by emotional turmoil, slumped on his chariot floor. His surrender to Krishna in *Shloka 7* marks a pivotal turning point—one that mirrors the moment in every seeker's life when humility replaces resistance, and a readiness to learn emerges.

Krishna, calm and smiling, begins his teaching not with battlefield strategies but with the highest spiritual truth: the eternal nature of the *Atma* (Self) and the transient nature of worldly identities, including the physical body. This profound teaching serves as the foundation upon which the rest of the Gita stands.

To re-familiarize Arjuna with his mortal identity and associated duty, Krishna introduces another vital facet of the Gita: *SVADHARMA*. The immortal knowledge of the Bhagavad Gita was handed to a warrior in crisis on the battlefield, emphasizing its uncontested utility for every one of us. Act we all must - and act we all will. But what action must we choose, and with what attitude must we execute it? Krishna succinctly but profoundly touches upon some central ideas of *Karma Yoga* - the Yoga of Action. Krishna teaches us through Arjuna the art of selfless action that skillfully transforms ordinary action into a path of inner growth.

When Arjuna's curiosity peaks, he asks, *"How does one established in Self-knowledge live and act in the world?"* Krishna's answer, encapsulated in the celebrated *Sthita-Prajna Lakshana*, not only amalgamates the secular and spiritual aspects of human existence but serves as both a goal and a guide for seekers. Through captivating poetry animating life's highest ideals, he enlightens us about the humanly achievable possibility of living with unwavering wisdom, peace, and clarity amidst life's storms.

Krishna concludes this chapter by presenting to us through Arjuna—the ultimate destination of *Self-realization*. He assures us that this masterfully designed odyssey is the only path out of a binding and sorrowful existence. It leads not only to material success and spiritual enlightenment but ultimately culminates in liberation from the repetitive cycles of birth and death

Core Themes of Chapter II: A Transformative Blueprint

The timeless teachings of Chapter II are directly relevant to our modern lives. Some of the key themes explored in this chapter include:

- **The Root of Human Suffering:** Why are we perpetually dissatisfied, even when surrounded by abundance?
- **The Highest Goal of Life:** Redefining success beyond material achievements.
- **Karma Yoga:** The art of performing with efficiency and focus, preparing the mind for higher possibilities and inner transformation.

- **Jnana Yoga:** Understanding one's true identity (*Atma*) as the source of enduring happiness.
- **Svadharma:** Performing one's duty in alignment with one's nature and role in society.
- **The Ideal of Sthita-Prajna:** The characteristics of one who has attained the highest goal of life.

Why is Chapter II titled *Sankhya Yoga?*

Sankhya in this context refers to the **knowledge of the *Atma* (true Self)**, the clear vision of our **eternal identity beyond the body and mind**. While the chapter also explores *Karma Yoga* and practical wisdom, the **ultimate purpose** of these teachings is to **lead the seeker to Self-knowledge (*Jnana Yoga*)**, making *Sankhya* the **core focus** of this chapter.

Why *Unlocking Human Potential*?

The title of our book reflects the transformative power embedded in Chapter II. Most people live far below their true potential, limited by fears, anxieties, and misguided goals. Krishna's teachings in this chapter call us **to rise above these limitations** and discover the boundless possibilities that lie within.

Imagine aiming for a small hill when a majestic mountain awaits you. This chapter asks us to set our vision on the **highest peak of human potential** and equips us with the tools to climb it—step by step, with confidence and clarity.

Krishna does not merely offer lofty ideals; he provides a **practical roadmap** to achieve them. By being introduced to the principles of *Karma Yoga*, *Jnana Yoga*, and *Svadharma* (one's intrinsic nature), we realize there is a time-tested method for aligning our actions with our higher goals, reducing the mental toll of daily challenges, and cultivating inner peace amidst external chaos.

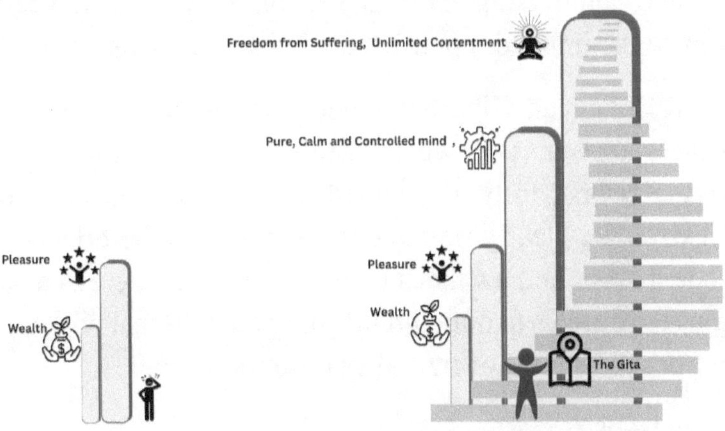

Fig: Unlocking Potential: The Gita Elevates Goals and Guides the Way

From Mortality to Immortality

At its heart, Chapter II is not just a philosophical discourse but an answer to humanity's deepest cry for liberation from sufferings, echoed timelessly in a wide array of spiritual literature. A heart-wrenching stanza in Adi Shankaracharya's *Bhaja Govindam*, attributed to one of his disciples, Nityanātha, pleads:

punarapi jananaṃ punarapi maraṇaṃ
punarapi jananī jaṭhare śayanam |
iha saṃsāre bahu dustāre
kṛpayā'pāre pāhi murāre ‖ 22 ‖

Again birth, again death,
Again, lying in the mother's womb!
It is indeed hard to cross this boundless ocean of saṃsāra,
O Krishna! By your infinite compassion,
Please liberate me from this ongoing transmigratory cycle.

Isn't this our collective predicament? Let alone freeing ourselves from endless cycles of birth and death – while alive, we want to live in peace and achieve our individual goals successfully. Yet, we are caught in stress-imbued repetitive cycles that deny us both.

The entire Bhagavad Gita, but especially Chapter II, in a nutshell, is Krishna's answer, as it were, to this human cry for help! For in it *Murari,* Krishna, fully acknowledges the incessant onslaughts of mortal existence, clearly points out what causes the affectation and diffidence thereof and awakens us to the fact that there is a way out. He begins to rouse us to our own infinite potential that will cheerfully take us from the shores of mortality to immortality.

Why This Book?

This book is not merely a commentary; it is a **study guide, a companion, and a practical manual** for anyone seeking to understand the relevance of the Bhagavad Gita in their lives. While the *First Step Into Bhagavad Gita* familiarized us with our inner chaos, this book assures us that there is a way out. It speaks not just to the intellect but also to the heart, offering profound wisdom while keeping the conversation relatable and contemporary.

Arduously compiled with the **author-trio's collective study, contemplation, application**, and **experience**, this book bridges the gap between **ancient wisdom and modern materiality**. Each shloka is explored in depth, breaking down complex philosophical ideas into clear, actionable insights that you can apply immediately.

Whether you are facing personal dilemmas, seeking clarity in your professional life, or simply longing for some semblance of inner peace, this book offers timeless solutions to modern challenges.

An Invitation to the Reader

Krishna assures us, *"Even a little practice of this wisdom can free you from great fear."* But "practice" is the key. This book is not meant for

passive reading. Reflect, question, and integrate its teachings into your daily life.

With open hearts, let us embark on this **transformative journey together**.

Let us begin.

—Project Self

Exploring Sankhya Yoga: Verse-by-Verse Journey

SHLOKA 1: A PORTRAIT OF HUMAN CHALLENGES

सञ्जय उवाच -

तं तथा कृपयाऽऽविष्टम् अश्रुपूर्णाकुलेक्षणम् ।

विषीदन्तमिदं वाक्यम् उवाच मधुसूदनः ॥1॥

sañjaya uvāca -

taṁ tathā kṛpayā"viṣṭam aśrupūrṇākulēkṣaṇam |

viṣīdantamidaṁ vākyam uvāca madhusūdanaḥ ||1||

Translation:

Sanjaya observed (*uvāca*):

To him [Arjuna] (*tvam*), who was overwhelmed (*avistam*) by deep compassion (*krpayā*) and saddled with sorrow (*visidantam*), whose eyes were brimming with tears and distress (*asrupurnakuleksanam*), Krishna (*Madhusudanah*) spoke (*uvaca*) the following (*idam*) words (*vakyam*)

[Sankya Yoga: 2.1]

At a Glance: Capturing the Spirit of the Shloka

Sanjaya continues to describe the unfolding scene at Kurukshetra to Dhritarashtra. A teary-eyed Arjuna, gripped by compassion and sorrow, is visibly distressed, completely incapacitated, and in desperate need of intervention. This chapter marks the commencement of the transformative dialogue between Krishna and Arjuna, which the world reveres as the Bhagavad Gita.

Commentary:

The opening shloka of the second chapter of the Bhagavad Gita marks the initiation of the life-transforming conversation between immortal Wisdom and mortal frailty. It dramatically illuminates the quintessence of the universal human experience. It captures a moment of profound inner turmoil that resonates with the heart of every person at life's crossroads. Arjuna, a warrior on the brink of battle, is overwhelmed with the same conflict we all face when confronted with challenging decisions that shake the very core of our beliefs and values. Emotionally besieged, intellectually torn, and physically incapacitated, Arjuna represents the complexity of our human condition— wherein strength falters in the throes of emotional vulnerabilities and decisions waver when confronted with moral doubt.

In the concluding moments of the first chapter, Arjuna is portrayed as '*sokasamvignamānasah*'—his heart heavy with the weight of sorrow. As we transition into the second chapter, Sanjaya expands this vivid portrayal, depicting Arjuna as a figure overpowered by a torrent of emotions.

'*Kripayāviṣṭam*' (engulfed by pity and compassion) shows he is rendered utterly motionless by shackling sentiments. '*Viṣīdantam*' (drowning in sorrow) and '*asrupūrṇa*' (with eyes full of tears) paint a picture of a warrior submerged in the waves of desolation, with '*akula īkṣaṇam*' (anxious eyes) reflecting utter anxiety and stress. Sanjaya's vivid description of Arjuna resonates with each of us facing life's inevitable battles. In Arjuna's paralysis, we see our own helplessness in and through life's sternest tests. His plight is a testament to our shared human journey.

Arjuna's overwhelming compassion, '*kṛpayāviṣṭam*,' often mistaken for a commendable trait, actually signifies the lack of emotional intelligence. Feeling is not the problem; our feelings must be tempered by clarity and wisdom. The Bhagavad Gita teaches us that emotions, even positive ones, should not cloud our judgment. It guides us step-by-step to cultivate this balance—to learn to harness our emotions so that they may serve us rather than enslave us as we navigate the complex odyssey of life.

The Bhagavad Gita spotlights our shared human plight, where unpredictable and often surprising twists and turns through life's unfoldment compel us to confront our desires and fears of uncertainty. The battle Arjuna faces represents the daily battles within us. At every unexpected twist and turn, overwhelmed by circumstance, clouded by emotions, and paralyzed by indecision, life asks us the crucial question: Are we equipped with the necessary wisdom to live our lives effectively?

At the start of the second chapter, Krishna, having been a silent observer so far, is poised to address Arjuna's crisis. His patient listening, characteristic of a seasoned counselor, a close friend, or even a well-wisher, teaches us the importance of empathy and understanding in resolving personal turmoil.

Mark how Krishna's abject silence gives Arjuna the space to unburden himself entirely of his confusion and overwhelming grief. Wisdom cannot be received by an incapacitated intellect that stands hostage to a mind in turmoil. Even though Krishna has not spoken a word throughout chapter one - he has taught us the greatest lesson of compassionately holding space for another as they unleash their inner tempest.

Sanjaya refers to Krishna as *Madhusudhana* (the slayer of the demon Madhu), symbolizing his ability to conquer both external and internal adversaries. External adversaries mean the enemy that stands on the side of *Adharma*—a subtle warning to Dhritarashtra of the inevitable annihilation of his evil-minded sons. Inner adversaries refer to Arjuna's binding attachments and fears thereof. *Madhusudhana*, the conqueror of outer and inner demons, is undoubtedly the ideal mentor, reassuring us of his ability to guide humanity through existential challenges.

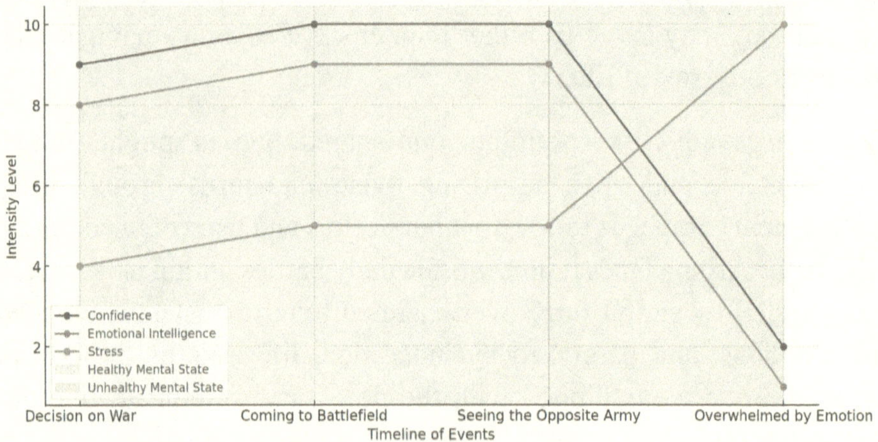

Fig: Arjuna's Emotional State Transition

Reflective Prompt

Reflect on a time when your emotions overwhelmed your judgment. In hindsight, did your impulsive actions turn out to be in your best interest?

When fear clouds the mind and chaos reigns, the quiet voice within—Krishna's whisper—guides us from confusion to clarity

SHLOKA 2: KRISHNA'S STRATEGY FOR EMOTIONAL RESILIENCE

श्री भगवानुवाच -

कुतस्त्वा कश्मलमिदं विषमे समुपस्थितम् |

अनार्यजुष्टमस्वर्ग्यम् अकीर्तिकरमर्जुन ||2||

śrī bhagavān uvāca -
kutastvā kaśmalamidaṁ viṣamē samupasthitam |
anāryajuṣṭamasvargyam akīrtikaramarjuna ||2||

Translation:

Bhagavan Krishna Said:

O Arjuna, where (***kutaḥ***) has this weakness (***kaśmalam***) come upon you at such a critical moment (***viṣame samupasthitam***)? This behavior is unbecoming (***anāryajuṣṭam***) of a noble person and will neither lead to heaven (***asvargyam***) nor bring honor (***akīrtikaram***), but only disgrace.
[Sankya Yoga: 2.2]

At a Glance: Capturing the Spirit of the Shloka

Krishna directly challenges Arjuna's sudden weakness and emotional breakdown at such a critical moment, stressing that this behavior is unworthy of a noble person and will only lead to disgrace, not honor. He reminds Arjuna that yielding to despair will not bring him happiness, success, or lasting fame. Krishna's words are a wake-up call, urging Arjuna to rise above his emotions and act with the strength and determination befitting a warrior.

Commentary:

In the heart of the battlefield, the air is thick with anticipation and the weight of duty is bearing down heavily on all present there. Foreseeing, as it were, the untoward consequences of Arjuna's emotional breakdown at the zero hours of battle, Krishna leaves aside spiritual sermons and hollers a call to action instead. Every student of the Bhagavad Gita wonders why. After all, Arjuna's gut-wrenching pleas are potent enough to move the sternest of hearts. We are sure they must have touched yours, too.

Think.

Arjuna, completely stranded by acute stress from his paralyzing sentiments, is in a state where compassionate, inspirational discourses, however resounding, would find no fertile ground to take root. Picture an athlete frozen at the opening whistle. The initial response of the coach must match the intensity of the emotional turmoil and what is at stake. Krishna's words serve as a clarion call, akin to a seasoned coach's stern pep talk before a life-defining performance aimed at reigniting the warrior spirit within Arjuna.

Kirshna's firm retort can also be likened to a strategic emotional intervention to jolt the lead commander back to reality. Picture this scenario: a military commander momentarily falters on the eve of a decisive operation. Their commander-in-chief steps in, not with gentle reassurances, but with a potent reminder of their role, the importance of the mission, and the stakes at hand. It is a psychological maneuver designed to activate the leader's intrinsic motivation and trained reflexes — a scenario mirrored in sports when a coach calls a timeout to refocus the team, using tactical language and a tone imbued with urgency and conviction. Such is the potency of Krishna's initial words to Arjuna — they are meant to resonate with the warrior's heart, stirring him from despondency to determination.

However, it is crucial to recognize that Krishna's stern approach is explicitly tailored to Arjuna's role as a warrior and his current emotional state. Had the distressed been a child, or a bereaved, the strategy would have been markedly different—employing soft words, a gentle embrace, or a reassuring kiss to soothe and comfort. This discernment in response underscores a profound understanding of human nature, emphasizing that while the call to action must be unyielding for a warrior like Arjuna, the essence of care and comfort must always adapt to the needs of the conflicted heart, bearing in mind the nuanced approach required in addressing the vast spectrum of human emotions.

Having said this, take yourself back to many instances in your life where you have seen a person (in real life or on the reel) in frantic, emotional, illogical distress - screaming, shouting, ranting, raving, and even threatening to do something completely irrational and especially detrimental in the heat of the moment. Has not the first human-to-human response in such scenarios been a stern shake of the shoulders or even a slap across the face just to recalibrate the person back to their senses?

At the onset of the second chapter, Krishna's direct address to Arjuna is both startling and poignant. It comes as a surprise to the warrior prince and the reader. Krishna, the personification of divine wisdom, questions Arjuna with a tone that cuts through the tension of the battlefield: *"kutastvā kaśmalamidaṁ viṣame samupasthitam?"*—

wherefrom to you, this disgrace, this cowardice, in such a critical moment? He uses the word '*kaśmalam*,' encapsulating all that is ignoble and disgraceful, a stark contrast to the valor expected of a warrior. The term '*viṣame samupasthitam*' signifies the criticality of the situation, where standing firm is not just expected but demanded by duty.

The term '*anāryajuṣṭam*' is pivotal, as Krishna rebukes the attitude unbecoming of '*ārya*'—not in the sense of race or creed but as a measure of character. An '*ārya*' is one who is noble, a person of honor and strength.

It is to be noted that, in the context of the Bhagavad Gita, *ārya*' does not indicate race; it epitomizes a noble-minded individual. This Sanskrit term has been historically misconstrued, particularly in Western scholarship, that propagated the notion of an 'Aryan race,' which was later appropriated by ideologies like those of Nazi Germany. However, these misinterpretations have no basis in the actual usage of the word within Sanskrit literature or in the teachings of the Buddha, where '*ārya*' consistently signifies nobility of spirit.

In Sanskrit dramas and classical texts, '*ārya*' is used to address a person of distinguished virtue — 'My dear *ārya*, noble-minded person'. Similarly, Buddha described his core teachings as the '*ārya-satyāni*' or the Noble Truths, further reinforcing the association of '*ārya*' with nobleness rather than race.

The following Sanskrit verse provides a clear definition of '*ārya*'.

"kartavyam ācaran karma, akartavyam anācaran |
tiṣṭhati prakṛtā cāre, saḥ vaḥ āryaḥ iti smṛtaḥ ||"

It states that an '*ārya*' is one who performs what is to be done (*kartavyam ācaran karma*), avoiding what should not be done (*akartavyam anācaran*), living a life of righteous conduct and discipline (*tiṣṭhati prakṛtā cāre*). This characterization concerns one's conduct and character, not race or nationality. It emphasizes that an '*ārya*' acts without hesitation or complaint, regardless of whether the duty is pleasant or unpleasant. Such a person does not discriminate between responsibilities and does not allow personal likes or dislikes to dictate their actions [1].

Krishna's use of '*anāryajuṣṭam*' is thus a decisive rejection of Arjuna's behavior, saying it does not befit the noble-minded. The deliberate use of '*arya*' is a clarion call to rise above pettiness and to live a life of discipline and honor. It has nothing to do with differences in skin color, height, or geographic origins. It is a call to be noble in thought and action, which Krishna emphasizes is essential for Arjuna at this crucial juncture of his life and, by extension, as it is for us in our respective battles.

Furthermore, Krishna's reprimand underscores that surrendering to despair is '*asvargyam*' and '*akīrtikaram*.' Krishna cautions Arjuna that his illogical stance of abandoning his duties will deny him well-deserved fame, honor, and prosperity in the present. And following the theory of Karma, as explained by Vedanta, will deny him future peace and happiness as well, symbolized here as heaven.

At this critical juncture, the exhortation is clear: one must rise above despondency, not yield to it. These words of Krishna are as impactful as would have been a physical shake-up of a person in impassioned desperation or that awakening slap across his face!

> **Reflective Prompt**
>
> *Reflect on any instance when you were emotionally paralyzed, and someone or something jolted you back to reality and the right action. Take a moment to offer gratitude for that intervention.*
>
> ---
>
> ---
>
> ---

Awaken from despair, for courage and clarity await your command

SHLOKA 3: RISING ABOVE DESPONDENCY

क्लैब्यं मा स्म गमः पार्थ नैतत्त्वय्युपपद्यते ।
क्षुद्रं हृदयदौर्बल्यं त्यक्त्वोत्तिष्ठ परन्तप ॥3॥

klaibyaṁ mā sma gamaḥ pārtha naitattvayyupapadyatē |
kṣudraṁ hṛdayadaurbalyaṁ tyaktvōttiṣṭha parantapa ||3||

Translation:

O Arjuna (***Pārtha***), do not succumb to unmanliness (***klaibyam***), for it ill suits a person of your stature (***naitat tvayi upapadyate***). Cast off this petty weakness of heart (***kṣudram hṛdaya-daurbalyam tyakta***) and rise up with resolve (***uttiṣṭha***), O vanquisher of foes! (***Parantapa***) **[Sankya Yoga: 2.3]**

At a Glance: Capturing the Spirit of the Shloka

Krishna interjects this unwarranted and fatalistic dejection with a powerful call to all of us through Arjuna: Rise above fleeting moments of weakness and reconnect with your inner strength. Allowing situational pressures to overwhelm you is beneath your true potential. Face life's challenges with unwavering courage and determination, recognizing that setbacks are not the measure of who you are but opportunities to awaken your resilience and tap into your boundless inner power.

Commentary:

Krishna employs a stern psychological approach to awaken Arjuna out of his stupor, urging him not to succumb to 'unmanliness'—a state unbefitting a warrior of his caliber. This exhortation is a reminder of the inherent strength and duty that define a warrior's essence. Krishna's approach is tailored, recognizing that the solution to an emotional quandary can only make headway in addressing the heart and spirit directly. Just as a coach might rally their strongest players with fervent words before a decisive play, Krishna seeks to ready Arjuna to fight and win this inevitable war by, first, reminding him of his own power and status.

In this pivotal shloka, Krishna directly pinpoints the crux of Arjuna's turmoil. The term *'klaibyam,'* which translates as unmanliness, reflects a spirit subdued by emotions, a heart that falters before the specter of adversity. Krishna implores Arjuna to not surrender to this frailty, this 'chicken-heartedness' utterly alien to his nature. The phrase *'Mā sma gamaḥ pārtha'* cries out to Arjuna, as it were, urging him to resist the pull of this meekness that seeks to claim him.

Why? Because *'naitattvayyupapadyate,'* – such a stance is unbecoming of Arjuna. It is a call to cast aside *'hṛdayadaurbalyam,'* the mental weakness that shackles one's spirit, labeled *'kṣudram'* for its pettiness, an ignoble blight upon a warrior's honor. The directive' *tyaktvā uttiṣṭha'* is both a provocation and a command – to shed this timidity and rise. To resurrect the innate strength that Arjuna is born with and has forgotten in the throes of his overwhelming emotions.

Valor Beyond Gender in Sacred Wisdom

In elucidating the term *'klaibyam'* as unmanliness within this context, it is imperative to clarify that the Bhagavad Gita advocates universal virtues applicable to all humanity, irrespective of gender identity. The scripture does not in any way endorse discrimination based on gender, race, or any other division. The reference to unmanliness here is not about gender but rather about the more "masculine" qualities of courage, determination, and the resolve to face challenges—attributes present in all genders, just in varying proportions. It is a call to embody the spirit of a warrior, which, in the vision of the Bhagavad Gita, is a metaphor for one who stands resolute in the face of life's adversities. This distinction is crucial for a contemporary understanding of the text to ensure its timeless messages are appreciated without misconstruing them through a narrow interpretative lens.

A Constructive Framework for Growth

Krishna's use of *'naitattvayyupapadyate,'* - this does not befit you, acknowledges and addresses behaviors or actions that deviate from one's highest potential. This transformative approach, masterfully employed by Krishna on Arjuna, rips past the boundaries of the ancient battlefield to offer timeless wisdom for personal growth and constructive communication for all of humanity down the ages.

The essence of *'naitattvayyupapadyate'* - does not befit you, is a profound reminder of our inherent capacity for nobility and greatness. Krishna's guidance to Arjuna underscores a vital distinction: our actions, mainly when they fall short of our potential, do not define our core selves. A constructive lens for personal growth, this admonition advocates for an approach that seeks to realign our behavior with our true nature rather than condemning our missteps. It champions resilience, encouraging us to recognize and correct our faults, inspired by the belief that our essence remains pure and undiminished.

In today's complex and fast-paced world, this message resonates with added significance, guiding us to face challenges with conviction in our inner virtues. Applied across various domains—whether in guiding the young, leading teams, or self-reflection—it motivates individuals to transcend their limitations. This ethos fosters a culture of appreciation and empowerment, where feedback is delivered with respect and dignity, nurturing a sense of self-worth, and encouraging continuous improvement.

Krishna's words to Arjuna affirm that each of us harbors untapped wellsprings of strength and nobility. It invites us to live in a manner that reflects our highest potential, steering our actions and interactions towards embodying the virtues that truly befit us. This timeless wisdom of the Bhagavad Gita urges us to live with integrity, honor, and purpose that resonate with our personal and collective journeys.

Arise, Awake and Act

Krishna's directive "get up and act" (*'tyaktvā uttiṣṭha'*) is a timeless exhortation to confront life's challenges with resilience and action. It is an affirmation that our moments of weakness do not define us; they serve as opportunities to tap into our inherent strength. We all face battles—health concerns, emotional upheaval, financial stress, or relational discord. Yet, within each of us is an untapped vigor, a reservoir of energy and strength waiting to be realized. We must not succumb to despair but rise with determination, embodying the fortitude that is our true essence.

The metaphor of clouds obscuring the sun powerfully illustrates our condition. While challenges may temporarily shroud our internal brightness, our true spirit remains steadfast and enduring. We are encouraged to face our adversities with courage and conviction.

Embodying this teaching would transform our narrative from weeping over troubles to standing firm and resolute. The Bhagavad Gita calls for empowerment and active engagement, urging us to awaken our dormant inner strength and confront problems head-on.

Swami Vivekananda, a prominent figure in the 19th century known for his progressive ideas and spiritual wisdom, deeply revered specific shlokas from the Bhagavad Gita, particularly Shlokas 2 and 3 of Chapter II. He passionately believed that grasping the essence of these shlokas was fundamental to understanding the Gita's profundity. The Bhagavad Gita's call to confront life's obstacles with unwavering courage particularly resonated deeply with his own vision.

An incident from Swami Vivekananda's life in Varanasi vividly illustrates his lived experience of this shloka's message. While walking through the city's narrow alleys, he encountered a group of aggressive monkeys blocking his path. Initially startled, Vivekananda attempted to flee, but the monkeys pursued him relentlessly. A stranger urged him to turn and face the monkeys. Summoning his inner strength, Vivekananda boldly confronted the creatures, and to his amazement, they retreated. Reflecting on this experience, Vivekananda shared: *"That is a lesson for all life — face the terrible, face it boldly."* He understood that by confronting challenges head-on, one can overcome them. Vivekananda famously declared, *"If we are ever to gain freedom, it must be by conquering the problems, never by running away. Cowards never win victories. You have to fight fear and troubles and ignorance if we expect them to flee before you."*

Swami Ji's appreciation for and repeated quoting of the Katha Upanishad's call to "Arise, awake, and stop not till the goal is reached" aligns seamlessly with the ethos of proactive engagement found in the Bhagavad Gita. He critiqued the submissive despondency that had beset India, advocating for a revival of inner strength and self-reliance. Vivekananda's clarion call for empowerment, echoing Krishna's message to Arjuna, remains a timeless inspiration, urging humanity to rediscover its inherent divine strength and confront life's adversities with unwavering determination and spirit. Together, these teachings form a cohesive framework for navigating life's challenges with courage, resilience, and unwavering determination, empowering individuals to realize their highest potential and achieve spiritual fulfillment.

Empowering Resilience

These two shlokas offer timeless wisdom on empowering those around us. In and through life's intriguing sojourn, each encounters their share of challenges and adversities, moments when self-doubt clouds the path ahead. Yet, as compassionate beings, we must uplift and strengthen one another in times of need. When a friend or loved one grapples with doubt or despair, our words and actions can kindle the flames of courage within them. We must remind them that their momentary weakness does not define their true essence, just as Krishna admonished Arjuna, "This doesn't befit you."

In the intricate web of social relations, our interactions can either diminish or enhance another's self-confidence. In the Indian epics, we find poignant examples of this principle at play. In the Ramayana, when Hanuman faced the daunting task of leaping across the ocean, a momentary lapse of confidence threatened to obscure his indomitable spirit. Yet, with the timely intervention of Jambavan, who extolled Hanuman's remarkable abilities, the mighty Hanuman was emboldened to overcome the insurmountable obstacle. Conversely, in the Mahabharata, we witness the tragic downfall of Karna, a formidable warrior whose confidence was eroded by the disparaging words of his charioteer, Shalya. These moving examples reiterate the profound impact of our words and deeds on the resilience and self-assurance of those around us.

Krishna's exhortation to Arjuna, framed within the context of their dialogue, serves as a blueprint for empowering others. By addressing

Arjuna as '*Partha*,' the son of Kunti, who was renowned for her courage, Krishna reminds Arjuna of his mighty parentage to shake him out of his emotional stupor. Krishna reminds Arjuna of his inherent and indomitable strength and valor to overcome internal and external adversaries by calling him '*Parantapa*,' the scorcher of foes. Krishna does not belittle Arjuna in his vulnerable moments but instead ignites the fire of determination within him, urging him to rise and confront life's challenges with unwavering resolve.

Thus, let us heed the call of Krishna and emulate his example by uplifting and empowering those around us, starting with ourselves. In a world often fraught with uncertainty and doubt, our positive self-talk anchored in a firm belief in our inner strength can pull us out of our darkest dungeons. Furthermore, our affirmative words of encouragement, which now come from established and experienced wisdom, can guide others towards their true potential. Let us strive to be like Krishna, fostering an environment where individuals, ourselves included, are emboldened to rise above their fears and insecurities and embrace their innate strength and courage. In doing so, we honor the timeless wisdom of the Bhagavad Gita and contribute to the collective upliftment of humanity.

Embrace the wisdom in Krishna's words to Arjuna as a guide for your own life. Confront challenges with courage, resilience, and determination, recognizing that momentary weakness does not define your true essence. Empower and uplift those around you, fostering an environment of encouragement and growth. Let the timeless teachings of the Gita inspire you to rise above fears and insecurities and embrace your innate strength and potential. Arise, awake, and act towards realizing your highest Self, and then step forward to contribute toward the collective upliftment of humanity.

Reflective Prompt

Have you been intentionally avoiding a particular fear or obstacle? Has your avoidance made it disappear? Does it not still lurk in the background and torment you in some way? How does the idea of confronting it directly make you feel?

Within you throbs the power to conquer every storm – rise and claim it

SHLOKA 4: ARJUNA'S QUEST FOR MORAL CLARITY

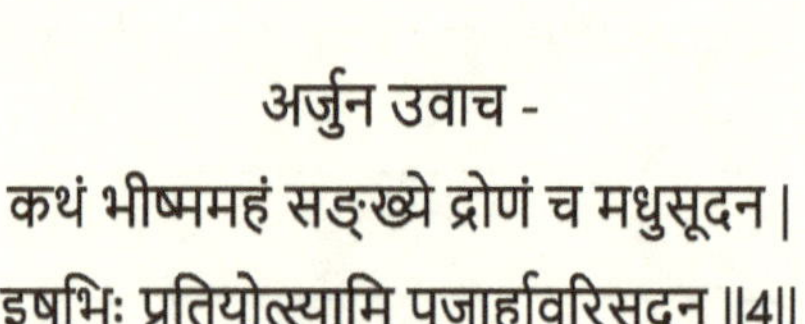

अर्जुन उवाच -
कथं भीष्ममहं सङ्ख्ये द्रोणं च मधुसूदन |
इषुभिः प्रतियोत्स्यामि पूजार्हावरिसूदन ||4||

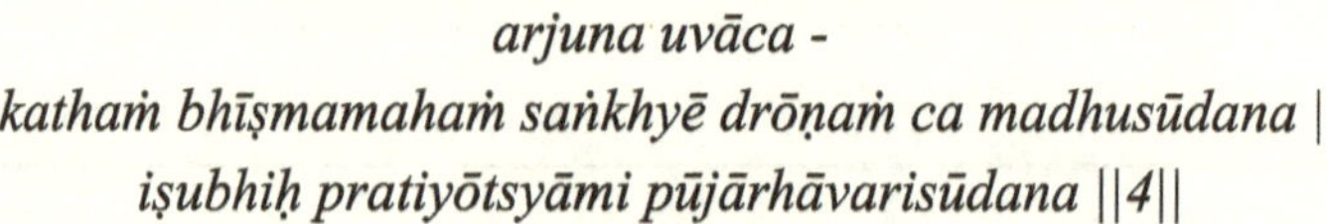

arjuna uvāca -
katham bhīṣmamaham saṅkhyē drōṇam ca madhusūdana |
iṣubhiḥ pratiyōtsyāmi pūjārhāvarisūdana ||4||

Translation:

O Madhusudana, how (***katham***) shall I ((***aham***) engage in battle (***saṅkhyē***) with arrows (***iṣu***) Bheeshma and Drona, who are worthy of my reverence (***pūjārhau***), O subduer of foes (***Arisudana***)?
[Sankya Yoga: 2.4]

At a Glance: Capturing the Spirit of the Shloka

Fulfilling one's responsibilities is never easy, especially when it requires going against personal preferences and risks impacting the emotions and expectations of those we hold dear. Such moments challenge us to confront the conflict between duty and attachment.

Commentary:

With both armies poised at the final frontiers of no doubt a cataclysmic but necessary war, the dialogue of the Bhagavad Gita begins to unfold in its spiritual entirety in the garb of a conversation between the Divine and mortal. In this pivotal fourth Shloka, we witness a subtle yet significant shift in Arjuna's attitude. Where abject dejection, just a little while ago, rendered him speechless and disarmed, we now hear the stirrings of a rational voice, validating, as it were, the efficacy of Krishna's emotionally resonant counsel. Within the rubble of emotional devastation, Arjuna begins to find his footing, his words no longer laced with the despondency of defeat but with the sincere curiosity of a man seeking viable solutions to his problems.

This transformation comes about because of Krishna's compassionate and empathetic presence, which meets Arjuna's emotional turmoil with a heart poised in understanding. Herein lies a profound lesson on the nature of emotional healing — that the path to clarity is often paved with the soft soil of heartfelt empathy rather than hard rocks of intellectual discourse. In and through Krishna's compassionate approach, we receive a powerful teaching: that before the intellect can be guided to the heights of spiritual enlightenment, the heart must first be grounded in emotional solace.

Arjuna's voice now carries the tone of logic and the sharpness of clearer thinking. His words now reveal a man not just caught in an emotional storm but painfully aware of the gravity of his situation. Arjuna's newfound rationality presents a logical challenge that honestly reflects his inner struggle: how can he, a seasoned warrior, reconcile the act of waging war against those who are the very pillars of his moral world? Bhishma, the embodiment of virtue and the family patriarch, and Drona, the mentor of all the Kauravas and Pandava forces, are amongst those dotting the enemy lines, no doubt - but they are also *his* grandfather and teacher whom he deeply loves and reveres.

By addressing Krishna as *'Madhusūdana'* (slayer of the demon *Madhu*) and *'Arisūdana'* (destroyer of enemies), Arjuna exposes the confusion he feels within. His chosen nomenclature is a poignant reminder to Krishna of the difference between past divine conquests and the present moral conundrum. Krishna was revered for killing demons, annihilating enemies, and destroying evil - but Arjuna is being asked to kill people who have always been his well-wishers, whom he cherishes so dearly, and who are worthy of every ounce of his love and respect. Arjuna's subtle approach pleads with Krishna, as it were, that this battle he is expected to fight, and win goes against his own emotional and spiritual convictions.

Arjuna's question pleads another critical issue. Is raising arms against one's teacher and grandfather not a sin? At first glance, a new student of the Gita, too, tends to be just as baffled by this predicament. Many debates have risen over this shloka, as Krishna seems to be sanctioning that as righteous, which Arjuna, or any human being, would consider unthinkable.

It is worth emphasizing here that Arjuna is misguided by his belief that actions in themselves are either good or bad. Vedanta repeatedly declares that no action as such is inherently good or bad - but the motive behind each action is what renders them so. An honorable action could carry a vicious motive behind it, and conversely, a malicious action could be supported by the noblest of all intents. Arjuna's present quandary falls under the second category. Unfortunately, Bhishma and Drona dot the lines of the army that stands on the side of unrighteousness (*adharma*). In this scenario, the incomprehensibly inhuman act of killing one's own teacher and grandfather becomes an act of the highest virtue due to the underlying motive of re-establishing righteousness (*dharma*).

In this vulnerable moment of genuine introspection, Arjuna grapples with the moral complexities of personal sentiments against obligation. His questions to Krishna echo the timeless inquiries of human hearts that seek to balance the scales of duty and love, right action and piety. Through Arjuna's introspective journey, the Bhagavad Gita offers guidance for all at the crossroads of difficult choices.

Confronting the Inner Battlefield: Ego, Habits, and the Quest for Self-Transformation

Through its allegorical narrative, the Bhagavad Gita intricately unfolds characters that represent the diverse aspects of the human psyche. We have touched upon these parallels in our preceding book, ***First Step into the Bhagavad Gita***.

Duryodhana epitomizes the restless mind, dominated by desires that drive one's intellect on a turbulent journey. In this state, the reins of control are elusive, with whims and whimsies guiding one's actions. Drona, conversely, symbolizes the ingrained instincts and *samskaras*—those deep-seated imprints from past actions and habits that quietly shape our present, subtly swaying our decisions and responses.

Bhishma stands as a symbol for the ego, that powerful sense of 'I' that wraps around the intellect like a sheath, obscuring its luminous essence with the veil of bodily identity. In the Bhishma state, one's true Self is forgotten, ensnared by the limitations and definitions imposed by the body and societal roles. This identification with the ephemeral body that perishes fosters the illusion of permanence within the impermanent.

Our journey with the ego commences right from our childhood, forming a bond that strengthens with time. This enduring relationship with our habits often vets us to vehemently defend it, crafting justifications for our actions, even when we recognize their detrimental nature. We become adept at pointing out the flaws in others, eager to cast stones, yet flinch at the prospect of turning the mirror on ourselves. The momentum of long-standing habits obstructs self-reflection and transformation. Engaging in external battles is more effortless than confronting internal adversaries, such as ego and our long-adhered to habits.

Arjuna's hesitation to fight Bhishma and Drona is not just a reluctance to engage in battle but a profound metaphor for our resistance to change. Just as Arjuna grapples with the idea of attacking those he reveres, we, too, struggle with challenging the deeply ingrained patterns and identities that we have come to respect and accept as part of ourselves. The Bhagavad Gita mirrors the internal conflict that rages within everyone. It encourages a deeper introspection and a braver confrontation with those hidden aspects of ourselves that hinder our spiritual evolution.

Reflective Prompt

Have you ever been in a situation where you had to choose between personal affinity and moral duty? What did you choose? How did your choice play out eventually?

The most brutal battles are fought not against daunting enemies without but raging conflicts within

Shlokas 5 & 6: Arjuna's Struggle with Dharma

गुरूनहत्वा हि महानुभावान्
श्रेयो भोक्तुं भैक्ष्यमपीह लोके |
हत्वार्थकामांस्तु गुरूनिहैव
भुञ्जीय भोगान् रुधिरप्रदिग्धान् ||5||

न चैतद्विद्मः कतरन्नो गरीयः
यद्वा जयेम यदि वा नो जयेयुः |
यानेव हत्वा न जिजीविषामः
तेऽवस्थिताः प्रमुखे धार्तराष्ट्राः ||6||

gurūnahatvā hi mahānubhāvān
śrēyō bhōktuṁ bhaikṣyamapīha lōkē |
hatvārthakāmāṁstu gurūnihaiva
bhuñjīya bhōgān rudhirapradigdhān ||5||

na caitadvidmaḥ katarannō garīyaḥ
yadvā jayēma yadi vā nō jayēyuḥ |
yānēva hatvā na jijīviṣāmaḥ
tē'vasthitāḥ pramukhē dhārtarāṣṭrāḥ ||6||

Translation:

It is far better for me to live on alms (*bhaikṣyam*) in this world than to kill these esteemed teachers (*mahānubhāvān*). Slaying them, even for the sake of wealth and desires (*arthakāmān*), would taint any pleasures I enjoy with the stain of their blood (*rudhira-pradigdhān*)
[Sankya Yoga: 2.5]

I am unable to determine what would be better (*garīyaḥ*)—to conquer them or to be conquered by them *(yadvā jayēma yadi vā nō jayēyuḥ)*. Arrayed before us are the sons of Dhritarashtra (*dhārtarāṣṭrāḥ*), whom, even in victory, we would not desire to outlive (*na jijīviṣāmaḥ*)
[Sankya Yoga: 2.6]

At a Glance: Capturing the Spirit of the Shloka

The next two shlokas witness Arjuna's heart wrenching stumble into an impossible choice bereft of a positive outcome whichever way he decides. A dilemma most humans face in lesser or greater proportion: I find myself torn between two difficult choices, both fraught with unfavorable outcomes. Part of me contemplates escaping the situation, even knowing it is not the right course. Yet, even if I follow through with my duty, I am left questioning whether success will truly bring satisfaction.

Commentary:

Amid the noisy battlefield of Kurukshetra, fortunately, Arjuna's logical faculties begin to pierce through the fog of his emotional turmoil. A problematic choice stares him in the face at this critical juncture, threatening to entangle him in unrecoverable outcomes. Here stands a warrior, deeply enmeshed in a web of confusion, facing a situation where neither option seems right. Arjuna's argument, laced with reason, highlights a fundamental human predicament: the challenge of choosing from options equally steeped in adversity - the proverbial *"choice between the devil and the deep sea."*

Arjuna deliberates aloud over his preference for a life of renunciation over the act of slaying the noble souls who stand before him. He ponders a life sustained by alms for himself—a path traditionally pursued by students and sannyasis, those who have renounced the material world in quest of spiritual enlightenment. The bewilderment presented by his duty to fight against his own kin weighs heavily upon him. The prospect of a world bereft of his revered elders and teachers is one he finds too bleak to contemplate.

Half convinced and half confused, he voices a perspective: engaging in battle driven by selfish desires for a kingdom and its associated pleasures is unjust. New students of the Bhagavad Gita tend to agree with Arjuna's stance almost immediately. After all, Arjuna is seen to be taking a noble stand towards renunciation. However, his arguments, while logical, miss the essentials.

Firstly, as gleaned in the previous shloka, the intent behind the war is pivotal. If this battle were waged out of selfish ambition, it lacks righteousness beyond every shadow of doubt. Yet, if its underlying motive is to uphold *dharma* and protect moral order, it is an entirely different scenario. After having exhausted all other means to attain peace, the principle of a *'Dharma Yudha,'* a righteous war, is to engage in battle only when failing to do so would result in greater evil. The bitter truth for Arjuna is that the noble warriors, Bhishma and Drona, have aligned themselves with Duryodhana's adharmic cause. Making way for the Kaurava forces to triumph would mean handing over the reign to a power that not only does not honor dharma but most unapologetically defies it, thereby plunging the kingdom into darkness.

World War II starkly reflects Arjuna's situation. Much like Arjuna's conflict, the allies had to align with the moral imperative of engaging in a war not for conquest but to defend human dignity against tyranny. The core tenet of *'Dharma Yudha,'* the righteous war, again came under the spotlight here: not waging it would lead to far greater suffering. The Allies fought to restore peace and uphold principles of humanity, mirroring the duty Arjuna is called upon to fulfill.

Secondly, let us examine Arjuna's consideration of taking up *sannyasa*, a life of renunciation, more closely. The renunciate's path is not for everyone but for those whose spiritual inclination renders the material world insignificant. Arjuna, inherently a raging warrior, is not suited at this stage in his personal evolution for a sannyasi's austere life seeped in contemplation. His warrior *(Kshatriya)* upbringing and corresponding disposition do not align with his idea of renunciation. And it definitely cannot be chosen as an alternative to battle.

The ancient and contemporary world is replete with cautionary tales of those who, facing crises, hastily adopt the life of renunciation despite it being in absolute contradiction to their innate tendencies or *vasanas*. Firstly, they become frustrated, suppressed, and repressed individuals unable to express their true selves. Such individuals often struggle and fail to adhere to the disciplines of *sannyasa*, leading them to commit unthinkable acts, not so much out of volition but forced by their core tendencies. This misalignment between one's nature and chosen path can prove harmful to society, as seen in news reports of those who misuse the respect accorded to renunciates.

Arjuna's acknowledgment of his confusion is commendable in these verses. Unlike in Chapter One, where he was vociferously defending his standpoint on the grounds of erroneous beliefs, he now recognizes his apprehension in its true light. This self-awareness is the first step towards seeking clarity. Krishna's empathetic engagement opens the door for Arjuna's introspection. A simple shift from illogical convictions to doubt transforms Arjuna into a seeker, primed for the wisdom Krishna is about to impart - wisdom that will illuminate the path not just for Arjuna but for humanity at large, teaching us how to navigate the complex battlefields of our own lives.

The Inner Struggle: Embracing Change for Personal Growth

Arjuna's struggle resounds the personal battles we all face when confronting ingrained habits and personality traits that hinder our growth. Subjectively, the verses shine a light on the human tendency to cling to familiar patterns, even when they are detrimental to our well-being. For instance, consider the struggle to curb a sweet tooth; the immediate pleasure derived from indulgence often overshadows the long-term health benefits of restraint. Similarly, Arjuna feels that without the presence and guidance of his elders, his life would be meaningless, even though their current stance threatens the greater good. This inner conflict is emblematic of our paralysis when attempting to change any deep-seated habit. However, there is a positive aspect in Arjuna's realization of his confusion. It signifies the first step towards transformation— a mere consideration that our current path may be flawed. This admission is a precursor to seeking guidance, much like an individual's recognition of unhealthy habits is the beginning of a journey toward self-improvement. Through this introspective lens, the shlokas not only enliven Arjuna's personal turmoil but also illustrate the beginnings of any individual's quest for a more enlightened self.

Reflective Prompt

Have you ever faced a situation where every choice seemed unfavorable? How did you navigate the dilemma, and what guided your decision-making process?

When every choice appears impossible let purpose, not preference, guide your steps

Shloka 7: From Despair to Discipleship

कार्पण्यदोषोपहतस्वभावः
पृच्छामि त्वां धर्मसम्मूढचेताः |
यच्छ्रेयः स्यान्निश्चितं ब्रूहि तन्मे
शिष्यस्तेऽहं शाधि मां त्वां प्रपन्नम् ||7||

kārpaṇyadōṣōpahatasvabhāvaḥ
pṛcchāmi tvāṁ dharmasammūḍhacētāḥ |
yacchrēyaḥ syānniścitaṁ brūhi tanmē
śiṣyastē'haṁ śādhi māṁ tvāṁ prapannam ||7||

Translation:

Overwhelmed by my weakness (***kārpaṇya-doṣa***) and confusion about what is to be done (***dharma-sammūḍha-cetāḥ***), I ask you: what is truly just (***yat-śreyaḥ syāt***)? Please tell me decisively (***niścitam brūhi tan me***). I am your student (***śiṣya***) seeking your shelter (***prapannaṁ***)—guide me (***śādhi māṁ***) [Sankya Yoga: 2.7]

At a Glance: Capturing the Spirit of the Shloka

This shloka is perhaps the most revered shloka of the Bhagavad Gita because had it not been for these words coming from Arjuna, Krishna would have never spoken. The quintessential act of humility and surrender to become a worthy receptacle for wisdom is beautifully portrayed through Arjuna's earnest plea: I am overwhelmed by the pressure of my situation and unable to see clearly. I seek your guidance to help me navigate the path of what is right and good.

Commentary:

Fatefully poised in the eye of the storm about to unleash upon the battlefield of Kurukshetra, we watch Arjuna transition from confused yet vehement intellectualization to a more subdued introspection. With Krishna's initial nonchalant approach to the situation, Arjuna was able to empty himself, as it were, of all his conflicting emotions. He now appears more cognizant of his helplessness in the face of the monumental challenge. He finally falls on his knees to solicit guidance from an intelligence wiser than his own. This moment in the storyline marks the crucial shift from his emotional paralysis to a conscious acknowledgment of his need for direction.

Arjuna, with newfound sobriety, confesses to Krishna, "My inborn nature (*svabhāvaḥ*) has been overwhelmed (*upahata*) by the bane of faint-heartedness (*kārpaṇya-doṣa*), and my mind is muddled regarding my duty (*dharma-sammūḍha-cetāḥ*)." In this state of earnest confusion, he beseeches, "Therefore, I am asking you (*pṛcchāmi tvām*) to guide me clearly (*niścitam brūhi tanme*) to what is truly beneficial for me (*yacchreyaḥ*)." Humbly, he surrenders, "I am your disciple (*śiṣyaste 'ham*), ready to be taught by you, who I turn to for refuge (*sādhi mām tvām prapannam*)." This plea transcends a mere call for help; it highlights the absolute necessity of surrendering one's ego to receive the light of wisdom.

Quest for Clarity Amidst Crisis

Shloka 2.7 of the Bhagavad Gita marks a pivotal transformation that resonates deeply with humanity's perennial quest for clarity amidst crises. Here, Arjuna embodies the archetypal seeker, confronting his vulnerabilities and acknowledging the paralysis of his will in the face of moral perplexity. This moment of surrender is emblematic of the first vital step towards wisdom: recognizing one's limitations and earnestly yearning for guidance. Arjuna displays profound humility, essential for any seeker of truth, by laying bare his turmoil before Bhagavan Krishna.

The Shloka animates the universal threefold path out of despair:

- Realizing the presence of a problem.
- Accepting one's inability to resolve it.
- Earnestly pursuing a mentor's guidance.

His shift from a state of confused conviction to the open vulnerability of a disciple, a '*shishya*,' catalyzes the transformative dialogue of the Bhagavad Gita. Without such readiness, even the wisdom of the world's most outstanding mentor would fall on deaf ears.

Arjuna's plea is a symbolic relinquishment of ego that allowed him to transition from a broken yet haughty warrior, no doubt at the helm of a mighty army, to a humble student in the presence of his teacher.

In and through life's undulating challenges, recognizing one's confusion marks the beginning of wisdom. Confusion can be categorized into two types. The first is an oblivious confusion, where one is lost in the maze of overwhelming predicaments and fails to recognize the state of disarray. Like a driver stubbornly believing they are on the right path despite all signs pointing otherwise. Such a person continues unchecked down a path of errors, compounding their difficulties. The second type is conscious confusion, where one is aware of their bewilderment and admits their need for direction. This is akin to a driver who, upon realizing they have veered off course, pulls over to seek help or consult a map. In this Shloka, Arjuna mirrors the latter. His stance of surrender, preceded by his admission of his confusion, opens the door to divine guidance. Acknowledging one's own disorientation becomes a pathway toward enlightenment. It creates a possibility to steer the lost traveler back to clarity and purpose.

In today's fast-paced world, where choices abound, and the pressure to succeed supersedes even common sense, this shloka offers a profound lesson in facing life's dilemmas. This ancient wisdom underscores the importance of humility in pursuing guidance as a foundational step toward overcoming challenges. Recognizing one's limitations, needing help, and actively seeking knowledge from the more experienced are not signs of weakness but strength. This approach, alongside helping us navigate personal and professional perplexities, also fosters an environment of learning and growth. One's openness to learning holds the key to success in any endeavor, making this timeless message innocuously woven into this shloka ever so relevant in the modern context.

Consider young entrepreneurs stepping into the competitive arena of startups, brimming with ideas yet uncertain of the path ahead. Amidst the excitement of innovation, they encounter unforeseen challenges that test their resolve. At this moment, like Arjuna, if they recognize the gap in their knowledge and experience, they will seek out a seasoned mentor who has navigated the uncertain waters of setting up fresh enterprise and can offer valuable advice with a sounder perspective. The willingness to become a 'shishya' - a humble student before the right mentors, especially at critical junctures, opens the door for inexperienced entrepreneurs to personal growth and creates possibilities for transforming challenges into opportunities for profound learning.

Kārpaṇya: The spiritual miserliness

The term '*kārpaṇya*' may incorrectly portray the image of a miser—a person abundant in resources yet stingy in their use. It is a word that paints the picture of self-imposed scarcity amidst plenty. The miser, who hoards wealth, refusing to either enjoy or share it, is seen as someone squandering the potential for a fuller life for oneself or for the aid of another. This notion of miserliness transcends the mere fiscal sphere and ventures into the spiritual realms in the teachings of the ancient scriptures.

The *Bṛhadāraṇyakopaniṣad* presents a profound interpretation of '*kārpaṇya*' in a spiritual context. It says, "The one who departs from this world without knowing this 'Immutable One' is a *kṛpaṇa*." (*Bṛhadāraṇyakopaniṣad 3.8.10*). Here, *kṛpaṇa* lives and leaves without delving into the depths of spiritual wisdom—the true treasure trove of the human experience. It is a metaphor for the squandering of our highest potential - the potential for discernment, or '*viveka*'—the ability to distinguish the real from the unreal, the transient from the eternal, the right from the wrong. This discernment, the hallmark of human beings, sets us apart from other species.

Arjuna, confused and perplexed by the immensity of the battle before him, refers to his own *kārpaṇya*, not in the material sense, but as a crisis of the spirit. He realizes that he is like a miser holding onto his confusion and sorrow when he has the opportunity—and the capacity to transmute it into liberation and joy. By uttering this word, Arjuna acknowledges that he is clinging to his suffering, unable to access the wisdom that lies within him, much like a miser who clings to wealth that is never utilized. In doing so, he mirrors our lives, challenging us to reflect on whether we are hoarding our inner resources, our potential for growth, and our capacity for wisdom. His plea to Krishna is on behalf of us all: to unlock the true wealth of understanding and to spend it generously pursuing a well-rounded life enriched with meaning beyond our material obsessions.

Beyond the Pleasant: Embracing the Path of Good

Arjuna finds himself at a juncture where the path forward is clouded by his emotions and doubts. Recognizing the inadequacy of his understanding, Arjuna turns to Krishna to illuminate the path of good (*shreyas*) over the path of the pleasant (*preyas*). This request underscores a universal dilemma: choosing between instant gratification and enduring virtue. Arjuna's plea reflects his deep yearning to align his actions with *dharma*, the principle that intricately weaves the fabric of the self into the grand tapestry of the cosmos.

The Katha Upanishad delves into this dichotomy with eloquence, stating:

"śreyaśca preyaśca manuṣyametastau samparītya
vivinakti dhīraḥ |
śreyo hi dhīro'bhi preyaso vṛṇīte preyo mando
yogakṣemādvṛṇīte ||"

Meaning, "Both the good (*shreyas*) and the pleasant (*preyas*) approach man. The wise, having examined both, distinguish them. Indeed, they prefer the good (*shreyas)* to the pleasant; the foolish, driven by fleshly desires, prefer the pleasant (*preyas*) for its immediate joy" (KU 1.2.2).

In this context, '*preyas*' is derived from '*prii*', meaning to please or delight, suggesting choices that provide immediate but transient pleasure. Conversely, '*shreyas*', from '*shri*', signifies true happiness and goodness, guiding us towards actions with lasting fulfillment. The essence of this teaching is that while enjoying life's pleasures (*preyas*) is not inherently wrong, such choices should not contradict the path of good (*shreyas*), which leads to true well-being and alignment with *dharma*.

Let us put this in the modern context by considering our daily lifestyle choices and the consequent status of our health. The path of pleasant (*preyas*) might lead us towards indulging in junk food, leading a sedentary lifestyle, and compromising heavily on sleep - all of which offer immediate gratification but negatively impacts our overall health over time. On the other hand, the path of good (*shreyas*) encourages balanced eating, regular exercise, and adequate sleep - choices that require more discipline and effort but award us with lifelong vitality and well-being. Just as Arjuna seeks Krishna's guidance to choose *shreyas* over *preyas*, we, too, face similar decisions daily. By selecting the path that aligns with our higher goals and well-being, we create for ourselves a life that, although sometimes challenging, is abundant with happiness and lasting fulfillment.

Becoming a Śiṣya: The Making of a True Knowledge Seeker

Arjuna's presentation of himself as a *'śiṣya,'* seeking guidance from Krishna, vividly journeys us through his profound transformation from warrior to disciple. This transition speaks volumes about the essence of learning and the role of a *'śiṣya'* or disciple in the Dharmic traditions. Arjuna's adoption of a *'śiṣya'* role is not just about seeking answers to his most bewildering questions but affirms his deeper commitment to the path of knowledge and wisdom.

In Sanskrit, three terms describe the spectrum of knowledge seekers: *'vidyārthī,' 'antevāsī,'* and *'śiṣya.'*

A *'vidyārthī'* possesses a desire for knowledge, a curiosity that sets the initial stage of learning. However, desire alone does not translate into understanding.

An *'antevāsī'* takes this further by actively engaging in the learning process, enrolling in courses, and seeking education. Yet, mere attendance does not guarantee comprehension.

The term' *śiṣya'* exemplifies the deepest dimension of learning. Derived from the root '*śiṣ*,' meaning to learn or be instructed, a *'śiṣya'* is someone genuinely committed to understanding and assimilating knowledge, distinguished by an earnest capacity to grasp and apply what is taught.

The term '*śiṣya*' goes beyond the individual to define one of the Dharmic traditions of India—Sikhism. The word 'Sikh' is derived from '*śiṣya*,' embedding the identity of a Sikh in the very nature of being a disciple. A Sikh is, therefore, one who is on a perpetual journey of learning and spiritual evolution, guided by the teachings of their Gurus. This principle is central to Sikhism, where the sacred scripture, the Guru Granth Sahib, is regarded as the eternal Guru, illuminating the path of its followers through its hymns and teachings. The essence of being a Sikh, much like being a '*śiṣya*,' is in the ceaseless striving for wisdom and understanding, a testament to the universality and enduring relevance of the concept of discipleship across cultures and time.

The Journey to Finding a True Guru

Arjuna's request to Krishna, "I am your *śiṣya*," underscores a pivotal shift from being a leader on the battlefield to embracing the humility of a student ready to follow and learn. This transformation reveals his readiness to receive wisdom as he moves beyond the ego and opens himself to the teachings of a Guru. The essence of being a '*śiṣya*' lies in one's active participation in learning, characterized by humility, dedication, and the sincere desire to evolve.

In the contemporary world, whether it is to navigate the complexities of career trajectories, ethical dilemmas, or personal growth, this attitude of a '*śiṣya*' endures. The modern '*vidyārthī*' begins with curiosity, and the '*antevāsī*' takes the necessary steps towards learning. But proper understanding and application of knowledge come only when one adopts the mindset of a '*śiṣya*.' An attitude that embraces humility and openness to guidance transforms challenges into opportunities for growth. It teaches us that in our quest for knowledge, the willingness to learn from those who have walked the path before us makes the wisdom of the past accessible and applicable to the present dilemmas.

Arjuna's surrender to Krishna as his Guru underscores the importance of choosing the right spiritual mentor. Krishna is venerated not merely as an extraordinary teacher but as the *'Jagat Guru'*—the teacher of the universe. His divine role as an incarnation of *Ishvara*, the Lord himself, is a testament to the ultimate source of guidance a seeker can aspire to.

"Guru" means "one who dispels darkness" with the light of knowledge. The Mundaka Upanishad qualifies a true guru as a *'shrotriya'*—well-versed in the sacred scriptures; and *'brahma-nishtha'*, deeply rooted in the ultimate Truth. Such a guide is well-rooted in the theoretical understanding of scriptural texts and embodies experiential wisdom from walking the path of enlightenment. Krishna, whose teachings form the essence of the Bhagavad Gita, exemplifies these supreme qualities of an ideal *Guru*.

In the modern landscape of spiritual questing, we are eternally challenged to seek and find the right *Guru*. Gone are the days of clear-cut roles. Today, enthusiastic, and unsuspecting seekers continually stumble upon an array of self-styled *gurus* whose outer guises and eloquent words can be misleading. Authentic spiritual mentorship is not gauged by the length of the beard, the color of robes, or erudite scholarship of the scriptures; but by the depth of wisdom, an uncompromising embodiment of the teachings, humility, and the capacity to impart transformative insights.

In an era bereft of conventional guarantees, seekers must vigilantly seek indicators of true wisdom and transformational influence in their mentors. In modern times, fully Self-Realized *Gurus*, as described by sage Angiras, are scarce. Thus, we often turn to *'upagurus'*, who can significantly advance our spiritual odyssey. A genuine *Guru* is one who not only imparts teachings but lives by them, guiding by example and translating esoteric principles into actionable, practical wisdom.

This quest for guidance is not exclusive to spirituality; it permeates all aspects of life, from career choices to personal development. The key lies in identifying mentors with theoretical knowledge and wisdom gleaned from lived experience. As a map is indispensable to a traveler, so is a living exemplar to the seeker of evolution. Arjuna's selection of Krishna as his mentor remains a powerful allegory for all who seek guidance: choose mentors who illuminate the path by their very being and whose lives are the very essence of their teachings.

The Bhagavad Gita's Approach to Mentorship

In the dialogue that unfolds within the Bhagavad Gita, there is a subtle yet profound lesson on the nature of guidance and its receptivity. Embodying the highest wisdom, Bhagavan Krishna refrains from imparting spiritual teachings to Arjuna until the moment is ripe. His initial response to Arjuna's turmoil is not a torrent of advice but a gentle nudge toward stability, highlighting that teaching can only commence when the student's mind is open and prepared. This readiness is beautifully captured in Arjuna's surrender, wherein he expresses a sincere willingness to learn, marking the commencement of Gita's more profound philosophical discourse.

A poignant Sanskrit shloka articulates this concept [3]:

"vācyam śraddhaḥ samēdasya prichchatasya viśeśathaḥ |
śradhda hīnasya tu prōktam ārāṇya ruthitōpamāḥ || "

This means that *"Teaching should be given to those who have faith and specifically ask for it. Offering guidance to one who lacks faith is like crying in the wilderness."* Krishna's patience and refrain from providing any transformative teachings right up to Arjuna's surrender emphasize the futility of offering guidance to someone who has yet to be ready or willing to value it. Just as Krishna awaits Arjuna's heartfelt plea, the verse underlines the importance of a receptive audience for meaningful instruction.

The distinction between advice and teaching is pivotal and is best described by the Chinese proverb: *"Give a man a fish, and you feed him for a day. Teach a man to fish, and you feed him for a lifetime."* While advice may provide a temporary solution, it breeds reliance on the advisor. On the other hand, teaching equips one with the skills for autonomous problem-solving, enabling the individual to navigate future adversities with assuredness.

The word *"śādhi"* in the shloka specifically reveals Arjuna's desire not just for temporary advice but for teachings that will empower him to do what serves his greatest good. Beyond answers to his immediate questions, he seeks a path to self-reliance and wisdom. The highest teaching, therefore, imparts the capacity to discern, decide, and act independently. By using the term *"śādhi,"* Arjuna expresses his readiness to be endowed with the knowledge that liberates and empowers him to become a self-sufficient seeker of truth.

Even in the academic world, the word education is derived from two different Latin roots—*"Educare,"* which means to train or mold, and *"Educere,"* which means to draw out. A good teacher undoubtedly plays a crucial role in training and molding a child. However, the best teachers can draw out the wisdom already inherent in the child by jumpstarting their own critical thinking and power of analysis.

Krishna serves not just as a problem solver in the throes of this paralyzing crisis. Through his revolutionary teachings, he empowers Arjuna to become self-sufficient in navigating life's complexities. This lesson remains particularly salient in an age marked by instant gratification of quick fixes. There are no quick fixes. As the famous quote by Gautama Buddha reads, *"No one saves us but ourselves. No one can, and no one may. We ourselves must walk the path."*

A well-meaning mentor guides us toward self-sufficiency, not reliance. The eternal message of the Bhagavad Gita implores us to seek enduring wisdom, evolve through diligent effort, and become self-reliant navigators of our lives.

As the Bhagavad Gita progresses from the battlefield context to the scared dialogue between Arjuna and Krishna brimming with universal and timeless teachings, we are reminded that the journey of Self-discovery and enlightenment requires the courage to acknowledge one's ignorance, the humility to seek guidance, and the wisdom to choose a mentor whose life embodies the truths they impart. Arjuna's sincere yearning and Krishna's profound mentorship set ablaze a dynamic that transcends epochs, cultures, and emphasizes the transformative power of the sacred *guru-shishya-parampara* or teacher-disciple relationship.

Reflective Prompt

Think about a time when you felt completely overwhelmed or confused by a situation. Did you acknowledge your need for direction? Who or what did you turn to for guidance? Pause with a heart full of gratitude for the timely help.

The first step to clarity is the humility to seek it

SHLOKA 8: THE LIMITS OF MATERIAL FULFILLMENT

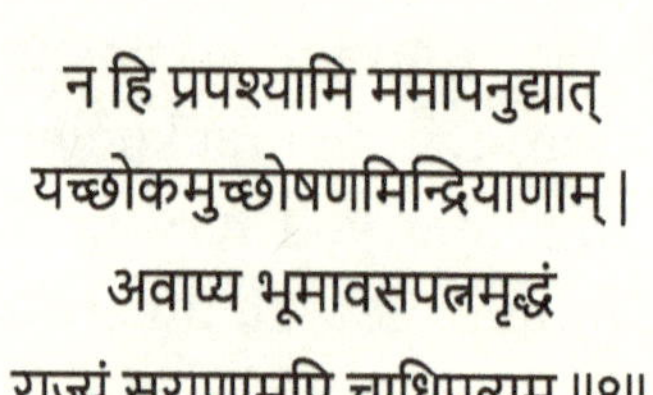

न हि प्रपश्यामि ममापनुद्यात्
यच्छोकमुच्छोषणमिन्द्रियाणाम् ।
अवाप्य भूमावसपत्नमृद्धं
राज्यं सुराणामपि चाधिपत्यम् ॥8॥

na hi prapaśyāmi mamāpanudyāt
yacchōkamucchōṣaṇamindriyāṇām |
avāpya bhūmāvasapatnamṛddhaṁ
rājyaṁ surāṇāmapi cādhipatyam ||8||

Translation:

I fail to see (***na hi prapaśyāmi***) how any wealth (***rājyaṁ***) or dominion
on earth (***bhūmāv asapatnam ṛddham***), or even command over the
celestial hosts (***surāṇām api cādhipatyam***), could dispel this grief
(***śokam***) that is drying up my senses (***ucchōṣaṇam indriyāṇām***)
[Sankya Yoga: 2.8]

At a Glance: Capturing the Spirit of the Shloka

A problem seen, is a problem half-solved. Arjuna's admission of his abject confusion is an incredibly positive sign of the possibility of a full recovery from his fall. His clear perception of where exactly he is stuck ploughs the fertile soil of his mind from which the right resolve can blossom - I am consumed by confusion and emotional overwhelm. Even the greatest achievements or rewards seem incapable of lifting this burden, leaving me uncertain and unmotivated to pursue my responsibilities.

Commentary:

In this poignant shloka, Arjuna realizes that the trappings of material success — power, wealth, and dominion — offer no solace to mental turmoil. His admission, *"Na hi prapaśyāmi"* (I do not see), reflects a moment of profound introspection, where the promise of even the most supreme worldly gains, "unrivaled prosperous kingdom on earth or overlordship over celestial hosts," is seen as futile against the grief "that has scorched my senses."

Arjuna's confession dramatically contradicts the popular notion that external achievements can be a panacea for inner distress. His distressed plea concedes that no amount of worldly opulence or authority can quench the mind's yearning for peace, nor can it overpower the sorrow that profoundly impacts the psyche and sensory experience. It warns, as it were, that unchecked earthly pursuits can leave one further distressed.

This shloka speaks volumes to a world that increasingly measures success by material accumulations and titles. It calls us to recognize that worldly conquests or possessions cannot appease inner turmoil. This recognition marks the first step toward a spiritual awakening, where the seeker turns away from the imaginary comforts of materialism and instead looks inward for enduring tranquility.

Ponder on this: Despite all the technological advancements and luxuries, there is a palpable sense of discontent and unfulfillment. But, like Arjuna, only a few realize that true contentment and relief from inner dis-ease come not from relentless acquisitions and enjoyment within the material world but from spiritual understanding and evolution of the mind and intellect. Even fewer are blessed with the right scriptural texts, guides, and teachers to see them through.

Arjuna's humble surrender to Krishna in the previous verse, "I trust you; you protect me, only you have to give me the solution," elicits the life-transforming wisdom of the Bhagavad Gita that follows. It inspires humanity to consider that perhaps only through spiritual enlightenment can one protect oneself from the constant onslaughts of life. It makes us aware that the desire to know, learn, and evolve must transcend all lower desires if we genuinely want to rise above the senseless battles of daily mortal existence.

By narrating this quintessential shift in Arjuna's perspective, Sanjaya highlights the value of seeking wisdom over material success and aspiring for a higher understanding that transcends the immediacy of temporal gain. This lesson is more relevant than ever in our contemporary world, where fundamental human struggles remain unchanged despite immense progress. The Gita gently lures us out of the illusory promises of this transient world by masterfully offering us a surer passage through worldly turmoil with its timeless wisdom.

Reflective Prompt

Reflect on a time when achieving a hard-chased material possession or goal left you feeling empty or unfulfilled. What does this teach you about where true contentment comes from?

No worldly treasure can soothe the ache of a restless heart

SHLOKA 9: ARJUNA'S MOMENT OF SURRENDER

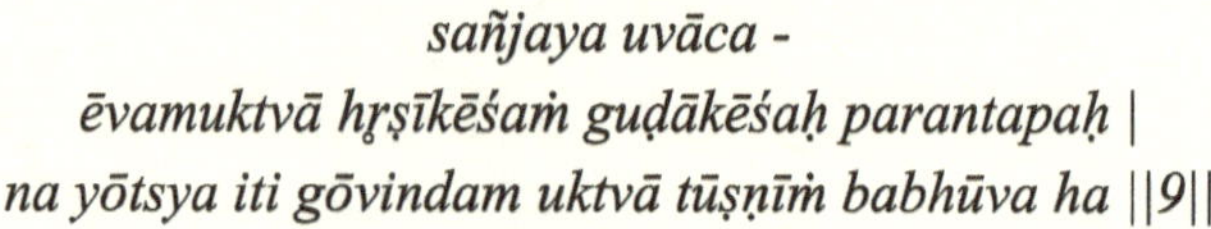

सञ्जय उवाच -

एवमुक्त्वा हृषीकेशं गुडाकेशः परन्तपः |

न योत्स्य इति गोविन्दम् उक्त्वा तूष्णीं बभूव ह ||9||

sañjaya uvāca -
ēvamuktvā hṛṣīkēśaṁ guḍākēśaḥ parantapaḥ |
na yōtsya iti gōvindam uktvā tūṣṇīṁ babhūva ha ||9||

Meaning:

Sanjaya narrates:

Amid the battlefield, Arjuna (***guḍākēśaḥ***, conqueror of sleep), the formidable warrior (***parantapaḥ***, scorcher of foes), addressed Krishna (***hṛṣīkēśa***, master of the senses), declaring decisively, 'I will not engage in battle' (***na yōtsya iti***). Having delivered these words to Krishna (***gōvinda***, provider of joy), he fell silent (***tūṣṇīṁ babhūva***, enveloped in profound stillness) **[Sankya Yoga: 2.9]**

At a Glance: Capturing the Spirit of the Shloka

Despite being highly skilled, Arjuna found himself overwhelmed and perplexed in a critical and high-pressure situation. Recognizing his state of helplessness, he took the vital step of seeking guidance from Krishna, highlighting the importance of self-awareness and seeking help from trusted and skilled individuals when faced with life's most challenging moments.

Commentary:

The 9th shloka of Chapter II marks a significant transition, both in the meter of the text and in the emotional landscape of its central character, Arjuna.

As the rhythm of the shloka shifts from the expansive *Trishtubh* to the more introspective *Anushtubh* meter, we witness Arjuna's internal conflict reaching a vital stillness. Sanjaya, who was granted divine vision by sage Vyasa, most brilliantly captures the gravity of the moment. He observes Arjuna, a warrior unrivaled in prowess, relinquishing the reins of his resolve to Bhagavan Krishna. It is a moment of profound surrender, signaling the readiness of the disciple to receive guidance from the divine teacher.

Arjuna's silence, as noted by Sanjaya, is, as it were, a loaded calm before the transformative storm of Krishna's teachings. His unwillingness to fight is not merely a refusal to engage in combat; it is an admission of the paralysis of his decision-making faculties. In acknowledging his limitations and seeking Krishna's counsel, Arjuna exhibits a vulnerability that is quintessential for genuine spiritual growth.

Modern psychology asserts that acknowledging moments of crisis can lead to significant personal transformation. The act of surrender, akin to Arjuna's admission of helplessness, is often the precursor to receiving help and gaining renewed strength. This idea is supported by contemporary research, which suggests that the admission of one's own limitations can be a catalyst for change that paves the way for personal development and psychological resilience.

This very pictorial shloka conveys a profound lesson in humility and the power of silence. In our contemporary world, where action is often emphasized over contemplation, the importance of quietude is frequently overlooked. Yet, as demonstrated by Arjuna's example, it is in the stillness of surrender that the human psyche is furrowed for the seeds of wisdom to be sown.

American talk show host Oprah Winfrey's resounding advice has helped millions around the world, *"When you don't know what to do - do nothing. You get still until you do know."*

As the battlefield evolves into a backdrop for an imminent spiritual discourse, Arjuna's bearing mirrors a universal experience. Just as a researcher stands before the unknown, admitting the limits of current knowledge and opening to new discoveries, or as a patient entrusts themselves to the expertise of a physician, Arjuna's stance teaches us the importance of trust and openness in the face of life's battles.

For a keen student of Vedanta, a question naturally arises here - why is Arjuna, a *Dhananjaya*, a winner of wealth and battles, relinquishing his very nature and duty in the face of the most important battle of his life? It becomes imperative to pause here and re-read all the preceding shlokas that bring us to this moment of the Bhagavad Gita's unfolding.

Up until now, Arjuna had forgotten the greater and, in fact, the only reason for this battle - that of the re-establishment of *dharma*. He had pitifully personalized the whole context. He had obliterated from his focus the fact that an entire nation looked up to the Pandavas to eradicate the evil that had gripped their lives and reinstate goodness. His refusal to engage in battle simply arose from self-pity that did not want to harm or, worse, kill his loved ones.

This shloka marks the end of his self-centeredness. Akin to human stamina, which falls short when working entirely for oneself - having forgotten the greater perspective, Arjuna is paralyzed with physical, mental, and intellectual fatigue. *He has lost the enthusiasm and passion for his work,* as it were. It is only when we work for higher ideals that include the well-being of all, including ourselves, that we can maintain our grit and determination to complete the tasks despite all odds.

Sanjaya's narration, yet again, unlocks avenues for the reader's own journey of Self-discovery. Arjuna's silence reflects our own moments of doubt and indecision. We are given a moment of calm to assess the reasons behind our inability to resolve whatever conflict confronts us. Through the warrior prince's dilemma, we are reminded that sometimes, the greatest obstacle on our path is ourselves. And that in those moments, the most significant act of courage is simply to pause, listen, and be willing to learn.

The ensuing discourse is a universal call to awaken the dormant seeker in each of us. This transition thus becomes a personal invitation to still our own inner conflicts, to listen for the wisdom that life offers, and to trust in the guidance that can steer us towards a path of true fulfillment and understanding.

In Their Names: The Essence of Guidance and Mastery

The names used for Arjuna and Krishna in the 9th shloka of the Bhagavad Gita unveil deep layers of insight into their characters and the overarching message of the epic. Sanjaya's choice of epithets— *Guḍākeśa* and *Parantapa* for Arjuna, and *Hṛṣīkeśa* and *Govinda* for Krishna reveal the depth of their core and the spiritual journey they have each undertaken.

The names used for Arjuna here, *Guḍākeśa*, which signifies mastery over sleep- contextually discipline and vigilance, and *Parantapa*, denoting his prowess in battle as the "scorcher of foes," paint a picture of a formidable warrior. Yet, these same qualities underscore a vital lesson: the outer victories and achievements, symbolized by martial prowess and astute alertness, do not necessarily equate to inner peace or resolve internal turmoil. This duality of Arjuna's character highlights the complexity of human nature, where strength and vulnerability coexist, and external successes cannot quench the inner thirst for deeper answers and solace.

In this shloka, we witness *Guḍākeśa,* the disciplined warrior, succumb to the emotional repercussions of the impending war. It is here that the juxtaposition of Arjuna's valor and his vulnerability lies exposed. Despite his legendary skills, Arjuna is engulfed by grief, illustrating that external triumphs alone cannot shield one from internal strife. The lesson is clear: life's battles are not just fought in the physical realm but within the complex corridors of the human psyche. It would behoove us to think of victory in which of the two battles would put us in better stead for life.

Krishna, addressed as *Hṛṣīkeśa,* or the 'Lord of the Senses,' epitomizes the mastery over the mind and senses, reflecting his role as the supreme guide capable of steering any being through life's tumultuous seas towards spiritual clarity and enlightenment. The name *Govinda,* rich with meanings that include the protector of cows, the sustainer of the Earth, and the revealer of the Vedas, encapsulates Krishna's multifaceted role as the guardian of *dharma,* the provider of sustenance, and the ultimate source of wisdom. In his guidance to Arjuna, Krishna transcends the role of a charioteer or friend, becoming the divine mentor who illuminates the path of *dharma* and spiritual liberation.

Krishna, as *Hrsikesa* and *Govinda,* stands as the beacon of hope and wisdom for Arjuna. The conversation that follows is not just a discourse on duty and righteousness but a deeper exploration of life's fundamental truths. We are privy to the transformation that ensues when *Guḍākeśa* surrenders to *Hṛṣīkeśa;* human frailty meets divine guidance, and the seeker ultimately finds refuge in sacred knowledge.

The contemporary relevance of these names and their meanings cannot be overstated. Like Arjuna, we strive for mastery over our professions and personal disciplines. We think they will ensure our happiness throughout life. Yet, we often find ourselves grappling with internal conflicts that no amount of external success can resolve. In these moments, seeking a *Hṛṣīkeśa*—a guide who can help us master our mind and elevate our understanding—becomes crucial for true growth and contentment.

Thus, the names *Guḍākeśa*, *Hṛṣīkeśa*, *Parantapa*, and *Govinda* encapsulate the essence of the Bhagavad Gita's teachings: true victory in life is achieved when we surrender our limited understanding to divine wisdom, move from self-centeredness to self-reliance, and transition from materially driven actions to enlightened actions.

The 9th shloka of Chapter II of the Bhagavad Gita, through the poignant narrative shift and the deliberate use of names for Arjuna and Krishna, offers a profound insight into the nature of the human struggle, the pursuit of wisdom, and the path to spiritual liberation. Arjuna stands at the crossroads of duty and despair. His surrender to Krishna symbolizes the universal journey toward understanding and enlightenment—a journey that requires the courage to confront one's deepest fears, humility, and willingness to seek guidance. Through this dialogue, the Gita overreaches its ancient origins, offering timeless wisdom that continues to guide individuals through the challenges of the contemporary world.

Reflective Prompt

Arjuna, though highly skilled, was unprepared for the emotional toll of the battle. Are there areas in your life where you rely solely on your skills without considering emotional or mental preparedness? How can you better equip yourself in these areas?

Even the mightiest sometimes need a hand to steady their gait

SHLOKA 10: SMILING WISDOM AMIDST CHALLENGES

तमुवाच हृषीकेशः प्रहसन्निव भारत |
सेनयोरुभयोर्मध्ये विषीदन्तमिदं वचः ||10||

tamuvāca hṛṣīkēśaḥ prahasanniva bhārata |
sēnayōrubhayōrmadhyē viṣīdantamidaṁ vacaḥ ||10||

Translation:

"O! Descendant of Bharata! In the middle (*madhye*) of both (*ubhayoḥ*) armies (*senayoḥ*), Krishna (*Hṛṣīkeśaḥ*), smiling (*prahasan iva*), told (*uvāca*) that [Arjuna] (*tam*) who is despair (*viṣīdantam*) this (*idam*) word (*vachaḥ*) [Sankya Yoga: 2.10]

At a Glance: Capturing the Spirit of the Shloka

Stationed between the two armies, at zero hours of battle, Krishna has just witnessed the otherwise indomitable warrior Arjuna's complete physical, emotional, and intellectual meltdown. With a calm and composed countenance, Krishna, the Master of the senses and mind, offers guidance not only to the confused warrior but to all of us. This masterfully portrayed moment illustrates that wisdom can bring clarity and strength in the face of life's most significant challenges. Krishna's smile conveys the promise of inner peace that emanates from the transformative power of knowledge. It reminds us that stability of mind and a thorough assimilation of spiritual knowledge can help us navigate even the most brutal battles - within and without.

Commentary:

In the heart of the battlefield, amidst the clamor and anticipation of imminent war, Sanjaya captures a profound moment of stillness within which quietly pulsates the highest spiritual wisdom to be imparted by a divine charioteer to a desolate warrior. Sanjaya addresses Dhritarashtra as Bharata to remind him, as it were, of his noble heritage, a poignant contrast to his actions.

Krishna, referred to as Hrishikesa, who has complete dominion over the senses and mind, stands calm and composed, starkly contrasting the chaos around him. His subtle yet significant smile is a harbinger of the profound teachings.

Krishna's smile amid this overwhelming turmoil would raise controversy in the mind of any student reading the Gita for the first time. But you see, Krishna's smile is a silent assurance of mastery over the looming confusion and disorder. Krishna is familiar with Arjuna's unconquerable proficiency on and off the battlefield. He knows Arjuna's current despondency comes not from his true nature but from a temporary surge of emotions. His smile reflects an understanding that these emotions will be rightly channeled with proper guidance, and the battle will be fought and won. Krishna's serene and confident smile displays the possession of a cure for the human crisis. Just like after a battery of medical tests, a doctor welcomes you with a jolly smile at your review appointment, even before disclosing the results. The doctor has a diagnosis and a treatment plan and is assured of the prognosis.

Krishna's smile also symbolizes the spontaneous joy that arises from a profound connection with the divine. It is a testament to the peace within a person who has mastered the mind. This independent state of happiness is the ultimate goal of all spiritual pursuits and the source of genuine and lasting contentment.

We often encounter situations that test our composure and jostle our mental balance. Krishna's comportment demonstrates that inner peace is achievable even when external circumstances are tense. Rather than succumbing to mind-driven fear and anxiety, as we most often are, his equanimous disposition encourages us to confront our difficulties with cheerful ease grounded in unshakable inner strength.

As explained in our introductory book, *First Step Into Bhagavad Gita*, the setting itself speaks volumes. Bhagavan Shri Krishna begins disseminating this Divine wisdom not in the tranquil seclusion of a forest or ashram but right where the heat of the conflict is. The battlefield, thus, becomes a metaphor for life, where often, the most profound insights dawn not on a yoga mat or within the confines of a meditation center but amid our daily struggles. The lightning flash of wisdom does not need to wait for that perfect moment of seclusion and solitude but can strike right where we stand, provided we are ready to listen.

Krishna's impending message, foreshadowed by his serene demeanor, articulates one of the Bhagavad Gita's core teachings: suffering is not a given but a choice. As the Buddhist saying made famous by Japanese author Haruki Murakami goes, *"Pain is inevitable. Suffering is optional.*" While continual physical and emotional onslaughts are inescapable aspects of human experience, the consequent suffering is a matter of individual perspective and choice.

The Bhagavad Gita illuminates the path from this suffering to liberation, emphasizing the distinction between transient pain and lasting suffering. It helps us understand that while we cannot always control the pains that come our way, it is very much within our grasp to manage and ultimately overcome them.

Corroborating the same, modern psychology keenly distinguishes between pain—a physiological and psychological response to stimuli and suffering - the narrative we weave around that pain. While pain is an unavoidable aspect of mortal existence, suffering is often the result of our resistance to that pain, our refusal to accept and understand it.

Consider the example of a patient suffering from chronic pain. While the physical discomfort is real, the extent to which the patient suffers emotionally and mentally is greatly influenced by their mindset. The famous scientist Stephen Hawking's remarkable life story exemplifies this distinction between pain and suffering. Though he was physically tied down by the excruciating pain of a debilitating disease, Hawking's mindset prevented this pain from morphing into suffering. Despite his physical limitations, his resilience and determination to contribute to cosmology without yielding to despair animate the Bhagavad Gita's core teaching to rise above life's challenges through wisdom and inner strength. They provide insight into human endurance and validate the power of the mind over the body's tribulations. The Gita instructs us not to cave into the onslaught of pain but to seek a deeper understanding of life's vicissitudes, thus transforming our relationship with suffering.

The battlefield that mercilessly stares Arjuna in the face is an analogy for the battlefield each of us hosts within our being. A smiling Krishna is ready to guide Arjuna from a place of desolation to one of enlightenment—an assurance to all of humanity, as it were, that with the proper counsel, a flight toward joy and liberation is possible even from the depths of despair.

In the very preliminary shlokas of this chapter, there is a promise of a journey from ignorance to knowledge, sorrow to contentment, and bondage to liberation. As Sanjaya continues his narrative, we at once realize that the wisdom of the Gita is as relevant now as it was on the battlefield of Kurukshetra thousands of years ago, offering solace and guidance to all who find themselves lost in the tempests of life.

Navigating the Spiritual Terrain: Two Distinct Teaching Methods

Sanatana Dharma uses two prominent teaching styles to guide seekers on their spiritual journey. The first style involves clearly outlining the ultimate destination right at the outset. This method can be likened to showing a climber the peak of the highest mountain from the valley below—it may appear daunting and unreachable at first. However, once the goal is established, the teacher guides the student step by step toward it. This approach helps students remember the final objective throughout the journey. A clear disadvantage, however, is that the sheer enormity of the goal might discourage some from beginning their journey.

The second approach adopts a more gradual method, revealing the path in stages without initially disclosing the destination. This can be likened to leading a climber up a mountain via a winding path, showing only the immediate next steps and not the mountain peak. While this method might ease students into the journey, reducing initial overwhelm, it carries the risk that students may settle for an intermediate stage, mistaking it for the goal, or deviate from the path due to a lack of understanding of the journey's full scope.

Though the Bhagavad Gita masterfully employs both styles through the brilliant dialogue between Teacher and student traversing all terrains of the human psyche - it is interesting to note that Krishna begins emphatically with the first teaching style, particularly evident from Chapter 2, Shloka 11. He starts with a profound exposition of the ultimate human goal—liberation from all suffering, or *Moksha*.

Krishna refrains from addressing Arjuna's immediate battlefield dilemma at once but instead sets the stage for a gradual and comprehensive spiritual elevation. This genius strategy helps students of the Bhagavad Gita understand that the teachings are not just aimed at resolving temporary crises but are designed to guide them toward eternal enlightenment, which can overcome every future obstacle. By revealing the ultimate truth upfront, Krishna's method prepares the seeker for a journey that aims for direct spiritual realization, albeit via a deeply philosophical exchange.

Krishna begins his discourse by introducing the ultimate goal of human life - without any comprehensible background. It may initially appear complex and unachievable for some. However, seekers need to be reassured that through the ensuing chapters, by bringing in the second teaching style, Krishna carefully leads us to this ultimate destination step-by-step. We solicit your patience and focus throughout the study of these verses. None of these teachings are beyond our grasp here and now. The instructions of the Gita are intended for understanding, practice, and realization in our immediate experience.

Reflective Prompt

Have you ever been in the position of counseling someone in a crisis? Knowing the crux of their problem and having a viable solution was it hard for you to suppress your smile? Do you see how a third-party perspective that looks at the problem but is not a part of it always bears a cheerful countenance qualifying them as true mentors?

From within life's unconquerable battles, the redeeming feature is always wise counsel. Seek it.

SHLOKA 11: THE WISDOM BEYOND SORROW

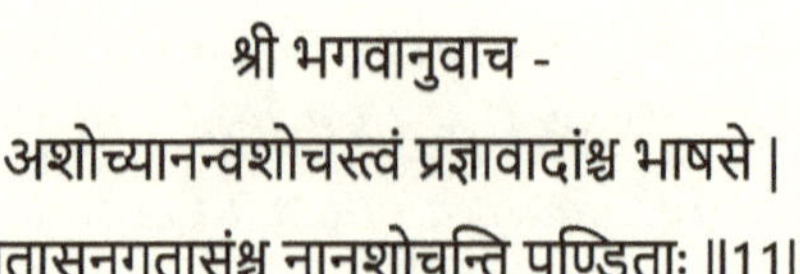

श्री भगवानुवाच -

अशोच्यानन्वशोचस्त्वं प्रज्ञावादांश्च भाषसे |

गतासूनगतासूंश्च नानुशोचन्ति पण्डिताः ||11||

śrī bhagavān uvāca -
aśōcyānanvaśōcastvam prajñāvādāmśca bhāṣasē |
gatāsūnagatāsūmśca nānuśōcanti paṇḍitāḥ ||11||

Translation:

Shri Bhagavan (**Krishna**) said:

You grieve for those beyond grieving (*aśōcyān*), and yet you speak like the learned (*prajñā-vādān*). Truly, the enlightened (*paṇḍitāḥ*) continuously weep (*na anuśōcanti*) neither for the living (*agatāsūn*) nor for the dead (*gatāsūn*). [Sankya Yoga: 2.11]

At a Glance: Capturing the Spirit of the Shloka

Understanding your true identity—who and what you are—beyond the body, mind, and intellect is the ultimate solution to all suffering. A person who realizes their essence as *Atma* [Consciousness] transcends perpetual worry over life's situations. They maintain a balanced perspective, fully engaged in life's challenges yet never overwhelmed, finding lasting peace and resilience through the knowledge of their unchanging, infinite nature.

Commentary:

Amid the clamor of the battlefield, this striking moment marks the beginning of Bhagavan Shri Krishna's teachings. His transformative discourse is a journey meticulously charted from the initial utterance of '*Asochyan*' in shloka 11 of Chapter II —signifying the futility of grief for what is impermanent—to the conclusive counsel '*ma suchah,' in* shloka 66 of Chapter XVIII - a directive to transcend sorrow. Herein lies the core intent of the Gita: meticulous guidance towards the alleviation of human suffering.

Krishna begins his teachings with a profound declaration that grief, as we know it, is unnecessary and highlights a path beyond the confines of suffering. By addressing Arjuna's despondency directly, Krishna extends his guidance to humanity, emphasizing that the lament over what is lost, what is yet to come, or what presently is, beyond a point, is misplaced. He underscores a vital truth: '*na anuśocanti paṇḍitāḥ*'—that the truly enlightened, those who have reached the pinnacle of wisdom, do not dwell in perpetual sorrow over the comings and goings of life, be it the loss of the departed, the anxiety for the living, or the uncertainty of the future.

This declaration is not a philosophical musing. It is a promise that while many of us are ensnared by the shackles of grief and suffering, a state of being exists—factual and accessible—where such afflictions no longer hold sway. And this transition from a state of constant worrying to one of transcendent wisdom is not merely aspirational but achievable.

Let us pause here to remind ourselves of where these words are being uttered. This peculiar setting of a roaring battlefield assures us that Spiritual edification—and the serenity it brings—is not the exclusive domain of the mystic or the ascetic but a pulsating potential within every one of us living in the material world - just waiting to be tapped into.

It is essential to distinguish between transient and perpetual sadness. The natural occurrence of sadness, a response to life's inevitable changes and losses, is part of what makes us inherently human. Yet, Krishna warns us against allowing this sadness to morph into *'anu śocanti,'* continual, deep-seated suffering that will diminish our capacity to live fully in the present.

The perpetual suffering, addressed by Krishna in this shloka, spotlights the predicament faced by countless individuals who find themselves imprisoned in their self-perpetuated woes, unable to break free from the shackles of past regrets and future anxieties. Modern society repeatedly faces this dilemma, where the shadows of the past and imaginations about the future often loom more pronounced than the reality of the present. This enduring anguish is akin to carrying the weight of an invisible burden, that distorts perception and impedes the ability to live fully in the now.

The Bhagavad Gita's teachings are not a call to emotionlessness. Emotions are powerful drivers of our actions—think about it: your best and worst decisions were likely influenced by strong emotions at the time. As human beings, we are endowed with the profound gift of emotions. Krishna encourages us to harness and channel them constructively rather than being overpowered by them.

By distinguishing between transient sadness and ongoing suffering, Krishna guides us into developing spiritual maturity that helps us to overcome life's inevitable pains without descending into perpetual sorrow. This path, as illustrated by the life of Buddha, who sought enlightenment to understand and overcome human suffering, underscores the profound quest at the heart of spirituality: to find peace amidst the turmoil, not by denying pain but by transforming our relationship with it.

Krishna's blunt assertion, *'na anuśocanti paṇḍitāḥ,'* unveils a timeless truth: genuine enlightenment transcends perpetual sorrow. The term *'paṇḍitā,'* often casually attributed to scholars or priests in modern discourse, has a more profound meaning in the context of the Bhagavad Gita. Here, it delineates not just an individual with an expansive scriptural acumen but one who has attained an intimate understanding of their true essence—who am I or what am I. This nuanced comprehension indicates a true *'paṇḍitā'* as an individual whose clarity about their own nature illuminates the path beyond the shadows of suffering. Krishna emphasizes that this profound realization of the true nature of the Self is quintessential to transcending all forms of suffering.

At the outset, Krishna addresses humanity's deepest existential struggle: the quest to break free from suffering. He reveals that true liberation cannot be found in external solutions but through an inward journey of Self-discovery. By understanding our true identity beyond the physical, mental, and intellectual realms, we transcend the cycles of sorrow tied to impermanence.

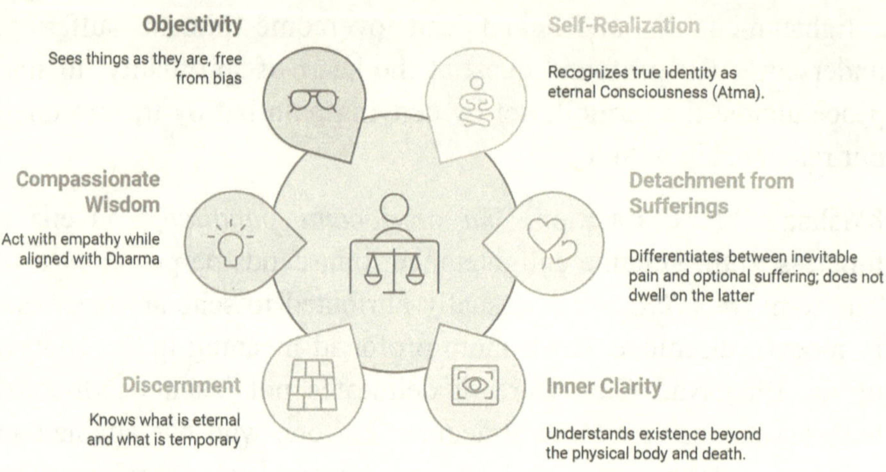

Fig: Characteristics of a "Pandita" (Enlightened Person)

Demystifying Enlightenment

When Krishna speaks of enlightenment as the means to transcend sorrow, the concept may initially seem abstract, mystical, and distant to the contemporary seeker. Understanding one's true identity might appear an esoteric pursuit reserved for the spiritual elites or those devoted to solitary contemplation. However, the Bhagavad Gita demystifies these preconceptions, emphasizing that enlightenment is neither an unreachable state nor the exclusive privilege of saints and sages. Instead, it is the intimate realization of our true essence—accessible to everyone, regardless of their role or station in life. As pointed out earlier, Krishna delivers this teaching to a warrior on a battlefield, underscoring its universal relevance for all, not just mystics or ascetics. This profound insight encourages us to shed the layers of conditioned identities and recognize that enlightenment is simply a return to our true Self—beyond the fleeting constructs of body, mind, and intellect.

This might seem out of the box as we are conditioned to view ourselves in the mirror of our bodies, minds, and intellect from an incredibly early age, accepting what we see and know as the totality of our existence. The Gita, however, challenges this deeply ingrained notion and invites us to question and explore reality beyond the confines of bodily identification.

Let us pause here to reflect upon a powerful analogy often cited by Adi Shankaracharya—a dream scenario: Imagine that in your dream, you are in Gangotri amidst the snow-covered Himalayas along the sacred banks of Mother Ganga. Within this dream, if someone were to inquire about your identity, you would naturally associate yourself with the body within that dream. Any harm to this dream body would cause you distress because, at that moment, your identities are intertwined. Yet, upon waking up, you realize that the dream body was not you. Your true essence—your Consciousness—remained untouched by the dream events.

When the dreamer realizes their true identity within the dream, it transforms into a lucid dream—a state where the dreamer becomes aware that they are dreaming. This awareness allows them to navigate the dream with the understanding that the sorrows and challenges within the dream are transient and do not define their true self.

Similarly, enlightenment or Self-knowledge in the waking state is the recognition that our identity transcends our physical form. In a lucid dream, the dreamer understands their actual state and gains a degree of control and detachment from the dream events - similarly, recognizing our true nature as Consciousness [*Atma*] provides a perspective that alleviates the inherent suffering within the ephemeral mortal life. We continue to deal with life's challenges, but from a vantage point of clarity and serenity, knowing that we are more than our experiences and that our essence remains untouched by the transient nature of the world. This awareness does not negate our worldly experiences but transforms our engagement with them. Sorrows and joys are experienced, but they no longer define us or dictate our state of being.

Enlightenment is not an esoteric state but a shift in perspective—a sound understanding of our existence that allows us to face life's challenges with newfound grace. It does not remove life's obstacles but changes how we engage with them, knowing that our true essence is eternal and unscathed by the transient nature of physical reality. This knowledge helps us skillfully navigate the tumultuous onslaughts of unavoidable earth-bound pains by resurrecting the calm composure of the Self that throbs within each one of us. Just as the awareness in a lucid dream alleviates the gravity of dream-world problems, Self-knowledge empowers us to transcend the suffering of our waking world, equipping us to handle life's trials with equanimity and grace.

Aspect	What Enlightenment Is	What Enlightenment Is Not
Nature	A shift in perspective—realizing one's true identity as Consciousness (*Atma*).	An abstract, mystical, or unattainable state.
Accessibility	Available to everyone, regardless of their life stage or role (e.g., a warrior like Arjuna).	Reserved exclusively for monks, saints, or ascetics.
Process	A practical understanding of existence that transforms daily living.	A withdrawal from the world or its responsibilities.
Impact on Emotions	Brings clarity and serenity, helping one navigate joys and sorrows with equanimity.	An escape from emotions or the elimination of all challenges.
Relationship with the World	Allows engagement with the world while understanding its transient nature.	Detachment from the world in a way that denies or avoids life's realities.

Analogy	Like waking up from a dream and realizing the dream events were transient and did not define your true self.	A magical transformation or otherworldly experience divorced from practical life.
Goal	Liberation from suffering through Self-realization and understanding the eternal nature of Being.	Avoidance of life's obstacles or a guarantee of constant happiness.
Application	Guides practical, everyday living by aligning actions with a higher awareness.	A theoretical or purely intellectual pursuit with no relevance to daily life.

Table: Demystifying Enlightenment

Rationale for Spirituality: Understanding the Gita's Call to Transcend Suffering

Shloka 11 encapsulates the foundational rationale for spiritual pursuit—a path discerned across spiritual traditions like Hinduism, Buddhism, Jainism, and Sikhism. This ancient wisdom, echoing through texts like the *Sāṅkhyakārikā* of the Sāṅkhya Darshana—one of the six classical schools of Hinduism—sheds light on spirituality as the only means to transcend human suffering.

The *Sāṅkhyakārikā*, an ancient text dating back to a time before its first known Chinese translation in 569 CE, begins with an exploration into the nature of happiness and the inevitability of suffering. It categorizes suffering into three types: *adhyātmika* (originating within oneself), *adhibhautika* (caused by others and external factors), and *adhidaivika* (resulting from natural forces). The text articulates a comprehensive inquiry into counteracting these sufferings, concluding that worldly remedies offer no permanent escape. This realization that material solutions falter in the face of life's more formidable agonies spurred spiritual luminaries like Buddha to seek answers beyond the tangible.

The essence of Krishna's teachings in the Bhagavad Gita echoes this timeless pursuit, offering enlightenment—understood as the profound realization of one's true nature—as the definitive resolution to life's endemic sorrows.

The words of Jesus Christ, *"If you continue in My word, you are truly My disciples. Then you will know the truth, and the truth will set you free"* (John 8:32-33), echo the same message found in Krishna's dialogue with Arjuna in the Bhagavad Gita. They reinforce that true liberation from suffering is possible primarily through Self-discovery and realizing our essence beyond the physical realm.

Beyond Grief: The Compassionate Clarity of the Enlightened

Krishna's assertion that the enlightened do not dwell in sorrow over the dead or the living may perplex a new student of the Gita. It naturally raises questions about empathy and humanity within the "enlightened.". Does enlightenment render one indifferent to the world's suffering? Far from it. Those who have attained true wisdom are the epitome of compassion. They unquestionably understand the inevitability of life and death as a spectacle of temporary appearance and disappearance within the eternity of unmanifest existence. This wisdom naturally fosters more presence and a deeper connection to all beings within every moment encountered.

Reflective Prompt

When faced with personal loss or disappointment, can you differentiate between natural sadness and prolonged suffering? Does the latter help in reversing the loss? How long will you allow suffering to obstruct life from flowing forward and look forward to what lies ahead?

Grieve not for what changes; embrace the eternal within

SHLOKA 12: TRANSCENDING LIFE'S CYCLE

न त्वेवाहं जातु नासं न त्वं नेमे जनाधिपाः ।
न चैव न भविष्यामः सर्वे वयमतः परम् ॥12॥

na tvēvāham jātu nāsam na tvam nēmē janādhipāḥ |
na caiva na bhaviṣyāmaḥ sarvē vayamataḥ param ||12||

Translation:

Never was there a time when I did not exist (***na tvā eva aham jātu na
āsam***), nor you (***na tvam),*** nor these kings of men (***na ime janādhipāḥ***).
Nor will there be a time hereafter (***na ca eva na bhaviṣyāmaḥ***) when any
of us shall cease to exist (***sarve vayam ataḥ param***)
[Sankya Yoga: 2.12]

At a Glance: Capturing the Spirit of the Shloka

The essence of all beings is eternal. There was never a time when we did not exist, and there will never be a time when we cease to exist. This declaration emphasizes that our true identity is imperishable.

Commentary:

In the previous shloka, Krishna presents the radical notion that those who have realized their true essence do not grieve for the living or the dead. If interpreted superficially, this assertion might seem cold or detached, bewildering a new student of the Bhagavad Gita.

Shloka 12 directly tackles this confusion, elucidating the nature of enlightenment and its relation to perception and grief.

Beyond Birth and Death: Understanding Our Immutable Nature

With utmost simplicity and clarity, Krishna declares a fundamental truth upon which the entire teaching of Advaita Vedanta is built: the inherent immortality of existence that transcends the apparent cycles of birth and death.

Piercing right through the illusion of mortality, Krishna asserts the timeless existence of all beings—beginning with himself, extending to Arjuna and, indeed, to all of humanity. By employing a deliberate double negative, Krishna not only negates the misconception of mortality but also reinforces the universal and timeless nature of our existence (*Atma*). This eternal truth applies to all, making no distinction between divine incarnations and mortal beings.

This knowledge, realized by those who have awakened to their true identity, accounts for the serene composure of the enlightened ones, or *panditas*, who remain anchored in the eternal continuity amidst the ephemeral flux of life and death. The unassailable knowledge of the undying nature of the Self [*Atma*] liberates them from every kind of transient sorrow.

Through this shloka, Krishna disentangles the confusion surrounding existence by asserting that at the heart of all life is an indelible constancy—our shared, immutable essence. This insight, profound in its simplicity, challenges us to redefine our understanding of existence, urging us towards a deeper exploration of our own eternal nature.

From Temporal to Timeless: Reexamining Our Identity

To understand and use the techniques to transcend mortal suffering professed by the Bhagavad Gita, we must primarily delve into the complexities of identity as perceived in daily life versus the eternal essence highlighted by Krishna.

In our daily lives, we perceive the self as a composite of the physical body, emotions, thoughts, and the sense of personal identity navigating the world. This notion, referred to in Vedantic terminology as *Ahamkara* (the "I-maker"), constructs our individual narrative, shaping who we believe ourselves to be based on experiences, memories, and perceptions.

Ahamkara functions as a necessary mechanism, allowing us to engage with the world meaningfully. However, it is a provisional construct, akin to the persona we adopt in a vivid dream. In a dream, we experience joy, suffering, and adventures as though they are real. A cut on the dream body feels like our pain, and its death feels like our end. Yet upon waking, we recognize these experiences as fleeting and distinct from our true self. Similarly, Krishna reveals that the identity we cling to in waking life—our body, thoughts, and emotions—is transient, while our true essence, *Atman* (the eternal Self), exists beyond these constructs.

This realization transforms our perspective. Just as awakening from a dream reveals the dream body's impermanence, recognizing *Atman* shifts our identity from the body, mind, and intellect to the eternal continuum of Consciousness. While this physical apparatus is essential for worldly engagement, it is not the entirety of who we are. Our essence exists beyond birth, growth, decay, and death, unbound by time's limitations.

Krishna encourages us to peel away the layers of *Ahamkara* to unveil the unchanging and undivided *Atman*. This deeper understanding allows us to live with clarity and detachment, much like a lucid dreamer who navigates the dream world with awareness of its impermanence. Enlightenment, therefore, is not about discarding *Ahamkara* but transcending its delusionary grip, seeing it as a tool rather than the entirety of selfhood. This holistic view enables us to view death not as an end but as a transition, placing our human experience within the broader context of eternity.

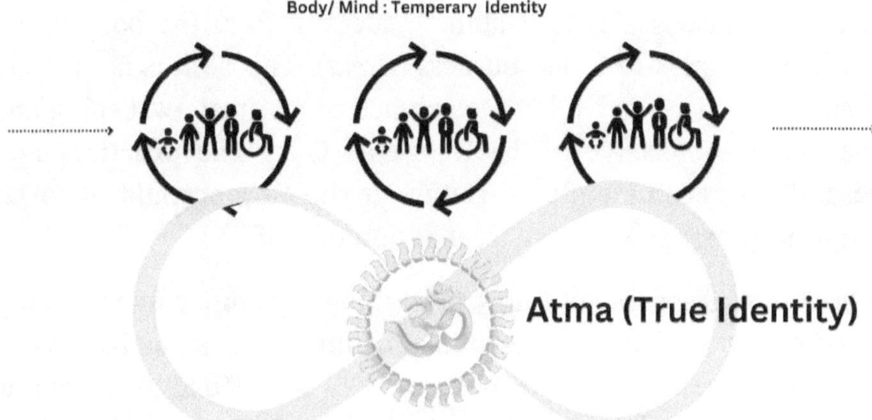

Fig: Our True Identity (Atma) is Eternal, While the Perceived Identity (Body) is Temporary

Why the Enlightened Do Not Suffer Perpetually

The enlightened ones, or *panditas*, have made this pivotal shift in perception. Their focus transcends the ephemeral and remains anchored in the Eternal, understanding that, at the core, nothing ceases to be. This profound realization explains why they do not succumb to perpetual grief (*nānuśōcanti paṇḍitāḥ*); **they recognize that at the most fundamental level, life's dramas do not alter the unchangeable essence of existence**.

This profound insight fosters a life of wisdom, joy, and equanimity, allowing them to fulfill worldly duties with a heart unburdened by the delusions of attachment and identity. They live fully in the world but are not of it; their actions are imbued with a deep understanding that **every thread of existence weaves together into a meticulous pattern within the eternity of the cosmos**. Death and birth become less intimidating, merely passing shadows in the light of the Atman.

By asserting this elevated state of the enlightened, Krishna offers a transformative solution to the enduring human predicament, which implicates a radical shift in identity from the body-mind-intellect complex to Consciousness (*Atma*). This shift is not merely a change in perspective but the essence of spiritual awakening and the ultimate objective of the Bhagavad Gita. **The practices and disciplines recommended throughout the Gita are laid down as steppingstones toward the Realization of Self.**

This Gita offers no solutions to making the impermanent body permanent; it highlights the eternal nature of Atman and shows us how to realize It as our true essence. The body, bound by its nature, cannot transcend its mortality, and the *Atma* does not need to attain immortality, for it is already beyond birth and death. Therefore, **the spiritual practices within the Gita are for shifting our identification from the mortal to the immortal aspect of our being**.

From time immemorial, seekers of Truth have pleaded for this shift through the ancient Vedic prayer:

'asato ma sad gamaya, tamaso ma jyotir gamaya, mrityor ma amritam gamaya'

Carry us from the unreal to the real, from darkness to light, and from the fear of death to the knowledge of our eternal nature.

The how might appear daunting, especially when approaching this text, void of clarity and understanding that comes with deep contemplation and insight. We aspire to demystify the process by guiding readers through the intricate nature of *Atma* that underpins our existence and illustrating how this shift in perception liberates us from the chains of perpetual sorrow. This exploration is not just an academic exercise but a journey toward understanding the eternal, unchanging truth of our being, paving the way for a life of deeper meaning and lesser grief.

Unveiling the Essence of *Atma*: From Corporeal to Eternal

Before proceeding, it is important to address potential confusion around the terms *Atma* and consciousness, as their meanings vary across different disciplines. In modern cognitive science, consciousness is often seen as a property of the mind, linked to awareness and perception. Likewise, the term *Atma* carries different meanings depending on its context. Adding to the complexity, the word 'soul' in some interpretations may evoke Judeo-Christian ideas of an ethereal essence subject to judgment, which can diverge from the Bhagavad Gita's vision.

The term '*Atma*' in Sanskrit fundamentally signifies "I" or "Self," its application varies widely based on the context, displaying a diverse spectrum of meanings. At its most basic level, '*Atma*' can denote the physical body, as when we describe physical attributes like height, saying, "I am 6 feet tall," here "I" refers to the body. In a different vein, when expressing emotions such as "I am sad," "I" points to the mind, encapsulating emotional states. So also, "I" refers to the intellect while saying, "I am thinking." Furthermore, when we discuss our existence in terms of birth, stating "I was born on a certain date," "I" encompasses the whole human being, integrating body, mind, and intellect. This multifaceted usage also extends to literary contexts, where "*atmakatha*," meaning autobiography, implies '*Atma*' as the individual human being narrating their life story. Conversely, "*Atmahatya*," translating to suicide, indicates an act done unto the physical self. Through these diverse usages, '*Atma*' embodies the essence of "I," morphing its reference to align with various aspects of individual existence, from the corporeal, emotional, and intellectual – to the composite being.

However, when we traverse the spiritual landscapes of the Bhagavad Gita, '*Atma*' assumes a profound connotation far beyond the mere corporeal, mental, or intellectual identity. It points to the quintessential essence of our being. This exploration is not about the ephemeral states of mind and intellect or the transient nature of our physical form but delves into the core of our existence—pure, immutable Consciousness.

This Consciousness is the constant, illuminating backdrop against which our thoughts, emotions, and sensations play out, unaffected by the content it reveals, like how the sun shines impartial to or unaffected by the earthly scenes it lights up. In a methodical and systematic exploration, Advaita Vedanta guides us to the realization that our true Self extends beyond the limits of our body, mind, and intellect. It reveals that the birth of the body does not mark our inception, nor does the body's death trumpet our cessation.

Advaita Vedanta recognizes *Atma* as non-dual Consciousness: eternal, indivisible, boundless, and the intrinsic reality of an individual. While '*Atma*' may signify the body, mind, intellect or individual identity in different contexts, its deepest, most authentic significance in Vedantic vision is this unalterable Consciousness. For clarity and emphasis, we might employ the term "*Satchitananda Atma*," pointing explicitly to the ever-present state of being that is our true nature.

Henceforth, to distinguish between the limited, contextual self and the universal, eternal Self, we will adopt the convention of using 'Self' (with a capital 'S') when referring to *Atma* in the ultimate sense and 'self' for its more restricted applications. This distinction aims to navigate the rich spiritual discourse on identity, ensuring a clear, modern understanding of these concepts as presented in the timeless wisdom of the Bhagavad Gita and Advaita Vedanta.

Consciousness Across Paradigms: Vedanta and the Scientific Frontier

In neuroscience or psychology, consciousness is seen as a cognitive function or an emergent property of the brain's complex activities tied to awareness and the processing of sensory inputs. Consciousness in the Spiritual context of the Bhagavad Gita transcends mere cognitive functions or sensory processing; it is not an emergent property of neural activities but the fundamental, unchanging essence of our being. This Consciousness (*Atma*) is not an entity that does or experiences; rather, it is the basis of experience itself, the ultimate subject that cannot be objectified.

A clear understanding of this distinction is vital for delving deeper into the teachings of the Gita. We must shift our view from a neurological analysis of consciousness to understanding It as an omnipresent, omnipotent, omniscient Presence that is the very substratum of existence. To prevent confusion, we will henceforth refer to this ultimate reality as 'Consciousness' (with a capital 'C') to keep with our ongoing exposition of '*Atma*' as this unchanging Consciousness.

Expanding upon the nuanced interpretation of Consciousness within Vedanta, it is compelling to note the emergence of alternative perspectives in the scientific community that resonate with these ancient insights. Particularly, the "Hard Problem of Consciousness," introduced by David Chalmers, challenges the prevailing scientific paradigm by questioning the very foundation of subjective experience, or qualia. This issue probes deeply into the enigma of how physical processes in the brain culminate in the rich landscape of human experience—how do the electrical and chemical machinations of the brain translate into the vivid sensation of color, the depth of emotion, or the subtleties of taste and sound?

To illustrate the quandary, let us compare the brain to a highly sophisticated computer. Science and technology have afforded us an understanding of how a computer processes data, executes programs, and performs complex tasks, akin to how neuroscience explains brain function, cognition, and control over bodily mechanisms. Yet, this analogy must be revised when confronting the experiential, subjective aspect of consciousness. The leap from the mechanical processing of information to the subjective feeling of 'seeing red' or the emotional euphoria from a melody remains inexplicable. This Hard Problem of consciousness suggests that Consciousness is not merely an emergent property of brain activity but could represent a fundamental aspect of the universe, as elemental as space and time.

Esteemed scientists have long-held views that resonate with Advaita Vedanta's profound tenets. This intersection of modern scientific thought and ancient wisdom highlights a growing appreciation for an integrated understanding of Consciousness.

Erwin Schrödinger, a seminal figure in quantum mechanics, extensively explored the philosophical dimensions of Consciousness and reality. His insights, expressed in 'What Is Life?' among other works, reflect a deep alignment with Vedantic principles. Schrödinger's concept of 'monistic idealism,' epitomized by his statement that *'The total number of minds in the universe is one,'* mirrors the Vedantic view of non-duality, where individual Consciousness *(Atman)* and the universal essence *(Brahman)* are fundamentally one and the same. His contemplations reveal a striking parallel between the principles of quantum mechanics and Vedantic vision, both challenging traditional views on the separateness of existence.

Similarly, Max Planck, the father of quantum theory, posited a revolutionary view that places Consciousness at the foundation of reality, suggesting that 'matter is derivative from consciousness,' a perspective that inversely challenges the materialistic approach of conventional science. Like Vedantic understanding, which positions Consciousness as the substratum on which the cosmos is projected, Planck's stance redefines our interpretation of the universe.

In contemporary times, thinkers like Roger Penrose and theoretical physicist Amit Goswami continue this exploration. Through his collaboration on the Orch-OR theory, Penrose suggests that quantum processes in the brain might play a crucial role in the manifestation of Consciousness, hinting at a complexity that classical physics fails to explain fully. This idea subtly echoes the Vedantic notion of the omnipresence and omnipotence of Consciousness. Meanwhile, Goswami champions a model of Consciousness-centric science, advocating a framework that mirrors the non-dual vision of Advaita Vedanta.

This evolving dialogue within scientific lobbies echoes the Vedantic view of Consciousness not as a derivative of material processes but as the fundamental reality from which the material universe springs. The exploration of Consciousness as potentially a basic feature of the universe aligns with the non-dualistic perspective of Advaita Vedanta, which sees Consciousness as the singular, unchanging essence permeating all existence. This perspective bridges ancient spiritual wisdom with contemporary scientific inquiry and invites a profound reevaluation of the quintessential position of Consciousness in the cosmos.

Aspect	Consciousness in Science	Consciousness in Vedanta
Definition	A cognitive function or emergent property of the brain's neural activities tied to awareness and sensory processing.	The fundamental, unchanging essence of being (*Atma*), the ultimate subject that enables experience itself, beyond sensory or cognitive functions.
Origin	Emerges from the complex interplay of electrical and chemical processes in the brain.	Eternal and independent of the body or brain; the substratum of existence itself.
Scope	Limited to sentience and awareness as linked to physical processes in the brain.	Omnipresent, omniscient, and omnipotent; transcends all physical and mental constructs.
Nature	An attribute or property of the physical brain, subject to scientific measurement and analysis.	The essence of identity; neither an attribute nor measurable, but the basis of all existence and awareness.
Analogy	Brain as a computer: consciousness as an emergent property akin to software generated by hardware.	Consciousness as the electricity that powers both the hardware (body) and software (mind), yet remains independent of both.
Temporal Status	Subject to physical changes, aging, and cessation with brain activity.	Eternal and unchanging; unaffected by birth, death, or the transformations of the body and mind.
Ultimate Goal	To decode how consciousness arises from brain activity and its implications for artificial intelligence and neuroscience.	To realize the Self Identity (*Atma)* as Consciousness, leading to liberation (*Moksha*) from the cycles of birth and death.

Table: Comparison of Consciousness in Vedanta and Modern Science

Shloka 12 declares that there is no birth or death for any being. It also affirms that those who identify with *Atma* - the ongoing eternal principle within do not grieve over the unstoppable changes that are part of material life. This assertion leads to questions about the apparent births and deaths that endlessly grip mortal reality with ecstasy and sorrow. The following shlokas unveil the metaphysical identity that remains unshackled from the chains of birth and death. They clarify the eternal nature of *Atma* and explain what it is that is born and dies.

> **Reflective Prompt:**
>
> Consider a time when you experienced loss or change—how might understanding an eternal essence within you have transformed your perspective?
>
> --
>
> --
>
> --

Wisdom blooms when we look beyond the fleeting to the Eternal within

SHLOKA 13: THE CONTINUITY OF EXISTENCE

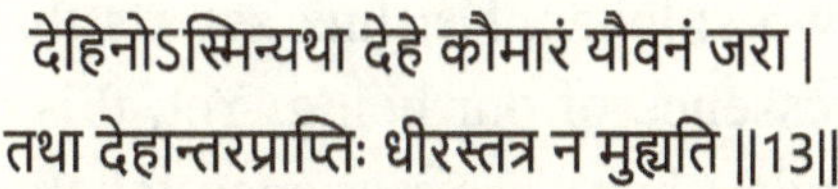

देहिनोऽस्मिन्यथा देहे कौमारं यौवनं जरा |
तथा देहान्तरप्राप्तिः धीरस्तत्र न मुह्यति ||13||

dēhinō'sminyathā dēhē kaumāraṁ yauvanaṁ jarā |
tathā dēhāntaraprāptiḥ dhīrastatra na muhyati ||13||

Translation:

Just as the embodied self (*dehinaḥ*) experiences transitions from childhood (*kaumāraṁ*) to youth (*yauvanam*) and then to old age (*jarā*) within this body (*dehe*), in the same way, it attains another body (*dehāntara-prāptiḥ*) after death. The wise (*dhīraḥ*) are not confused or deluded (*na muhyati*) by this understanding **[Sankya Yoga: 2.13]**

At a Glance: Capturing the Spirit of the Shloka

Krishna uses another very relatable analogy here to ascertain the continuity of life after the death of the physical body. Just as the dweller in this body experiences stages of childhood, youth, and old age, similarly, it acquires a new body after death. The wise understand this transition and are not confused or worried by it.

Commentary:

In the preceding two shlokas, Krishna asserts that neither birth nor death touches the essence of our being. Yet, this declaration starkly contrasts the everyday human experience wherein birth and death seem not only real but are inevitable. This apparent contradiction raises a pertinent question: if beings are indeed eternal, as Krishna suggests, then who undergoes the process of birth and death? And what does happen after death?

Shloka 13 directly addresses this obvious query. The resolution we find here is fundamental to understanding the metaphysical continuity of existence, a core tenet of the Bhagavad Gita, around which all its other life-transforming teachings revolve.

To navigate this profound inquiry, it is essential to understand the integral components that constitute human existence: the physical body (*Sthula Sharira*), the subtle body (*Sukshma Sharira*), the causal body (*Karana Sharira*), and the Consciousness (*Atma*).

The physical body consistently goes through birth, growth, aging, decay, and death. The subtle mind and intellect also express themselves through evolving thoughts, emotions, and intelligence. The causal body remains inaccessible to us. Consciousness illuminates the external world and inner thoughts and feelings. The subtle mind, intellect, and causal facet no longer manifest when the body ceases to function, leaving the body inert and insentient. Failing to view a human being as this amalgamated entity, we often think of the death of the physical body as terminal and absolute. We consider the body's birth as our birth and the body's death as our death. But is this accurate? Let us systematically explore each component through the lens of Advaita Vedanta to understand what happens to each through the processes of birth, growth, decay, disease, and death.

Note: Vedanta speaks of three bodies—physical, subtle, and causal—to provide a framework for understanding the layers of our identity. While we have mentioned the causal body (Karana Sharira) above, we will not explore it in detail at this stage, focusing instead on the physical and subtle bodies alongside Consciousness (Atma).

Physical Body (*Stula Sharira*)

The physical body, or *Sthula Sharira*—where *"stula"* means "physical" or "tangible"—is the most immediate and perceivable aspect of our existence. It is the medium through which we engage with the external world, processing stimuli via the organs of perception (such as the eyes and ears) and performing actions through the organs of action (like the hands and feet). Any impairment in this physical apparatus—diminishing vision or hearing loss—directly impacts our ability to perceive and interact with our surroundings.

This body encompasses all that is material and perceptible: muscles, bones, organs, nerves, and the brain. It serves as the vessel for our physical existence, subject to the natural laws of birth, growth, decay, and eventual death. Medical science primarily addresses this aspect of our being, treating illnesses, injuries, and physical aging.

In daily life, we often equate our identity with the physical body, marking significant milestones—birth, growth, aging, and death—by its transformations. This identification, though natural, limits our understanding of existence, as it confines our sense of self to what is tangible and temporary.

Krishna's teachings challenge this narrow view, urging us to see ourselves beyond the physical body. This shift in perspective begins the journey toward realizing our deeper identity beyond the temporary nature of the physical form.

Subtle Body (*Sukshma Sharira*)

The subtle body, or *Sukshma Sharira*, comprises 19 elements in Vedantic teachings. These include the mind (*manas*), intellect (*buddhi*), capacities of the five sensory organs (*jnanendriyas*), the powers of the five organs of action (*karmendriyas*), and the five *pranas*. *Unlike* the physical body, the subtle body is intangible and cannot be seen or touched. It represents the non-material aspects of our being.

The physical body, on its own, is inert and incapable of perception, action, or thought. It is the subtle body that animates and enables it to perceive, act, and function. For example, the eyes, as part of the physical body, merely serve as tools for capturing visual data, but the ability to interpret and understand this information resides in the subtle body. Similarly, while the ears facilitate hearing as part of the physical body, comprehension and processing of sounds occur through the subtle body. Neural impulses generated in the physical brain are tangible, but the thoughts and emotions they manifest are intangible, belonging to the subtle body.

By governing thoughts, emotions, and sensory perceptions, the subtle body transforms the physical body into a living, responsive entity. However, the subtle body requires the physical body as a medium to interact with the material world. When the physical body ceases to function, the subtle body loses its means of expression but continues its existence, awaiting another physical form.

To illustrate this relationship, consider the example of an Apple MacBook. The laptop's hardware—its screen, keyboard, CPU, and sensors—represents the physical body. However, the hardware alone cannot perform tasks; the software, representing the subtle body, makes the device functional. The software determines the laptop's capabilities, from running applications to processing data, yet it is intangible. Even when loaded with terabytes of data, the laptop's physical weight remains unchanged, emphasizing the non-material nature of these functions. This highlights the distinction between the physical hardware and the intangible yet vital software that animates it

Understanding the distinction between the physical and subtle bodies is critical to grasping the teachings of Advaita Vedanta. While the physical body undergoes birth, aging, and eventual death, the subtle body transcends these physical changes, continuing its journey beyond the demise of the physical form. This distinction underscores the idea that neither the physical body nor the subtle body encompasses the entirety of our Being, paving the way for exploring the ultimate dimension of human existence—Consciousness (*Atma*).

Returning to the MacBook analogy: when the hardware becomes obsolete, the valuable software and data are not discarded but transferred to a new device. Similarly, at death, the subtle body transitions from an old or diseased physical form to a new one. The old hardware is left behind, while the subtle body continues its journey, seeking a new physical body to manifest its functions. This process, governed by the law of *karma*, highlights the continuity of existence beyond the physical realm.

Consciousness (*Atma*)

Beyond the physical and subtle body lies the third and most fundamental dimension of our existence: *Atma*, or Consciousness. As seen in Shloka 12, *Atma* is the pure Consciousness or *Chit*, which is the core of our being, the awareness that animates our thoughts and emotions and enables our actions. It is the awareness that allows us to perceive and interpret our inner and outer world.

Advaita Vedanta describes *Atma* through three defining aspects: ***Sat, Chit,*** and ***Ananda***:

1. ***Chit* (Pure Consciousness)**: Refers to the illuminating awareness by which we experience everything. It is the inner light that enables us to see, hear, smell, taste, and feel. This Consciousness is not a function of the body or mind but their enabler. It is the essence of who we are at the deepest level.

2. ***Sat* (Existence)**: Represents the foundational reality upon which everything else depends. *Sat* is the eternal and unchanging essence of the universe, the substratum that sustains all phenomena. While the physical body and the material world are subject to change and decay, *Sat* underlies and supports their very existence. It is the fundamental Being that remains constant through the transient nature of the empirical world.

3. ***Ananda* (Wholeness)**: Often translated as bliss, Ananda refers to the intrinsic completeness (*Paripoornata*) of *Atma*. It signifies the unlimited contentment experienced within—a profound sense of fulfillment that is not dependent on anything external. This inner joy arises naturally from realizing one's true nature as *Atma*, transcending the limitations and suffering tied to the physical and subtle bodies.

Reverting to the Apple MacBook example: The hardware represents the physical body, and the software represents the subtle body. However, the most crucial element is electricity, without which neither the hardware nor the software can function. Similarly, Consciousness is the most fundamental aspect of our existence, enabling both the physical and subtle bodies to operate. Just as a laptop needs both hardware and software to function powered by electricity, our physical and subtle bodies need Consciousness to manifest.

Thus, *Atma*, the true Self, is not subject to birth and death, which affect the physical body. This eternal, limitless Consciousness persists beyond all physical changes and experiences. The Bhagavad Gita declares *Atma*—**this eternal Consciousness—as our true identity**. While we often equate ourselves with the body, mind, and intellect, these are merely tools or instruments through which Consciousness expresses itself. By identifying solely with the physical or subtle body, we limit ourselves to the transient and overlook the eternal essence that defines who we are. Recognizing Consciousness as our true Self (*Atma*) shifts our perspective, freeing us from the cycle of sorrow and attachment tied to impermanence.

This insight bridges the apparent contradiction between Krishna's assertion of our infinite nature and the everyday visuals of birth and death.

Aspect	Physical Body (Sthula Sharira)	Subtle Body (Sukshma Sharira)	*Atma* (Consciousness)
Definition	The tangible, material aspect of our existence.	The non-physical component consisting of mind, intellect, senses, and vital energies.	The fundamental, eternal awareness that illuminates all experiences and enables existence.
Composition	Muscles, bones, organs, and other physical elements.	19 elements: mind (manas), intellect (buddhi), 5 sensory capacities, 5 action powers, 5 pranas.	Pure existence (*Sat*), consciousness (*Chit*), and inner wholeness (*Ananda*)
Function	Engages with the world through sensory perception and physical action.	Processes thoughts, emotions, and perceptions; governs interactions with the world.	Enables the existence and awareness of both the physical and subtle bodies.
Visibility	Visible and perceivable.	Invisible and intangible.	Non-objectifiable; the unchanging witness of all experiences.
Changeability	Constantly changing: birth, growth, decay, and death.	Evolves with thoughts, emotions, and desires; transitions after physical death.	Eternal, unchanging, and unaffected by physical or mental states.
Dependency	Depends on the subtle body for sensory and motor functions.	Relies on the physical body for expression and action. Depends on consciousness for awareness	Independent; neither born nor dies, and sustains all experiences without dependence.
Lifespan	Temporary; begins with birth and ends with death.	Temporary but much longer than physical body; transitions between bodies across lifetimes.	Eternal; persists beyond all changes in the physical and subtle bodies.

Table: Comparison of Physical Body, Sutle Body and Atma

Reconciling the different dimensions of Human Identity

We have explored in detail the different dimensions of human identity: the physical body (*Stula Sharira*), the subtle body (*Sukshma Sharira*), and Consciousness (*Atma*). Together, they form the composite human being. Our usual identification is with the physical body, the most tangible and visible aspect of our existence. As Mr. X or Ms. Y, that begins with the birth of our physical body. Our existence is viewed upon the timeline marked by the changes in this body: infancy, childhood, youth, adulthood, and old age. These morphing physical attributes, emotions, and thoughts define our identity through these varying phases of life. Because our identity evolves through this timeline and ceases with the death of the physical body, we view ourselves as temporary, defined by the lifespan of the physical body. However, this is only a partial understanding of who we indeed are.

Vedanta insists upon a continued existence after the death of the physical body. The subtle body that houses our mind and intellect moves into a new physical body in a process known as transmigration or reincarnation. Thus, while the physical identity of Mr. X or Ms. Y is temporary, the subtle body seeks new expressions through new physical forms. One subtle body can have many physical bodies and, thus, many physical identities through multiple lifetimes. For instance, Mr. X in this life could have been Ms. A in a past life and might be another being in the next life.

To understand this better, let us revisit our previous example of an Apple MacBook. We transfer the software and data to a new device when the hardware becomes outdated. The new laptop has a different physical form, but the stored information from the old device remains intact. Similarly, the subtle body transitions to a new physical body, carrying the essence of the individual's emotions and thoughts. The type of body that the subtle body moves to is governed by the law of Karma, which we will explore through the later chapters of the Bhagavad Gita.

However, even the subtle body is not our absolute identity. Our fundamental identity is rooted in *Atma*, or pure Consciousness. *Atma* is the eternal, unchanging awareness that underlies all experiences. Unlike the physical, and subtle bodies, which are subject to immediate and eventual cessation respectively, *Atma* persists for eternity. It is our elemental essence beyond our physical, mental, and intellectual attributes.

When Krishna states that there was never a time when we did not exist and that there will never be a time when we cease to exist, he refers to our eternal Being—*Atma*. Our experiences of birth and death are tied to our identification with the physical body, but our true Self, *Atma*, transcends these temporal events.

Decoding Shloka 13

Modern scientific discoveries highlight the body's constant state of renewal. Barring a few neural exceptions, most cells regenerate every 7 to 10 years, altering our physical makeup entirely. Despite such profound cellular transformation, our sense of Self—our core identity—remains unaltered.

In Shloka 13, Krishna employs this natural process of change to illustrate a deeper metaphysical reality. He declares that just as the body steers through various life stages within a single lifetime, the subtle body, too, shifts from one physical form to another across multiple lifetimes. Despite the demise of a particular physical body, this continuity of existence is emphasized in the phrase "*dehāntaraprāptiḥ*," indicating the acquisition of a new body.

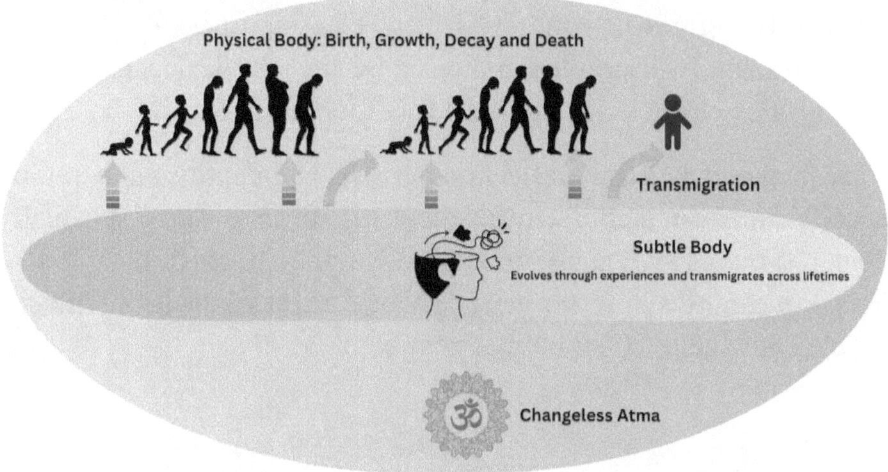

Fig: Transition of the physical body and subtle body and changeless Atma

Krishna stresses the importance of a steady, discerning mind to comprehend this continuous flow of existence. Individuals with such a mind harbor a depth of emotional, intellectual, and spiritual maturity that enables them to look beyond the superficial changes of the physical world. This wisdom allows them to remain undisturbed by the death of the physical body, viewing it merely as a transition and not the end, akin to the body's various stages through the natural aging process.

The cycles of birth and death are understood within the larger context of an eternal existence that endlessly expands beyond the confines of any one physical form. Referencing our earlier example, just as we do not mourn the loss of old hardware when we upgrade to a newer computer model – wholly identified with the *Atma*, the wise remain unaffected by the changes in the perishable body - their own and others.

In modern parlance, these individuals maintain an 'unflappable' nature in the face of life's inevitable transformations and endings. Those who begin to align with their true identity are equipped to face life's transitions with grace and steadiness, recognizing that what truly defines us—the essence of Consciousness or *Atma*—is immortal and ever-present, unbound by the physical changes and endings that characterize our worldly experiences.

This shloka invites us to reflect on our sense of identity, encouraging a shift from a material-centric view of life to a more spiritually centered one. This change in basic assumptions gives us a life of deeper meaning and lesser grief, where the fear of death is replaced by the knowledge of our eternal nature.

Reflective Prompt

Think about the transitions in your life, from childhood to adulthood. What part of you has stayed constant through these changes, and how does that shape your understanding of who you truly are?

Life's transitions cannot touch the timeless essence of your being

SHLOKA 14: ENDURE THE FLUX

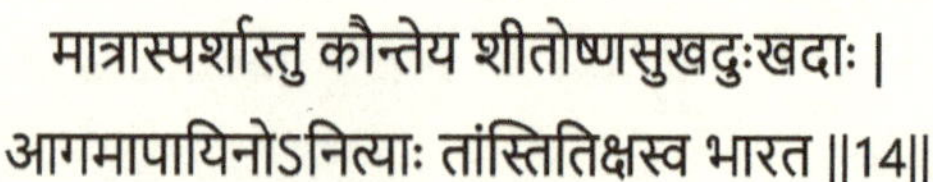

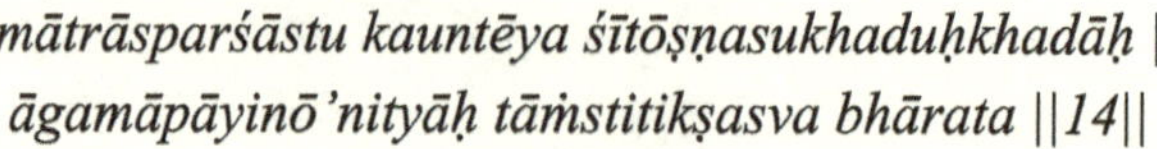

mātrāsparśāstu kauntēya śītōṣṇasukhaduḥkhadāḥ |
āgamāpāyinō'nityāḥ tāṁstitikṣasva bhārata ||14||

Translation:

O Son of Kunti (Kaunteya)! The interactions of the senses with
their objects (***mātrāsparśāḥ***) produce sensations like cold and heat,
pleasure and pain (***śīta-uṣṇa-sukha-duḥkhadāḥ***). These sensations are
impermanent (***anityāḥ***), coming and going (***āgama-apāyinaḥ***). Endure
them with patience (***titikṣa***), O Descendant of Bharata (***Bhārata***)!
[Sankya Yoga: 2.13]

At a Glance; Capturing the Spirit of the Shloka

Understanding our true identity as *Atma* (Consciousness) helps us transcend the fear of death. However, life constantly presents us with a range of experiences—some pleasant, others challenging. To live effectively and with resilience, we must recognize that these experiences, born from interactions with the world, are impermanent (*anityāḥ*). By cultivating steadiness and endurance (*titikṣa*), we can navigate life's fluctuations with grace and clarity.

Commentary

In the unfolding narrative of the Bhagavad Gita, Krishna transitions seamlessly from affirming the eternal nature of *Atma* to addressing the tangible realities of daily life.

Krishna clarifies that while the *Atma* endures through all time, space, and causation, our earthly experiences do not. Think. We are constantly steering through a world rife with challenges—health issues, personal losses and setbacks, relationship turmoil, and the like. These inevitable happenings are profoundly felt by all of us, directly shaping the unfolding of our lives in innumerable ways. Abiding in the immortality of the *Atma* does help alleviate the fear of death, but it does not exempt us from the trials and pains of mortal existence.

This shloka emphasizes two prerequisites for a successful material and spiritual life: **endurance and resilience**. Krishna acknowledges that our body will invariably face changes that manifest as physical sensations—like heat and cold—and our mind will be confronted by varying emotional states—like joy and pain. They will affect us, no doubt, but they are temporary. Explaining their fleeting nature, Krishna encourages us to cultivate a steadfast spirit. This does not mean dismissing our problems; we could not even if we tried. **While inhabiting this body, these human afflictions cannot be treated as mere illusions and be ignored but must be viewed as aspects of mortal existence to be faced head-on**. What helps us do so is a clear cognition of their momentary nature.

While Krishna asserts our eternal identity as *Atma*—unchanged and unscathed through all experiences—he also acknowledges the practical challenges of daily life. He encourages us to endure these inconsistencies with fortitude, reminding us that 'this too shall pass.' It is a clarion call to actively engage with life's challenges, armored by this practical insight. Doing so renders our every action fitting to navigate this world of change while we remain anchored in the unchangeable. This equilibrium is essential for living our lives with wisdom and grace. Ultimately, what cannot be cured must be endured, reinforcing the importance of resilience and cheerful forbearance through the undulated topography of human experience.

Decoding Shloka 14

The term *'mātrāsparśāḥ'*—the interaction of senses with the world—highlights how our sensory perceptions measure and interpret experiences. *'sparśa'* translates as touch, encompassing all forms of sensory exchange, while *'mātrā'* implies a measurement. This process of sensory measurement determines our experiences of heat (*'uṣṇa'*) and cold (*'śīta'*), pleasure (*'sukha'*), and pain (*'duḥkha'*). People interpret these sensations differently based on their mindset, circumstances, and experiences. For example, a chilly day may invigorate someone who enjoys wintry weather but incapacitate another who despises the cold.

Krishna emphasizes that these sensory experiences are *'āgamāpāyina'* and *'anityāḥ,'* - transient and ever-changing, respectively. In layperson's language, "they come and go." Just as the weather seamlessly shifts from cold to warm and back again, our reactionary experiences of pleasure and pain are equally fleeting. No physical or emotional state lasts forever. For instance, the pain of a financial downturn or the grief from losing a loved one is real and life-altering, but like all things, it will pass.

Krishna advises '*titikṣasva*' - to endure these fluctuations with fortitude. Here, '*titikṣa*' means to endure, to bear with resilience. This endurance is not passive resignation but an active engagement with life's challenges, armed with a thorough understanding of their impermanent nature. It stresses a mindset that understands and accepts the ebb and flow of worldly experiences and engages accordingly, much like a seasoned sailor who knows how to helm stormy seas by making anticipatory adjustments to his sails in line with changing winds and currents.

To put this into a modern context, consider the stresses of daily work life—demanding projects, challenging coworkers, and non-negotiable deadlines. While these can produce unthinkable stress and anxiety, recognizing their inevitability and eventual transience helps us plan ahead, maintain our composure, and manage our reactions. This approach does not eliminate challenges but empowers us to face them more effectively.

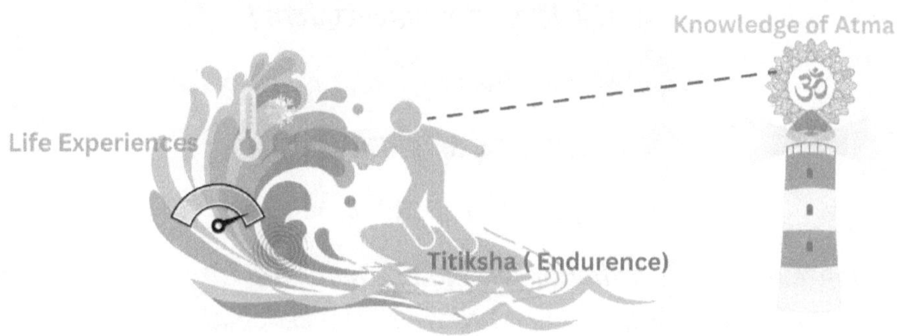

Fig: Titikha: Resilience Amidst Life's Inevitable Flux

Titiksha: Cultivating Resilience Amidst Life's Inevitable Flux

Titiksha is a beautiful Sanskrit term that exemplifies the spirit of resilience and fortitude. This term trumpets one's ability to maintain composure and steadfastness amidst life's inevitable challenges, which include physical discomforts, emotional upheavals, and psychological stresses. Krishna emphasizes that while these adversities are unavoidable, they are inherently transient. And it is possible for every striving seeker to cheerfully endure these fleeting trials rather than resist them in vain or succumb to them in despair.

In engineering terms, just as materials undergo endurance tests to gauge their durability under varying conditions, humans, too, are tested by such fluctuations of life. A metal might excel in enduring heat but falter under freezing conditions. Similarly, individuals have varying thresholds for what they can endure—what is trivial for one might be traumatic for another. Also, an overwhelming circumstance through a particular phase of one's life may be a breeze to maneuver at another point. This variability underscores the importance of developing robust inner strength to withstand all of life's diverse challenges.

Shankaracharya, in his seminal work *Viveka Chudamani*, eloquently defines Titiksha as:

सहनं सर्वदुःखानामऽप्रतिकारपूर्वकम् ।

sahanam sarvaduhkhanam apratikarapurvakam

चिन्ताविलापरहितं सा तितिक्षा निगद्यते ॥

chintavilaparahitam sa titiksha nigadyate

"Endurance of all afflictions without countering aids, and without anxiety or lament is said to be titiksha." (Vivekachudamani 25)

This definition clarifies that endurance does not mean suffering in silence; instead, it is about meeting life's difficulties without internal resistance or emotional turmoil. It is the capacity to face discomfort and pain without letting them disturb our clarity of mind and consequent peace.

The practical application of *Titiksha* in daily life can be likened to the wisdom of knowing how to tackle unpredictable waves while surfing the ocean. Just as seasoned surfers master the art of diving under a threatening wave to avoid being swept away and riding the more negotiable ones, we, too, can learn to navigate the waves of life's challenges with stability and grace. As famously said by Jon Kabat-Zinn, American professor emeritus of medicine and creator of Stress Reduction Clinic at the University of Massachusetts Medical School: *"You can't stop the waves, but you can learn to surf."*

Moreover, the idea of the "threshold of pain" in neurological terms speaks to our individual capacities to handle discomfort. Some may endure more, some less, but the goal for each person is to expand their threshold through physical and emotional strengthening. This aligns with the modern medical perspective, as noted by Dr. Steven E Brena. He points out that endurance can be seen as our ability to control our response to sensory input so that our performance remains unimpaired despite pain.

Titiksha, which is traditionally defined by scriptural texts as spiritual endurance and personal resilience, also holds significant value in the corporate world. It proves crucial for navigating challenges and uncertainties in today's fast-paced and often volatile business environment. This ancient principle teaches professionals to endure and thrive amidst adversities by viewing them as opportunities for innovation and growth. Within the corporate context, *Titiksha* would mean cultivating a mindset that regards setbacks as temporary and transformative, encouraging a proactive approach to objective problem-solving. This ability to maintain composure and persistence in the face of difficulties is essential for leaders and teams alike, driving the development of a resilient organizational culture that can adapt and prosper under any circumstance.

***Titiksha*, therefore, is a dynamic quality that empowers us to accept and transcend life's inevitable hardships**. It teaches us to "bear with" rather than "break under" the pressures of existence, fostering a resilience that is both liberating and enlightening. This stoic endurance is the key to navigating the dualities of comfort and discomfort, pleasure and pain, which are but transient phases in and through human experience.

Titiksha is a life-transforming practice that refines our character and elevates our spiritual pursuits. Thus, it is not only a strategy for survival but also a pathway to profound personal growth and spiritual emancipation.

In conclusion, through this oft-quoted verse, Krishna hands us a practical guide for navigating the human condition. By recognizing the transient nature of our daily physical and mental experiences and understanding that 'this too shall pass,' we can face life's inherent challenges with more remarkable poise and solidity. This teaching provides a living framework that honors our eternal, unchanging nature as *Atma* while acknowledging our incessant earthly struggles.

Reflective Prompt

Can you think of an instance when an untoward circumstance got the better of you? Did you resist it with anger and resentment? How did this approach impact the circumstance? After studying this shloka do you think you can handle a comparable situation in the future with fortitude and grace?

In life's shifting tides, endure with grace, for every wave must fade

SHLOKA 15: FROM ENDURANCE TO ENLIGHTENMENT

यं हि न व्यथयन्त्येते पुरुषं पुरुषर्षभ |
समदुःखसुखं धीरं सोऽमृतत्वाय कल्पते ||15||

yaṁ hi na vyathayantyētē puruṣaṁ puruṣarṣabha |
samaduḥkhasukhaṁ dhīraṁ sō'mṛtatvāya kalpatē ||15||

Translation:

O Arjuna, the noblest among men (***Purusharshabha***)! The person (***purusham***) who is not afflicted (***na vyathayanti***) by these dualities (***ete***)—pleasure and pain (***sukha-duhkha***)—and who remains balanced in both (***samaduhkhasukham***) with a steady mind (***dhiram***), is indeed fit (***kalpate***) for immortality (***amritatvaya***) [Sankya Yoga: 2.15]

At a Glance: Capturing the Spirit of the Shloka:

A wise person, embodying resilience (*Titiksha*) and clarity (*Viveka*), maintains equanimity through life's inevitable highs and lows. This steadfast balance is the foundation for unlocking life's greatest potentials, achieving material excellence and Self-realization.

Commentary:

Shloka 15 continues to build upon the wisdom gleaned from earlier declarations that the Self (*Atma*) is our real identity, and earthly experiences, though undeniable and palpably felt, are transitory. Here, Krishna deepens our understanding of the transformative power of *Titiksha*, the spirited endurance that equips us to navigate life's inevitable fluctuations. He encourages us to meet life's highs and lows with grace, declaring endurance (*Titiksha*) as the cornerstone of spiritual growth.

The shloka carries an inspiring promise: Those who maintain equanimity in the face of pleasure and pain unlock the highest potential of human existence. Krishna emphasizes that enduring worldly fluctuations with discernment leads to ultimate liberation— freedom from the cycles of birth and death.

Elevating the Aspirant

Krishna addresses Arjuna as '*Purusharshabha*,' - prominent among human beings. This title is highly symbolic for those earnestly trekking the spiritual path. By using such a distinguished title, Krishna encourages Arjuna and every seeker to stand tall not only upon the bedrock of their material achievements but deeply rooted in their ethical and spiritual stature. The comparison is with the bull, which stands out distinctively among its species with its sheer presence and strength. The spiritual aspirant should also be prominent among humans for their unwavering commitment to higher principles amidst life's fluctuating circumstances of joy and suffering that the majority fall prey to.

It is important to address the use of *'Purusha'* in *'Purusharshabha.'* While traditionally translated as 'man,' in Vedanta, it refers more broadly to any individual who inhabits a body. The word finds its root in *'Pura,'* meaning a dwelling or body. The use of masculine terminology here, and in many languages where male gender is often the default, should not be viewed as gender discrimination but as a grammatical convention. In translating and interpreting these texts, the focus remains on the universality of the teachings applicable to all human beings, regardless of gender, emphasizing that spiritual achievements transcend mortal identities.

The Pillars of Spiritual Prominence: Resilience and Equanimity

Krishna identifies the qualities that elevate an individual to *'Purusharshabha'* - prominent among human beings. Prominence in the spiritual context does not merely rest upon material laurels but results from mastering one's internal responses—primarily through the practice of *Titiksha*, or resilience. He underscores the importance of maintaining composure through life's varied experiences - *'sama dukha sukham'* - joyous or painful. According to Krishna, a genuinely great individual remains unaffected (*na vydhayanti*) by life's vicissitudes, maintaining balance and control in all situations.

This capacity for equanimity does not hail indifference but applies a deep understanding of one's internal landscape to effectively manage and understand emotions. It calls for a disciplined response rather than impulsive reactions or irritation, which can escalate into anger and violence. In our fast-paced world, where patience is frequently tested—from everyday traffic jams to high-pressure deadlines—Krishna's teachings remind us that patience is an active practice for preserving inner peace.

As famously said by Austrian philosopher and holocaust survivor Viktor E. Frankl:

"Between stimulus and response, there is a space. In that space is our power to choose our response. In our response lies our growth and freedom."

The life of Sardar Vallabhbhai Patel offers a poignant example of this principle in action. Known for his critical role in India's freedom struggle, Patel demonstrated extraordinary inner strength during a crucial moment in his personal life. When informed of his wife's demise during a court proceeding, Patel chose to focus on the task at hand, only allowing himself to mourn after the fulfillment of his professional duties. His emotional resilience was not due to a lack of love for his wife but arose from a profound capacity to manage personal grief while fulfilling public responsibilities. Such fortitude exemplifies Krishna's ideal of stability and endurance amidst life's inevitable challenges. Patel's ability to navigate personal loss while upholding his professional integrity highlights the honor of cultivating character strength and resilience—qualities essential for spiritual enlightenment and any significant personal achievement.

Sri Ramakrishna's allegorical song, *"Re man, tumi krishi kaj jano na,"* highlights the importance of developing our inner capacities. He compares human potential to a fertile field that, if properly tended, can yield a rich spiritual harvest. This analogy serves as a reminder of the transformative power of self-discipline and persistent effort in leading a fruitful life and realizing one's true spiritual nature.

In the teachings of Shantideva, a revered figure in Buddhist philosophy, endurance is lauded as a fundamental virtue along the spiritual journey. Shantideva portrays endurance as an active, essential strength that sustains and nurtures the growth of all other spiritual attributes. In the absence of endurance, no other qualities can be sustained.

In the Gospel of Matthew, Jesus Christ iterates, *"By your endurance, you will gain your lives."* (Luke 21:19). These words stress the necessity of steadfastness in the face of trials and tribulations. Christ teaches that enduring hardships tests faith and strengthens it, leading to spiritual preservation and deeper fulfillment.

With this teaching, Krishna provides a compelling framework for material and spiritual fulfillment, emphasizing that the ability to endure personal trials with an inner strength and resolve paves the way to achieving the highest human potential. This approach no doubt enriches one's spiritual journey, but it also fortifies one's character through wisdom and consequent resilience.

'Etē na vyathayantē' specifically points out that a person endowed with *Titiksha* is not disturbed by *'mātrāsparśāḥ'*—sensory experiences of the changing world, which affect the senses, mind, and intellect. This steadfastness is essential for maintaining a clear, undisturbed mind amidst life's inevitable changes, allowing one to face and control situations effectively.

Krishna emphasizes that individuals who maintain this equilibrium—*'sama dukha sukham'*—do not merely survive life's challenges but thrive through them as they do not allow these fluctuations to disrupt their mental peace.

Furthermore, Krishna connects this clarity and stability to the ultimate spiritual goal—Enlightenment. He uses the term *'Amritavaya'* to explain that enlightenment involves a shift in identity from associating oneself with the mortal body, mind, and intellect to identifying with the immortal Consciousness (*Atma*). This realization facilitates one's transcendence of the limitations imposed by bodily existence.

This realization does not imply that the physical body will become immortal. It is about acknowledging and embracing the eternal nature of *Atma*. This shift is akin to moving from experiencing life as an unalterable reality to recognizing it more as a lucid dream, where one becomes aware of a persisting truth beyond the temporary and fluctuating bodily experiences. Thus, enlightenment is about understanding and internalizing the immortal nature of one's true Self.

Krishna concludes the shloka by describing such an individual as '*dhira*', which is typically translated as courageous. But here, *dhira* represents a wise person characterized by deep understanding, emotional resilience, and intellectual stability, enabling them to remain composed and steadfast in any situation. The term originates from the roots '*dhi*' (to hold or sustain) and '*ra*' (possession), accentuating one's capacity to maintain emotional and intellectual steadiness amidst life's trials.

In this shloka, Krishna reiterates that mastering *titiksha* – steadfast endurance through all of life's encounters is not only essential to navigate the material world successfully but is an absolute prerequisite for a seeker to qualify for that state of meditation that culminates in immortality.

Reflective Prompt

Are you able to sit still in meditation? Or beyond a few moments does your mind get pulled into regrets over the past, anxieties for the future, and a million things to accomplish in the present? What can you do to approach the seat of meditation with a clearer and more balanced mind?

Resilience steadies the heart, clarity lights the path to greatness

SHLOKA 16: DISTINGUISHING THE UNCHANGING FROM THE TRANSIENT

नासतो विद्यते भावः नाभावो विद्यते सतः |
उभयोरपि दृष्टोऽन्तः त्वनयोस्तत्त्वदर्शिभिः ||16||

nāsatō vidyatē bhāvaḥ nābhāvō vidyatē sataḥ |
ubhayōrapi dṛṣṭō'ntaḥ tvanayōstattvadarśibhiḥ ||16||

Translation:

There is no independent existence (***na bhāvah***) for the relative (***asatah***), and there is no non-existence (***na abhāvah***) for the absolute (***satah***). The essence (***tattva***) of both these (***anayoḥ ubhayoḥ***) is understood (***dṛṣṭah***) by the seers of Truth (***tattva-darśibhiḥ***). [Sankya Yoga: 2.16]

At a Glance: Capturing the Spirit of the Shloka

Shloka 16 urges us to distinguish between the fleeting and impermanent (*Asat*) and the unchanging Reality of the eternal essence (*Sat*). It reminds us that while the transient aspects of life—our possessions, identities, and experiences—appear real, their existence is temporary and derived from the eternal substratum. True wisdom lies in x-raying through the transient and grounding ourselves in the eternal substratum, leading to a life of clarity, balance, and freedom from undue attachment to the impermanent.

Commentary:

This seemingly technical shloka reveals a core truth: our perception of life shifts with our viewpoint. Much like how, on a long scenic drive, the landscape varies for everyone riding the same car depending on their seat and individual affinities - our spiritual progression shapes our understanding of and consequent interaction with life. Life may be meaningful and coherent to those well advanced on their spiritual path, whereas it might seem perplexing and fraught with struggle for beginners or those not yet on the path.

An American teacher of courses in self-improvement, Dale Carnegie's quote animates this thought succinctly:

"Two men looked out from prison bars,
One saw mud, the other saw stars."

Until now, Krishna has been highlighting humanity's extremely limited identification with the body-mind-intellect complex restricted to the confines of birth and death. He has emphatically declared that our physical presence is a temporary vehicle for navigating the earthly realm, but it is not our complete identity. Our true nature is the eternal Consciousness (*Atma*)—unaffected by the ephemeral phases of birth, life, and death.

Yet, Shlokas 14 and 15 acknowledged that we cannot ignore our body, mind, and intellect while inhabiting this world. While agreeing with the inevitability of life's challenges, these shlokas stressed the importance of *Titiksha*—endurance born from a deeper understanding of life's transient nature—an essential quality for remaining gracefully equanimous through life's ups and downs.

Shloka 16 now encapsulates the core of Vedantic wisdom, **clearly discerning between what is real and eternal (*Sat*) and what is relatively real and transient (*Asat*)**. Krishna masterfully decodes the complexity of Absolute Reality and its inextricable relation to our self-identity.

Essense of the shloka:

The essence of this shloka clearly distinguishes between *Sat* and *Asat*, terms representing Absolute and relative realities, respectively. Krishna begins this shloka by asserting that *Asat*, which can be understood as anything impermanent, possesses no inherent existence or '*bhāva*.' This means that its existence is temporary and dependent upon *Sat*, the ultimate Reality.

In contrast, *Sat*, which represents the eternal essence, is characterized by a ceaseless existence; it cannot be negated or rendered non-existent. Krishna explains that all perceived existences of the transient world (*Asat*) derive their seeming reality from their relationship to *Sat*, the enduring truth. The shloka concludes by noting that those who thoroughly understand the ultimate Reality effortlessly discern this profound distinction between *Sat* and *Asat* and function masterfully in the world that mercilessly consumes those who do not.

Krishna explains that while our worldly identities tied to the body, mind, and intellect may seem real, they are ultimately fleeting and dependent on the eternal reality of *Atma*, which is independent and everlasting. This foundational knowledge underpins the Vedantic view of existence, drawing a clear line between that which is permanently real and only temporary.

Absolute and Relative Exitance: Understanding *Sat* and *Asat*

The concepts of *Sat* and *Asat*—are pivotal to understanding the essence of Vedantic teachings. These terms serve as foundational principles that delineate the nature of Absolute and temporary Realities.

Sat, also known as *Satyam* in a Vedantic context, signifies the Absolute Reality or **the truth that remains unchanged across time—past, present, and future**. The ancient Rishis of India clearly defined *Sat* as '*Trikala Abaditam*,' which means that which is not negated (*abaditam*) in the three periods of time (*trikala*) – present, past, and future. *Sat* represents the unchanging, eternal truth that exists independently through all time and space without any reliance on external factors. The term *Satyam* here should not be limited to the ethical dimension of truthfulness but understood in its broader metaphysical context as the Absolute Reality.

***Sat* is characterized by its permanence and independence**; it does not depend on anything else for its existence or recognition. This enduring nature is intrinsic, manifesting continuously without beginning, persisting unaltered, and extending without end. Derived from the Sanskrit verb '*as,*' meaning to be or to exist, the term '*Sat*' fundamentally underscores existence and reality itself, thus establishing it as the core of being and the underlying truth of the universe.

A poignant reflection of this truth is found in the Chandogya Upanishad, which states:

'*Sadeva somyedamagra asid ekameva advitiyam,*' meaning, in the beginning, dear boy, this (universe) was only Absolute Reality (*Sat*), one without a second. This profound statement highlights that only the undifferentiated state of *Sat* existed before the universe manifested.

On the other hand, *Asat* **refers to something that does not have an independent existence-** it is temporary and transient. Unlike *Sat*, *Asat* pertains to all with a beginning and an end, subject to change and extinction. It encapsulates all perceptible phenomena and forms that interact with our senses but do not exist independently; their existence is contingent upon *Sat*.

This transient nature of *Asat* is eloquently described in the Māṇḍūkya Upaniṣad Kārikā by Gauḍapāda:

'ādau ante ca yannāsti vartamāne'pi tat tathā;

Vitataiḥ sadṛśāḥ santo avitathā iva lakṣitāḥ.'

Translating to, what does not exist at the beginning and the end, does not truly exist in the present either; though it seems to be real (*Sat*), it is characterized as not real (*Asat*).

This shloka highlights that anything that does not persist before its appearance and after its disappearance and only exists transiently is deemed *Asat*, thereby emphasizing its ephemeral nature.

Another term that can express the concept of '*Asat*' in Vedantic literature is '*Mithyā*.' This term should not be misunderstood as indicating something purely illusory or non-existent. Instead, '*Mithyā*' describes the relative or dependent reality of objects that seem real within the constraints of time and space but ultimately revert to their fundamental substratum, which is '*Sat*.'

It is crucial to distinguish '*Mithyā*' from '*Tuccha*,' a term that denotes absolute non-existence, something that can be entirely disregarded. **While '*Tuccha*' has no practical impact or relevance, '*Mithya*' plays a significant role and cannot be ignored.** When something exists and can be experienced in the present it cannot be deemed as unreal.

A classic example widely used across Vedantic teaching traditions to further articulate this point is that of a pot made from clay. The pot, representing *Asat* or *Mithya,* is merely a functional form of clay from which it originates. It is molded from clay and utilized, and it may eventually break. Despite the various transformations the pot undergoes, the underlying reality of the pot—the clay symbolizing *Sat*—remains constant. The pot's existence is dependent entirely on it for its reality, the clay.

Therefore, while the pot as *Asat* or *Mithya* must be acknowledged in its transient form for its practical value, it lacks permanence and should not be confused with the absolute, unchanging reality of clay. Just as the clay was present in and through the pot's formation existence and continues after its physical destruction, so does *Sat* exist before, during, and after the material manifestations of *Asat.* This enduring presence of *Sat* provides the foundational reality for all forms of *Mithya,* which arise from and return to it.

Aspect	Sat (Absolute Reality)	Asat (Relative Reality)
Definition	The unchanging, eternal essence of existence.	The temporary, ever-changing phenomena perceived by the senses.
Existence (Bhāva)	Exists inherently and continuously across time.	Apparent existence; arises and dissolves within Sat.
Non-Existence (Abhāva)	Non-existence is impossible; always present.	Has a beginning and an end; non-existent before creation and after destruction.
Dependency	Independent; the source and substratum of all.	Entirely dependent on Sat for its existence. Arises from and dissolves back into Sat.
What is	Consciousness *(Atma)* in every living being which is nothing but Absolute Reality of the Universe *(Brahman)*	Body, mind, emotions, objects, thoughts, and sensory experiences.
Longevity	Permanent and timeless.	Temporary; exists within the constraints of time and space.

Illustrative Example	The clay (*Sat*) that remains constant through all forms.	The pot (*Asat*) made of clay, which changes form and eventually ceases to exist.
Goal	To realize and shift our identity to *Sat*, the eternal essence.	To understand the temporary nature of the body and all objects in the universe, enabling detachment and clarity.

Table: Sat & Asat

Analyzing Existence: What Qualifies as Sat and Asat?

Let us now explore what in the universe qualifies as *Sat* (Absolute Reality) and what constitutes *Asat* (relative or temporary reality). This will help highlight the practical applications of these foundational Vedantic principles.

Asat encompasses everything in the universe that has a temporary existence. This category includes all material objects, living beings, varying mental states, and intellectual stances. These are *Asat* because they come into being, dynamically change, and ultimately cease to exist. Their existence depends on something more fundamental.

Material Objects: Every tangible object around us, from simple utensils like a clay pot to complex structures like vehicles and skyscrapers. While they serve functional purposes, their existence is temporary, subject to wear, tear, and destruction.

Living Beings: All organisms, including humans, animals, and plants. Without exception, they all undergo the unavoidable stages of birth, growth, change, disease, decay, and death.

Mental States and Intellectual Stances: Emotions and thoughts arise, change, and eventually fade over time, entirely dependent on the physiological, emotional, and intellectual states of the beings experiencing them.

The universe, with all its galaxies, stars, and planets, also comes under *Asat*. These bodies assumed existence at some point and will cease to exist at another, conforming to cosmic laws that govern them.

In stark contrast to *Asat*, *Sat* is defined as existing beyond the constraints of time and space—unchanging, eternal, and independent. Nothing within our direct sensory experience qualifies as *Sat*, as everything accessible to us undergoes change and is subject to decay. Through their groundbreaking subjective investigations, the ancient sages of India identified a fundamental, unchanging reality behind this world of change. **They named this enduring reality *as Brahman*, the Absolute Reality.**

Symbolized by the sacred sound of ॐ (OM), *Brahman* is understood as vast and infinite. It is derived from the root *'bṛh'* which signifies growth or expansion. This indicates that Brahman is the expansive foundation upon which all temporal phenomena manifest.

Brahman's eternal, unchanging reality is beautifully described across several Upanishads, each affirming its absolute nature. In *Shvetashvatara* Upanishad, the sage declares, *"Oh Children of Immortality, I have discovered that which is behind all changes—the fundamental Reality that is Brahman."* The same is affirmed in the Mundaka Upanishad, which states, *"Brahman alone is all this—pure, immortal, and timeless, existing beyond all spatial and temporal bounds as the highest Reality of the universe."*

Similarly, the Chandogya Upanishad meditatively reflects: *"All this is indeed Brahman. From It arises, by It subsists, and into It dissolves,"* encouraging a serene acceptance of life's ever-changing phenomena as expressions of *Brahman*. These teachings collectively highlight that everything in the universe, visible or not, stems from and returns to *Brahman*, fitting perfectly with the Vedantic definition of *Sat* as the authentic, unchanging essence of all existence.

An investigation of the nature of *Brahman* or *Sat* leads us to a pivotal question: Is this fundamental reality matter, energy, or something else entirely? Through their prolonged meditative insights, the ancient sages of India arrived at a revolutionary understanding. They discerned that **the essence of *Sat*, the core substance from which the universe springs, is not material nor mere energy but Consciousness itself, referred to as '*Cit*' in Sanskrit.**

Consciousness is not a passive or inert force but the active, dynamic foundation from which all matter and energy derive. It infuses every particle, moment, and entity within the universe. We can, therefore, unequivocally assert that ***Sat*, or Absolute Reality, is fundamentally Consciousness**. Vedanta expresses this truth most eloquently: *Sat* is always *Cit-Atman*, meaning that the most essential and accurate state of being (*Sat*) is indistinguishable from Consciousness (*Cit*). The implication here is profound: **what is real and eternal (*Sat*) must inherently be conscious (*Cit*), and vice versa.**

This inseparable nature of *Sat* and *Cit* suggests that the **truest expression of reality is self-existent Consciousness**. Look closely—this is a practical truth that each of us experiences directly. Every moment of our life is permeated by consciousness, underscoring our personal and continuous engagement with this fundamental aspect of reality. This Consciousness, or Sat-Cit, forms the unshakeable core of all that exists. It offers a gateway to understanding the universe not as a collection of disparate elements but as a unified field of Consciousness

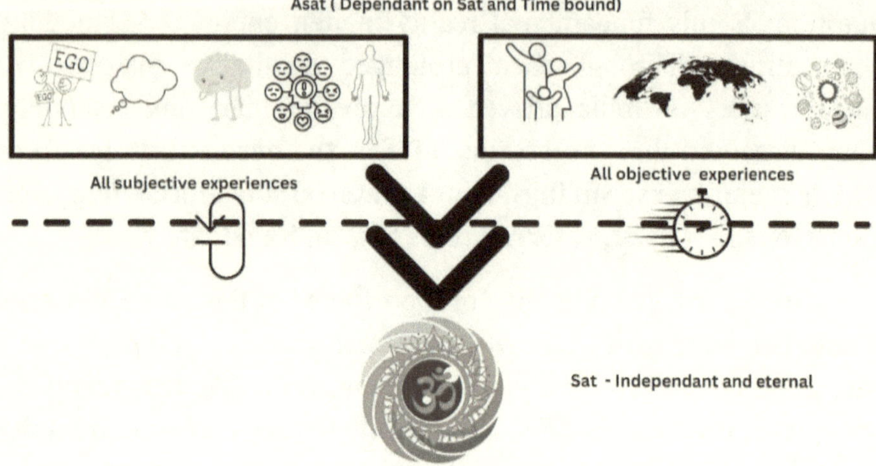

Fig: Sat and Asat

Unveiling the Unity: Connecting Individual Consciousness with Universal Brahman

The fundamental substratum of the universe is *Brahman,* and its intrinsic nature is Consciousness. From Shlokas 11-12, Krishna revealed that our identity is not confined to the body, mind, and intellect but is *Atma,* which is pure Consciousness. This means that the essential nature of our *Atma* is that of *Brahman*, the fundamental Reality of the universe.

This core teaching of Vedanta is encapsulated in celebrated Mahavakyas, such as *'Tat Tvam Asi'* (Thou Art That). This powerful aphorism bridges the gap between individual identity and foundational Reality, illustrating that *'Tat'*—that which is *Brahman*, the Absolute Reality of the universe—and *'Tvam'*—you, the individual Self—are fundamentally the same. The word *'Asi'* establishes this profound identity, declaring that our true nature as *Atma* is not different from the ultimate Reality, *Brahman*.

In this shloka, Krishna explains that while our bodily identity is transient and therefore falls into the category of *Asat,* our true *identity* as *Atma* is eternal, categorizing it as *Sat*. This *Sat*, pulsating within us, though not palpable by our limited physical apparatus, is dynamic and alive with the same vibrant force that constitutes the entirety of the universe as *Brahman*. The Bhagavad Gita helps us understand the transience of our physical nature while elevating our perspective to recognize and embrace our eternal identity, aligning our individual Consciousness with the Absolute Reality, *Brahman*.

The Permanence of Sat and the Transience of Asat

Krishna's core message in this shloka becomes clear considering what we now understand: for *Asat*, there is no enduring existence (*'bhāva'*), and for *Sat*, non-existence (*'abhāva'*) is impossible. This distinction helps us discern the eternal from the ephemeral.

Asat, which includes everything in the universe, from our physical, mental, and intellectual faculties to everything else encompassed within the vastness of the cosmos, lacks independent existence. *Asat* is bound by time and is, therefore, temporary. It emerges, changes, and eventually ceases to exist. Recognizing this impermanence is vital; it liberates us from undue expectations and the existential angst associated with the transient nature of worldly phenomena. There is no reason to be overly concerned with the impermanence of *Asat*, as its transient nature is a fundamental aspect of its existence.

Conversely, *Sat*, symbolized by *Atma* or Consciousness, embodies permanence and independence. Unlike *Asat*, *Sat* is not subjected to the constraints of time. It has existed in the past, exists in the present, and will continue to exist in the future. This eternal, unchanging nature of *Sat* is our true identity. Understanding this, we can shift our allegiance away from the transient (*Asat*) and anchor it in the eternal (*Sat*), recognizing that our essence, our true Self endures permanently.

By comprehending this crucial distinction, we realize that while the physical world and our experiences are valuable for our temporal existence and growth, they should not be the ultimate focus of our life's pursuits. Instead, our efforts should be spiritually directed towards realizing and embracing the permanence of *Sat*—our true nature. This evolving understanding offers profound peace of mind. It aligns us with the eternal, unbounded nature of our existence, thus paving the way for ultimate liberation or *Moksha* while awarding us noteworthy material success.

Knowers of Truth Differentiate external (Sat) from transient (Asat)

Krishna concludes this shloka by highlighting that the discerning seers, known as '*tattvadarśibhiḥ*,' have grasped the distinction between *Sat* and *Asat*. '*Tattva*' signifies the essential nature or truth of something, transcending mere sensory observations or superficial appearances. For example, unlike the illusion that the Earth is flat, based on sensory perception, *tattva* reflects deeper truths, such as the Earth's roundness confirmed by scientific inquiry.

These enlightened seers recognize *Sat*, the eternal and unchanging reality, exists perpetually and independently. *Asat*, by contrast, appears real but lacks intrinsic existence, deriving its apparent reality from *Sat*. With this understanding, the seers navigate life's impermanence with a deep appreciation of *Asat's* transient nature. They understand that while elements of *Asat* continually interact with our senses, they should not form the basis of our existential beliefs. This wisdom encourages shifting from transient to enduring realities—from *Asat* to *Sat*.

Krishna underscores that our true Self, the *Atma*, is not limited to the ephemeral world but expands into the unchanging *Sat*—pure, infinite Consciousness. This insight transforms our overall approach to life by stabilizing us upon a resolute foundation amid the ever-changing physical world.

Tattvadarśins, who internalize this knowledge, do not lament the natural transitions of *Asat*, like growth, change, disease, decay, and death. Nor do they rejoice in birth. They comprehend that their essential identity as *Atma* remains unaffected by these changes. The wise recognize *Sat* and *Asat* for what they are. They have no doubt that while *Asat* is characterized by change and dependency, *Sat* remains independent and eternal. This wisdom frees them from excessive grief and attachment, aligning them with the timeless truth of existence.

Recognizing the temporariness of *Asat* and the constancy of *Sat no doubt* provides us spiritual solace through good and bad times. But it also equips us with the resilience to face life's victories and trials with equanimity. This balance is achieved through the previously discussed quality of *Titiksha*—gracefully enduring the triumphs and trials of the material world while anchored in the knowledge of our eternal nature.

Thus, Krishna advises humanity to cultivate a deeper perception of reality and remain firmly anchored in *Sat* to successfully navigate the good, bad, and indifferent we constantly experience in the world of *Asat*. Doing so enables us to live meaningfully in the temporal world while remaining spiritually connected to the eternal, achieving a harmonious balance between our earthly aspirations and ultimate spiritual truth. This dual approach fosters the quintessential quality of equanimity, one of the central tenets of Krishna's teachings in the Bhagavad Gita.

Bridging Materialism and Spirituality

In our modern era, where materialism often dominates personal and societal priorities, the teachings of Shloka 16 gain profound relevance. Material objects and pursuits, while necessary for our daily transactions and survival, are inherently transient. Recognizing them as '*Asat*'—lacking permanent existence—can lead to a healthier perspective on life.

This spiritual stance is being increasingly echoed in contemporary scientific thought. The initial views of classical materialism are being questioned as scientists delve deeper into the nature of reality. For instance, the famous physicist Robert Millikan expressed skepticism about materialism, describing it as *"the height of unintelligence."* Albert Einstein also touched upon this, suggesting that what we perceive as matter merely manifests a more fundamental field, stating, *"We have in today's physics two realities. One matter, the other the field. Both cannot be true, for the field alone is true. Matter is only a condensation of that field."* This mirrors the Vedantic view where the ultimate Reality—*Sat*—is seen as the only truth, and all material forms are temporary manifestations.

Understanding the temporary nature of all material phenomena and recognizing our more profound connection to the eternal '*Sat*' allows us to navigate life with greater clarity and peace. This shift in perspective is crucial for personal well-being and addressing the global challenges of consumerism and environmental degradation. Embracing the Vedantic vision of *Sat* and *Asat* helps to cultivate a sense of responsibility and sustainability, acknowledging that while we engage with the material world, our ultimate values and goals should reflect something more enduring.

Thus, the ancient wisdom of the Bhagavad Gita continues to offer valuable insights into living harmoniously in an increasingly complex material world, which is only made possible by staying deeply connected to our spiritual dimension.

Reflective Prompt

Is your current perception of reality wholly centered around your health, family, career, possessions, and social engagements? Do the constant changes in these external factors keep you stressed and anxious? How might what you studied in this shloka help alleviate some of that inner turmoil?

Know the eternal within, and let the temporary flow like a gentle stream

SHLOKA 17: INDESTRUCTIBLE AND OMNIPRESENT

अविनाशि तु तद्विद्धि येन सर्वमिदं ततम् |
विनाशमव्ययस्यास्य न कश्चित्कर्तुमर्हति ||17||

avināśi tu tadviddhi yēna sarvamidaṁ tatam |
vināśamavyayasyāsya na kaścitkartumarhati ||17||

Translation:

Understand (*viddhi*) that (*tad*) by which (*yena*) all this (*sarvam idam*) is pervaded (*tatam*) [*Atma*] to be indestructible (*avināśi*). No one (*na kaścit*) is capable (*arhati*) of bringing about (*kartum*) the destruction (*vināśam*) of this changeless *(avyayasya)* eternal essence (*asya*)
[Sankya Yoga: 2.17]

At a Glance: Capturing the Spirit of the Shloka

Atma, our true identity, is indestructible, unchanging, all-pervading, and singular, forming the foundation of everything in existence. By anchoring ourselves in this timeless awareness, we discover the unity of all beings and the unwavering essence that binds us to the cosmos as one.

Commentary:

In previous shlokas (11-16), we learned that our core identity - *Atma* is not just eternal (*nitya*) but also the Absolute Reality (*Sat*) of the universe.

In this shloka, Krishna further reinforces the eternal nature of *Atma* by emphasizing its indestructibility (*'Avināśi'*). He also introduces two other critical dimensions of *Atma*: *Avyaya*- its immutable consistency through time, and *Sarvagata* – its all-pervasiveness.

Atma (Consciousness) is not limited to any particular form or place; It is omnipresent, pervading the entire cosmos. This suggests a singular, unified existence animating in and through the myriad forms of life. This declaration asserts that the essence permeating the whole universe is one and indivisible. To deepen our understanding of our spiritual identity, let us use these profound revelations to build upon previous discussions.

Beyond Destruction: The Permanence of *Atma*

Krishna's powerful proclamation, *"Avināśi tu tadviddhi,"* urges us to recognize the indestructible nature of *Atma*. This statement reinforces our previous reflections—that *Atma*, our true essence, is eternal (*Nityaḥ*). Yet here, Krishna expands the nature of *Atma* from merely eternal to indestructible. He unequivocally affirms that *Atma* cannot be destroyed.

The term *'avināśi'* is the opposite of *'vināśi.'* The latter refers to that which is perishable or destructible. By declaring *Atma 'avināśi'*,

Krishna emphasizes that unlike physical entities that undergo creation and destruction, such as the pots in the previously discussed metaphor of the pot and the clay, the underlying essence—*Atma*, akin to the clay in the metaphor—remains unaffected and unharmed. While pots can break, the clay—representing *Atma*—persists, underscoring its timeless and indestructible nature.

Krishna uses the directive '*viddhi*' to stress the importance of this knowledge. '*Viddhi*' implies an in-depth, internalized understanding. It is a call to fully grasp and absorb the truth that *Atma* is beyond destruction. It urges us to internalize this truth as a fundamental aspect of our existential awareness.

In the second part of the shloka, Krishna states, '*kaścit vināśam kartum na arhati*,' which translates to no one can bring about the destruction of this [*Atma*]. This assertion logically concludes: **if *Atma* is genuinely indestructible, then no force, human or divine, can cause its demise.**

Adi Shankaracharya's commentary asserts that not even *Īśvara* (the Lord) can destroy the *Atma*. This does not question the boundary of divine power but reasons the fundamental oneness of *Īśvara* and *Atma*. Since both *Īśvara* and *Atma* are manifestations of the same ultimate Reality—*Brahman*—the idea of destruction does not hold. There is no distinction between the destroyer and the destroyed when both are the same *Brahman*. Think. Who can destroy whom? Thus, destruction, in the sense of ceasing to exist altogether, is impossible for *Atma*.

Through these teachings, Krishna connects the eternal and indestructible attributes of *Atma* to a broader spiritual framework encompassing the non-duality of *Īśvara* and *Atma*. This perspective is spiritually liberating as it elevates our perception of self beyond the temporal and transient to the realm of the eternal and immutable.

Atma Everywhere: The Eternal Fabric of Existence

Krishna unveils another essential dimension of *Atma* in this shloka: *'yena sarvam idam tatam'* - its all-pervading nature. This means that this universe of ours, including our body and mind (*idam*), is pervaded, or filled with That (*tatam*), indicating Absolute Reality or Fundamental existence (*Sat*). Sat, essentially our own *Atma* or Consciousness, infuses every aspect of the cosmos, thereby underpinning the existence of everything in the universe.

When Krishna declares the universe as being pervaded by this fundamental existence (*Sat*), it is crucial to grasp the unique nature of this pervasiveness. Unlike a fragrance that permeates a room but is separate from the room's contents, the pervasiveness of *Sat* is fundamentally different. **Sat does not exist as a separate layer; it constitutes the essence of all that exists**. Every object in the universe is not just filled with *Sat* but is a manifestation of *Sat*. This means that the universe and everything within it is an expression of this fundamental Reality, not separate but one and the same.

The idea that one thing can pervade everything is perplexing. However, it can be simplified with our previous analogy of clay and pots. Imagine hundreds or thousands of pots, each varying in shape, color, and size. Despite these differences, all pots share a common essence—clay. It is this clay that gives form and existence to the pots. If we remove the clay, the pot ceases to exist. Similarly, *Sat,* the fundamental Reality, constitutes the core substance of all material objects. This Reality extends to every aspect of the universe— from far-off celestial bodies like galaxies to all perceptible and imperceptible matter on Earth.

Author Kamal Ravikant articulates this truth beautifully for the modern reader:

"I promise you that the same stuff that galaxies are made of, you are. The same energy that swings planets around the stars makes

electrons dance in your heart. It is in you, outside you, you are It. It is beautiful. Trust in this. And you and your life will be grand."

Adi Shankaracharya enhances this understanding by connecting it to the Puranic vision of Bhagavan Vishnu, derived from the Sanskrit root *'Vish,'* meaning to pervade. Vishnu, therefore, is not just a deity confined to religious narratives but represents the pervasive Reality that saturates the entire universe. The descriptor *'Veveshti Vyaapnoti iti Vishnuh'*—He who pervades everything, highlights that this divine essence, Vishnu, is nothing but *Sat*, which is omnipresent and immutable, infusing every particle and space within the cosmos.

What becomes of *Sat* at the end of any universal life cycle? Despite the dissolution of forms, which we now know as *Asat,* the eternal *Sat* remains unaffected. While the transient *(Asat)* relies on the eternal *(Sat)* for its manifestation, the eternal does not depend on the transient. During the universe's cycle, *Sat* appears as the differentiated world of forms; however, beyond these cycles, it exists in an undifferentiated state. This relationship affirms that the essence of existence *(Sat)* remains intact and unchanged regardless of the transformations within the universe of forms.

Modern scientific pursuits have consistently sought a unified theory of existence. Ancient Vedantic wisdom already pinned down this unity, asserting a singular fundamental reality *(Sat)* from which all diversity arises. While science continues to probe material and energetic dimensions, Vedanta clearly says that all matter and energy derive from and are manifestations of a singular Reality—*Sat.*

Krishna assures us that *Atma* is eternal and the ubiquitous essence of existence—ever-present in all things. This understanding helps us recognize our universal connection with the entirety of creation. It helps us reconcile the transient phenomena our physical bodies are momentarily a part of with the enduring Reality *(Sat)*, our true essence *(Atma)*.

The Essence of Existence: How *Atma* Pervades the Universe

In this exploration, clarifying the relationship between *Sat*, the foundational Reality, and our true self, *Atma*, is essential. While it is evident that every material object originates from *Sat*, the connection between this fundamental Reality and our core identity, *Atma*, might seem less direct.

Like all objects, our physical body is a manifestation of *Sat*. Yet, the link between *Sat* and *Atma* needs explicit clarification.

Sat underlies every material entity; at its core, it is Consciousness or *Cit*. Consciousness enables each living being to be aware of their thoughts and emotions. It is the light that illuminates our awareness. According to Vedantic vision, matter itself originates from this Consciousness. Viewing the universe from this perspective, both non-living matter and living entities manifest from *Sat*, expressed in its purest form as *Cit*.

Therefore, as we observe the universe, we recognize that all elements, living or not, are manifestations of *Sat*. In living beings, while the physical form is made of matter (derived from *Sat*), the essence of life, or awareness, directly expresses *Cit* or pure Consciousness. Hence, the entire cosmos is pervaded by *Sat*. In its most sublime form, *Sat* as *Cit* is equivalent to *Atma*—our innermost essence. Moreover, in its most refined essence, *Sat* as *Cit* directly corresponds to *Atma*—our true nature.

To summarize, every object and being in the universe is not only permeated by *Sat* but is a manifestation of it. **The purest expression of *Sat* is Consciousness, which is unequivocally declared as our *Atma*.** Thus, in its myriad forms and existences, the entire universe is imbued with *Atma*, illustrating the profound unity and interconnectedness of all existence.

The Immutable Core: Understanding *Atma* as Avyaya

In this shloka, Krishna introduces the term *'Avyaya,'* to highlight the unchanging or immutable dimension of *Sat,* the fundamental Reality of the universe. Derived from the root *'vaya'* (to change or diminish), prefixed by 'a-' (indicating negation), *'Avyaya'* translates directly to unchanging or immutable. This description of *Sat* as *Avyaya* emphasizes its role as the immutable foundation upon which the transient phenomena of the universe manifest and dissolve.

Consider the analogy of a vast ocean with waves continuously forming and disbanding on its surface. While the waves transform constantly, the depth and vastness of the sea—remain unchanged. Similarly, *Sat* underlies the ever-changing universe of forms and phenomena. Despite the endless transformations occurring within the material world, from the birth and death of stars to the fleeting thoughts and emotions within us, *Sat* remains untouched and perpetually consistent like the water of the ocean.

This unchanging nature of *Sat* as *Avyaya* offers a practical framework for understanding existence. Every change we perceive in the universe, physical or subtle, occurs against the backdrop of this unchanging Reality, highlighting that a stable, changeless entity underpins the dynamism of existence.

A crucial point to note here is that when *Sat*, the fundamental Reality of the universe, is *avyaya* –unchanging, it presents a compelling reflection on our true identity, Consciousness (*Atma*). We have recognized that the purest nature of *Sat* is *Cit* (Consciousness) and that *Cit* is our *Atma* or identity. Thus, if *Sat* is *Avyaya,* so too is *Cit,* and consequently, our true identity, *Atma,* is also unchangeable. This is precisely the insight Krishna aims to impart. **While our perceived identity of body, mind, and intellect is ever subject to change from birth to death, our actual identity, *Atma*, does not undergo any change**. This realization forms the core teaching of Krishna in the Bhagavad Gita, which firmly asserts our eternal essence amidst the temporal world. It offers a stable foundation from which to view the transformative nature of our existence.

One *Atma*, Infinite Expressions: The Unity of Existence

In this shloka, Krishna also invites us to ponder another profound yet subtle dimension of *Atma*: its singularity. Having established that *Atma* is eternal, all-pervading, and the absolute Reality of the universe, we encounter an intriguing question: How many *Atma* are there? Given the countless living beings, does each possess a separate *Atma*? Advaita Vedanta clearly states that there is only one Reality *(Sat)*, which is pure Consciousness, singular and non-dual. This implies that, **fundamentally, the true identity of all beings is one and the same.**

To understand this better, let us take the space and pots analogy often used in traditional Vedantic teachings. If multiple pots are placed in a room, each appears to contain a separate portion of space. However, upon smashing the pots, it becomes evident that the space within them is continuous and undivided. Similarly, although individuals appear distinct due to physical, mental, and intellectual differences, the *Atma* within each is the same, continuous Reality.

Another powerful Vedantic example is the Sun's reflection in multiple buckets of water. Each bucket may show a distinct reflection, suggesting multiple suns, but only one Sun exists. The medium (the water in the buckets) creates the illusion of different suns reflecting in different buckets. In the same way, the apparent distinction among individual Consciousnesses, *Atma,* arises due to the different "containers" or bodies, minds, and intellect we possess.

These analogies, while helpful, are not without their limitations. They should not be viewed as complete representations of the Truth but as tools to aid our understanding of these profound concepts.

Another common query: If *Atma* is universal, why do we experience Consciousness limited to our senses and knowledge? It is because of the "equipment" we use—our bodies, minds, and intellect, which are different and distinct in each of us. Just as electricity powers a supercomputer and a simple calculator differently based on their capacities, so does the universal Consciousness (*Atma*) manifest differently in everyone according to the limitations and capabilities of their physical, mental, and intellectual forms.

The *Śvetāśvatara* Upanishad articulates the essence of non-duality in Vedanta, beautifully:

eko devaḥ sarvabhūteṣu gūḍhaḥ sarvavyāpī sarvabhūtāntarātmā.

"The one Divine is hidden in all beings, all-pervasive, and the inner self of all."

This shloka asserts that the one divine essence pervades and constitutes the core Self of every being in the universe.

In conclusion, the profound revelation of the Bhagavad Gita is **Atma Ekah—there is only one *Atma*.** Regardless of individual differences, our fundamental identity is unified in the singular, eternal essence of existence and Consciousness. This revolutionary vision weaves all of existence into a cohesive whole, emphasizing our interconnectedness and the unified nature of all that is.

This shloka continues to unravel the multifaceted nature of *Atma*, our true essence. It reaffirms the eternal nature of *Atma* by describing it as *Avināśi* - indestructible, *Sarvagata* - omnipresent, and *Avayaya* - immutable, reinforcing its unchanging nature amidst the transient cosmos. Together, these insights lead to a profound realization: despite the multitude of living beings, there exists only one *Atma*, unifying all in its singular, undivided essence and indestructible.

Insight	Explanation
Atma is Eternal	It exists beyond birth, death, and destruction.
Atma is All-pervading	It is the foundation of everything in existence, from the smallest particle to galaxies.
Atma is Immutable	It remains unaltered despite the transient nature of the physical world.
Atma is One	Though it appears as though there are many individual selves, *Atma* is singular and unified, the essence of all beings.

Reflective Prompt

Do you consistently find yourself getting perturbed by the physical, mental, and intellectual differences between you and those around you? Do you tend to fixate on a "my way or the highway" attitude in life? How does this affect your interpersonal relationships? How might this lesson on one unified Consciousness help you navigate your relationships with greater ease?

The essence of all beings is one—indestructible, timeless, and whole

SHLOKA 18: ETERNAL *ATMA*, FLEETING BODIES

अन्तवन्त इमे देहाः नित्यस्योक्ताः शरीरिणः |
अनाशिनोऽप्रमेयस्य तस्मादृध्यस्व भारत ||18||

antavanta imē dēhāḥ nityasyōktāḥ śarīriṇaḥ |
anāśinō'pramēyasya tasmādyudhyasva bhārata ||18||

Translation:

The bodies (***dehāḥ***) of the embodied Self (***sharirinah***), which is eternal (***nityasya***), indestructible (***anashinah***), and beyond measure or comprehension (***aprameyasya***), are indeed perishable (***antavantah***). Therefore, O Bharata (***Arjuna***), stand up and fulfill your duty (***yudhyasva***) [Sankya Yoga: 2.18]

At a Glance: Capturing the Spirit of the Shloka

Life's challenges often stem from our deep identification with the impermanent—our physical, mental, and intellectual identities. Krishna reminds us that while our bodies are destined to perish, our true essence, the *Atma*, is eternal, indestructible, and beyond the grasp of time. Rooted in the timeless truth of our unchanging Self (*Atma*), we can face life's battles with clarity and courage.

Commentary:

In this shloka, Krishna continues to build upon what he had declared in Shloka 11, that knowledge of one's identity as *Atma* alleviates the existential dread surrounding life and death. Krishna previously unfurled the attributes of our true Self, the *Atma*, as fundamental, eternal, all-pervasive, and non-dual. Here, he expands upon the description of *Atma* as '*anāśina*' (indestructible) and '*nitya*' (eternal) by introducing an essential new dimension: '*aprameya*'—indicating that *Atma* is immeasurable and beyond the grasp of ordinary sensory perception and logical inference.

Krishna makes it unequivocally clear that while *Atma* remains eternal, the physical and subtle bodies we identify with—are transient, subject to birth, change, growth, disease, decay, and ultimately, death. **This teaching directly addresses humanity's greatest fear: the fear of death, presenting a liberating perspective that transcends the finite to draw from the infinite realms of existenc**e. The transient nature of our corporeal forms does not signify the cessation of existence. The *Panditas* (those enlightened with this Truth) embody a fearless approach to life and live free from suffering.

Eternal (*Nitya*) Indestructibility (*Anāśina*)of *Atma*

In this shloka, Krishna reiterates the immortal characteristics of *Atma*, which he has emphasized throughout his discourse: "*nityasya śarīriṇaḥ anāśinaḥ.*" *Atma*, our true identity, is described as *'nitya'* (eternal) and *'anāśina'* (indestructible). The term *'nitya'* has its roots in *'ni'* (direction or progression) and the suffix *'tya.'* When combined, they define a continuous, unending state. This portrays *Atma* as existing endlessly beyond the bounds of time and change.

Similarly, *'anāśina'* is derived from the root *'nāśina'* (to perish or destroy) with the prefix *'a'* denoting negation. Together, *'anāśina'* powerfully asserts that *Atma* is imperishable and cannot be destroyed by any means. This immutability highlights the contrast between the enduring nature of *Atma* and the transient nature of the physical and subtle bodies that we often mistake as our true selves. By declaring *Atma* as *'nitya'* and *'anāśina,'* Krishna aims to dissolve the fear associated with impermanence and death, redirecting our focus towards realizing our eternal essence that transcends physical existence.

Transience of the Physical and Subtle Bodies

Contrasting sharply with the eternal nature of *Atma*, Krishna highlights the inherent transience of our physical and subtle bodies, which form critical aspects of our current identity as human beings. The term *'antah'* (having an end) underscores the inevitable mortality of these bodies. Unlike *Atma*, described as *'nitya'* (eternal) and *'anāśina'* (indestructible), our physical and subtle bodies are bound within the confines of birth, growth, change, disease, decay, and death. The word *'śarīriṇah'* is emphasized in the plural, pointing to both the physical body, which can be touched and felt, and the subtle body, comprising the core of mental and intellectual impressions, which together participate in life's experience. Krishna asserts that these components of our existence are *'asat'*—not the ultimate truth and transient. While the physical body ceases to exist at death, the subtle body, carrying the mental and intellectual impressions, may continue to transmigrate but is still not permanent.

The Unseen Self: Exploring *Atma*'s Incomprehensible Nature

In our everyday lives, we identify closely with our physical and subtle bodies, the tangible aspects of our existence. This identification is rooted in our direct experiences; we perceive our bodies through sensory input and comprehend our emotions and thoughts through our mental and intellectual faculties. In this shloka, Krishna acknowledges that while our bodies are easily perceivable and relatable, *Atma*, our true essence, is not. He describes *Atma* as *'Aprameya'* (beyond the scope of ordinary sensory perception and logical reasoning). *'Aprameya'* comes from the Sanskrit prefix *'a'* (indicating negation) and the root *'ma'* (to measure). *Atma* cannot be quantified or grasped through the five senses, feelings, or analytical thought.

This inherent incomprehensibility of *Atma* explains why we typically identify with our physical and subtle bodies. It is like how, in a dream, we mistake our dream bodies for our real selves, accepting their limitations and experiences as our own. Despite knowing the truth about our identity, aligning with the reality of the waker from within the dream state is impossible. The waker's identity in this different order of reality is temporarily *'Aprameya'*—not perceivable. In the dream, the dream body and world seem immediate and perceptible, while the true identity of the waker is ungraspable.

Similarly, in waking life, our body, mind, and intellect are readily perceivable and available, making it easy and natural to identify with them. In contrast, our true identity, *Atma*, cannot be comprehended by our sense organs, mind, or intellect. It is the substratum of our physical and subtle faculties, no doubt, yet is beyond our grasp - *'Aprameya.'*

An obvious question then begins to trouble every sincere seeker: If *Atma* cannot be known through regular means of perception, emotion, and thought, how can one ever truly identify with It and establish It as one's real identity?

Scriptural texts and the experiential teachings of great Masters serve as '*Pramana*'—pointers that help us understand what lies beyond the reach of our sensory, mental, and intellectual capabilities. Although they cannot describe *Atma* directly—they help us remove false notions and misidentifications. They guide us in peeling away the layers of identity we construct around our body, mind, and intellect, dispelling the illusion much like becoming lucid in a dream. Realizing you are dreaming can dramatically shift your experience of the dream; similarly, scriptural teachings can help move our perception from identifying with our transient bodies to recognizing our true Self as *Atma*.

This realization of our broader existence, whether in a dream or the waking world, evolves our understanding of ourselves and the world by removing the ignorance that veils our true nature. It frees us from the fears and suffering tied to bodily existence and ushers us into a life of more profound wisdom and peace aligned with our eternal essence.

Embracing the battle of life

Krishna concludes this shloka with a powerful directive: Therefore, fight on ('*tasmat yuddhyasva*'), on the pretext that Arjuna's reasons for avoiding the battle do not hold against his more significant duty to uphold *dharma*. This command is not just for Arjuna on that battlefield of Kurukshetra but is a clarion call for humanity to meet life's challenges without fear or excessive worry. Krishna stresses that while our physical bodies are born to eventually perish, our *Atma* lives on - eternal and indestructible. Krishna's message reverberates through all time and space, urging us to act courageously and fulfill our responsibilities, firmly rooted in understanding our eternal nature beyond the ephemeral physical existence.

It is crucial to understand that Krishna's order to "fight" is contextual, pertaining to the specific duty of Arjuna as a warrior on a particular battlefield. This should not be misconstrued as an endorsement of violence. In his commentary, Adi Shankaracharya elucidates that Krishna's instruction aims to clear the obstructions of sorrow and confusion that cloud judgment and action. His advice is directed not towards promoting battle but towards encouraging righteous action (*'dharma'*) in the face of challenges. Therefore, the exhortation to "fight" symbolizes a call to uphold oneself, engage actively with difficulties, and strive to remove personal and universal suffering. The battlefield of Kurukshetra is symbolic of understanding and overcoming the internal and external conflicts we encounter daily, guided by deep spiritual wisdom and an unwavering commitment to virtue.

Without Knowledge of *Atma*	With Knowledge of *Atma*
Fear of death and attachment to body	Acceptance of body's transient nature
Over-identification with roles	Balanced engagement with detachment
Anxiety in facing challenges	Courage and equanimity in action
View life as finite	Recognize eternal essence in existence

Table: How the Experiential Knowledge of Atma Transforms Action

In this shloka, Krishna masterfully addresses existential concerns about life and death by distinguishing between the eternal *Atma* and our transient physical and subtle bodies. He clarifies that while our bodies are temporary and designed to end, *Atma*—our true identity—remains unchanged by the ravages of time, inspiring us to live a life of enlightened action and deep spiritual integrity.

In encouraging Arjuna to fight on, Krishna uses the battlefield as a metaphor for life's challenges, guiding us to transcend physical limitations and embrace our *dharma* with courage. This profound message, central to the Bhagavad Gita, does not advocate for literal conflict but a committed pursuit of righteousness in the face of all incapacitating adversities.

Reflective Prompt

Are you often overwhelmed by the fear of loss, aging, or death? How might seeing yourself as an eternal Consciousness beyond the limitations of the body transform the way you view these experiences and embolden your approach to life?

The body may fade, but the Self shines eternal, untouched by time or tide

SHLOKA 19: NEITHER DOER NOR RECEIVER

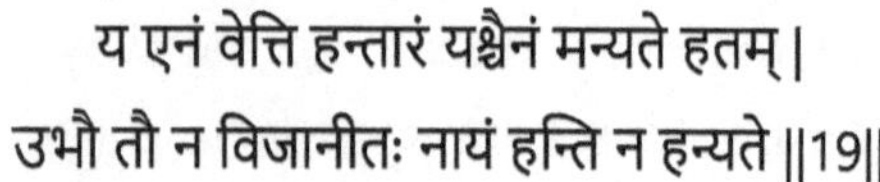

य एनं वेत्ति हन्तारं यश्चैनं मन्यते हतम् ।
उभौ तौ न विजानीतः नायं हन्ति न हन्यते ॥19॥

ya ēnaṁ vētti hantāraṁ yaścainaṁ manyatē hatam |
ubhau tau na vijānītaḥ nāyaṁ hanti na hanyatē ||19||

Translation:

Whoever thinks this [*Atma*] kills (*hantāram*) or is killed (*hatam*), both are mistaken (*na vijānītaḥ*). This [*Atma*] neither kills (*na hanti*) nor can it be killed (*na hanyate*) [Sankya Yoga: 2.19]

At a Glance: Capturing the Spirit of the Shloka

Atma, our true Self, is eternal and uninvolved, neither acting as an "agent" nor serving as an "object" of action. The roles of doer and experiencer belong solely to the transient physical, mental, and intellectual identities we mistakenly associate with ourselves. Recognizing that *Atma* remains untouched by actions and their outcomes liberates us to engage in the world with clarity and detachment, grounded in the timeless and unchanging essence of our being.

Commentary:

From shlokas 11 to 25, Krishna methodically reveals the essence of our true nature, which extends beyond the transient identities tied to our physical, mental, and intellectual faculties. While these aspects are crucial for navigating our earthly existence, they do not define our true identity. Our core identity is *Atma*, the eternal Consciousness that is the foundation of existence, untouched and unchanged by the temporal world.

Shloka 19 deepens our understanding of *Atma* by emphasizing that it is neither the doer of actions (*'Akarta'*) nor the experiencer of their results (*'Abhokta'*). Actions and consequences belong to the body, mind, and intellect but do not affect the eternal Self. This profound insight reassures us that while we navigate the responsibilities and challenges of worldly life, our true Self remains untouched, unaffected, and eternally serene.

By directly quoting a mantra from the *Katha Upanishad* (Chapter 1, Section ii, mantra 19), Krishna not only validates his teachings through the authoritative scriptural tradition of *Sanatana Dharma* but also honors the Upanishads as a primary source of spiritual knowledge (*pramāṇa-grantha*). This methodical referencing connects the seeker more logically to the otherwise hard-to-grasp Upanishads - a revered dialogue of spiritual inquiry and enlightenment that has guided ancient saints, sages, and advanced spiritual seekers alike for millennia.

Atma is Beyond Doership and Enjoyership

Krishna clarifies a common misconception of doership and enjoyership with vivid imagery of a battlefield, where it is natural for a warrior to believe they are the killer or the killed. However, Krishna points out that anyone so identified with their physical and subtle bodies would naturally hold such beliefs because they have not understood their true nature - *Atma*. If identified with the *Atma*, they would rest assured that they are neither the agent (*'karta'*) of any action nor the recipient (*'bhokta'*) of any action's consequences.

'Enam' in this verse refers to *Atma*, which is self-evident, eternal (*nitya*), and forms the basis of all existence (*sat*), beyond the reach of ordinary perception (*aprameya*). When Krishna discusses the *'hantā'* (killer) and *'hatam'* (killed), he emphasizes that *Atma* neither engages in killing nor can it be killed. The *Atma* transcends action and its effects—it is neither *'kartā'* (the doer) nor *'bhokta'* (the enjoyer of action).

Krishna's insight extends beyond the battlefield to all aspects of life. When engaging in daily activities like working, eating, exercising, or sleeping we often identify ourselves as the initiators and enjoyers of these actions. However, Krishna explains that these are attributes of a temporary provisional identity tied to the body, mind, and intellect. This is akin to a dream, where the dream identity appears to perform actions and experience their results. Still, the actual self—the waker now temporarily dreaming in the bed—remains unaffected.

Just as the waker lends consciousness and existence to the dream identity but is not affected by the happenings in the dream, *Atma* enables our worldly identity to act and experience without being involved in or altered by these activities. This understanding helps us recognize that while we may experience doership and enjoyership, these are not qualities of our true Self, *Atma*, but of a temporary identity handling our current life circumstances.

We cannot discount the provisional requirement of this temporary identity (*ahamkara*) in our day-to-day lives. While we live, we must perform actions that naturally incur results, whether maintaining the body, caring for the family, achieving professional success, or even studying or teaching the Bhagavad Gita. Krishna is not negating this identity; he is educating us to understand that this current identity is not our complete identity as *Atma* and that *Atma* is not affected by the actions of the *ahamkara*.

A person with this knowledge will continue to perform actions but identified with *Atma* instead of their physical and subtle apparatus. This is like someone acting in a lucid dream, **performing actions, and enjoying results with the knowledge that they are beyond those actions and results.**

Many crucial teachings of the Bhagavad Gita revolve around the understanding that *Atma* is uninvolved in worldly actions. One critical derivation is that if *Atma* is *akarta* and *abhokta,* it is free from all karmic bonds. Consequently, *Atma* accrues no merit (*punya*) or sin (*papa).* As a result, *Atma* is not bound by the laws of karma and reincarnation.

Aspect	Misconception	Truth About *Atma*
Doership	*Atma* performs actions (e.g., killing, fighting).	*Atma* is **Akarta** (non-doer).
Experience of Results	*Atma* experiences the results of actions.	*Atma* is **Abhokta** (non-enjoyer).
Subject to Change	*Atma* is affected by actions and changes.	*Atma* is unchanging and eternal.
Association with the Body	*Atma* is tied to the body's actions.	*Atma* is distinct and unaffected by the body.

Table: The Atma does not act, nor is it acted upon

Influence of this shloka on Ralph Waldo Emerson:

American philosopher Ralph Waldo Emerson, captivated by the profound spiritual insights of the Bhagavad Gita, poeticized the central theme of this shloka in his poem 'Brahma,' reflecting the mystical and eternal aspects of the Self precisely as described by Krishna:

> *'If the red slayer think he slays,*
> *Or if the slain think he is slain,*
> *They know not well the subtle ways*
> *I keep, and pass, and turn again.'*

Emerson's words echo the Bhagavad Gita's declarations about the illusion of death and the eternal, uninvolved nature of *Atma*. His poem seamlessly bridges the gap between Eastern spirituality and Western literary expression, accentuating the universal relevance and enduring appeal of these spiritual truths.

In this Shloka, Krishna continues to build upon the transcendent nature of *Atma*, emphasizing that it is neither the doer of actions nor the experiencer of their results. He clarifies that our perceived identity—the self we think we are while engaged in daily activities and interactions—is not our true Self. Krishna reveals that *Atma* exists beyond these ephemeral roles as *'akarta'* (non-doer) and *'abhokta'* (non-enjoyer). This wisdom frees us from the misconceptions we typically hold about our existence and consequent crippling attachments.

Krishna challenges our conventional understanding of self, guiding us step-by-step to recognize that what we often consider our identity is merely a temporary manifestation, not the eternal *Atma*.

Reflective Prompt

Do you sometimes feel trapped by the identities and roles society has assigned you? Would understanding your true Self to be beyond all roles and identities infuse greater authenticity and freedom in all your activities and relationships?

The Atma does not act, nor is it acted upon—it simply shines, eternal and free

SHLOKA 20: BEYOND BIRTH AND DEATH

न जायते म्रियते वा कदाचित्

नायं भूत्वा भविता वा न भूयः |

अजो नित्यः शाश्वतोऽयं पुराणः

न हन्यते हन्यमाने शरीरे ||20||

na jāyatē mriyatē vā kadācit

nāyaṁ bhūtvā bhavitā vā na bhūyaḥ |

ajō nityaḥ śāśvatō'yaṁ purāṇaḥ

na hanyatē hanyamānē śarīrē ||20||

Translation:

This (Atman - The Consciousness) is never born (***na jāyate***), nor does it ever die (***na mriyate***). Once it comes into existence (***bhūtvā***), it never ceases to exist (***na bhūyaḥ***). It is unborn (***ajah***), eternal (***nityaḥ***), unchanging (***śāśvataḥ***), and ancient yet ever-new (***purāṇaḥ***). The Self (***Atman***) is not destroyed (***na hanyate***) when the body (***śarīra***) is destroyed. **[Sankya Yoga: 2.20]**

At a Glance: Capturing the Spirit of the Shloka

While the body, mind, and intellect undergo growth, transformation, and decay, our true essence, *Atma*, is eternal, unchanging, and beyond the cycles of birth and death. Recognizing this unalterable nature of *Atma* frees us from the sorrows tied to life's impermanence, enabling us to live with serenity and resilience amidst change.

Commentary

In the previous shloka, Krishna explored how *Atma*, or Consciousness, is neither the initiator nor the recipient of actions within the world. It is the fundamental Reality that animates all objects and activities emerging and dissolving within the confines of time, space, and causation.

Think. When something acts or is affected by action, it invariably undergoes change. Every action transforms the actor or the acted upon in some way. Neither remains the same.

Given that *Atma* is neither an agent of action nor affected by action, it follows that *Atma* persists changeless. Like the previous one, this declaration emphasizing the immutable nature of *Atma* is also quoted from the Katha Upanishad (Chapter 1, Section ii, Mantra 18).

Note that this shloka is presented in the distinct *triṣṭubh* meter, differing from the usual pattern, to ensure it resonates uniquely and captures the listener's attention. The shift in meters highlights the timeless, unaltered essence of Consciousness and stresses the eternal dimensions of *Atma*.

Krishna begins this shloka with two potent declarations that set the foundation for understanding *Atma*: **it is never born (*na jāyate*), nor does it ever die (*na mriyate*).** These statements highlight that *Atma* stands beyond the typical life-death continuum that every being in the material realm is subjected to. He elaborates that *Atma* does not transition from non-existence to existence and vice versa or change forms, like a pot from clay or a seed to a plant. *Atma* is changeless, existing eternally without beginning (*na bhūtvā*) or end (*na bhavitā*).

Krishna concludes by clarifying the relationship between *Atma* and the body: even when the body is destroyed (*hanyamāne śarīre*), *Atma* is not (*na hanyate*). This distinction stresses that while the physical body undergoes changes and perishes because it is susceptible to alterations (*vikāra*), *Atma* does not. It is *Nirvakara*.

Atma is commonly misunderstood as an intrinsic attribute of the body, and thus we tend to equate our existence to varying bodily conditions. Krishna's proclamation initiates a crucial discernment (*viveka*) that while the body is transient, our true essence, *Atma* is eternal and unmodifiable.

Understanding *Atma* and our core essence to be one and the same frees us from the illusions and sufferings tied to the unavoidable affectations of body, mind, and intellect. Aligning us with our eternal essence, which is untouched by the transient nature of the material world, this wisdom enables us to live with a greater sense of detachment and serenity.

Aspect	True Self (*Atma*)	Perceived self (Physical, Mental, Emotional)
Existence	Unchanging (Avyaya)	Constantly changing
Perception	Beyond ordinary perception	Perceptible to senses
Action	Neither the doer nor the experiencer	Subject to actions and their consequences
Death	Beyond birth and death	Bound by birth and death

Table: True Self Vs Perceived self

**Delving deeper into the intrinsic qualities of our true essence -
Atma:**

The fullness of *Atma* cannot be articulated in words. Any semantic description of *Atma* can only point towards what *Atma* is. Verses like these at best serve as those necessary pointers to give seekers a close enough description of its totality.

Let us take a closer look at some of the words used in this shloka to describe *Atma*:

Ajaḥ **(Unborn)**: Any being born must necessarily die, making its existence finite and limited to a specific period. *Atma* is not born when we are born, nor will it die when we die. It was, is, and will forever continue to be. *Atma* is infinite.

Nityaḥ **(Eternal)**: *Atma* never ceases to be. A previously discussed analogy of the ocean helps us understand its eternal nature. Countless waves rise, dance upon, and then crash into the ocean; the ocean beneath persists eternally. Similarly, myriad beings are born, exist for a while, and then die, but *Atma* persists eternally.

Sāśvataḥ **(Changeless)**: *Atma* is the changeless Reality upon which all changes occur. Vedanta categorizes the changes that all physical objects undergo into six stages: existence in potential (*asti*), birth (*jāyatē*), growth (*vardhatē*), transformation (*vipariṇamatē*), decay (*apakṣīyatē*), and finally, death (*vinaśyati*). Krishna asserts that *Atma* does not undergo any of these changes and, therefore, remains untransformed.

Purāṇaḥ **(Ancient)**: No point in time can be pinned as the beginning of *Atma*. It is ancient. It has existed from time immemorial.

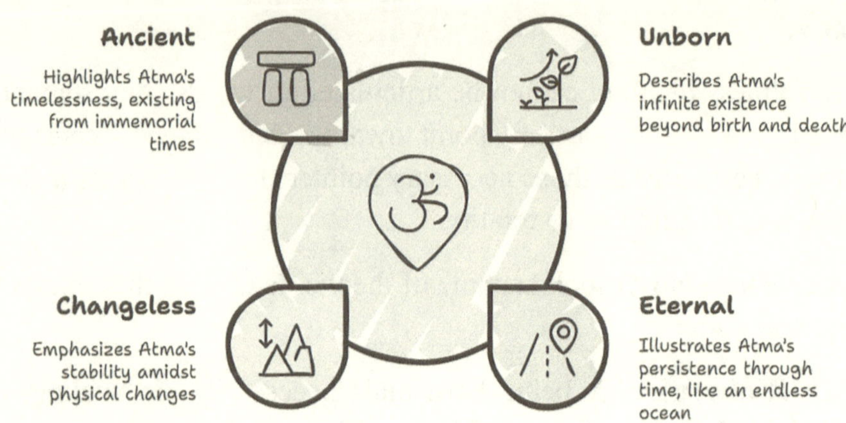

Fig: Nature of Atma

Recognizing these transcendental qualities of *Atma* as our core qualities can profoundly shift our perception of self and the universe as we slowly but surely begin to realize that we are beyond the transient and the perishable.

Adi Shankaracharya's Insight

Through his incisive commentary on this shloka, Adi Shankaracharya emphasizes that *Atma*, our true identity, is untouched by the six-fold modifications that affect all physical entities: birth, existence, growth, transformation, decay, and death. He argues that since *Atma* is devoid of change or transformation, it inherently transcends the physical processes observable in the material world.

Shankaracharya declares that *Atma* is *'aśocya'* (not a source of sorrow) by asserting that it is free from all forms of modification. If *Atma* is unchangeable and cannot be subjected to or cause suffering, it stands beyond the realm of sorrow. This perspective challenges the typical human experience where sorrow often stems from various changes—a process that *Atma* is not subjected to.

Shankaracharya contends that *Atma* is characterized by '*ānanda*' (fullness). Aligning with this understanding of *Atma*, our true essence must necessarily be void of grief and suffering, supporting Krishna's assertion in Shloka 11 that one who truly knows *Atma* transcends sorrow.

An alignment with this pivotal conclusion by Shankaracharya provides us with a firm footing to overcome existential grief. We can attain a more profound sense of detachment and peace by realizing that our true Self is eternal and blissful, unaffected by worldly changes. Furthermore, Shankaracharya's discussion integrates these metaphysical insights into a broader spiritual context, demonstrating how even theoretical knowledge of these attributes of *Atma* can profoundly influence personal growth and liberation from suffering. This connection between intellectual understanding and experiential wisdom sets apart Shankaracharya's teachings, which emphasize the transformative power of this ancient insight.

Krishna assures us that understanding the unchangeable, eternal nature of *Atma*—exempt from birth, death, and all intermediate transformations—frees us from misapprehensions that lead to sorrow. This realization fortifies our spiritual foundation, aligning us with the true essence of our being that remains untouched by temporal changes.

Reflective Prompt

Reflect on the ways you relate to changes and transitions in your life. How might your perspective shift if you identified yourself with Atma - unchanging and eternal?

Beyond the hands of time - Atma is the essence of all that is and will be

SHLOKA 21: REDEFINED SELF IDENTITY

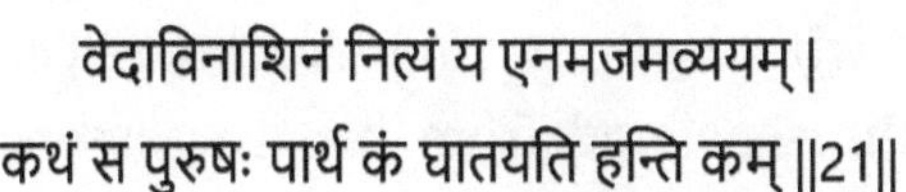

वेदाविनाशिनं नित्यं य एनमजमव्ययम् |
कथं स पुरुषः पार्थ कं घातयति हन्ति कम ||21||

vēdāvināśinaṁ nityaṁ ya ēnamajamavyayam |
kathaṁ sa puruṣaḥ pārtha kaṁ ghātayati hanti kam ||21||

Translation:

O Arjuna (***Pārtha***), he who understands (***veda***) that the *Atma* is indestructible (***avināśinam***), eternal (***nityam***), unborn (***ajam***), and unchanging (***avyayam***), how can such a person (***sa puruṣaḥ***) kill (***hanti***) or cause another to be killed (***kaṁ ghātayati***) [Sankya Yoga: 2.21]

At a Glance: Capturing the Spirit of the Shloka

The one who identifies with the *Atma* - the indestructible, eternal, unborn, and unchanging essence - how can they consider themselves as the performer or victim of any action?

Commentary:

In this shloka, Krishna addresses Arjuna's immediate dilemma on the battlefield: killing his relatives or being the cause of their deaths. Identified with the body, mind, and intellect complex, Arjuna has completely disassociated from his true essence and is steeped in ignorance. His non-apprehension of Reality creates all these misapprehensions, agitations, and grief around a straightforward task before him.

Having clarified in the earlier shlokas that our essence, *Atma*, is immune to the six modifications that physical bodies undergo, Krishna now emphasizes that *Atma* does not initiate any action, nor is it affected by its consequences. When thoroughly internalized, this knowledge about the nature of *Atma* helps seekers understand that their current identity, often conflated with the body, mind, and intellect, is distinct from their true, unchanging essence. Recognizing this distinction is crucial to navigating the material realm with wisdom and peace and for spiritual growth, as it shifts one's identification from the transient to the eternal.

Knowing Self as *Atma*: The Ultimate Goal of a Spiritual Seeker

This shloka primarily emphasizes that the ultimate goal of every spiritual seeker should be deep, experiential knowledge of one's true identity as *Atma*, or Consciousness. Krishna uses the term *'Vēdāḥ,'* which means 'one *must* know.' This directive is not merely about reading scriptures or familiarizing oneself with religious doctrines superficially but attaining a direct, transformative knowing of one's true nature.

While the word *Veda* typically refers to the foundational scriptural body of knowledge in *Sanatana Dharma*, here *'Vēdāḥ'* is employed as a verb indicating urgent action—**know yourself at the deepest level.**

Krishna has extensively covered the nature of the *Atma* (Self) in preceding shlokas: *'Avināśinam'* (indestructible), *'Nityam'* (eternal), *'Ajam'* (unborn), and *'Avyayam'* (immutable). These pointers distinguish *Atma* from everything changing and ephemeral, including the physical body, mind, and intellect, subject to the six modifications discussed earlier. Slowly beginning to disidentify with the temporary aspects and identify with the eternal *Atma* within shifts a seeker's focus from the perishable body to the imperishable essence of Consciousness.

This crucial inward journey entails a two-step process. The first step is distinguishing *Atma*, or Consciousness, from the physical form. Typically, we perceive Consciousness as another aspect of our body due to its close association with our experiences. To advance spiritually, one must recognize that Consciousness, though operating within the body, exists independently of it.

Understanding this distinction is a prerequisite for the second step, identifying with the Self. Without gaining, contemplating, and experiencing scriptural knowledge, our identification with the transient physical aspects of our being becomes deeply ingrained, and the body feels like the beginning and end of our existence.

However, Krishna challenges this deep-seated identification. He invites us to see the body as transient, likening it to an iceberg—solid and distinct, but ultimately just a temporary formation of water that will eventually dissolve back into its fundamental state. Just as the iceberg, though appearing separate, is nothing but a solidified state of water, which it returns to upon melting, our physical form is merely a temporary configuration of the five elements arising from and merging back into the same sea of Consciousness. Despite the apparent differences between our bodies, minds, and intellects, our true essence is *Atma—Sat* (existence) and pure Consciousness. Everything is intrinsically nothing but *Atma*, revealing a profound and permanent unity underlying all fleeting diversity.

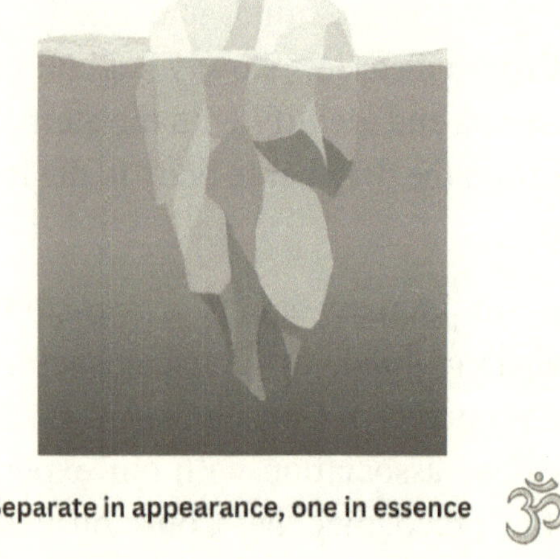

Fig: Everything is intrinsically nothing but Atma

This recognition requires active, persistent effort through '*nidhidhyāsanam*'—a sustained contemplation on this teaching that shifts the sense of 'I' from the physical to the spiritual, from the changing to the unchanging. This change in basic assumptions is what Krishna terms '*Vēdāḥ*'—the internalized and experiential knowing that our true identity is *Atma* (Consciousness), not the body.

Aligning with the eternal, immutable *Atma* liberates the seeker from the extreme vicissitudes of physical existence and consequent sorrows. **This state of being, wherein the unshakeable knowing 'I am the *Atma*' replaces the previous misconception that 'I am the body,' is the pinnacle of Self-realization, offering the necessary detachment and peace from the incessant dramas of worldly life.**

Krishna further elucidates the profound implications of fully identifying with *Atma*. **When individuals realize they are not just associated with *Atma* but at the core are *Atma*, the characteristics traditionally attributed to *Atma* transform into personal truths**. Rather than merely viewing *Atma* as *'akartā'* (not the doer) and *'abhoktā'* (not the enjoyer), the enlightened individual affirms, 'I am *akartā*; I am *abhoktā*.' This pivotal shift helps one transcend limiting physical, mental, and intellectual identifications and embrace the limitless aspects of unchangeability and immortality.

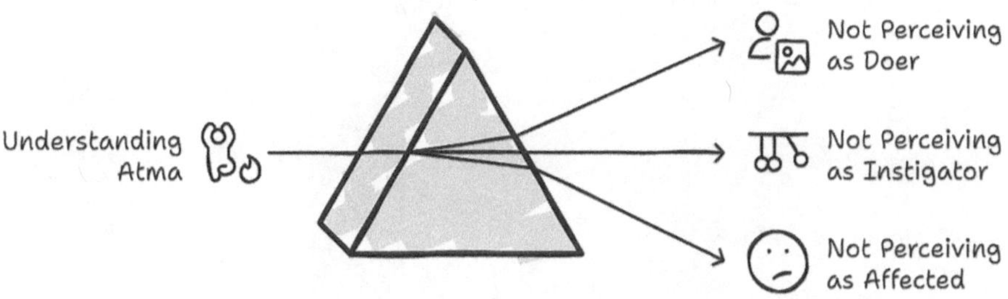

Fig: Atma is neither a doer nor enjoyer

Krishna emphasizes that with this profound understanding, the spiritual seeker no longer perceives themselves as the doer of actions *(karta)*, the instigator of actions (*kārayitah*), or as being affected by actions (*bhoktā*). He poses rhetorical questions to underline this insight: 'How can that *Atma* kill anyone (*kaṁ hantim*)?' and 'How can that *Atma* instigate anyone to kill (*kaṁ ghātayatim*)?' Framed within the context of the Mahabharata war, the notion of 'killing' is metaphorical, extending to all our day-to-day actions, feelings, and thoughts. Thus, one who truly knows *Atma* steps beyond the usual roles and becomes *'akartā,'* a liberated being. This individual recognizes that while the body-mind-intellect complex may engage in actions as they ought to, their core essence, *Atma*, exists beyond the initiations and ramifications of these activities and remains unaffected.

Krishna continues to clarify the profound distinction between our true and eternal Self and perceived and transient selves. This shloka, in particular, emphasizes that knowing oneself as *Atma* — indestructible, eternal, and immutable — fundamentally alters one's interaction with the world. No longer bound by the illusions of doership and enjoyership, the enlightened seeker transcends the limitations imposed by physical, mental, and intellectual identities, freeing themselves to perform their duties to the best of their ability. It paves the way for a deeper engagement with life, rooted in the unchanging truth of *Atma*.

Reflective Prompt

If you genuinely began to believe that you were neither the instigator of actions nor the receiver of the results of those actions, how might this transform your interactions with objects and beings of this world?

Beyond the fleeting roles, I am the eternal whole

SHLOKA 22: DEATH AS TRANSITION, NOT END

वासांसि जीर्णानि यथा विहाय

नवानि गृह्णाति नरोऽपराणि |

तथा शरीराणि विहाय जीर्णानि

अन्यानि संयाति नवानि देही ||22||

vāsāṁsi jīrṇāni yathā vihāya
navāni gṛhṇāti narō'parāṇi |
tathā śarīrāṇi vihāya jīrṇāni
anyāni saṁyāti navāni dēhī ||22||

Translation:

Just as a person discards old, worn-out clothes (***vāsāṁsi jīrṇāni***) and takes on new ones (***navāni),*** in the same way, the embodied self (***dēhī***)—comprising the subtle body (***sūkṣma śarīra***)—sheds aged bodies (***jīrṇāni śarīrāṇi***) and assumes new ones (***navāni śarīrāṇi***) [Sankya Yoga: 2.22]

At a Glance: Capturing the Spirit of the Shloka

Just as a person casts off worn-out clothes for new ones, the subtle body discards an old physical body at death and adopts a new one at birth, while the *Atma* remains unaffected and unchanged.

Commentary:

In this shloka, Krishna employs a simple yet profound analogy to illuminate the enigma surrounding death and rebirth. He explains that our current self-identity as human beings is composed of three distinct elements: the physical body, which includes all that is tangible; the subtle body, which encompasses our faculties of perception, emotion, and thought; and the *Atma*, the eternal Consciousness that animates both the physical and subtle bodies. At the moment of death, the physical body ceases to exist, the subtle body transitions to a new physical form, and the *Atma* remains unchanged, eternal and all-pervading

Krishna illustrates this transition through a brilliant metaphor: just as we discard worn-out clothes and don new ones, the subtle body sheds the old physical body and adopts a new one to continue its journey.

This vivid comparison helps demystify the process of death and rebirth, highlighting that death is not an end but merely a change in the guise through which the subtle body expresses itself. Meanwhile, the *Atma*, unaffected by these changes, persists in its pure state.

Exploring the Depths:

Physical Body as Temporary Garment

Krishna begins by comparing the physical body to old clothes that are discarded when they wear out: *'vāsāṁsi jīrṇāni yathā vihāya'* (just as a person sheds worn-out clothes). This imagery starkly portrays the body as something temporary and replaceable, emphasizing that death is merely the end of the body's utility, not the end of existence.

With all its functions and attributes, the body serves as a vessel for life's journey, akin to clothes that temporarily adorn and protect the physical form but are ultimately dispensable.

Subtle Body as the Continuer of Experience:

The subtle body, which encompasses the programming that generates perceptions, actions, emotions, and thoughts, acts like the wearer of these clothes. It survives the physical body and transitions to new forms: *'navāni gr̥hṇāti narō'parāṇi'* (takes up new ones). This transition is steered by the law of karma, which determines the nature of the future physical form. Unlike the physical body, which disintegrates, the subtle body carries forward across different lifetimes.

Atma as the Unchanging Witness:

Most importantly, Krishna underscores the constancy of our true identity -the *Atma* amidst these transitions. The *Atma* remains unaffected by the death of the physical body or the movements of the subtle body. It is the eternal witness, never worn out, never renewed— immutable and imperishable. This distinction between the *Atma* and the other aspects of our being helps clarify the true nature of the Self as separate from the physical, mental, and intellectual constructs we often mistake for our real identity.

Modern Parallel to Enhance Understanding:

As looked at earlier, Krishna's analogy can be likened to an old computer upgrade to a new one. The software (subtle body) that contains all the programs, data, and preferences is transferred to a new machine (a new physical body). The electricity powering the computer (*Atma*) remains the same, unaffected by the change in hardware. This modern analogy helps concretize our understanding of change and continuity in the process of birth and death in a relatable way.

This clarity about the physical body's temporality and the subtle body's transmigration, facilitated by the constancy of *Atma*, is intended to foster a deeper connection with our true identity and a detachment from the material aspects of existence.

Clarifying Misconceptions on Transmigration:

To reiterate the core teachings of this shloka, it is essential to understand the distinct roles of each aspect of our being during the death and rebirth process:

- **Physical Body:** What dies is the physical body. It is compared to discarded worn-out clothing that loses its utility value.
- **Subtle Body:** The subtle body transmigrates. This aspect, comprising our emotional and intellectual patterns, moves from one physical form to another, driven by karma, to continue its journey of experiences.
- *Atma:* The *Atma* remains completely unaffected by these transitions. It does not die, nor does it transmigrate. It is the eternal, unchanging witness enlivening these innumerable cycles of birth and death.

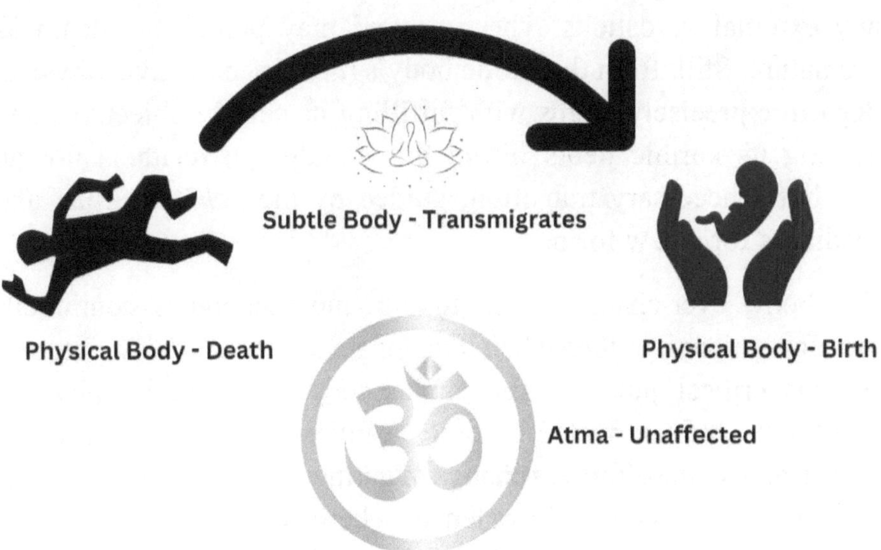

Fig: Physical Body, Subtle Body & Atma

Deciding When to Change Bodies

In describing the process of death and rebirth, Krishna employs the metaphor of changing clothes to articulate the finitude of the physical body. However, this analogy might prompt questions about the untimely deaths of the young, whose bodies are not worn out. To clarify, the concept of 'old' is subjective and determined by the indweller, the *dehī,* rather than bodily conditions or adverse external circumstances.

For example, the tradition of royalty wearing clothes only once before considering them old or car rental businesses considering cars outdated after just a year illustrates that 'oldness' is a relative and functional decision, not an absolute state determined by physical wear and tear or the number of years things have been in use.

This personal determination of the 'right time' to discard the body underscores a profound spiritual truth: the physical body's readiness for death is judged by the subtle body residing within it, not by any external yardsticks. The bereaved may perceive a death as premature. Still, from the subtle body's (*dehī*) perspective, physical departure precisely aligns with fulfilling its earthly objectives and settling its karmic debts. From this standpoint, death is not an end but a necessary transition, guided by the *dehī's* journey and readiness for a new form.

The body, ever-changing and time-bound, undergoes continuous transformation; it is shed when it no longer serves the *dehī's* purpose. At this critical juncture, the subtle body, unbound by physical constraints and unaffected by time, seamlessly transitions to a new vessel, akin to the effortless change of garments. This cycle represents a natural progression of existence, where the only constants are change and the ongoing journey of the subtle body.

Fearless in the Face of Death

Understanding and identifying with our eternal, unchangeable *Atma* can profoundly impact how we face life's ultimate certainty: death. When fully embraced, this wisdom grants extraordinary composure and fearlessness at the time of death.

As depicted in Plato's dialogues, Socrates faced his death with remarkable wisdom and serenity. His distressed and tearful disciples surrounded him as he prepared to drink the hemlock. Yet, Socrates alone remained calm, chastising his followers for their sorrow. His fearlessness stemmed from a deep recognition of his true Self as separate from his physical body. When asked by Crito, one of his followers, about how he should be buried, Socrates replied with insightful levity, 'Crito, you must first catch me, the real me, before you ask that question,' highlighting his belief in his immortal Self, which would not perish with his body. He advised them to treat his body like any other, portraying his detachment from the physical form.

Socrates's profound understanding mirrors Krishna's teachings that our existence does not end with death. His ability to dissociate his true Self from his body at his life's end demonstrates the ultimate realization of spiritual teachings.

In recent history, figures like Swami Vivekananda have echoed this sentiment, declaring that a nation, or any individual who fears death, cannot achieve greatness. True valor and greatness emerge from confronting and accepting the inevitability of death without fear, embodying the teachings that the *Atma*, our true Self, is beyond death.

These historical instances serve as powerfully lived examples of the spiritual truths Krishna discusses. They inspire us to internalize and experiment with these profound insights. Recognizing and embracing our true nature as the eternal and immutable *Atma* enables us to face life and death with courage, transforming our existential experience.

In this shloka, Krishna reconciles the observable phenomena of death and birth with the immortality of the *Atma*. He explains that while the physical body—comparable to worn-out clothes—is discarded at death, what transmigrates is the subtle body, adhering to the laws of *Karma*. This transition does not signify the end of existence but a change in the form through which the subtle body continues its journey. The *Atma*, our true essence, in contrast, remains untouched and unchanged, neither dying nor migrating. By understanding these distinctions, we gain clarity on the mechanics of life and death. Aligning with the eternal truth of our spiritual essence helps dissolve the fear of death, thereby injecting a newfound clarity and confidence into our overall approach to life and a calm acceptance of the inevitable end.

Reflective Prompt

Do you fear death as the end of your existence? How might adopting the perspective of the Atma as eternal help alleviate your fears?

What you wear is transient, who you are is eternal

SHLOKA 23: THE UNTOUCHED ETERNAL

नैनं छिन्दन्ति शस्त्राणि नैनं दहति पावकः |
न चैनं क्लेदयन्त्यापः न शोषयति मारुतः ||23||

nainaṁ chindanti śastrāṇi nainaṁ dahati pāvakaḥ |
na cainaṁ klēdayantyāpaḥ na śōṣayati mārutaḥ ||23||

Translation:

Weapons (***śastrāṇi***) cannot cut this *Atma* (***na enaṁ chindanti***), fire (***pāvakaḥ***) cannot burn it, water (***āpaḥ***) cannot wet it, and wind (***mārutaḥ***) cannot dry it (***śōṣayati)*** **[Sankya Yoga: 2.23]**

At a Glance: Capturing the Spirit of the Shloka

The *Atma* is indestructible and cannot be affected by ordinary means of destruction that impact the body or other physical objects.

Commentary:

As knowledge progresses from the known to the unknown, familiar concepts and analogies are employed to further illustrate the incomprehensible nature of *Atma*. By using relatable terms, the indestructibility of *Atma* is conveyed with greater clarity and precision.

This shloka spins off the *Pancha Bhoota* model, a conceptual framework from the ancient Indian worldview that says all matter is made up of a permutation and combination of the five fundamental elements or '*bhootas*': earth (*Prithvi*), water (*Apa*), fire (*Agni or Pavaka*), air (*Vayu)*, and space (*Akasha)*. Krishna vividly highlights how each element, representative of different states of matter, interacts and affects the physical body but has no effect on *Atma.*

In order of subtlety, by Cosmic laws, the gross cannot affect the subtle. As the saying goes, *"Stone walls do not a prison make nor iron bars a cage."* Inescapable prison walls can arrest your physical body but not your thoughts. *Atma* is the subtlest aspect of our composite whole and transcends the nature or effect of any of these elements and, hence, cannot be destroyed by any of them.

Krishna begins by discussing weapons, a manifestation of the earth element known for its solidity. He acknowledges that weapons can cut and destroy physical forms but asserts that they cannot harm the *Atma*. Fire, too, can burn to ash the body but cannot touch the *Atma*. Even space, the subtlest of all elements, cannot be destroyed by weapons or fire; how can *Atma*, which is subtler than space, be?

Water can percolate into porous objects and wet them - but *Atma* is all-pervading and has no emptiness; hence, it cannot be permeable. How can water wet it? *Atma* alone exists with no gaps to fill.

Wind or air cannot dry it as drying is a dehydration process that extracts water from molecules. *Atma,* pervading every atom of existence, holds no specific molecules from which water can be drawn and emptied. Thus, wind or air representative of the gaseous state, can desiccate and deplete the body, but it cannot dry or burn the *Atma.*

Krishna underscores the profound difference between the body's vulnerability and *Atma*'s invulnerability with these graphic examples.

He acknowledges that the body is susceptible to affectation from these five elements - but the *Atma* transcends them all and stands beyond their physical constraints and alterations.

Fig: Atma: Untouched by Nature's Forces

Krishna's systematic analysis using the *Pancha Bhoota* model elaborates upon *Atma*'s indomitable nature, offering a clear and vivid perspective on why it transcends all physical boundaries and conditions. It illuminates the path for seekers to recognize and internalize their true, undying Self.

Reflective Prompt

In moments of fear or doubt, can you pause and reflect on the timeless, untouchable essence within you? How might this change the way you face challenges?

Unscathed by weapons, untouched by fire, unwet by water, unshaken by storm—

SHLOKAS 24 & 25: THE ETERNAL AND UNCHANGING REALITY

अच्छेद्योऽयमदाह्योऽयम् अक्लेद्योऽशोष्य एव च |
नित्यः सर्वगतः स्थाणुः अचलोऽयं सनातनः ||24||

acchēdyō 'yamadāhyō 'yam aklēdyō 'śōṣya ēva ca |
nityaḥ sarvagataḥ sthāṇuḥ acalō 'yaṁ sanātanaḥ ||24||

अव्यक्तोऽयमचिन्त्योऽयम् अविकार्योऽयमुच्यते |
तस्मादेवं विदित्वैनं नानुशोचितुमर्हसि ||25||

avyaktō 'yamacintyō 'yam avikāryō 'yamucyatē |
tasmādēvaṁ viditvainaṁ nānuśōcitumarhasi ||25||

Translation:

This *Atma* (**ayam**) cannot be cut (**acchedyaḥ**), nor can it be burned (**adāhyaḥ**); it cannot be moistened (**akledyaḥ**), nor can it be dried (**aśoṣyaḥ**). It is eternal (**nityaḥ**), all-pervading (**sarvagataḥ**), unchanging (**sthāṇuḥ**), immovable (**acalaḥ**), and most ancient yet new (**sanātanaḥ**). **[Sankya Yoga: 2.24]**

This *Atma* (**ayam**) is said to be unmanifest (**avyakta**), unthinkable (**acintya**), and unchanging (**avikārya**). Therefore, knowing (**viditvā**) this, you should not grieve (**anuśocitum**). **[Sankya Yoga: 2.25]**

At a Glance: Capturing the Spirit of the Shloka

Atma, our true identity, is eternal, unchanging, and unaffected by the forces that shape the material world. It is ever-present, all-pervading, stable, the most ancient, and always relevant. Beyond the reach of perception and inference, the *Atma* transcends the body and mind. Recognizing this unshakable inner truth offers clarity and peace amidst life's challenges and frees us from all suffering.

Commentary

Through shlokas 11 to 25, Krishna methodically unveils the various dimensions of *Atma*, affirming its indestructible nature. Addressing humanity's deepest existential fear—the fear of death—Krishna offers a transformative insight. He elucidates that our perceived identity, tied to the body and mind, is not our true Self. We are *Atma*, the eternal Consciousness, impervious to any manner of destruction. Shloka 25 marks the conclusion of this discourse, paving the way for further exploration of these teachings from logical and pragmatic viewpoints in subsequent shlokas.

The Self-Evident Nature of *Atma*

'*Ayam*' in these shlokas refers to the our true identity-*Atma*. *Atma* is self-evident, requiring no external proof of its existence. It is the foundational Consciousness that makes all perception possible. Just like if a torch is shining, we do not need evidence of the batteries within. The batteries enable the torch to shine - without them, there would be no light. You do not need another torch to prove the presence of batteries within the first torch. They are self-evident.

Everything in the universe becomes known through *Atma*, not vice versa. Therefore, repeating in Shloka 24 in a passive voice precisely what he said in Shloka 23 in an active voice, Krishna emphasizes that '*ayam*'—*Atma* is the all-pervasive presence impervious to physical damage—that cannot be cut, burned, wetted, or dried. Any means and methods known and unknown to mankind cannot harm or destroy the *Atma*. This added emphasis is crucial to distinguishing *Atma*'s permanence and immutability from everything else in the material world.

Let us examine some of the terms used in these shlokas to indicate the absolute indestructibility of *Atma*.

***Nitya* (eternal or everlasting):** The Sanskrit word '*Nitya*' derived from the root '*Ni,*' suggesting depth or permanence, and combined with the suffix '*tya,*' forms an abstract noun that emphasizes a constant, unalterable state. By describing *Atma* as *Nitya*, Krishna reiterates that though objects and beings of the world are at the mercy of the laws of time, space, and causation - *Atma* is beyond the world, therefore, remains untouched and unharmed by worldly onslaughts.

It is crucial to understand that our true nature is not something that comes into being or ceases to exist; rather, it is a permanent state of being. This inherent immortality, when understood and internalized, addresses the existential dread of non-existence that is primarily responsible for a life inhibited by the overwhelming fear of death. Recognizing oneself as *Nitya* - fundamentally eternal shifts one's perspective from the shackles and dread of a finite existence to a liberating sense of an infinite state. This realization reinforces an essential knowledge of continuous existence beyond the physical demise of the body and impactfully transforms our approach to life.

***Sarvagataḥ* (All-pervading):** *Atma* is not confined by the physical boundaries of time and space that define bodily existence. It is the foundational essence underlying the microcosm, and the macrocosm, like a dreamer's mind, pervades the entire dream. Within the dream, each character and landscape, though perceived as separate, is actually a manifestation of the dreamer's own mind. Just as the dream is a unified creation of the dreamer's mind, everything in our universe is imbued with the essence of *Atma*, reflecting a fundamental oneness.

Recognizing that *Atma* permeates every aspect of existence enables us to look beyond illusions of separateness, fostering a profound connection to the universe and a deeper understanding of the intrinsic unity that links all life forms. This realization broadens our perception of self and nurtures a sense of universal kinship and interconnectedness.

'Sthānuḥ' (stable) conveys stability, not in the mundane sense of physical immobility, but as an existential constancy that transcends the usual dynamics of time and space. Just as a massive banyan tree remains steadfast at its base despite its freely swaying branches, *Atma* remains constant amidst the flux of the universe. This stability at the base symbolizes that, at its core, *Atma* is unaffected by the cosmic play of creation, preservation, and dissolution.

'Achalaḥ' (Immovable) complements the idea of *'Sthānuḥ'* by negating any possibility of displacement. Movement implies shifting from one place where you are to a place that you are not. But *Atma* is all-pervading. There is no place it does not already exist. Think. *Atma* will move from where to where when it is already everywhere? This rhetorical question reinforces *Atma*'s quality of omnipresence—movement within itself is a paradox, and thus, *Atma* is described as immovably firm. All displacements and movements are empowered by *Atma*, but *Atma* itself does not move.

Distinguishing between *'Sthānuḥ'* and *'Achalaḥ'* deepens our understanding of *Atma*'s profound steadiness and dependability. In the worldly context, things considered stable still experience shifts or disturbances at some level. However, *Atma*, being the ultimate truth, exhibits absolute stability and firmness—unmoved at any level. It is a state of being that transcends physical laws, reflecting a higher-dimensional reality where change is non-existent. Consistently tapping into this firm stability within through all the glaring vicissitudes of life will award us peace, dexterity, and enduring happiness that none of our worldly dependencies can.

***Sanatanah* (Ancient, Ever Relevant):** If time is defined as the interval between two experiences, time begins with the second experience. But *Atma*, as we have studied earlier, existed at the first experience. Therefore, *Atma* existed before time. It is *Sanatanah*, ancient.

Although most ancient, *Atma* is eternal and ever-present, making it the oldest yet continually pertinent Reality. Unlike modern theories requiring empirical evidence for validation, *Atma*'s timeless nature is affirmed through ages of wisdom, not confined to recent discoveries or experimental data. The Sanskrit root *'Sanat,'* denoting enduring continuity, highlights *Atma*'s eternal nature, unchallenged by time and unrestricted by spatial confines. All the above descriptions of the nature of *Atma* assure seekers that *Atma* is not a fleeting philosophical notion but a perennial truth recognized by sages and spiritual masters across various epochs and cultures. Its unchanging nature makes it a reliable foundation of spiritual inquiry, deeply rooted in tradition yet always relevant to contemporary life and beyond.

Additionally, it is noteworthy that Hinduism was originally known as *'Sanatana Dharma,'* which means a way of life oriented towards realizing the eternal and continuously relevant nature of *Atma. Sanatana Dharma* is a spiritual culture that emphasizes a higher life path that guides individuals toward their own timeless truth.

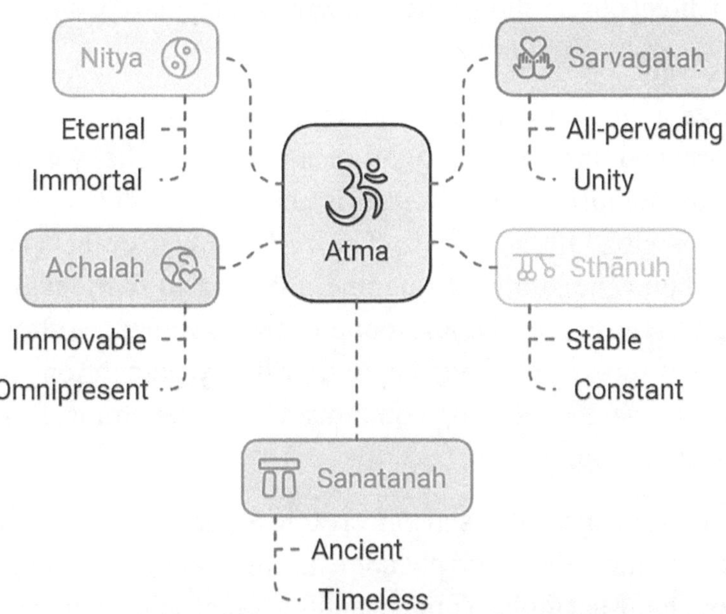

Fig: Atma: Imperishable, Untouched, Unchanged

Shloka 25 concisely recapitulates the previous shlokas, reinforcing key ideas. The qualities described here collectively emphasize the transcendent dimension of *Atma*—qualities that defy conventional perception and thought, highlighting its immutable essence. Through this summarization, Krishna aims to solidify the understanding that while the nature of *Atma* is repeatedly described using different terminology, its depth and significance warrant reiterated contemplation.

***Avyakta* (Unmanifest):** Our senses can only perceive the world because it appears before us in manifest form. They cannot perceive the *Atma* that remains unmanifest in and through all these physical manifestations. In a world where we are accustomed to valuing only what can be perceived or proven, the idea of *Avyakta* challenges us to acknowledge the existence of realities beyond our sensory experiences. It pushes the boundaries of what we consider 'real' by positing that the most fundamental aspects of existence might lie beyond direct observation, hidden within the depths of Consciousness itself.

***Achintya* (Inconceivable):** Unlike the world, *Atma* cannot be fully grasped through thought or inference. The world is an object of comprehension. *Atma* is the subject that enables the comprehension of the world. Think. How can objects be used to apprehend the subject? Imagine a person looking at the stars through a telescope. The telescope is an instrument with which a person can look at galaxies beyond ordinary perception. But can the person turn the telescope on himself and view himself through its lens at any point?

Another reason the *Atma* is inconceivable is because it fundamentally differs from the objects and phenomena our intellects are equipped to analyze. Our usual tools of understanding—reasoning, analyzing, and categorizing—are based on distinctions and separations, while *Atma* is a seamless unity, a singular existence that underpins all dualities. Thus, *Atma* is self-evident and intrinsic, beyond every possibility of validation through thought processes.

***Avikarya* (Unchangeable):** The oft-quoted words of Greek philosopher Heraclitus, *"The only constant in life is change."* True, but unlike the observable world around us, which undergoes constant modification, *Atma* remains perpetually unchanged. This enduring stability of the *Atma* can be likened to the unchanging nature of a person's mind amidst the ever-evolving scenarios of a dream. No matter how dynamic our life experiences might be, the fundamental essence of *Atma*, like the mind of the person dreaming, remains unaffected by temporal and fast-shifting projections of the dream or of life.

Contemplating this immutable aspect of *Atma* offers a grounding perspective of the ever-changing physical world, reminding us that a state of permanence and stability exists at our core.

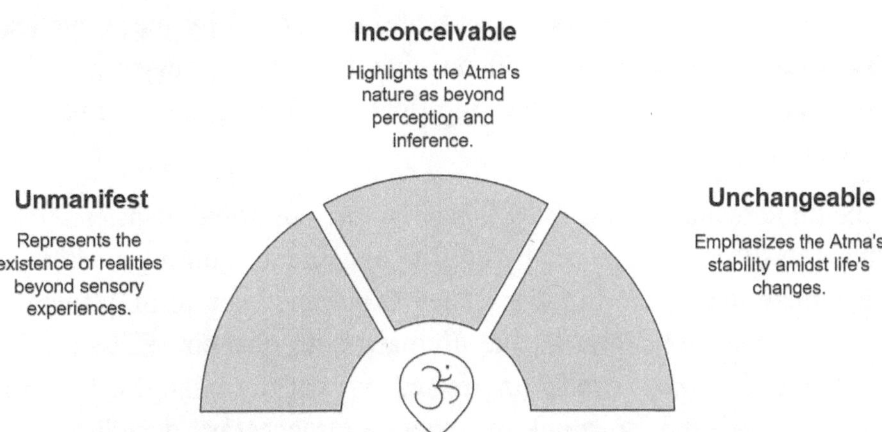

Fig: Atma: Unmanifested Reality beyond perception and inference

The description of these *Avyakta*, *Achintya*, and *Avikarya* dimensions of *Atma* assert a profound, unmanifested Reality beyond sensory perception, thought, and change. They invite us to expand our understanding of the Self and encourage a deeper, more introspective grounding into our true nature to successfully navigate the material world.

Paramarthika and *Vyavaharika*: The Dual Realities of Existence

In the extensive discourse from Shlokas 11 to 25, Krishna elucidates the nature of *Atma* as distinct from the empirical world, asserting that *Atma* exists in a higher order of reality. The visible and tangible empirical world is subject to time and space and is defined by Vedanta as *'Vyavaharika Satyam'* or transactional reality. This means that while the world proves its existence in and through everyday interactions, it possesses a conditional and temporary reality.

In contrast, *Atma* is described as *'Paramarthika Satyam'*—the Absolute Reality, which remains constant and unchanging. This Absolute Reality underpins the existence of all empirical phenomena without being affected by their transformations. While the material world undergoes constant changes—birth, growth, decay, disease, and death—*Atma* remains immutable, untouched by these cyclical processes. This unmanifest, inconceivable, and unchangeable nature of *Atma* lends existence to the empirical world, yet it does not partake in its transient attributes.

The understanding that *Atma* is beyond the empirical manifestations helps to discern the eternal from the ephemeral, guiding seekers to recognize that while the world they experience is real on a relative level, it does not represent the ultimate truth of their existence. By realizing that the *Atma* is unaffected by worldly changes, one can cultivate a deeper spiritual awareness and necessary detachment to navigate life with a firmer resolve and greater serenity. This insight is crucial for spiritual growth and leads to a liberated state of being, where the true essence of life is understood beyond the superficial layers of experienced reality.

In concluding this profound section, Krishna asserts that understanding the true nature of *Atma* renders grief unnecessary in the face of death. The teachings up to this point clarify that while the physical body may perish, the *Atma,* our true essence, endures eternally. This realization helps us see beyond the immediate pain of loss.

Krishna emphasizes that the *Atma* is singular and all-encompassing, dissolving the illusions of separation and multiplicity. Recognizing that there is one *Atma* manifesting in myriad forms helps dissolve the sharp sting of grief. Such an enlightened perspective sees the continuity of existence beyond the apparent finality of death, providing profound peace and stability amidst life's inevitable changes and unavoidable end.

Although Krishna acknowledges that mourning is a natural response to the physical departure of beings, he explains why it should be tempered by the knowledge of *Atma*'s eternal nature. This understanding does not at once erase grief but transforms its context, offering a deep, abiding peace that comes from recognizing our infinite nature and unending connection to all existence. Such insight ensures that grief does not overwhelm our ongoing experience of life. No matter who comes or who goes, as is commonly said - *"the show must go on!"*

Through shlokas 11 to 25, Krishna systematically unfolds the eternal, unchanging, and indestructible nature of *Atma*, which equips us with revolutionary perspectives that liberate us from our greatest fear associated with death. Understanding that death is merely a transition of forms, not an end to our actual being, enables us to live our lives with greater clarity, freedom, and peace.

Sanskrit Term	Meaning	Explanation
Nitya	Eternal	Beyond birth and death; unchanging in nature.
Sarvagataḥ	All-pervading	Present everywhere, in everything, without exception.
Sthānuḥ	Stable	Constant and unwavering despite the dynamics of time and space.
Achalaḥ	Immovable	Omnipresent, with no possibility of displacement.
Sanatanah	Timeless	Existed before time, enduring through all ages, and relevant for eternity.
Avyakta	Unmanifest	Beyond sensory perception, hidden in all manifestations.
Achintya	Inconceivable	Cannot be grasped by thought or reasoning, as it is the enabler of all comprehension.
Avikarya	Unchangeable	Immutable and unaffected by the transformations of the physical world.

Table: Dimensions of Atma

Reflective Prompt

How does recognizing Atma as your true, eternal identity influence your understanding of death? How will this knowledge of your inherent immortality change your current approach to life?

\---

\---

\---

In the silence of existence lies the indestructible essence of being

Shloka 26: Rational Calm Amid Life's Certainty

अथ चैनं नित्यजातं नित्यं वा मन्यसे मृतम् ।
तथाऽपि त्वं महाबाहो नैवं शोचितुमर्हसि ॥26॥

atha cainaṁ nityajātaṁ nityaṁ vā manyasē mṛtam |
tathā'pi tvaṁ mahābāhō naivaṁ śōcitumarhasi ||26||

Translation:

O mighty-armed Arjuna (***Mahabaho***), even if you think of (***manyase)*** the *Atma* (***enam***) as constantly being born (***nitya-jatam***) or constantly dying (***nityam mṛtam***), you should not grieve (***na śocitumin arhasi***) this manner (***evam***). [Sankya Yoga: 2.26]

At a Glance: Capturing the Spirit of the Shloka

Even if life is seen as beginning at birth and ending at death, mourning its inevitable cycle is unnecessary. In the material world, change and impermanence are the only constants, and embracing this reality allows us to face loss and transitions with composure. By cultivating strength and clarity, we can rise above fear and sorrow, focusing instead on living fully and purposefully.

Commentary

Krishna's brilliance as a teacher is evident in his systematic addressing of life's problems from multiple perspectives. In Shlokas 11-25, he approaches the issue from a spiritual standpoint, explaining the eternal nature of *Atma*. From Shlokas 26-30, he shifts to a practical perspective, providing reasoning that appeals to logic and everyday understanding. In Shlokas 31-33, he presents a dharmic perspective, emphasizing duty and righteousness as foundational principles. Finally, in Shlokas 34-37, he offers an argument from a worldly, materialistic viewpoint. A great teacher meets each student where they are by offering wisdom according to their capacity of understanding—so that no one is left behind in the journey to the truth. By addressing the problem from these four distinct angles—the spiritual, the practical, the dharmic, and the earthly—his words resonate with people at various stages of development, ensuring that this quintessential knowledge equips all to live a more balanced and fearless life.

In this shloka, Krishna shifts his argument by acknowledging that not everyone can conceptualize themselves as the eternal, undying *Atma*. He uses *'atha cha,'* meaning 'even if,' to accept the alternative point of view held by most. He consoles, even if you think of yourself as *'nityaṁ jātaṁ'* (being born) and *'nityaṁ mṛtaṁ* (constantly dying)—like most others in the material world do—there is still no need for deep sorrow (*'na śocitumarhasi'*).

This view echoes the materialistic philosophy from the Charvakas of the Vedic period to the observances of modern scientists who believe that life begins at birth and ends with death, denying the existence of an independent *Atma*. They view *Atma* or Consciousness not as eternal but merely as an attribute of the body. Even if one adopts this perspective, Krishna argues that extreme grief over life's only constant death is unnecessary.

Krishna addresses Arjuna as *Mahabaho* (mighty-armed) to remind him of his indomitable strength and valor, which do not befit his current state of anxiety and fear.

> **Reflective Prompt**
>
> *How do you typically respond to the idea of death—your own or that of others? Can viewing death as a natural and inevitable part of life help you approach it with less fear and sorrow?*
>
> --
>
> --
>
> --

Even if all ends, grief is but a shadow before the light of understanding

SHLOKA 27: ACCEPT THE UNAVOIDABLE

जातस्य हि ध्रुवो मृत्युः ध्रुवं जन्म मृतस्य च |
तस्मादपरिहार्येऽर्थे न त्वं शोचितुमर्हसि ||27||

jātasya hi dhruvō mṛtyuḥ dhruvaṁ janma mṛtasya ca |
tasmādaparihāryē'rthē na tvaṁ śōcitumarhasi ||27||

Translation:

For that which is born (*jātasya*), death (*mṛtyuḥ*) is certain (*dhruvaḥ*),
and for the dead (*mṛtasya*), birth (*janma*) is certain (*dhruvaṁ*).
Therefore (*tasmāt*), over the inevitable (*aparihārye arthe*), you should
not (*na*) grieve (*śōcitum arhasi*) [Sankya Yoga: 2.27]

At a Glance: Capturing the Spirit of the Shloka

Some things in life are inevitable, and there is no sense in worrying about what cannot be changed. Birth and death are certainties for every living being, so instead of fearing or grieving excessively over them, we should accept these natural cycles as part of existence.

Commentary:

This shloka offers one of the most practical pieces of wisdom: **to accept what cannot be changed.** You do not need to be a Vedanta scholar or even believe in the concept of *Atma* to at least recognize the pragmatism in this truth. Even if you see yourself merely as the body, you cannot resist life's cyclical process. Anything born is destined to die—this is an immutable cosmic law. Just as we celebrate birthdays to mark the beginning of life, we must also accept that life will eventually end. Denying or ignoring this reality does not alter it; closing our eyes to the inevitable does not make it disappear.

Although we can all plainly see that death is inevitable, we often struggle to apply this understanding in our own lives, particularly when death strikes close to home. It is easy to philosophize mortality when it affects others, but this knowledge becomes unavailable when it involves our loved ones or us. Krishna's straightforward instruction here encourages us to internalize this reality—that death is a certainty for all that is born (*jātasya mṛtyuḥ dhruvam*).

Think. Can anyone, however powerful, escape death? No being incarnated physically, be it then, Rama, Krishna, or Jesus, could avoid the natural cycle of life and death. No one can evade these laws of existence. Accepting this truth allows us to live more fully in the present, with less attachment to what is transient and more focus on what truly matters.

Just as death is inevitable for the living, birth is equally certain for those who have passed away (*dhruvaṁ janma mṛtasya ca*). This idea, deeply rooted in dharmic traditions, highlights the cyclical nature of birth and death, governed by the law of karma. While this cycle may not be provable by science, it breathes sheer logic.

The key lesson from this shloka is that life and death are intrinsic aspects of physical existence. Resisting these natural processes results in sorrow, while acceptance brings peace. Krishna urges us, through Arjuna to not grieve over situations beyond our control, referred to as *'aparihārye' arthē'* (choiceless situations). These realities cannot be altered by any means—neither by human effort, knowledge, nor divine grace. The intelligent response to such unpleasant facts is total acceptance.

When we resist these unavoidable realities, we often direct our frustration toward others, the world, or "God." We must slowly bring our minds into a mode of acceptance by studying and meditating upon these teachings. In Vedanta, God is viewed as our higher potential—by praying, we tap into our inner strength and psychological resilience. Thus, with the two-pronged approach of knowledge and surrender, we can cultivate the inner strength to face these inescapable phenomena with equanimity and grace.

Transcending Grief: Universal Wisdom on Life's Cycles

The Stoic philosopher Epictetus encouraged his students to scrutinize their lives and environment. He advised them to discern what lay within their power to change or control and gracefully accept things beyond their influence. Birth and death, two inevitable aspects of existence, are prime examples of what lies beyond human control. Epictetus taught that once we recognize the limits of our influence, we can free ourselves from unnecessary anxiety and sorrow. Rather than constantly battling against the inevitable, we should cultivate indifference toward things we cannot change.

Regarded as one of India's foremost yoga gurus, BKS Iyengar— founder of world-famous Iyengar Yoga—implored his students to *"live happily and die masterfully."* His widely quoted words, *"Yoga teaches us to cure what need not be endured and endure what cannot be cured,"* echo Epictetus' thoughts on happenings beyond human jurisdiction.

In a poignant tale, a grieving mother, Kilvani, who had lost her only son, sought Buddha's help to bring her child back to life. Buddha asked her to fetch a mustard seed from any house where no one had ever died. As she journeyed through the town, door to door, the weight of her grief deepened as she realized that death had touched every family. It spares no one—it is the universal law governing all life.

John Hay's poem The Law of Death recounts the same story with striking imagery:

> "And then from door to door, she fared,
> To ask what house by Death was spared.
> Her heart grew cold to see the eyes
> Of all dilate with slow surprise:
> 'Kilvani, thou hast lost thy head;
> Nothing can help a child that's dead.
> There stands not by the Ganges' side
> A house where none hath ever died.'"

Through Buddha's poignant advice, *"Murmur not! Bow, and accept the common lot,"* Kilvani realized that her grief stemmed from the erroneous belief that she alone had suffered such loss. This story highlights the central message of Shloka 27: It is futile to grieve over the inevitable and teaches us to accept life's impermanence with wisdom and fortitude.

The above exposition brings us to the absolute sensibility embedded in the Serenity Prayer, made famous by the work of Alcoholics Anonymous during the 20th Century:

"God grant me the serenity,
To accept the things I cannot change;
Courage to change the things I can;
And wisdom to know the difference."

We face all kinds of circumstances throughout our lives. Some are within our control, and some are not. This prayer rightly solicits the poise to accept what cannot be changed, the fearlessness to change what we can, and most importantly, the wisdom to know when to act and when to surrender in faith.

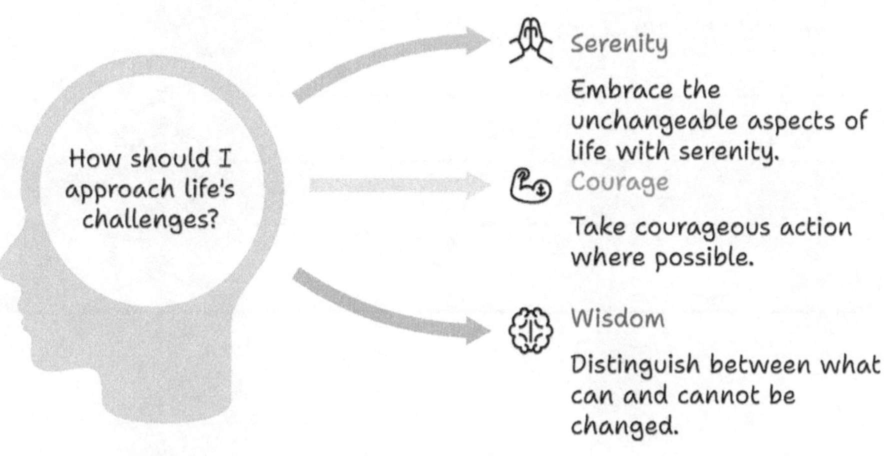

Fig: Serenity Prayer

Words of freelance writer and blogger Samuel Rodenhizer are most befitting here: *"For all your days prepare and meet them ever alike. When you are the anvil, bear- when you are the hammer strike."*

Reflective Prompt

Reflect on a time when resisting a circumstance beyond your control brought about unwarranted stress and anxiety. How did it influence your actions in that moment? And the outcome? How would you approach a comparable situation in the future armored with this knowledge?

Acceptance of the inevitable is the gateway to inner peace

SHLOKA 28: LIFE'S FLEETING DANCE

अव्यक्तादीनि भूतानि व्यक्तमध्यानि भारत |
अव्यक्तनिधनान्येव तत्र का परिदेवना ||28||

avyaktādīni bhūtāni vyaktamadhyāni bhārata |
avyaktanidhanānyēva tatra kā paridēvanā ||28||

Translation:

O Bhārata! All beings (***bhūtāni***) are unmanifest (***avyakta***) in their beginning (***ādīni)***, manifest (***vyakta***) in their middle state (***madhyāni***), and return to being unmanifest (***avyakta-nidhanāni***) in the end. So why grieve (***paridēvanā***) over this. **[Sankya Yoga: 2.28]**

At a Glance: Capturing the Spirit of the Shloka

Living beings were not present before birth and will not continue in their current form after death. The manifestation of any particular physical form in this world is momentary along the inexhaustible cosmic timeline. Even the greatest figures who left a lasting impact on the history of the world have come and gone. Understanding the existential play of appearance and disappearance, there is no reason to grieve over the impermanence of any worldly form or expect an eternal existence for it.

Commentary:

In this shloka, Krishna continues offering a clear and practical perspective on life, reminding us that the beginning and end of all living beings are unknown to us. He says, '*avyaktādīni bhūtāni*' (all beings are unmanifest before birth), '*vyaktamadhyāni*' (manifest in the middle), and '*avyaktanidhanāni*' (unmanifest again after death). This reveals a fundamental truth: living beings exist in an unmanifest, invisible form before birth and after death. They manifest in form only briefly in between. Our current existence, from birth to death, is just a tiny flicker in the vastness of time.

English poet and cultural critic Mathew Arnold articulates the thought beautifully: "*Life is an arrow shot from the darkness, flutters in the light for a while and vanishes back to darkness.*" Our lives follow a similar pattern. We appear in manifest form from the unmanifest for a little while and merge back into the unmanifest again.

This understanding helps us recognize the futility of grieving over the inevitable. We do not know where we come from at birth or where we will go after death. Our life dances briefly between the womb and the tomb. It behooves us to realize that every life is a passing phenomenon, and clinging to the idea of permanence in something inescapably transient only leads to unnecessary suffering.

A striking declaration in the *Sanatsujātīya* section of the Mahabharata's Śānti Parva, too, captures the essential nature of life as a journey from the unmanifest to the manifest and back again: *adarśanāt āpatitaḥ punaśca adarśanam gataḥ* — we came from the unseen, and we return to the unseen.

Krishna reminds us of these immutable facts and urges us to stop fixating on things that cannot be changed, as this causes unnecessary attachment and sorrow. Life constantly moves forward like an arrow in flight, and we cannot halt or reverse it. Therefore, there is no benefit in lamenting the ephemerality of worldly existence. Krishna asks, *'Tatra kā paridēvanā'*—what is there to grieve about?

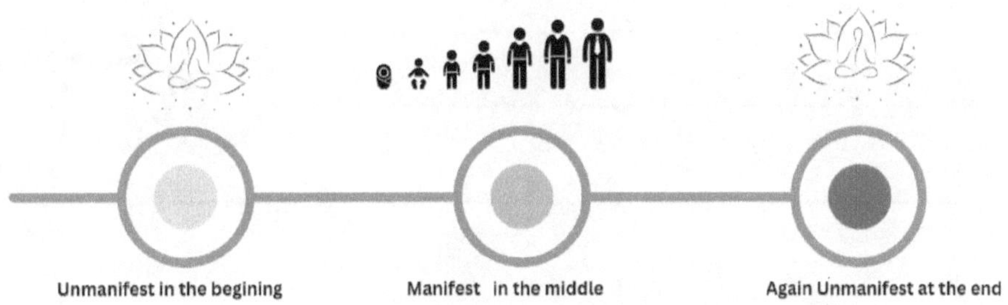

Fig: Life's fleeting dance

It helps to internalize that the past and future are beyond our perception. What truly matters is how we live in the present. Swami Rama Tirtha, one of the first notable teachers of Hinduism to lecture in the United States, is known to have hollered, *"Your only duty in life is to be cheerful."*

This shloka reminds us that life is cyclical - punctuated with brief appearances and disappearances. Dwelling on what cannot be changed only causes uncalled-for suffering. Instead of grieving over the impermanence of life, Krishna encourages us to live with wisdom and acceptance.

Reflective Prompt

Knowing that life is fleeting, how can you focus more on living fully in the present rather than being consumed by regrets of the past or anxieties about the future?

What appears must fade; what fades will reappear

SHLOKA 29: THE GREATEST WONDER

आश्चर्यवत्पश्यति कश्चिदेनं
आश्चर्यवद्वदति तथैव चान्यः |
आश्चर्यवच्चैनमन्यः शृणोति
श्रुत्वाऽप्येनं वेद न चैव कश्चित् ॥29॥

āścaryavatpaśyati kaścidēnaṁ
āścaryavadvadati tathaiva cānyaḥ |
āścaryavaccainamanyaḥ śṛṇōti
śrutvā'pyēnaṁ vēda na caiva kaścit ||29||

Translation:

Some look upon the *Atma* as a wonder (***āścaryavat paśyati***), others speak of it as a wonder (***āścaryavat vadati***), and still others hear of it as a wonder (***āścaryavat śṛṇoti***). Yet, even after hearing about it (***śrutvā'pi***), most people cannot comprehend it at all (***na ca ēva veda***)

[Sankya Yoga: 2.29]

At a Glance: Capturing the Spirit of the Shloka

The *Atma* is incredibly subtle and not easily understood. Though self-evident as the consciousness within us, the senses or intellectual analysis cannot fully grasp it. As such, it is often seen as a wonder. Some look upon it with awe, others speak of it as a curiosity, and many hear about its nature. Yet, despite this, most people still fail to truly understand it.

Commentary

In this shloka, Krishna emphasizes the profound difficulty in comprehending the nature of *Atma*. He acknowledges that even though *Atma* is ever-present and self-evident as our own Consciousness, it remains a mystery to most people. The word *āścarya,* wonder, captures the essence of this shloka, expressing both astonishment and admiration for the *Atma*.

When a person who has long believed themselves to be a limited being, bound by time and space, hears about their true identity as the indestructible, eternal *Atma*, it comes across as a profound wonder. Being taught that one's existence does not end with the death of the body and that they are, in fact, the foundational reality of the universe is nothing short of awe-inspiring.

When a Self-realized master speaks about it, it often sounds like a wonder to others. Because the *Atma* cannot be articulated in words. All descriptions are mere pointers. One must identify with *Atma* to know *Atma*. Truths like the unity of all beings, the interconnectedness of everything in the universe, and how all these disconnected entities are, in fact, manifestations of one single, eternal consciousness are concepts beyond human comprehension or direct experience. They contradict the ordinary perception of separateness in the world. Hence, hearing about *Atma* also creates tremendous wonder in a listener.

Atma is the very substratum that pervades through every atom of existence. It is omnipotent, omnipresent, and omniscient. It lies beyond human faculties despite being the power behind their functioning. The senses cannot perceive it. The mind cannot feel it. Intellect cannot conceptualize it. In this context, the word *āścarya*, wonder, highlights the difficulty of comprehending something so subtle and beyond the reach of the senses, mind, and intellect. Though it is talked about, taught, and meditated upon, very few realize it. Most people do not understand it even after hearing about it.

Shloka 29, cited from the Kathopanishad (Chapter 1, section ii, verse 7), highlights the astonishing paradox of Self-realization. Despite the *Atma* being ever-present and self-evident, the limitations of our senses, mind, and intellect make it challenging to understand. The greatest wonder is that even though it is within us and has been emphatically spoken about down the ages, it continues to elude us, remaining one of the greatest mysteries of existence. This makes the quest for Self-knowledge a profoundly enchanting journey.

Looking at *Atma* as a wonder can also be analyzed from another angle:

We spend our entire lives seeking fulfillment in objects, beings, and worldly achievements. However, despite attaining all our desires, a nagging sense of incompleteness lingers. That is because what we continually search for outside is already within us. When people realize their true nature as *Atma*, they discover that the greatest security and happiness is not in the external world but in their own being. This realization that the source of true fulfillment lies within and not outside is one of life's greatest wonders.

Another wonder for the student of spirituality is the realization that while we may hear and speak about *Atma* as eternal, all-pervasive, and indestructible, it feels like a distant concept, something separate from ourselves. However, when one attains Self-realization, it is wondrous to discover that all that was studied and spoken of was never about something external but our own true nature.

Thus, *Atma* reveals itself as a wonder through multiple levels of our experience: its nature, the realization of its presence, and the understanding that what we seek outside is within us. Even though *Atma* is self-evident, the journey toward its realization is one of the most enigmatic experiences in life.

Ponder on the following poem by John Godfrey Saxe, which pictorially animates the central message of this shloka most wonderfully:

The Blind Men and the Elephant

It was six men of Indostan
To learning much inclined,
Who went to see the elephant
(Though all of them were blind),
That each, by observation
Might satisfy his mind.

The first approached the elephant,
And, happening to fall
Against his broad and sturdy side,
At once began to bawl:
"God bless me! But the elephant,
Is nothing but a wall!"

The second feeling of the tusk,
Cried: "Ho! what have we here,
So very round and smooth and sharp?
To me tis mighty clear,
this wonder of an elephant
is very like a spear!"

The third approached the animal,
And, happening to take,
The squirming trunk within his hands,
Thus boldly up and spake:
"I see," quoth he, the elephant
Is very like a snake!"

The fourth reached out his eager hand,
And felt about the knee:
"What most this wondrous beast is like,
Is mighty plain," quoth he;
""Tis clear enough the elephant
Is very like a tree."

The fifth, who chanced to touch the ear,
Said: "E'en the blindest man
Can tell what this resembles most;
Deny the fact who can,
This marvel of an elephant,
Is very like a fan!"

The sixth no sooner had begun
About the beast to grope,
Than, seizing on the swinging tail
That fell within his scope,
"I see," quoth he, "the elephant
Is very like a rope!"

And so these men of Indostan,
Disputed loud and long,
Each in his own opinion

Exceeding stiff and strong,
Though each was partly in the right,
And all were in the wrong!

So, oft in theologic wars
The disputants, I ween,
tread on in utter ignorance
Of what each other mean,
And prate about the elephant
Not one of them has seen!

The men's physical blindness prevented them from knowing the full magnitude of the elephant. Each thought he knew what it was, and yet none knew it at all. Similarly, our limited mortal faculties steeped in spiritual blindness cannot conceive the idea, let alone know *Atma* in totality. And so, it remains a mystery—a wonder!

Reflective Prompt

Do you still find it hard, if not impossible, to believe that the unbroken peace and happiness you seek reside within? Can you dare to turn inward at least a small portion of your worldly quest? How do you plan to begin?

The greatest wonder lies within, beyond sight, thought, or word

SHLOKA 30: BEYOND GRIEF

देही नित्यमवध्योऽयं देहे सर्वस्य भारत |
तस्मात्सर्वाणि भूतानि न त्वं शोचितुमर्हसि ||30||

dēhī nityamavadhyō'yaṁ dēhē sarvasya bhārata |
tasmātsarvāṇi bhūtāni na tvaṁ śōcitumarhasi ||30||

Translation:

O Bhārata! This *Atma* (***dēhī***), residing in the bodies (***dēhē***) of all beings is eternal (***nityam***) and cannot be slain (***avadhyaḥ***). Therefore, you should not grieve (***na śocitumarhasi***) for any of these beings (***sarvāṇi bhūtāni***) [Sankya Yoga: 2.30]

At a Glance: Capturing the Spirit of the Shloka

Everything in this universe, including our body, mind, and intellect is subject to change and eventual death. However, the end of the body, mind, and intellect is not the end of our existence. Our true identity is *Atma*—the eternal Consciousness within—which is never subject to change or destruction. With this understanding, we can rise above sorrow, recognizing that death is not truly an end but a transition.

Commentary

In this shloka, Krishna recaps the teaching that began in Shloka 11, emphasizing that no situation in life, including the fear of death, warrants excessive worry or emotional breakdown. He has addressed this issue from two perspectives:

1. The spiritual view that reveals our true identity as the eternal *Atma*.
2. The practical view that reminds Arjuna and all who identify primarily with the physical body that the *Atma*, the true self, is indestructible (*nityam avadhyaḥ*), while the body is certainly perishable. Therefore, there is no sense in seeking permanence in the body.

The first key lesson is that the mortal body (*dēha*) is subject to birth, growth, change, disease, decay, and death. While we can take the necessary steps to look after the body as best we can, we cannot alter or halt these modifications that everyone must undergo. It is a natural part of life, and we all know it. The problem lies in acceptance. Accepting the body's impermanence is the first step toward developing mental solidarity for life's unavoidable losses. Though we do not know when or how death will come, accepting its certainty can help us live every moment of life with firmer resolve and face death with greater courage and peace.

Studying, contemplating, and practicing the teachings of *Sanatana Dharma* can help us slowly but surely slip into this mode of acceptance. The words of German Philosopher Arthur Schopenhauer affirm the author-trio's experiential view, *"In the whole world, there is no study so beneficial and so elevating as the Upanishads. It has been the solace of my life; it will be the solace at my death."* As we explained in our first book of the **Gita Odyssey Series,** the Bhagavad Gita is the distilled essence of the great Upanishads which hold all the secrets of life and beyond.

The second key lesson is recognizing that behind this mortal body lies our real identity—the *Atma*, the indweller (*dēhī*). The body is temporary (*anityaḥ*), but the *Atma* is eternal (*nityaḥ*). Once we begin to entertain this truth more fervently, the death of the body will no longer shock us as profoundly. Be it the death of our loved ones or our own. While the loss of life will always bring sadness, spiritual wisdom can help us navigate the sorrow with dignity and grace. Though grief lingers quite strongly for a while, we have all experienced that life goes on. We forget the maxim, "This too shall pass," and get lost in the loss. These teachings keep us from being swept away in ways that incapacitate us entirely in the present. We begin to glean that life is like a train journey where different passengers get on and off continually. We cannot sit to mourn beyond reason each exit. We thus learn to move forward without being paralyzed by loss.

Lastly, for those who feel that death is a finality, Krishna explains that the demise of the physical body does not mark the end of the journey. The subtle body journeys on for a while.

Krishna emphasizes that the *Atma*, so elaborately described in earlier shlokas as indestructible (*avinashi*) and eternal (*nityaḥ*), resides in all beings (*sarvasya dēhē*). There are many beings in the world, but the indwelling *Atma* in all is one and the same. *Atma*, the essence of Consciousness (*caitanyam*), endures even when the body perishes. Therefore, there is no need to excessively grieve over the death of any being - living or dead.

We can intellectually accept the mortality of others but struggle to use the same understanding when it comes to ourselves or those closest to us. Krishna reminds us to apply these understandings universally; accepting the inevitability of death allows us to better manage its emotional impact. Krishna says, *'Na tvaṁ śōcitumarhasi'*—you should not grieve. Excessive grief will not delay or halt mortality.

Death is inevitable, but we must still do our best to alleviate the suffering of those who are sick or in pain. With all the medical advancements, we must not refrain from extending lives wherever possible. However, despite our best efforts, we must gracefully accept a terminal diagnosis or death as part of life's natural order. Resistance or excessive grief only causes unnecessary suffering. Neither can change facts.

How to approach life and death for greater peace?

Fig: How to approach life and death

In conclusion, this shloka sums up the teachings of accepting life's inevitable cycles of birth and death. By recognizing the impermanence of all bodies and the eternity of the one *Atma* that dwells within all, we can navigate life's challenges with greater peace and understanding. By accepting what cannot be changed, we free ourselves to focus on performing our duties without being overwhelmed by sorrow.

Reflective Prompt

How can internalizing the inevitability of death and aligning more firmly with the eternal truth of Atma bring more peace and purpose to your daily life?

What perishes is not you; what endures is your truth

Shloka 31: Living True to Your Svadharma

स्वधर्ममपि चावेक्ष्य न विकम्पितुमर्हसि ।
धर्म्याद्धि युद्धाच्छ्रेयोऽन्यत् क्षत्रियस्य न विद्यते ॥31॥

svadharmamamapi cāvēkṣya na vikampitumarhasi |
dharmyāddhi yuddhācchrēyō'nyat kṣatriyasya na vidyatē ||31||

Translation:

Considering your own *dharma* [as a warrior] (*svadharma*), you should not waver (***na vikampitum arhasi***). For a warrior (*kṣatriya*), there is no greater duty than to engage in a righteous battle (***dharmyāddhi yuddhāt***).
[Sankya Yoga: 2.31]

At a Glance: Capturing the Spirit of the Shloka

Everyone has an intrinsic nature displaying unique qualities, called *svadharma* in Sanskrit. We need to recognize our *svadharma* and align our responsibilities and actions accordingly. Following one's *svadharma* adorns life with a meaningful purpose and brings great fulfillment.

Arjuna is a warrior. His highest duty and *svadharma* is to engage in a righteous battle. Despite all obstacles, we should not hesitate to follow our *svadharma*.

Commentary

After explaining the futility of grieving over the inevitable, Krishna now focuses on guiding us through Arjuna to stay true to our innate nature and fulfill our duties, even when they seem challenging.

There are two important reasons for us to do so. First, through Shlokas 31-33, Krishna stresses the importance of aligning one's actions with one's *svadharma*, or intrinsic nature, from a dharmic standpoint. In Arjuna's case, it was to fight a righteous battle keeping in line with his warrior status. Then, in subsequent verses (34-37), Krishna assures us that only by fulfilling our duties in line with our natural disposition can we accrue prosperity, success, and honor in the world. Thus, Krishna highlights the importance of *svadharmic* action and the dangers of inaction, both spiritually and practically.

Navigating Life through Svadharma: Unlocking Your Unique Path

In this shloka, Krishna introduces the concept of *Svadharma*, the distinctive essence that defines each individual. *Svadharma* refers to the intrinsic qualities that make something what it is. For example, the *svadharma* of sugar is to sweeten, or the *svadharma* of fire is to burn. Similarly, we each have core qualities that uniquely make us who we are. For some, this might manifest as intellectual gifts, such as in research or philosophy; for others, it may be practical skills like engineering or creative talents in art and music. *Svadharma* is essentially our nature—our personal blueprint for how we are meant to act, thrive, and contribute to the world.

However, it is important to note that *svadharma* is not a property of the *Atma*, which is eternal and unchanging, but rather a quality of the subtle body—our mind and intellect. Since the subtle body evolves with time and experience, so too can our *svadharma*. The path that feels right for us might shift as we mature or encounter new experiences. This dynamic nature of *svadharma* means that we should remain open to change, embracing new roles and responsibilities as they arise while staying attuned to our core nature.

Aligning with our *svadharma* is crucial for living a life of fulfillment and purpose. When we align our actions and careers with our intrinsic nature, we experience flow, ease, and efficiency. Straying from this path and acting contrary to our true nature often leads to feelings of restlessness, dissatisfaction, and inner conflict. For instance, imagine someone with a deep affinity for numbers and analysis, like an accountant, being forced into the role of an artist or poet—they would struggle and feel out of place. Similarly, an entrepreneur stuck in a job that does not allow them to express their creative or leadership skills will feel stifled. This is the potential downside of free will—it allows us to choose paths that may not align with our true selves, resulting in internal turmoil and dissatisfaction.

How to achieve fulfillment and success in life?

Align with Svadharma

Leads to fulfillment and success

Stray from Svadharma

Causes dissatisfaction and inner conflict

Fig: How to achieve fulfillment in life

Modern research too is producing similar inferences. In the well-known book *Atomic Habits*, James Clear discusses how success often stems from finding and nurturing one's *svadharma*. He elaborates this with examples of elite athletes like Usain Bolt and Michael Phelps. Bolt and Phelps did not become great because they simply worked harder than others—they excelled because their physical attributes naturally aligned with their sports. Usain Bolt's long legs and explosive power made him an ideal sprinter, while Michael Phelps' unique wingspan and long torso made him a natural swimmer. Both athletes thrived because they followed their *svadharma,* which helped them achieve greatness in their respective fields.

Svadharma extends beyond physical abilities and speaks to our inner motivations and spiritual calling. Take, for example, the great Indian saint Swami Vivekananda. Although highly intelligent and capable of success in various fields, his nature was deeply inclined toward spirituality and service. Even as a young man, Vivekananda was drawn to more profound questions about life and sought the guidance of spiritual masters. His meeting with his guru, Ramakrishna Paramahamsa, awakened his true *svadharma*, leading him to dedicate his life to spiritual growth and the upliftment of humanity. His spiritual journey was not merely a career choice but a natural alignment with his inner calling.

Identifying and living by your *svadharma* can lead to material success and spiritual fulfillment. When you work in harmony with your intrinsic qualities, your actions become more sustainable, your success more achievable, and your happiness more lasting. Just as a runner thrives on the track and a swimmer takes to the pool as does a fish to water, we must each find the space—professionally, creatively, and spiritually—where we effortlessly align with our *svadharma* and flourish.

The lesson here is simple: do not chase external goals just because they are convenient, appealing, glamorous, or easy. Instead, ensure your choices are deeply rooted in your *svadharma*—your core nature. When we align with who we truly are, we begin to live a meaningful life that feels natural and fulfilling.

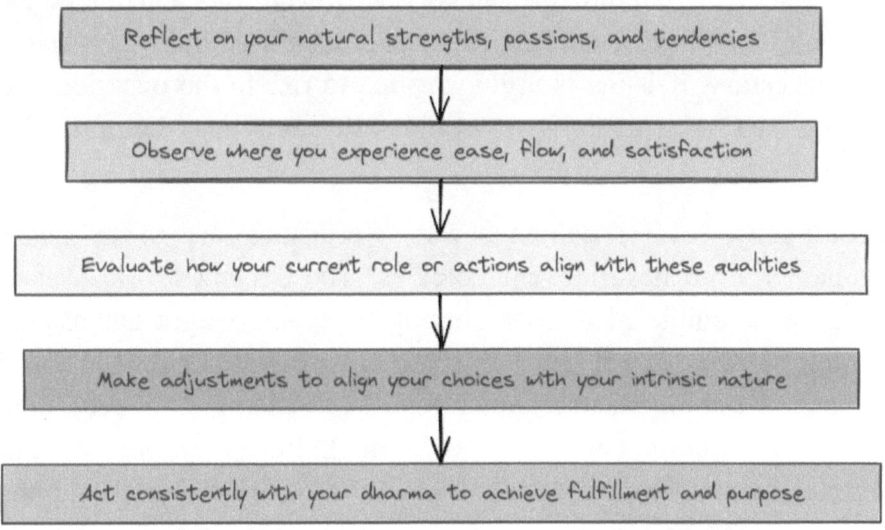

Fig: Steps to Identify and Align with Your Svadharma

Krishna's Direct Appeal to Arjuna

In this shloka, Krishna expounds on the concept of *svadharma* by applying it directly to Arjuna's situation on the battlefield. Krishna urges Arjuna to reflect on his *svadharma* as a warrior (*kṣatriya*) and to act in alignment with it. Engaging in a righteous war (*dharmyāddhi yuddhāt*) is a moral duty and the most noble expression of character for a warrior.

Krishna acknowledges that war is not easy, and the challenges it presents—such as facing death, destruction, and the moral complexity of killing—are immense. Yet, for Arjuna, who is a warrior, avoiding battle would mean acting against his essential nature. This would lead to a loss of purpose and tremendous inner conflict. Difficult though it may be, engaging in a righteous war would help him fulfill his duty of upholding *dharma*—the moral and social order.

Krishna's use of the phrase *dharmyāddhi yuddhāt*—righteous war—clarifies that not every battle is noble. Wars of aggression and conquest do not fall into this category. However, wars that defend the weak, uphold justice, and restore social order are not only permissible but necessary. Krishna is urging Arjuna to rise to the occasion and engage in a battle that aligns with his true nature and the principles of *dharma*.

Historically, several righteous wars were necessary to safeguard humanity from destructive ideologies. The Second World War is a classic example of nations coming together to fight against the tyranny of the Nazi regime. The war was fought not for territorial expansion but to preserve human dignity, freedom, and justice. Had the Allied forces not acted, the world might have been plunged into an era of extreme oppression and genocide. Krishna's teaching finds expression in this scenario, which affirms that defending human values and freedom sometimes requires the difficult choice of engaging in battle. Fulfilling our duties, even when challenging or uncomfortable, is essential to live in alignment with our nature.

Despite being aligned with our *svadharma,* we sometimes cannot take the right action due to various constraints and circumstances. Consider a soldier whose *svadharma* is to fight but is forced to fight in the lines of tyrannical forces. Imagine the *dharmic* conflict he would feel within. Krishna reinforces that there is no greater opportunity for a warrior than to fight a just war. On the battlefield of Kurukshetra, Arjuna's svadharma, as a warrior, brought him to the center of a righteous war. Through this battle, he is entitled to express his inner nature, fulfill his responsibility, and stand by *dharma*. Think. Can there be a more incredible blessing than this for any human being?

This can be likened to anyone staying true to themselves and fulfilling their responsibilities in life, even when those duties are challenging. A doctor might face the arduous task of treating patients during a pandemic, or a leader may have to make tough decisions during a crisis. In all such cases, the essence of Krishna's message remains to align your actions with your *svadharma,* face your challenges with courage, and recognize that fulfilling your duty is not only an obligation but a path to inner contentment.

Avoiding the battle, Arjuna would betray his nature as a warrior, shun his duty, and hinder the greater cause of justice - defy *dharma*. Krishna authoritatively concludes that there is no greater opportunity for a warrior than to fight a righteous battle.

Clarification on Krishna's Advice to Arjuna

It is essential to understand that Krishna's counsel in this shloka, encouraging Arjuna to engage in battle, is specific to Arjuna's *svadharma* as a warrior. Arjuna's duty as a protector of justice and order required him to engage in war when necessary. If Krishna had been speaking to a student, a philosopher, or a merchant, the advice would have been entirely different, tailored to their *svadharma* and role in society. The Bhagavad Gita is often misunderstood as a war-mongering scripture. But it is, in fact, a dialogue that emphasizes duty, righteousness, and living in alignment with one's true nature.

Krishna's words are not a blanket endorsement of violence or war. Instead, it is a call to action for individuals to fulfill their duties, even when difficult. Arjuna, a warrior, a warrior, he must establish justice through righteous warfare. Interestingly, Mahatma Gandhi, who considered the Bhagavad Gita his mother, fought for India's freedom through *ahimsa* - the principle of non-violence. The core message of the Gita is to live with integrity and fulfill one's responsibilities, whatever they may be, in alignment with the principles of *dharma*.

Reflective Prompt

Pause to look at how you are currently engaged with life. Are you being true to yourself? Is your occupation in line with your core nature? Is what you do contributing to the greater good of all? How can you better chart your life to be aligned with your *svadharma?*

Recognize and align with your true calling; it will bless you with a materially and spiritually fulfilling life

SHLOKA 32: OPPORTUNITY IN SVADHARMA

यदृच्छया चोपपन्नं स्वर्गद्वारमपावृतम् |
सुखिनः क्षत्रियाः पार्थ लभन्ते युद्धमीदृशम् ||32|

yadṛcchayā cōpapannaṁ svargadvāramapāvṛtam |
sukhinaḥ kṣatriyāḥ pārtha labhantē yuddhamīdṛśam ||32||

Translation:

O Pārtha, only the fortunate warriors (***sukhinaḥ kṣatriyāḥ***) come across such a battle (***yuddham īdṛśam***), which has arrived by chance (***yadṛcchayā upapannam***) and opens the gates to heaven (***svargadvāram apāvṛtam***) [Sankya Yoga: 2.32]

At a Glance: Capturing the Spirit of the Shloka

Performing bounden duties is essential, even when they oppose personal preferences or appear complicated. By staying true to our *svadharma*, we open doors to opportunities for progress and fulfillment, materially and spiritually. If you pause to look back at your life so far, you will realize that often, the performance of the most challenging duties has eventually led to the greater good of yourself and all concerned.

Commentary

In this shloka, Krishna continues to encourage Arjuna to fulfill his duty as a warrior, even though it defies his will and volition. Krishna explains that this rare opportunity to fight in a righteous war (*dharmyāddhi* yuddhāt) should be embraced even when it appears unexpectedly (*yadṛcchayā cōpapannaṁ*).

The opportunity to act in alignment with one's *svadharma* is a rare privilege. Arjuna's duty as a strong and courageous warrior is to protect society and defend righteousness. Though war is undesirable and carries significant risks of losing one's life and causing harm to others, Krishna emphasizes that Arjuna's war is justified because it is being fought for a noble cause. Engaging in a righteous war serves the greater good and enables a warrior to fulfill his *dharma* and thus evolve spiritually.

To understand this better, let us consider the example of healthcare workers during the COVID-19 pandemic. Much like how Arjuna did not seek out battle, these workers did not choose the pandemic. Yet, when it struck, they recognized their duty and fulfilled it despite personal risks. Many doctors, nurses, and frontline workers put their lives on the line to save others. Their *dharma* was to care for the sick and protect society, and though some may have lost their lives, their actions were aligned with their higher purpose. In that process, they were also faced with heart-wrenching decisions, such as not allowing a dying patient to see their loved ones. However, in the larger karmic scheme, acting by one's dharma, even when it leads to personal sacrifice or difficult choices, ensures spiritual progress and conducive conditions in future lives.

Krishna's reference to the "open gate to heaven" (*svargadvāram-apāvṛtam*) alludes to favorable conditions that one inadvertently garners for future lives through the performance of selfless *dharmic* actions. Even if the immediate outcome involves personal loss, fulfilling one's duty in ways that benefit the whole accrues *punya* (good merit). Arjuna would secure his own spiritual progress through the accumulation of *punya* by engaging in this righteous war.

In conclusion, Krishna urges us to rise above our self-inflicted emotional entrapments and recognize the opportunities we are given to fulfill our *svadharma*. While fulfilling our duties may sometimes go against our personal wishes, it aligns with cosmic order. By embracing our responsibilities, no matter how difficult, we progress spiritually, accumulate positive karmic merit, and pave the way for favorable conditions in future lives. When followed with integrity, fulfilling one's duty is the path to spiritual expansion and ultimate liberation.

Reflective Prompt

Recall a specific time when you had to respond to your call of duty against your wishes. Did you succumb to your resistance, or did you act? How would you apply what you have learned to a comparable situation in the future?

Align with your duty, and the universe aligns with you.

SHLOKA 33: THE COST OF NEGLECTING SVADHARMA

अथ चेत्त्वमिमं धर्म्यं सङ्ग्रामं न करिष्यसि |
ततः स्वधर्मं कीर्तिं च हित्वा पापमवाप्स्यसि ||33||

atha cēttvamimaṁ dharmyaṁ saṅgrāmaṁ na kariṣyasi |
tataḥ svadharmaṁ kīrtiṁ ca hitvā pāpamavāpsyasi ||33||

Translation:

But if you refuse to engage (***na kariṣyasi***) in this righteous war (***dharmyaṁ saṅgrāmaṁ***), then by abandoning (***hitvā***) your duty (***svadharmaṁ***) and honour (***kīrtiṁ***), you will incur (***avāpsyasi***) sin (***pāpam***) [Sankya Yoga: 2.33]

At a Glance: Capturing the Spirit of the Shloka

Shunning responsibilities out of fear, laziness, strong aversions, or discomfort does not befit virtuous people. Failing to act when duty calls damages reputation and leads to negative consequences, both in this life and in the ensuing karmic unfoldment.

Commentary

In the previous shloka, Krishna highlighted the benefits of performing *svadharmic* actions. In this shloka, he emphasizes the negative outcome of shying away from one's *svadharma*. For Arjuna, a natural warrior, his *svadharma* is to fight in a righteous war, and refusing to do so would mean abandoning his duty. Krishna explains that avoiding this battle would result in dishonor and the accumulation of *pāpam* (negative karma).

Nothing is more critical to a warrior than his honor. Krishna masterfully plays on this weakness and warns Arjuna that this omission would result in losing his honor and reputation (*kīrti*), causing him immense suffering.

It is to be noted that there are two kinds of *pāpam*: one from doing something wrong (*niṣiddha-karaṇam*) and the other from failing to do what should be done (*vihita-akaraṇam*). Arjuna's refusal to fight a just war falls under the latter—omission, or *pratyavāya-pāpam*. By not engaging in this dharmic war, Arjuna would fail to protect justice and risk sowing the seeds for negative consequences for himself, both in this life and in future ones.

Krishna's message is clear: even if performing one's duty is difficult or uncomfortable, neglecting it can have far-reaching consequences, including karmic repercussions that extend beyond this lifetime. For Arjuna, failing to act by his *svadharma* would not only tarnish his legacy but also lead to spiritual regression, potentially condemning him to suffering in future lives.

Duty and Integrity: Lessons from the Gita for Modern Life

Krishna's advice to Arjuna in the Bhagavad Gita remains profoundly relevant in the modern world. His call to fulfill one's duties, even when difficult, applies to everyone, regardless of profession or circumstance. We often face situations where we must engage in uncomfortable actions that defy our personal preferences. However, neglecting those responsibilities for any reason has far-reaching and long-term consequences.

Let us revisit the example used in the exposition of the previous verse. Much like Arjuna, frontline workers of the COVID-19 pandemic did not want to be in a situation where their lives were at risk. Yet, despite the long hours, emotional stress, and personal risk, they stepped up to fulfill their duty when the crisis arose. They knew shirking their responsibilities during such a grave world crisis would mean allowing the virus to spread, significantly harming society. By acting by their professional *dharma,* they upheld ethical values and societal order, much like Krishna urges Arjuna to do on the battlefield.

Krishna's teachings remind us to rise when duty calls, even if it goes against our immediate wishes. The consequences of avoiding responsibility are not just external, like loss of respect or credibility, but internal as well, leading to guilt, dissatisfaction, and negative karmic consequences.

In our personal and professional lives, we often face moments where the right course of action is not easy. We struggle while confronting a tricky situation at work, fulfilling family responsibilities, or making a decision that requires personal sacrifice. Krishna stresses here that failure to act in alignment with our duty leads to negative consequences, both in the present and future. Just as Arjuna's avoidance of his warrior duty would have led to total disarray in the kingdom, personal disgrace, and spiritual devolution, neglecting our responsibilities leads to missed opportunities for fulfillment and peace in the immediate present and spiritual growth in the future.

Footnote: Understanding Pāpam

'Pāpam' is often loosely translated as "sin," which confuses readers, especially those familiar with the biblical concept of sin. In Vedanta, *'pāpam' refers* to the negative consequences of actions—either by commission (doing something wrong) or omission (failing to do what should be done). It is not equivalent to the "original sin" concept in the biblical sense. While biblical sin is often associated with a moral transgression against divine law, *'Pāpam'* in Vedanta is more about accumulating adverse karmic effects due to actions out of alignment with *dharma* (righteousness) and cosmic order. Vedanta focuses on self-correction and learning through experience, emphasizing karmic consequences over moral judgment.

Reflective Prompt

Reflect on a time when you shunned a demanding responsibility due to fear, laziness, strong aversion, or discomfort. What effect did this omission have on your own conscience and the lives of others involved? How might things have been different if you had simply done what should have been done?

Honor lies in duty fulfilled, not in the comfort of avoidance

SHLOKAS 34-36: REPUTATION AT STAKE

अकीर्तिं चापि भूतानि कथयिष्यन्ति तेऽव्ययाम् |
सम्भावितस्य चाकीर्तिः मरणादतिरिच्यते ||34||

भयाद्रणादुपरतं मंस्यन्ते त्वां महारथाः |
येषां च त्वं बहुमतः भूत्वा यास्यसि लाघवम् ||35||

अवाच्यवादांश्च बहून् वदिष्यन्ति तवाहिताः |
निन्दन्तस्तव सामर्थ्यं ततो दुःखतरं नु किम् ||36||

akīrtiṁ cāpi bhūtāni kathayiṣyanti tē'vyayām |
sambhāvitasya cākīrtiḥ maraṇādatiricyatē ||34||

bhayādraṇāduparatam maṁsyantē tvāṁ mahārathāḥ |
yēṣāṁ ca tvaṁ bahumataḥ bhūtvā yāsyasi lāghavam ||35||

avācyavādāṁśca bahūn vadiṣyanti tavāhitāḥ |
nindantastava sāmarthyaṁ tatō duḥkhataraṁ nu kim ||36||

Translation:

People will speak endlessly of your dishonor (***akīrtiṁ***), and for someone who has been honored (***sambhāvitasya***), dishonor (***akīrtiḥ***) is worse than death (***maraṇāt***) [Sankya Yoga: 2.34]

Great warriors (*mahārathāḥ*) will think that you have withdrawn from the battle out of fear (*bhayāt raṇāt uparatam*). Having earned their respect (*bahumataḥ*), you will fall into disgrace (*lāghavam*)
[Sankya Yoga: 2.35]

Your enemies (*tavāhitāḥ*) will speak many cruel and unspeakable words (*avācyavādān*), ridiculing your abilities (*nindantas tava sāmarthyam*). What could be more painful (*duḥkhataram*) than that?
[Sankya Yoga: 2.36]

At a Glance: Capturing the Spirit of the Shlokas

The importance of fulfilling one's responsibilities is presented from a worldly perspective. The loss of respect and honor in society can be devastating, especially for an honorable person. When someone fails to rise to the occasion, they risk being seen as a coward, tarnishing their reputation among peers and opponents. In addition to this internal sense of failure, they may face harsh criticism and ridicule from those around them, including adversaries who will mock their abilities. The pain of losing one's dignity and enduring public disgrace creates a ripple effect of negativity throughout one's life. Such a life is more painful than death for a person of good repute.

Commentary

After emphasizing the importance of doing one's duty from a philosophical perspective in the earlier verses (31–33), Krishna now highlights a more worldly and materialistic point of view.

In Shlokas 34–36, Krishna emphatically states the untoward bearings turning away from duty has on one's standing in society. This compelling assertion resonates with everyone, even those who may not be spiritually inclined. Throughout the Bhagavad Gita, Krishna's continually shifting stances to cater to the intellect of the spiritually and materially inclined showcase his brilliance as a teacher.

Krishna's words to Arjuna holler the social consequences of refusing to fight in the Mahabharata war. Being a highly respected warrior (*mahārathāḥ*), Arjuna would incur tremendous disgrace if he withdrew from the battle. People would speak of his disrepute for generations; for someone honored throughout his life, such dishonor would be worse than death.

Furthermore, Arjuna's peers and fellow warriors, who had once respected him, would now think that he had retreated out of fear (*bhayād*), not because of any noble reason. His enemies would go even further, mocking his abilities (*nindantastava sāmarthyam*) and spreading unmentionable insults, which would be far more painful for Arjuna to endure than the battle itself. For a warrior, losing his reputation is akin to losing his entire identity. William Shakespeare's words from Julius Ceasar ring true here: *"The evil that men do lives after them; The good is oft interred with their bones."* It does not matter how much fame and honor Arjuna has garnered throughout his life - this single dishonorable retreat from a righteous war would drown it all in a puddle of shame.

Krishna's message holds immense relevance for our day-to-day lives in the modern world. While we may not necessarily be warriors on a battlefield, every one of us faces challenges that demand action. Whether in our professional, personal, or public lives, avoiding our duties or failing to meet expectations threatens our self-worth and respect in society.

In the corporate world, if a leader or manager avoids making a tough decision because it is discomfiting or might make them unpopular, they risk losing credibility and respect in the eyes of their colleagues and subordinates. This loss of trust can damage their reputation and career.

In conclusion, Krishna emphasizes that doing one's duty is not only essential from a *dharmic* perspective but also from a material one. Disregarding duties leads to a loss of dignity and respect. In modern life, we may not face literal battles, but we face challenges that require us to rise to the occasion. Even when complex, fulfilling our obligations allows us to uphold our personal integrity and build trust in ourselves and in the minds of others. The consequences of failing to shoulder our responsibilities are far more painful than the discomfort of executing them, however difficult they may be. Krishna reminds us that avoiding these challenges only brings more tremendous suffering.

Consequences of Duty Fulfillment

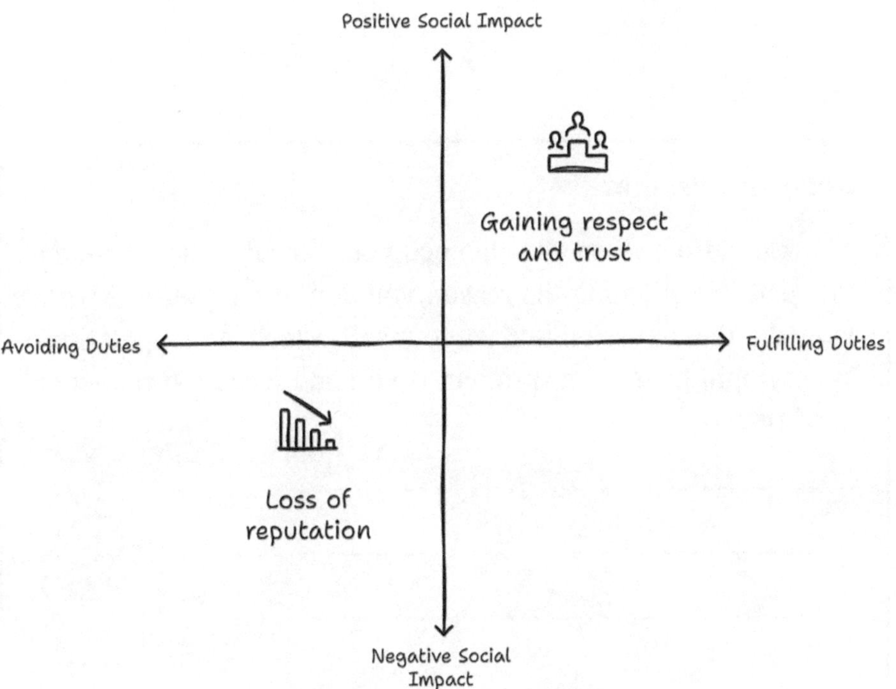

Fig: Consequence of Duty Fulfillment

Reflective Prompt

Think of a time when you shunned your bounden duty. Spend a moment investigating the reason you comforted yourself with. How did that omission impact your self-esteem and reputation? What might have been different if you had faced the challenge head-on?

Honor lost in inaction is a wound deeper than any battle

SHLOKA 37: DHARMA ALWAYS REWARDS

हतो वा प्राप्स्यसि स्वर्गं जित्वा वा भोक्ष्यसेमहीम् |
तस्मादुत्तिष्ठ कौन्तेय युद्धाय कृतनिश्चयः ||37||

hatō vā prāpsyasi svargaṁ jitvā vā bhōkṣyasēmahīm |
tasmāduttiṣṭha kauntēya yuddhāya kṛtaniścayaḥ ||37||

Translation:

If you are killed (**hatāḥ**), you will attain heaven (**svargam**). If you are victorious (**jitvā**), you will enjoy the earth (**bhokṣyase mahīm**). Therefore, rise up (**uttiṣṭha**), Kaunteya [son of Kunt], and resolve to fight (**kṛtaniścayaḥ**)! [**Sankya Yoga: 2.37**]

At a Glance: Capturing the Spirit of the Shloka

Fulfilling your duty with determination is always rewarding, regardless of the outcome. If you succeed, you will enjoy the tangible results of your efforts, including recognition and achievement. If you do not succeed, your efforts are not wasted; they accumulate valuable experience and good karmic credits, which will benefit you in the future. The key is approaching your responsibilities with clarity and commitment, assured that you gain something meaningful either way.

Commentary

After giving Arjuna exhaustive reasons to engage in battle from both the spiritual and material standpoints, Krishna concludes his sermon on the importance of fulfilling one's duty by highlighting the direct and indirect benefits of doing so. Krishna declares that aligning with *dharma* only accrues benefits regardless of the outcome. **Whether successful or not, the result of dutiful action backed by pure intention is always rewarding**.

Krishna fully acknowledges the possibility of both outcomes - Arjuna losing his life or winning the war. Krishna assures Arjuna that if Arjuna were to be killed in battle (*hatō*), he would gain entry into heaven (*svarga*) as a reward for performing his *dharmic* duty. Krishna reminds him that according to the *dharma-śāstra,* a warrior who dies fulfilling his duty attains *svarga* and, in future lives, draws unto himself even better circumstances due to his virtuous actions. Arjuna's earlier concern about incurring sin (*pāpa)* is dismissed by Krishna, who clarifies that no sin will come to him who is engaged in righteous warfare, only spiritual elevation.

If Arjuna wins the battle (*jitvā)*, he will enjoy the immediate fruits of his victory—earthly rewards, such as ruling the kingdom (*bhokṣyase mahīm*). Thus, Krishna assures Arjuna that he is in a win-

win situation with absolutely nothing to lose. Lovingly addressing him as *Kaunteya* (son of Kunti), Krishna urges Arjuna to rise (*uttiṣṭha*) and fight with firm resolve (*yuddhāya kṛta-niścayaḥ*), knowing he will only stand to gain in victory, or death. Krishna's call for Arjuna to stand up is both a physical and psychological encouragement to overcome his inner reticence and fulfill his duty as a warrior.

In modern times, the message of this shloka remains profoundly relevant, especially in moments of crisis where fulfilling one's duty with courage and determination is critical. One such example is the firefighters who risked their lives during the tragic events of 9/11 at the World Trade Center. These brave individuals rushed into the burning buildings, fully aware of the dangers they faced, yet they did so out of a sense of duty to save others. Many died through this selfless endeavor, but so many more lives were saved in the bargain. Their act of unprecedented courage left an indelible mark on society. They did not let fear of personal safety deter them from performing their duties, and today, they are remembered as heroes who sacrificed themselves for the greater good. Their legacy continues to inspire generations.

Regardless of the outcome, resolutely fulfilling one's responsibilities always yields benefits. Whether one succeeds or faces failure, the effort put into upholding *dharma* by any human in their personal or professional lives leaves a lasting impact. Fulfilling one's duty brings honor; even if the results are not immediate or tangible, such actions become the foundation for a better future.

Should one engage in duty despite uncertain outcomes?

Winning the Battle

Immediate rewards and victory

Losing in Battle

Spiritual elevation and karmic reward

Fig: Dharma always rewards

Reflective Prompt

Reflect on the idea that even in failure, acting with integrity and commitment can yield spiritual or personal growth. How have your past efforts, even those that did not lead to success, contributed to your growth today?

The path of dharma brings only gain, never loss

Shloka 38: Act with a Steady Mind

सुखदुःखे समे कृत्वा लाभालाभौ जयाजयौ ।
ततो युद्धाय युज्यस्व नैवं पापमवाप्स्यसि ॥38॥

sukhaduḥkhē samē kṛtvā lābhālābhau jayājayau |
tatō yuddhāya yujyasva naivaṁ pāpamavāpsyasi ||38||

Translation:

By making pleasure and pain (***sukha-duḥkha***), gain and loss (***lābha-alābha***), victory and defeat (***jayājayau***) equal in your mind, prepare for battle (***yuddhāya yujyasva***). In this way, you will incur no sin (***pāpam avāpsyasi***) [Sankya Yoga: 2.38]

At a Glance: Capturing the Spirit of the Shloka

Approach all actions with a balanced mind, treating success and failure, pleasure and pain, and gain and loss the same. This equanimous attitude, free from binding attachment to outcomes, leads to true success. Acting with clarity and poise ensures your actions amass no negative mental impressions or karmic consequences.

Commentary

In Shloka 38, we see a transformative shift in Krishna's discourse-from *why* one must fulfill their duties to *how* they should be carried out. From Shlokas 11-37, Krishna has exhaustively explained that fear—including the greatest fear, the fear of death—should not prevent us from doing what needs to be done. He has assured us that dutifully aligning our actions with *dharma* leads to material success and spiritual growth. Continuing to address Arjuna's primary concern about accruing sin from fighting this war (Chapter I:36, 39), Krishna now introduces a revolutionary approach to action known as *Karma Yoga*—a central teaching of the Bhagavad Gita.

Karma Yoga, or the Yoga of Action, provides a practical roadmap for engaging in mundane or spiritual duties without allowing them to overwhelm or drain us. The essence of Karma Yoga lies in performing our actions with equanimity without getting overly anxious about the result. Adopting this approach makes our actions more focused, efficient, and less exhausting. This mindset enhances the quality of our efforts and serves as a tool for spiritual growth.

Krishna begins exploring the principles of Karma Yoga right up to Shloka 53 of this chapter, showing us how to apply this profound wisdom to our everyday lives. These teachings help us navigate life's complexities while maintaining inner balance, making them as relevant in today's fast-paced world as they were in ancient times. Whether it be significant career decisions or small, mundane tasks, the principles of Karma Yoga ensure that we perform our activities with clarity, calmness, and spiritual fortitude.

Equanimity in Action: The Key to Success

Samatvam (equanimity) is the central message of this shloka: "Treat *sukha-duḥkha* (pleasure and pain), *lābha-alābha* (gain and loss), and *jaya-ajaya* (victory and defeat) the same." To approach every triumph or setback with a steady mind. This mental balance allows us to act efficiently in the present by not getting emotionally incapacitated by worrying over the outcomes. It ensures that we remain unperturbed by the inevitable fluctuations of life.

By adopting this mindset, Krishna reassures Arjuna that he will not incur *pāpam* (sin). When we act with equanimity and detachment, we align ourselves with the natural order of *dharma* and gather no negative karmic consequences. The privileged human experience is not meant to be dotted with one success, joy, or gain after another. It is justified and honored by the grace and resilience we exude when encountering all the glaring opposites in the world. As Swami Dayananda Sarasvati beautifully articulates: *"Success in life is nothing but the capacity to face success and failures."* A successful person, therefore, is not someone who avoids failure altogether but someone who can face both outcomes without being too emotionally disturbed.

Success and Failure: A Balanced Approach

Life is a necessary admixture of success and failure. No one person experiences constant success or incessant failure. As Isaac Newton most succinctly describes this immutable law of life, *"what goes up must come down."* A balanced attitude ensures that we remain unperturbed by these unstoppable waning and waxing phases of life. One of the foundational teachings of the Bhagavad Gita is *samatvam*—remaining balanced in *sukha-duḥkha* (pleasure and pain), *lābha-alābha* (gain and loss), and *jaya-ajaya* (victory and defeat).

When the mind is in balance, we are less likely to become arrogant or make rash decisions while hurtling around in euphoric joy. As we have often rightly heard, "The higher you fly, the harder you fall." A balanced mind also helps us learn from failure and use those lessons as steppingstones toward future success rather than be paralyzed by it. A mind uncontrollably swept away by these opposites gains nothing eventually.

Equanimity and Emotional Intelligence

Modern psychology, particularly the work of Daniel Goleman on emotional intelligence, echoes the essence of Krishna's teaching. Goleman highlights that emotional intelligence—the ability to manage emotions and remain calm under pressure—is critical to success in life and work. People with high emotional intelligence can regulate their emotional responses in ways that positively impact their future.

Scientific findings on how the brain reacts to stress and pressure validate this ancient wisdom. When we face demanding situations, the amygdala, or the brain's emotional center, can trigger a "fight or flight" response. This often leads to impulsive reactions driven by fear, anger, or anxiety. However, as Goleman suggests, we can interrupt this automatic response by cultivating self-awareness and self-regulation and responding with clarity and calmness. This is precisely what Krishna teaches Arjuna—to maintain mental equanimity, avoid knee-jerk reactions, and approach his challenge with a calm, steady mind.

Practical Example: First Responders and Crisis Management

The practicality imbued in this teaching can be gleaned from a modern-day example of firefighters. These individuals are trained to stay composed, make impromptu decisions, and act efficiently despite the chaos around them. Consider firefighters rushing into a burning building. They would be unable to perform their duties effectively if they were overwhelmed by fear or panic. However, rigorous training and mental discipline equip them to maintain equanimity, precisely navigate the crisis, and save lives.

Just as firefighters must remain calm under pressure to do their job effectively, we must cultivate mental equipoise to handle life's challenges. By doing so, we ensure that our actions are free from impulsive reactions and their negative consequences.

In conclusion, we should learn to approach every situation in life-good, bad, or indifferent with a calm and balanced mind. Krishna does not promise a life free from failure; instead, he teaches us how to deal with both triumphs and setbacks with a sense of inner calm and strength. By creating this mental steadiness, we can act with greater clarity and purpose, free from the emotional turbulence that often clouds judgment. This is a key tenet of *Karma Yoga*, which awards every seeker practical wisdom to live a fulfilling life as they continue to work towards Self-realization.

Reflective Prompt

Think about a time when you felt overwhelmed by either joy or disappointment. How did this emotional state affect your decision-making? What would change if you approached similar situations with a calm, balanced mindset?

Equanimity is the bridge between effort and wisdom

Shloka 39: From Sankhya to Yoga

एषा तेऽभिहिता साङ्ख्ये बुद्धिर्योगे त्विमां शृणु।
बुद्ध्या युक्तो यया पार्थ कर्मबन्धं प्रहास्यसि ॥39॥

ēṣā tē'bhihitā sāṅkhyē buddhiryōgē tvimāṁ śṛṇu |
buddhyā yuktō yayā pārtha karmabandhaṁ prahāsyasi ||39||

Translation:

This wisdom, which has been explained to you so far, pertains to
Sāṅkhya (*ēṣā tē'bhihitā sāṅkhyē*). Now, listen to the teaching on Yoga
(*yōgē tvimāṁ śṛṇu*). Equipped with this knowledge (***buddhyā yuktō***),
O Arjuna (***pārtha***), you will free yourself from the bondage of karma
(***karmabandhaṁ prahāsyasi***) [Sankya Yoga: 2.39]

At a Glance: Capturing the Spirit of the Shloka

Krishna has exhaustively covered the knowledge of the Self thus far. However, understanding our true identity is not enough; we must learn how to live in ways that align with this knowledge. He now introduces the path of Yoga, which teaches us how to reduce mental strain, live efficiently, and progress materially and spiritually. By practicing this Yoga, we can free ourselves from the bondage of actions (*Karma*) and move toward realizing our highest potential..

Commentary

This shloka marks a shift in Krishna's teaching. He begins by saying, 'So far, I have taught you about the nature of the *Atma (eṣā te'bhihitā sāṅkhye),* referring to Self-knowledge, or *Atma jñānam,* which distinguishes the eternal *Atma* from the temporary body, mind, and intellect. The word *sāṅkhya* meaning knowledge of the Self—' the truth of oneself' or *Atma* (derived from *saṁyak kyāyatē, ātmatatvam yasyām sa sāṅkhy*a), forms the essence of the wisdom in the Upanishads and has been the central theme of Krishna's guidance in the earlier shlokas. Krishna emphasizes that understanding the *Atma* is a prerequisite for any spiritual seeker. It provides the reason and means to release oneself from mortal confusion and grief. This chapter is aptly called *Sankhya Yoga* because its primary teaching is knowledge of the *Atma.*

It is important to note that although the chapter is titled '*Sāṅkhya Yoga,*' it does not exclusively focus on *Sāṅkhya.* In fact, it is often said Chapter II offers a sweeping view of the entire Bhagavad Gita. Similarly, in other chapters of the Gita, while the chapter title does project the central theme of the chapter, other significant topics are also woven into the discussion. For example, although the twelfth chapter is called Bhakti Yoga, '*bhakti*' (devotion) is expounded even more elaborately in the eleventh chapter, where Arjuna is awestruck by Krishna's divine magnificence.

After introducing us to our identity as *Atma* (*eṣā te 'bhihitā sānkhye*), Krishna says, 'Now, listen to the teaching about Yoga' (*buddhiryoge tvimām śṛṇu*). This raises a natural question: Why is Yoga necessary if the knowledge of the Self (*Atma jñānam*) alone frees us from suffering and ultimately leads to liberation? Is it an alternative path to knowledge? No. However, specific prerequisites must be met to realize and experience our identity as Consciousness (*Atma*) beyond the body, mind, and intellect.

Although Self-knowledge is the only means to liberation, many people are not yet ready to fully grasp and live this knowledge. Just as a student must prepare and pass an entrance exam to pursue advanced studies in medical school, one must first prepare oneself to be receptive to the profound truths of Self-knowledge.

Even if one hears the most excellent teachings about the *Atma,* without a pure, calm, and disciplined mind (*Antahkarana Śuddhi*)—referred to as *adhikaratvam* in traditional Vedanta—this knowledge will remain theoretical and disconnected from direct experience. This is why Krishna introduces Yoga as the disciplinary path that purifies and stabilizes the mind. Through Yoga, one can overcome the obstacles that prevent the realization of oneself as the *Atma*.

The Sanskrit word '*Yoga*' comes from the root '*Yuj*,' which carries multiple meanings depending on the context. In this context, the appropriate meaning is *Yuj Samādhau,* referring to Yoga as discipline and control. This refers to the physical and mental discipline required to prepare for Self-knowledge. *Samādhi,* often interpreted as meditative absorption, is also the state of mental calmness, focus, and control. Here, '*Sama*' means balance or equanimity, and '*Dhi*' means mind. Together, *Samādhi* means the balanced and composed mind necessary for receiving Self-knowledge. Krishna emphasizes that Yoga, in this sense, refers to any practice that purifies and disciplines the mind by removing the obstacles of *Mala* (mental impurities) and

Vikshepa (mental disturbances). We have explained these terms in detail in our preceding book, ***First Step Into Bhagavad Gita***.

Krishna is about to expound *Buddhi Yoga*, where '*Buddhi*' refers to a particular mental attitude. Another common name for *Buddhi Yoga* is *Karma Yoga,* which refers to performing proper actions with the right attitude. The revolutionary teaching Krishna presents is that any action—whether spiritual, like prayers or meditation, or even mundane activities like commuting, work, cooking, or bathing—can be transformed into a practice for purifying and controlling the mind (*Antahkarana Śuddhi*).

Thus, Karma Yoga expands into a broad spectrum of practices, including *Bhakti Yoga, Ashtanga Yoga, Dhyana Yoga,* and *Hatha Yoga.* Depending on the specific activities, these practices are given different names, but they all fall under the broader discipline of Karma Yoga when performed with the right attitude.

Many of the Yoga disciplines we see in the modern world—like devotion or physical postures—fall under the broader discipline of Karma Yoga if they are performed with the proper intention and mindset.

Krishna concludes by saying, *buddhyā yukto yayā pārtha karmabandham prahāsyasi* -- 'Endowed with this Yoga, you will be free from the bondage of *Karma*. Through Yoga, one not only purifies the mind but also frees oneself from the bondage of *Karma*, which compels one to act or react to situations. In this context, Karma refers to the indirect results we acquire through our willful actions. These accumulated *Karmas* manifest as mental tendencies in our current life and become the cause of future births. Many of us may have experienced moments where we are compelled to act in a certain way, even against our conscious will. This compulsion arises because our past actions create mental tendencies that influence our behavior, accumulating more *Karma*. Over time, these tendencies shape our future actions and even determine our future births. Many individuals are unaware of how mental tendencies limit their freedom of choice in actions.

Therefore, Yoga is essential for breaking this cycle. By practicing Yoga, one can gradually reduce the influence of past Karmas on present actions, paving the way to attain the necessary qualifications for pursuing Self-knowledge and be liberated from all Karmic bonds and suffering.

Aspect	Karma Yoga	Jnana Yoga
Definition	The discipline of performing activities with proper attitude	The pursuit of Self-knowledge to realize one's true identity as *Atma*.
Primary Goal	Purification of the mind (*Antahkarana Shuddhi*).	Direct realization of the Self (*Atma Jnana*) for liberation (moksha).
Focus	Equanimity of the mind	Contemplation, inquiry, and reflection on Vedantic teachings.
Mental State Required	Develops calmness, focus, and emotional balance.	Requires a calm and purified mind as a prerequisite.
Role in Spiritual Path	A preparatory step to make the mind eligible for Jnana Yoga.	The ultimate step that leads to liberation and freedom from bondage.
Outcome	Mental Purity and Mental Stability	Direct realization of the *Atma* as eternal, unchanging Consciousness.
Key Practices	Bhakti Yoga (devotion), Upasana Yoga (meditation), Ashtanga Yoga (discipline).	Listening (*Shravana*), reflection (*Manana*), and deep contemplation (*Nididhyasana*).
Suitability	For those still bound by likes, dislikes, and attachments.	For those with a pure, focused, and disciplined mind.

Table: Understanding Karma Yoga and Jnana Yoga

Clarification: Karma Yoga and Jnana Yoga Are Not Parallel Paths

There is a common misconception in modern spiritual circles that *Karma Yoga, Jnana Yoga, Bhakti Yoga,* and *Raja Yoga* are separate and parallel paths, each suited to different temperaments. For instance, *Karma Yoga* is thought to be for the active, *Bhakti Yoga* for the emotional, and *Raja Yoga* for the meditative. However, according to the teachings of Advaita Vedanta, *Karma Yoga* is not an alternative to *Jnana Yoga*; instead, it is a preparatory step to make one eligible (*adhikaratvam*) for Jnana Yoga, the pursuit of Self-knowledge. Advaita Vedanta expounds on two broad stages in the spiritual journey:

Step 1: Karma Yoga: this includes various disciplines such as Dhyana Yoga, Bhakti Yoga, and Ashtanga Yoga to purify the mind and make it calm, focused, and free from the pull of likes and dislikes.

Step 2: Jnana Yoga: where a calm and focused mind actively seeks Self-knowledge to realize one's true identity as *Atma*. While Karma Yoga is indispensable for mental preparation, Jnana Yoga is the direct and only means of liberation (*moksha*). Therefore, these are not parallel paths but sequential steps; no one can skip this progression.

*Note: As we progress further in the Gita, we encounter another discipline called **Upasana Yoga**, which is also part of **Karma Yoga**. Upasana Yoga focuses on controlling and calming the mind through devotional practices, meditative techniques, and sustained focus on the divine. It complements the other aspects of Karma Yoga, aiding in mental discipline and spiritual alignment*

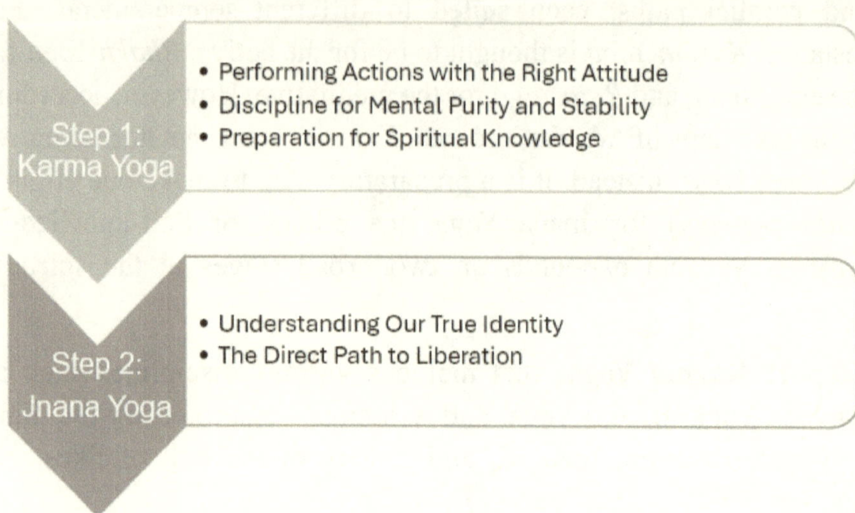

Fig: Karma Yoga and Jana Yoga are complementary paths

Clarification: Sankhya in the Bhagavad Gita vs. Sankhya Darshana

It is essential to clarify that the word '*Sankhya,*' as used in this shloka and in the title of the chapter, has no direct connection with the *Sankhya Darshana* founded by Maharshi Kapila. In the context of the Bhagavad Gita, '*Sankhya*' refers to Self-knowledge, or *Atma Jnana*—the knowledge of the true Self distinct from the body, mind, and intellect. This aligns with Vedanta's non-dual (Advaita) vision, where the ultimate Reality is singular, and the *Atma* is identified with *Brahman*. In contrast, *Sankhya Darshana* is one of the six classical schools of Indian philosophy and posits two fundamental realities: *Purusha* (Consciousness) and *Prakriti* (Matter). This dualistic framework fundamentally differs from the monistic (Advaita) teaching of the Bhagavad Gita. Hence, when Krishna speaks of '*Sankhya*' in the Gita, it should be understood as referring to knowledge of the *Atma,* not the philosophy of *Sankhya Darshana.*

Reflective Prompt

You have been introduced to your core identity as Atma—Supreme Consciousness. Can you accept this as your truth, or does it seem too theoretical? What identifiable factors prevent you from knowing yourself as the immutable, indestructible, eternal Self?

Discipline purifies; wisdom liberates.

SHLOKA 40: EVERY STEP COUNTS

नेहाभिक्रमनाशोऽस्ति प्रत्यवायो न विद्यते ।
स्वल्पमप्यस्य धर्मस्य त्रायते महतो भयात् ॥40॥

nēhābhikramanāśō'sti pratyavāyō na vidyatē |
svalpamapyasya dharmasya trāyatē mahatō bhayāt ||40||

Translation:

In this path [of Karma Yoga], there is no loss from an unfinished attempt (***abhikramanāśaḥ***), nor is there any adverse result (***pratyavāya***). Even practicing a little of this dharma (***Karma Yoga***) protects one (***trāyate***) from great fear (***mahatō bhayāt***) [Sankya Yoga: 2.40]

At a Glance: Capturing the Spirit of the Shloka

Karma Yoga is a path where every effort counts, and there is no risk of failure or negative consequences from incomplete practice. Unlike other pursuits, even small steps on this path yield meaningful benefits. There is no need to worry about not reaching an end goal or facing setbacks; whatever little you can practice will still accumulate as progress and offer protection.

Commentary

Before even diving into its detailed explanation, Krishna glorifies the ease and security of Karma Yoga, generating a sense of excitement and curiosity in the listener. This is another glaring visual of Krishna's effective teaching method—to present the benefits of a particular practice and capture the student's attention for what is to come.

Krishna begins the shloka with '*na iha abhikramanāśaḥ*'-in this path of Yoga, there is no wasted effort, even if the practice is incomplete. Many actions follow an "all or nothing" rule in our day-to-day lives. For example, if you start a project but leave it unfinished, you often lose the benefit of all the accumulated effort and must begin again. Whether taking up an exercise or diet regime, studying, or even practicing certain religious rituals, incomplete efforts often yield no results. But Krishna reassures us that Karma Yoga is different. Even if one only partially practices it or pauses the effort for any reason, nothing is lost – one continues to progress. Your effort into Karma Yoga is like building character—each small step is cumulative, adding to your development. If you are distracted or interrupted midway, you will not start from nothing. You resume precisely where you left off.

Krishna continues, '*pratyavāyō na vidyatē*,' meaning there is no risk of adverse effects or harmful consequences from Karma Yoga. In other areas of life, there could be negative results if we make mistakes or leave things incomplete. For example, if someone stops an antibiotic course prematurely, their condition might worsen. In such cases, the incomplete action results in *'pratyavāya'* or adverse outcomes. But in Karma Yoga, Krishna assures there is no fear of negative consequences.

Krishna then makes a powerful statement, *"svalpam api asya dharmasya trāyatē mahatō bhayāt,"* meaning that even a small practice of Karma Yoga can protect one from great fear. In contrast to material actions, which require completion to yield results (like digging a well, where you only benefit if you reach water), Karma Yoga offers palpable inner growth, even from partial effort. Regardless of how much effort is exerted, every practitioner will gain mental clarity, emotional resilience, and spiritual progress in varying degrees.

In Karma Yoga, no effort is wasted. For instance, even if a person digging a well does not find water, the inner transformation is already underway if the action is performed with the right attitude. Without the spirit of Yoga, incomplete tasks may feel like wasted effort, but in Karma Yoga, the process itself ensures growth, making every step meaningful. Ralph Waldo Emerson poeticizes this thought, *"It's not the destination. It's the journey."*

Krishna highlights the inclusive nature of Karma Yoga. It is not an "all or nothing" path. There is no need to compare oneself with others or feel discouraged by someone else's progress. Neither should we judge how others tread this path. Everyone can practice at their own pace, whatever effort is made will yield benefits. No action is too small to be meaningful. Even small, consistent steps in Karma Yoga lead to noteworthy results over time.

An undeniable outcome of Karma Yoga is the gradual development of *'yoga buddhi,'* or emotional intelligence. As one practices Karma Yoga, one's mind settles and becomes more focused. Over time, Karma Yoga helps develop the *'buddhi'* (intellect) Krishna repeatedly mentions throughout the Gita. This *'buddhi'* integrates emotion, reason, and willpower, enabling one to navigate life with clarity, purpose, and inner calm. This transformative development of the intellect becomes a powerful tool for personal and spiritual growth.

Furthermore, the practice of Karma Yoga offers immediate protection from the great fear of *samsāra*—the endless cycle of suffering (*'mahatō bhayāt'*). Although progress along this journey may be gradual, and not easily noticeable, inner growth starts from the first step, and momentum builds over time. Even if liberation is not fully realized in this lifetime, the spiritual growth achieved through Karma Yoga is never lost. Krishna reassures us later in the Gita that no spiritual effort is wasted, and any progress made will carry forward into future lifetimes.

Karma Yoga is an antidote to fear and confusion. Even a little practice can bring peace of mind and protect one from the fear of failure and uncertainty of results. As Krishna emphasizes in this shloka, the path of Karma Yoga is not about immediate success or attaining perfection. It is about the process itself, where every step, no matter how small, contributes to personal growth and ultimate liberation.

By starting on this path, a person begins to reverse the cycle of *samsara*, gradually moving toward *moksha* or liberation. Even if life circumstances interrupt one's practice or thwart full participation, the transformative power of Karma Yoga ensures that every effort made offers spiritual protection and progress.

Encouragement for Spiritual Seekers

Krishna's assurance is particularly comforting for those overwhelmed by the vastness of the spiritual path. Many seekers worry, "How can I cross the ocean of *samsara*? I am not a sage or yogi. I am but an ordinary human with many limitations and weaknesses." Krishna dispels such discouraging thoughts, reminding us that perfection is not expected all at once. Even small actions, such as a short prayer, a moment of mindfulness, a genuine act of service, or even an ordinary worldly activity performed in the spirit of Yoga, create momentum toward spiritual progress. The cumulative nature of Karma Yoga ensures that no effort is wasted, and each small step builds upon the last.

Karma Yoga is not about taking anything to its logical end or achieving perfection. It is about engaging sincerely, at one's own pace, with the right attitude of *'Buddhi Yoga.'* Bhagavan's assurance that even a small effort can yield excellent results reminds us that faith, persistence, and consistent practice matter more than the scale of the effort. Just as a tiny spark of fire can set ablaze an entire forest, even a little practice of Karma Yoga protects one from the great ills of life.

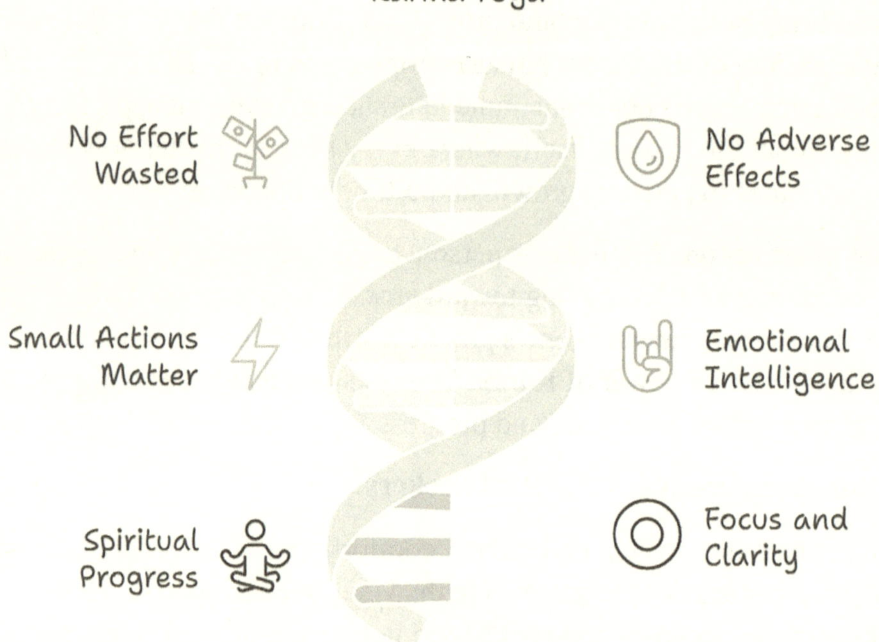

Fig: Benefits of Karma Yoga

Swami Vivekananda's Reflections

Swami Vivekananda, one of the most practical monks of modern times, was deeply inspired by the teachings of Karma Yoga. His thoughts on the essence of Krishna's message are as follows:

"There is no danger that you can overdo it. If you do even a little of it, this yoga will save you from the terrible round of birth and death. This is teaching on the practical side. Believe, therefore, in yourselves, and if you want material wealth, work it out; it will come to you. If you want to be intellectual, work it out on the intellectual plane, and intellectual giants you shall be. And if you want to attain to freedom, work it out on the spiritual plane, and free you shall be and shall enter into *Nirvana*, the Eternal Bliss. But one defect in the Advaita was its being worked out so long on the spiritual plane only, and nowhere else; now the time has come when you have to make it practical. It shall no more be a *rahasya*, a secret, it shall no more live with monks in caves and forests, and in the Himalayas; it must come down to the daily, everyday life of the people; it shall be worked out in the palace of the king, in the cave of the recluse; it shall be worked out in the cottage of the poor, by the beggar in the street, everywhere; anywhere it can be worked out. Therefore, do not fear whether you are a woman or a *shudra*, for this religion is so great, says Lord Krishna, that even a little of it brings a great amount of good. A very small amount of dharmic work performed brings a large amount of result. If this statement of the Gita wanted an illustration, I am finding every day the truth of that great saying in my humble life."

Swami Vivekananda's powerful words reinforce Krishna's teaching that Karma Yoga is accessible to everyone, regardless of background or circumstance. Whether one is a king or a commoner, monk or householder, the transformative power of Karma Yoga can be practiced in every aspect of life. Even small, sincere efforts on this path offer immense benefits, protecting us from the fears of life and guiding us closer to spiritual liberation.

Reflective Prompt

Do you get dejected when you do not see immediate results for your concerted effort in any field? Henceforth, can you endeavor to approach the same efforts in the spirit of Karma Yoga? Knowledge is not power. Applied knowledge is power. Try it to realize it.

In the journey of Karma Yoga, even the smallest spark ignites great transformation

SHLOKA 41: FROM DISTRACTION TO DETERMINATION

व्यवसायात्मिका बुद्धिः एकेह कुरुनन्दन |
बहुशाखा ह्यनन्ताश्च बुद्धयोऽव्यवसायिनाम् ||41||

vyavasāyātmikā buddhiḥ ēkēha kurunandana |
bahuśākhā hyanantāśca buddhayō'vyavasāyinām ||41||

Translation:

In the pursuit of liberation [*mokṣa*], O Arjuna, descendant of the Kurus (***Kurunandana***), there is one clear and resolute understanding (***vyavasāyātmikā buddhiḥ***). But the thoughts of those who lack discernment (***avayavasāyinām***) are scattered, branching out endlessly (***bahu-śākha hyanantāḥ***) [Sankya Yoga: 2.41]

At a Glance: Capturing the Spirit of the Shloka

Clarity of purpose, focus, understanding of the ultimate goal, and the role of each spiritual practice (*sadhana*) are the essential qualities that distinguish a Karma Yogi. With a well-defined purpose, a Karma Yogi walks the spiritual path firmly resolved, recognizing that every practice, appropriately done, leads toward Self-realization. In contrast, those lacking this clarity are scattered in their approach. Without a clear understanding of their goal or the various paths available, they jump from one practice to another, distracted by the endless variety of methods, without fully committing to any or getting anywhere.

Commentary

In this shloka, Krishna highlights the difference between the focused and determined mind (*vyavasāyātmikā buddhi*) and the scattered, unfocused mind (*bahuśākhā*). *Vyavasāyātmikā buddhi* refers to a clear, focused, and resolute mind. Karma Yoga emphasizes a unified, concerted effort toward spiritual growth, where every thought, emotion, and action aligns with the goal of *moksha*—the experiential realization of one's identity as Consciousness beyond the body, mind, and intellect. This single-pointed focus enables a person to harness their mental energy effectively, creating a deep sense of purpose and direction in life.

It does not mean that a Karma Yogi neglects worldly pursuits when they keep *moksha*— spiritual liberation—as their highest goal. The clarity of the primary goal helps align all other supporting goals perfectly. For example, consider a person traveling from Thiruvananthapuram to New York with a layover in Dubai for some shopping. If they mistakenly prioritize shopping over catching their connecting flight, they risk missing their primary objective of reaching New York. However, if they plan their shopping, remaining ever-focused on their onward journey, they can achieve both without compromising the primary goal.

Similarly, when a Karma Yogi keeps *moksha* as their top priority, they pursue personal and professional goals fully cognizant of their temporary nature and do not get lost in those pursuits. This mindful approach allows the Karma Yogi to excel in the material realm without losing sight of spiritual goals. Krishna wants us to cultivate this focused and determined mind (*vyavasāyātmikā buddhi*).

In contrast, the *avyavasāyī*—those with a scattered or unfocused mind—lack clarity and determination and are easily distracted. Krishna describes this mindset as *bahuśākhā*—many-branched and endless—reflecting a mind constantly pulled in different directions. On the spiritual path, this refers to people who lack clarity about the ultimate goal of life. Innumerable desires pull their mind in all directions. Their focus shifts from one worldly pursuit to another, thinking that each new achievement will bring security or lasting happiness. However, once they achieve one goal, they realize it does not bring with it the anticipated fulfillment, so they chase another, entrapped in a never-ending loop of dissatisfaction.

Many lack clarity about their true purpose, even within the religious or spiritual domain. Some believe heaven to be the ultimate destination and that surrendering to a particular God or performing specific rituals will secure their place there. Others may desire to inhabit higher realms like *Vishnuloka* or *Shivaloka*. Some misguided believe that acts of violence against non-believers will bring them closer to salvation. These are all examples of a lack of clear understanding, leading to scattered efforts and a constant shift from one practice or belief to another.

Krishna's emphasis on *vyavasāyātmikā buddhi* is akin to the scientific principle of focused energy. Like a laser beam, which is powerful because its light rays are concentrated into a single point, a person with a focused mind can penetrate deeper into any chosen endeavor, achieving more remarkable results. On the other hand, scattered light diffuses without much effect - similarly, a scattered mind tugged in all directions cannot progress in material or spiritual life.

Great individuals like Swami Vivekananda and Mahatma Gandhi had an extraordinary impact because they harnessed and channeled their mental energy toward a single goal. Their thoughts, words, and actions gushed in one direction, creating a powerful force of influence. Krishna encourages us to ensure that our mental energy is not dispersed in endless pursuits but is instead integrated and consciously channeled toward our chosen goal. A unified mind is not only a prerequisite for spiritual progress but also for secular pursuits of life.

Aspect	Focused Mind (*Vyavasāyātmikā Buddhi*)	Scattered Mind (*Bahuśākhā Buddhi*)
Purpose	Clear and well-defined	Undefined or confused
Mental State	Calm, steady, and resolute	Restless, distracted, and wavering
Energy Utilization	Concentrated and efficient	Diffused and wasteful
Approach to Goals	Persistent and systematic	Impulsive and inconsistent
Outcome	Progress toward liberation and success	Stagnation and dissatisfaction

Table: Focused Vs Scattered Mind

Sādhanas and Spiritual Confusion

Unlike other spiritual traditions, Hinduism offers many spiritual practices (*sādhanas*). Voluminous scriptures comprising the *Vedas*, the *Itihasas*, *Sutras*, and the *Puranas*, along with their commentaries and sub-commentaries, prescribe different *sādhanas*. For instance, in some places, the emphasis is on *pūja* (ritual worship); in others, it is on *japa* (chanting), while others recommend meditation, *bhajans* (devotional singing), or pilgrimage. These diverse options often leave people confused.

A perfect example of this is the spiritual columns in The Hindu newspaper, which feature a different recommendation every day. One day, you might read that simply doing the 'Who am I' inquiry will lead to instant liberation. The next day, the column might suggest raising the kundalini as the only way to freedom. And then, on another day, you will see that uttering *'Sri Rama Rama Rameti'* is enough to attain *moksha* (liberation). You are left wondering, "Which practice should I follow? Which one is the real path?[2]"

Even the stories from our scriptures confuse and bewilder. One text says Dhruva and Prahlada attained liberation through intense *tapas* (austerity), while another story might suggest that singing alone led someone to enlightenment. Then, there is the story of Dharma-Vyadha, a butcher who attained *moksha* by simply doing his duty [2].

Krishna addresses this confusion directly in this shloka by emphasizing the need for clarity. He points out that a true Karma Yogi clearly understands the ultimate goal *(moksha)* and the role of each *sādhanā* along the way. Without this clarity about the means and ends (*sādhanā and sadhya*), one risks misunderstanding or misusing spiritual practices.

The Importance of Clarity in the Spiritual Path

In this shloka, *vyavasāya* means *niścaya*—a clear understanding of what one seeks and how one intends to pursue it. This clarity is essential for spiritual growth.

The Bhagavad Gita declares that your true nature is Consciousness beyond the body, mind, and intellect. As stated in the *Mahavakyas*, this Consciousness is *Brahman*, the ultimate Reality (*Pranjanam Brahma* or *Ayam Atma Brahma*). Since you are already the supreme Brahman, the only thing that can liberate you is the direct experiential knowledge of your true Self. To acquire this knowledge, you must seek a qualified teacher and desire to learn and evolve through wisdom.

However, even when teaching is available, knowledge is not guaranteed to take root immediately. Why? Because it requires a mind that is free from distractions. It is not enough to be an adult physically; the mind must be mature and prepared to grasp this knowledge. This preparation is accomplished through Karma Yoga—a life of action performed with a prayerful attitude and without binding attachment to the results.

The choice for a spiritual seeker lies not in the type of practices but in their lifestyle: either as a *householder* following Karma Yoga or as a *sannyasi* (renunciant) pursuing knowledge exclusively. Both chosen paths require the seeker to purify the mind through Karma Yoga, and both must ultimately seek Self-knowledge for liberation. Even a sannyasi must gain *antaḥkaraṇa śuddhi*—purification of the mind—through disciplined practices of Yoga before the knowledge of the Self can dawn.

As studied in the previous shloka, Karma Yoga and Jnana Yoga are sequential steps on the same path. Once purified of impurities (*mala*) and disturbances (*vikshepa*) through Karma Yoga, the mind qualifies for Jnana Yoga, where the ignorance of the Self is removed through knowledge. Whether they choose the path of renunciation or remain engaged in worldly life, this is a two-step process for all seekers. Krishna stresses that spiritual progress requires this clear understanding: the focus and determination to purify the mind through Karma Yoga and then the pursuit of Self-knowledge through Jnana Yoga.

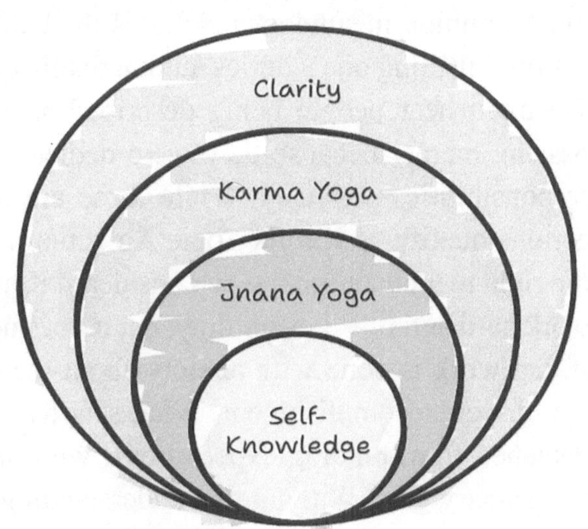

Another challenge for many seekers is the lack of clarity on what Karma Yoga truly entails. While a Karma Yogi understands the path clearly, Karma Yoga is often misunderstood and difficult to grasp. Karma Yoga is one of the most challenging concepts in Advaita Vedanta to fully comprehend, even more so than the nature of the *Atma* and the connection between *Jiva* and *Ishvara*. There has long been a lot of misinformation about Karma Yoga, even in Krishna's times. In modern times, the confusion has only grown, with numerous books, talks, and articles contributing to misinterpretations. Swami Dayananda Saraswati wisely remarked, *'Sometimes we must unlearn what we have learned to truly understand.'*

Krishna illuminates Karma Yoga in Shlokas 40–46 before delivering its precise definition in Shloka 47. Let us explore some common misconceptions about Karma Yoga that are prevalent today. Understanding Karma Yoga is the first step in a seeker's spiritual journey. It provides the foundation needed to navigate the spiritual path skillfully.

Merely Fulfilling One's Duties is Not Karma Yoga: One of the most common misunderstandings is the belief that working hard or simply fulfilling one's duties automatically qualifies as Karma Yoga. We often hear people being described as Karma Yogis after their passing merely because they were dedicated workers or took their responsibilities seriously. While these are admirable traits, not all actions qualify as Karma Yoga. An action must be performed with the right mental attitude to be considered Karma Yoga. A person may work hard and fulfill every duty, but it does not count as Karma Yoga if that work is done with anxiety about the outcomes or a sense of ego-driven accomplishment. What sets Karma Yoga apart is action detached from binding expectations; with one's spiritual growth as the primary goal. Without this understanding, even the most diligent work remains ordinary karma, not Karma Yoga.

Karma Yoga is Not Acting Without Expecting Results: Another widespread misconception is that Karma Yoga means acting without expecting results. People often define Karma Yoga as 'You have the right to perform your actions, but not to the results thereof,' frequently misinterpreted as action with total disregard for the outcome. Such a mindless attitude is both unrealistic and impractical. No one in the world, including Krishna, acts without expecting results. You go to work expecting a salary, buy a car expecting it to run, or teach someone with the hope they will learn. Karma Yoga teaches that one should not be attached to the results in a binding way—meaning, the results should not disturb your mental equilibrium. It is not the expectation of results that is the issue, but the attachment and dependency on those results for your sense of self-worth or happiness that Karma Yoga seeks to transform. When you let go of this attachment, the same actions become Karma Yoga.

Karma Yoga is Not About Acting Without Desire: A third misunderstanding is that Karma Yoga means acting entirely without desire - often framed as selfless action or *'nishkama karma.'* While it is true that enlightened beings act without personal desires, for most seekers, actions are naturally driven by desires—whether it is the desire for security, success, or even spiritual growth. The critical difference is that in Karma Yoga, one performs actions with desires without binding attachment.

Even desires for professional success, cooking a meal, or performing social service can be Karma Yoga if aligned with *dharma* and performed with the right mental attitude. Understanding that having desires does not disqualify someone from practicing Karma Yoga is essential. Karma Yoga is about learning to engage with those desires in ways that promote spiritual progress rather than attachment.

Fig: Common Misconceptions about Karma Yoga

These are just a few popular misconceptions that cloud the proper understanding of Karma Yoga. We encourage readers to reflect deeply on these points. As Krishna emphasized, when Karma Yoga is genuinely understood, it can lead to a significant leap forward on the spiritual path. It is not about renouncing actions or desires but about performing them with clarity and the right attitude. We will continue to explore and clarify more such points about Karma Yoga through the ensuing verses. We encourage you to approach this exploration with a willingness to unlearn and relearn as needed to experience the transformative power of Karma Yoga.

Harnessing the Power of Focus: From the Gita to Modern Research

The importance of focus and clarity, as emphasized in this shloka, closely aligns with the insights from Daniel Goleman's book *Focus: The Hidden Driver of Excellence*. Goleman explains that sustained attention and a single-point focus are crucial for achieving success and cultivating emotional intelligence and resilience. In modern neuroscience, research shows that a scattered mind, which Krishna describes as *'bahuśākhā'* (many-branched), leads to inefficiency and mental fatigue. The brain's energy is divided across too many tasks or distractions, reducing clarity and productivity. On the other hand, when one engages with a *'vyavasāyātmikā buddhi'*—a focused and determined mindset—neural pathways in the brain strengthen around the task at hand, leading to greater creativity, emotional regulation, and efficiency. On the spiritual path, clarity of purpose and focus not only sharpens the mind but also fosters inner peace and progress. Similarly, modern research suggests cultivating mindfulness and focus for overall well-being.

Reflective Prompt

Take a moment to reflect upon all your current pursuits in life. Are you 100% certain that this is what you genuinely want? What have you pitched as the highest goal for yourself? Does what you are currently pursuing support that?

In the clarity of purpose lies the strength to achieve the infinite

SHLOKAS 42, 43 & 44: BEYOND RELIGIOUS MATERIALISM

यामिमां पुष्पितां वाचं प्रवदन्त्यविपश्चितः |
वेदवादरताः पार्थ नान्यदस्तीति वादिनः ||42||

कामात्मानः स्वर्गपराः जन्मकर्मफलप्रदाम् |
क्रियाविशेषबहुलां भोगैश्वर्यगतिं प्रति ||43||

भोगैश्वर्यप्रसक्तानां तयाऽपहृतचेतसाम् |
व्यवसायात्मिका बुद्धिः समाधौ न विधीयते ||44||

yāmimāṁ puṣpitāṁ vācaṁ pravadantyavipaścitaḥ |
vēdavādaratāḥ pārtha nānyadastīti vādinaḥ ||42||

kāmātmānaḥ svargaparāḥ janmakarmaphalapradām |
kriyāviśēṣabahulāṁ bhōgaiśvaryagatiṁ prati ||43||

bhōgaiśvaryaprasaktānāṁ tayā'pahṛtacētasām |
vyavasāyātmikā buddhiḥ samādhau na vidhīyatē ||44||

Translation:

Those who do not have clarity (***avipaścitaḥ***) speak (***pravadanti***) flowery words (***puṣpitāṁ vācam***), O Arjuna (***Pārtha***), delighting in the rituals of the Vedas (***vēda-vāda-ratāḥ***) and claiming there is nothing beyond them (***na anyat asti iti vādinaḥ***) [Sankya Yoga: 2.42]

Those who are full of desires (***kāmātmānaḥ***), focused on heaven (***svargaparāḥ***) as the ultimate goal, speak of many special rituals (***kriyā-viśeṣa-bahulāṁ***) that promise better births (***janma-phala***), the fruits of rituals (***karma-phala***), all aimed at attaining pleasure and power (***bhōgaiśvarya-gatiṁ***)
[Sankya Yoga: 2.43]

Those attached to pleasure and power (***bhoga-aiśvarya***), with their minds carried away (***apahṛta-cetasām***), by these flowery words lack the focused understanding (***vyavasāyātmikā buddhiḥ***) mental stability (***samādhi***) necessary for spiritual growth
[Sankya Yoga: 2.44]

At a Glance: Capturing the Spirit of the Shloka

In modern life, many people lack clarity about their true purpose or goal, leading them to focus on short-term pleasures and material gains. Without a clear understanding of their higher purpose, they get carried away by desires for wealth, power, and sensory pleasures, believing these to be the ultimate achievements. Their priorities become misaligned, chasing after activities that only serve temporary satisfaction. True spiritual progress and Self-realization requires clarity, focus, and a sense of purpose—qualities that cannot be cultivated while worldly distractions consume one's mind.

Commentary:

In these three shlokas, Krishna shifts his emphasis from the Karma Yogi to those who lack clarity about the ultimate goal of life (*Karmi*). These people, referred to as *avipaścitaḥ* (the unwise), are shrouded in the belief that ultimate success lies in wealth, power, and the fulfillment of desires. As Krishna says, they are *kāmātmānaḥ*—embodiments of materialistic desires. Their actions and even religious practices are not aligned with the pursuit of inner growth or spiritual liberation; instead, they aim to fulfill sensory desires in this life or hanker after heavenly rewards. Krishna sympathizes with them but also points out the limitations of their understanding. Unlike the Karma Yogi, who has *vyavasāyātmikā buddhi* (a focused and determined mind), these individuals have scattered minds (*bahuśākhā*), distracted by endless desires and ambitions, which makes it difficult for them to progress spiritually.

According to Krishna, the issue is not that people seek success and pleasure—these are natural human desires. He criticizes the undue importance placed on these material goals at the expense of inner growth. These individuals think they can achieve peace and happiness by performing rituals in exchange for sense pleasures. However, they fail to realize that true fulfillment and lasting peace come not from external pleasures but from inner growth and Self-realization. Their focus on *bhoga* (pleasure) and *aiśvarya* (power) fogs the mental clarity needed for spiritual advancement.

Such people naturally lack *Vyavasāyātmikā buddhi*—the single-pointed focus needed to attain higher spiritual realization. Their minds are pulled in many directions, leaving no room for the stability and focus *(samadhi) required* for inner growth. In this way, their obsession with pleasure and power (*bhogaiśvarya prasaktānām*) clouds their ability to see beyond temporary, worldly gains. As a result, they remain alien to the deeper purpose of life, which lies in understanding one's true nature and moving toward liberation (*moksha*).

The four Vedas—Rig Veda, Yajur Veda, Sama Veda, and Atharva Veda—form the foundational scriptural knowledge of Sanatana Dharma. Each Veda is broadly divided into two sections: **Karma Kanda**, which focuses on ritualistic practices, and **Jnana Kanda**, which reveals the nature of our true identity, the *Atma*.

The *Karma Kanda* section of the Vedas prescribes numerous rituals to fulfill material desires, ensure prosperity, and secure a place in heaven. One such ritual is the *āvahanti hōma*, which invokes wealth, food, clothing, and cattle:

"āvahantī vitanvānā | kurvāṇā cīramātmanaḥ | vāsāṁsi mama gāvaśca |

annapānē ca sarvadā | tatō mē śriyamāvaha | lōmaśāṁ paśubhiḥ saha svāhā"

(Taittiriya Samhita 1.4.1)

This translates as: *"May prosperity always expand for me. Let me always have ample clothing, food, drink, and cattle. Bestow upon me wealth, prosperity, flourishing livestock, and abundance."*

These rituals reflect the Vedic recognition of material needs, acknowledging that wealth, food, and comforts are essential for life. However, Krishna's blatant criticism is aimed at those who make material gains their ultimate goal, ignoring the higher purpose of Self-realization or at least continued spiritual growth. Their perspective, *'nānyad astīti vādinaḥ'* - there is nothing beyond this—relegates the Vedas to solely being a means to achieve material benefits and heaven. He critiques this narrow focus, calling it the "flowery language" of the unwise, and urges seekers to look beyond rituals toward inner growth.

Although Vedic rituals, known as *Vaidika karmas*, were integral to daily life, during the Mahabharata war, people were overtly obsessed with ritualistic practices for material gains. In these verses, Krishna directly challenges this view, arguing that an obsession with *bhoga* (pleasure) and *aiśvarya* (power) scatters the mind and hinders spiritual progress.

Religious Materialism

Krishna's criticism of those who pursue material gains and heaven through Vedic rituals is relevant even today. Although ancient ritualistic practices are primarily extinct, this archaic mindset persists in modern religious practices across various traditions. Many visit temples, churches, mosques, or other places of worship to seek blessings for health, wealth, and success in worldly life. For many, religion becomes a transactional relationship with the divine, where worship is offered in exchange for material gains. For others, it is outright beggary donning the garb of devotion.

The concept of heaven as the ultimate goal continues to dominate many spiritual traditions. The promise of eternal pleasure and enjoyment is glorified as a reward for faith or righteous behavior. For instance, the *Garuda Purana* describes heaven as a place filled with celestial gardens, musical performances by divine beings, and free-flowing rivers of nectar. Similarly, the Bible depicts heaven as a realm of eternal joy, and in the Quran, paradise is described as a place of abundant sensory delights. While these descriptions may offer comfort and hope, Krishna warns against becoming fixated on such heavenly rewards. The purpose of human life is to transcend the pursuit of worldly and celestial pleasures and realize the Self (*Atma*).

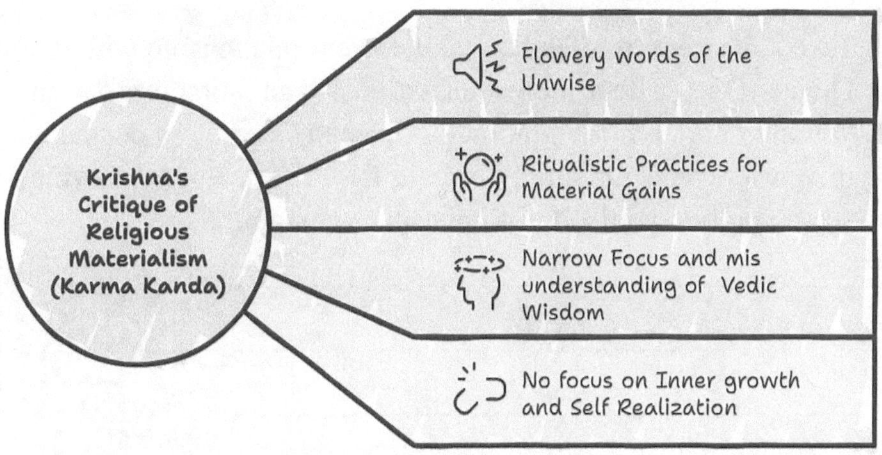

Fig: Religious materialism

Reflective Prompt

Take a moment to reflect on your current relationship with the Divine. Does it feel more transactional than worshipful? Can you incorporate more gratitude in place of ceaseless demands in your prayers? Or simply bask in the Presence of the Divine when you find yourself in a holy space next time?

Rise above the flowery promises; walk the path of inner truth

SHLOKA 45: THE MINDSET OF A KARMA YOGI

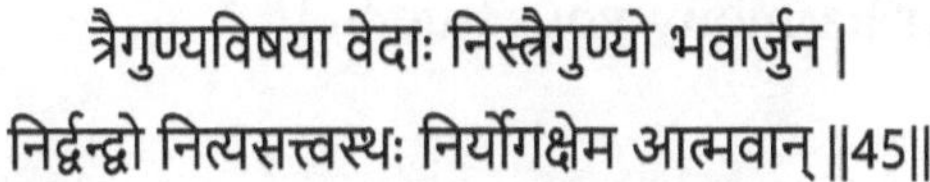

traiguṇyaviṣayā vēdāḥ nistraiguṇyō bhavārjuna |
nirdvandvō nityasattvasthaḥ niryōgakṣēma ātmavān ||45||

Translation:

Oh Arjuna! The Vedas [Karma Kanda] deal with the realm of the three gunas [qualities of nature] (***traiguṇyaviṣayāḥ***). Transcend these three gunas (***nistraiguṇyaḥ***). Be free from the dualities (***dvandvas***) of life, be ever established in sattva [goodness or harmony] (***nityasattvasthaḥ***), free from concerns over acquisition and preservation (***yoga-kṣema***), and be mindful of your true self (***ātma-vān***) [Sankya Yoga: 2.45]

At a Glance: Capturing the Spirit of the Shloka

Much of daily life revolves around material pursuits and sense pleasures. Shift your focus beyond these conventional goals to the recognition of your true identity as *Atma*. It is essential to rise above the constant pull of dualities—such as success and failure, pleasure and pain, gain and loss—and let go of concerns over acquiring or preserving material possessions. You can transcend worldly distractions and move toward deeper spiritual fulfillment by staying grounded in inner harmony your true Self.

Commentary

In this Shloka, Krishna guides us on the qualities and mindset of a true Karma Yogi, offering insight into the personality, thinking patterns, and the ultimate goal of someone genuinely on the path of Yoga. A Karma Yogi transcends the conventional pursuit of material gains and sense pleasures, focusing instead on inner growth and spiritual wisdom. This shift involves maturing beyond traditional religious practices—the rituals and rewards—and engaging in life more reflectively.

The Karma Yogi understands that true fulfillment comes not from accumulating material objects but from inner growth and Self-realization. By shifting focus, the Karma Yogi rises above temporary pleasures and dualities, embracing a more expansive, mindful way of living.

Krishna says, *Traiguṇyaviṣayāḥ vedāḥ,* meaning that much of the knowledge in the material world, including religious scriptures, is centered on material accomplishments. In fields like Computer Science, Biology, or Physics, the focus tends to be on external achievements—health, wealth, and comfort. This also holds true in the realm of religion. The *Karma Kanda* portion of the Vedas and sections of other scriptures often emphasize rituals or practices for attaining worldly success or securing a place in heaven. Many people engage in religious practices primarily for material benefits, treating them as a means to gain promotion, health, job security, family wellness, and ultimately, heaven—what can be described as religious materialism.

Krishna introduces a pivotal point about the dual nature of the Vedas and guides us through maturing from "lower religion" to a higher, more spiritual way of life.

Going Beyond the Gunas: *Nistraiguṇya Bhava*

Krishna says, *Traiguṇyaviṣayāḥ vedāḥ*—the Vedas deal with the three *guṇas* (qualitative texture of mind and intellect) - *Sattva, Rajas,* and *Tamas*, which symbolize the material world and its cycles of pleasure, agitation, and sorrow.

The *guṇas* are the fundamental qualities shaping all experiences in the material world. *Sattva* represents equanimity, purity, and serenity. *Rajas* drives desire and action, often causing restlessness and agitation. Meanwhile, *Tamas* represents inertia and ignorance, leading to confusion or sorrow. The Vedas, particularly the *Karma Kanda,* focus on helping people navigate the material aspects of life influenced by these *guṇas*.

Krishna does not dismiss the Vedas or the pursuit of material gains. He acknowledges that the Vedas prescribe rituals and actions for fulfilling desires, attaining wealth, and securing a place in heaven. However, he urges us not to remain stuck in this lower level of understanding. While worldly responsibilities and desires are important, a higher calling—the spiritual dimension—transcends these material concerns.

Krishna's advice —*Nistraiguṇyo bhavārjuna - to go beyond the gunas* -encourages us not to be compulsively led by these gunas. But how does one do that? Existing gunas are not something we can directly get hold of or change at will. To become *nistraiguṇya,* the first step is to recognize that material achievements—whether driven by *sattva, rajas,* or *tamas*—are temporary and limited. Instead of being overwhelmed by desires, pleasures, or even rituals for heavenly rewards, we must focus on a more enduring and meaningful goal: spiritual growth and Self-realization.

Krishna's message is not about renouncing worldly desires entirely but about not being consumed by them. Just as we may enjoy entertainment or pursue a respectable job, we should understand that these are secondary to the ultimate purpose of life: inner growth and realization of the *Atma*—our true, eternal Self. By setting a higher goal of spiritual realization, we can limit being uncontrollably pulled into lower ways of living by the gunas.

The way to be *nistraigunya* - go beyond the gunas is, primarily, to elevate our priorities. Fix a higher ideal. Rituals for material pleasures have their place, but they should not be the ultimate objective. An undeterred focus on our highest ideal will help us gain control of the otherwise unbridled expression of gunas.

Transcending Dualities: *Nirdvandvo Bhava*

Another way to transcend the gunas is to rise above the pairs of opposites—'*Nirdvandvo Bhava*'. Life will inevitably present dualities: success and failure, joy and sorrow, gain and loss. These experiences are brought about by our past actions, known as *prārabdha karma,* and gunas magnetize accordingly. No matter how much we prioritize spiritual growth, dualities are part of life's cycle. Krishna advises developing mental strength to withstand these fluctuations without losing balance. Consciously choosing how we respond to them.

Just as physical immunity strengthens through exposure to challenges, our mental resilience grows by facing life's difficulties with wisdom. Problems will arise naturally and facing them with equanimity without letting them drain our mental energy is essential. This ability to maintain balance in life's ups and downs is called *nirdvandvata*, a key to preserving mental energy and staying centered.

Cultivating *Sattva*: *Nityasattvastho Bhava*

Krishna encourages us -*Nityasattvastho Bhava to* be established in *Sattva* at all times. *Sattva* represents mental purity and wisdom, giving us the discriminative power to prioritize *dharma* (righteousness) and *moksha* (liberation) over *artha* (wealth) and *kama* (pleasure). This awareness, known as *nitya-anitya vastu viveka,* helps us realize that our ultimate peace and security come from spiritual strength, not material achievements.

To maintain this awareness, we must continually engage with sources of wisdom—whether through sacred texts, wise teachers, or spiritual companionship (*satsanga*). These sources help strengthen our connection to *sattva* and keep us focused on higher spiritual goals.

Freeing Yourself from Anxiety: *Niryogakshema Bhava*

Krishna also asks us to transcend the persistent human worry over *Yoga* (acquisition) and *Kshema* (preservation). Most people expend significant mental energy in securing and preserving what they have. While material possessions are necessary for survival, they should not be our source of ultimate security.

Krishna declares in Chapter 9, Shloka 22:

"Ananyāścintayantō māṁ yē janāḥ paryupāsatē |
tēṣām nityābhiyuktānām yoga-kshemaṁ vahāmyaham ||"

"I take care of the *yoga* and *kshema* of those who, with unwavering focus, worship me."

True strength comes from staying singularly focused on your immutable, indestructible, and eternal aspect—*Atma*, the Self. *Niryogakshema bhava* reminds us not to dissipate our energy worrying about survival but to trust that when we align with our higher Self, the rest will take care of itself.

Be Alert and Deliberate in Life: *Atmavān Bhava*

Krishna concludes by urging Arjuna to be *ātmavān*—to live with awareness and alertness. This means leading a deliberate life, not one swept along by circumstances or societal expectations. Too often, people lead mechanical lives, simply going through the motions of education, career, marriage, and family because "everyone else is doing it." Krishna advises us to avoid this trap and live purposefully, making conscious decisions that align with our higher goals.

Krishna advises staying vigilant and remembering that life's material stages are intermediaries and not the ultimate destination. Let them not distract you from the fundamental goal of spiritual growth and Self-realization. Adi Shankaracharya reiterates, *apramattaḥ bhava*—"Do not be careless."

While stops along a long bus journey for rest and refreshment are essential, they are not the destination. A wise traveler keeps the final goal in mind and does not get so lost at a particular stop as to miss the bus. Similarly, the stages of life—such as secular education, career, and family are necessary but not the ultimate purpose of human life. They are in place to support our journey toward spiritual growth and Self-realization.

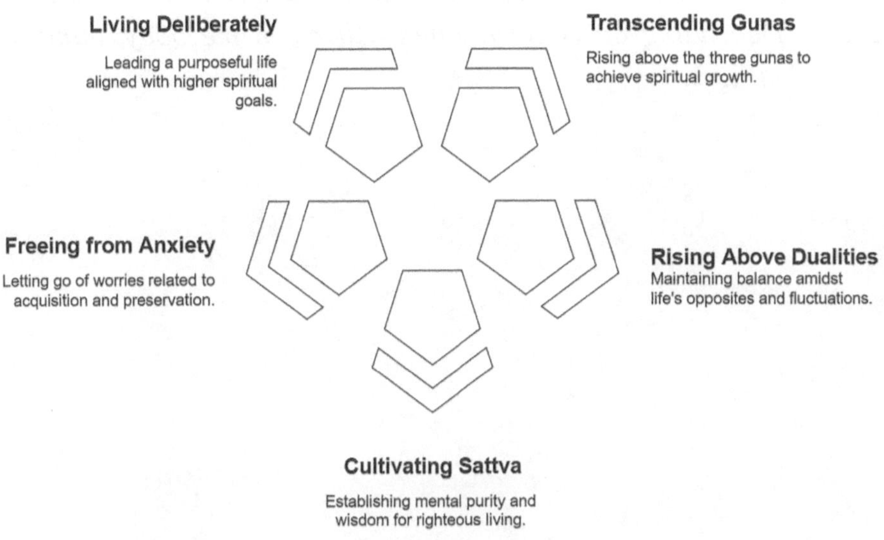

Fig: Path of a Karma Yogi

Beyond Scriptures and Religion

Many approach the Vedas or other scriptures primarily to gain material benefits. However, Krishna emphasizes that the scriptures offer much more than rituals for worldly gains. Once these profound teachings of Vedanta begin to become lived experiences only then will our obsession with the world slowly begin to lessen. If you imbibe and exude the qualities mentioned in just this shloka - having transcended gunas, free from the pairs of opposites, ever-alert, established in *Sattva*, and unconcerned with material acquisitions or protection - think - would you continue to need external guidance? No. You would be free of the crutches of religion itself. In the words of Swami Chinmayananda, *"One who is beyond the gunas has no more use for the Vedas - he is the Master, thereafter, to amend the Vedas or to add to them; he is the Master, who shall give the Divine sanction for the very Vedic declarations."*

Note: *In this verse, Atma (Atmavān Bhava) refers to the mind, not Consciousness. Sanskrit is a context-sensitive language, and the meaning of a word must be interpreted based on its specific usage. Depending on context, Atma can mean the body, mind, or Consciousness.*

Reflective Prompt

Are you living life deliberately, making conscious choices that align with your values and spiritual aspirations? Or are you going through the motions, shaped by societal expectations? How can you bring more awareness to your decisions?

Rise above the fleeting; anchor in the eternal

SHLOKA 46: GOING BEYOND SCRIPTURES

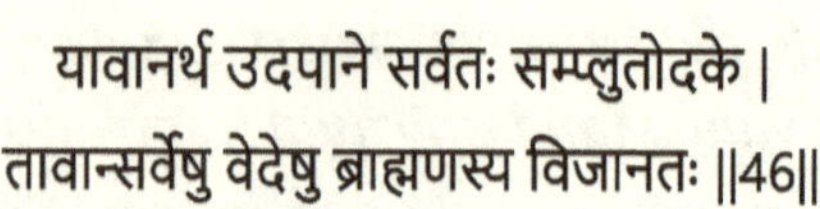

यावानर्थ उदपाने सर्वतः सम्प्लुतोदके |
तावान्सर्वेषु वेदेषु ब्राह्मणस्य विजानतः ||46||

yāvānartha udapānē sarvataḥ samplutōdakē |
tāvānsarvēṣu vēdēṣu brāhmaṇasya vijānataḥ ||46||

Translation:

To the one who has realized the Self (***brāhmaṇasya vijānataḥ***), all the
Vedas (***sarvēṣu vēdēṣu***) are as useful as a small reservoir (***udapānē***)
when there is a flood of water everywhere (***samplutōdakē***)
[Sankya Yoga: 2.46]

At a Glance: Capturing the Spirit of the Shloka

A person who has realized their true identity (*Atma*) experiences a deep, all-encompassing fulfillment that surpasses all worldly pleasures and material gains. While achievements like wealth, status, and relationships offer limited joy, spiritual wisdom and establishment in the Self bring a sense of complete contentment. Such a person no longer depends on external objects or even the guidance of scriptures for their happiness.

Commentary

Krishna encourages seekers to remain undeterred on the path of Karma Yoga despite the challenges and effort involved by citing its ultimate reward in this Shloka. He acknowledges that the disciplined life of a Karma Yogi may seem arduous compared to the carefree life of the uninitiated. However, Krishna explains that the reward—*moksha* (liberation)—is worth every effort. *Moksha*, a state of infinite joy, contentment, and freedom from suffering, far outweighs the temporary pleasures and comforts of worldly life.

Krishna explains that the fulfillment *(ānanda)* gained through spiritual wisdom and liberation is all-encompassing. It surpasses the worldly pleasures of wealth, status, relationships, or material achievements we typically seek. He does not dismiss the happiness that comes from worldly success but points out that such happiness is limited and fleeting.

In contrast, moksha offers infinite satisfaction. By seeking *moksha*, one does not lose the pleasures of the world; instead, with a detached mindset engages more profoundly with them when they appear. Karma Yoga ultimately leads to this infinite joy, where worldly pleasures are naturally included, without the suffering that typically accompanies them.

A Karma Yogi does not miss out on anything. Instead, they attain a state where all worldly joys are enjoyed within the infinite fulfillment of *moksha*. The finite worldly pleasure cannot contain the infinite, but all finite joys are naturally included in the infinite state of *moksha*. This makes the pursuit of Karma Yoga a worthy and profoundly fulfilling endeavor.

Krishna further points out that a sagacious person *(vijānatah)*, one who has understood the nature of life, realizes the fleeting nature of material gains and seeks the lasting fulfillment of *moksha*. The '*brāhmaṇa*' in this Shloka is not defined by caste but by their discernment and wisdom *(vivēka)*. '*Brāhmaṇa*' in this context refers to anyone with spiritual insight and clarity of mind to see beyond surface-level pleasures and strive for the higher goal of Self-realization.

Krishna uses a powerful analogy. He compares worldly pleasures, achievements, and even the benefits of ritualistic practices to a small well of water *(udapānam)*, which offers limited utility, such as drinking water. In contrast, *moksha* is likened to a vast lake or reservoir *(sarvatah samplutōdakē)* that provides the benefits of the well and so much more. Krishna's point is that while the well may fulfill specific needs, a vast reservoir can meet those needs and provide additional benefits—like irrigation, bathing, and sustaining life on a larger scale.

Fig: Vishayananda Vs Atmananada

The message is clear: worldly pursuits, symbolized by the small well, offer finite and temporary pleasures. These pleasures—such as wealth, status, relationships, or success—are fragile, and just as a well can dry up, these sources of happiness can fade or disappear over time. In contrast, *moksha*, symbolized by the vast reservoir, offers infinite and enduring fulfillment that encompasses and surpasses all the limited joys of worldly life.

The infinite joy of *moksha* includes all the finite pleasures and rewards that one can attain through rituals (*kāmya karma*) or material pursuits. By achieving spiritual liberation, a person does not miss out on the temporary pleasures of the world; instead, they gain something far more significant—a sense of inner completeness and peace that makes the pursuit of finite pleasures seem insignificant in comparison. This comparison underscores the explosive power of spiritual wisdom (*Atma jñāna*).

Krishna tells Arjuna that if he genuinely wants lasting happiness and fulfillment, he must seek *moksha,* not merely the temporary pleasures of life. To attain *moksha*, one must practice Karma Yoga— acting in the world with the right attitude and with a focus on inner growth. Like the vast lake, *moksha* provides a state of fulfillment that includes all the world's joys without limitations, making it the highest and most worthwhile pursuit for a wise person.

Through this vivid analogy, Krishna emphasizes the importance of shifting focus from material gain to the pursuit of spiritual liberation, clarifying that while worldly pleasures are not to be rejected, they are ultimately minor and fleeting compared to the infinite joy and peace that come with Self-realization.

When the Scriptures Become Secondary

Krishna dares to say what so few religious leaders do: the ultimate goal is to go beyond all practices, rituals, and even sacred texts to experience the truth directly. Scriptures, though invaluable as guides, are merely a means to an end, not the end itself. The Vedas and all sacred texts illuminate pathways to worldly gains and spiritual wisdom. However, once a seeker attains the knowledge of their true self (*Atma*) as Consciousness, earthly pleasures, and even the scriptures themselves lose their significance.

Scriptural texts are not meant to be clung to forever. Once the knowledge within them culminates into lived wisdom and the truth is realized, the scriptures, which served as roadmaps, are no longer necessary. Just as a roadmap is discarded once one reaches their destination; a spiritually realized person no longer needs the guidance of scriptures to navigate or transcend mortal existence. They have reached a state of *moksha*—freedom and infinite contentment.

The 14ᵗʰ-century teacher Vidyāraṇya expresses this truth beautifully in his Vedantic text, *Pañcadasi*:

"Granthamabhyasya medhāvi jñāna-vijñāna-tatparaḥ;
Palālamiva dhānyārthī tyajet grantham-aśeṣataḥ"

"Like a person searching for rice husks in the paddy to extract the grain, the intelligent seeker studies the scriptures to grasp their essence, then discards the books entirely—just as one discards the husk after taking the grain."

Books are just tools that help us reach the truth. Once the truth is realized, we no longer need books. The focus shifts from erudite scholarship to direct experience. Sri Ramakrishna explained this through the analogy of a letter: when you receive a letter listing the things you need, you do not keep reading the letter over and over. You take the letter, get what you need, and discard it. Similarly, the true purpose of sacred texts is to guide us toward spiritual realization, not to be worshipped endlessly. We have extensively expounded on this misstep by spiritual seekers in our book, ***First Step Into Bhagavad Gita.***

Other religions also echo the same thought. In the Bible, it is said: "The letter killeth, but the spirit giveth life" (2 Corinthians 3:6). This is a reminder that clinging to the literal words of scripture without understanding their deeper spiritual meaning can lead to stagnation, whereas living by the spirit of those teachings leads to growth and freedom.

The same teaching is resounded in Islamic mysticism. Maulana Jalaluddin Rumi, in his *Masnavi*, writes:

Man ze Qurān maghz rā bardāstam;

Ustukhān pese sagāṅ andakḥtam

"I have drawn the marrow from the Qur'an and the dry bones I have thrown to the dogs."

Here, Rumi emphasizes that the essence of spiritual teachings within the marrow truly matters, while the dry bones can be discarded once the marrow (truth) is ingested.

Go beyond the scriptures. They are undoubtedly necessary initiators, but do not become dependent on them. In our book, **First Step Into Bhagavad Gita**, we have dedicated an entire section to this and exhaustively explained how if *shravanam* (listening to and reading the scriptures) is not followed by *mananam* (contemplation) and *nidhidhyasanam* (direct experience through application), the knowledge becomes redundant, and no spiritual progress is achieved. The scriptures serve as a tool to guide us toward Self-realization and should be reverentially used as such. But once that realization occurs, they serve no purpose. For a realized person, this thought will create no conflict, but it is essential for seekers still on the way to understand that they must make an effort to meditate upon and realize the truth within the scriptures rather than being endlessly stuck in them.

Going beyond Scriptures

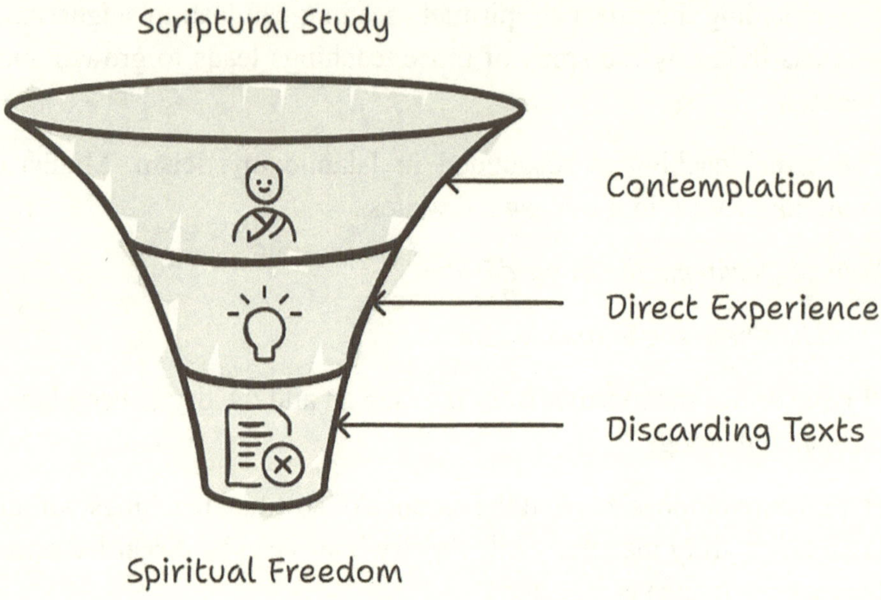

Fig: Going Beyond Scriptures

This profound message reminds us that spiritual growth cannot be achieved by accumulating knowledge, performing rituals, or following dogma. It is achieved only by working toward realizing the truth within and continually living from that place of ever-evolving freedom and joy. Once we attain full realization, we naturally set aside the roadmap and remain anchored in the fullness of that realization forever.

Reflective Prompt

In your personal or professional life, are there 'road maps' or guidelines you depend on too much? How can you transition from reliance on them to mastery over your own path?

*The husk serves the grain—scriptures serve truth,
then fall away*

SHLOKA 47: KARMA YOGA DEMYSTIFIED

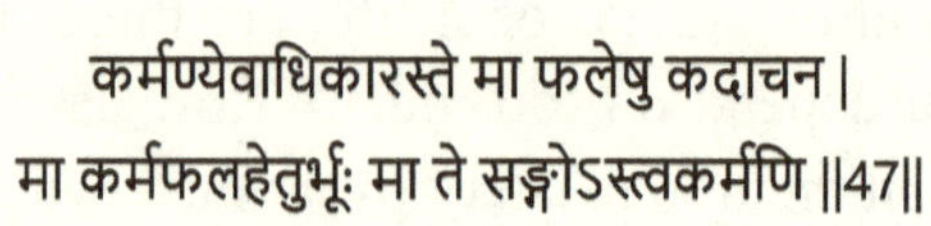

karmaṇyēvādhikārastē mā phalēṣu kadācana |
mā karmaphalahēturbhūḥ mā tē saṅgō 'stvakarmaṇi ||47||

Translation:

Your *(te)* choice (**adhikāraḥ**) is in action (**karmaṇi**) only (**eva**), never (**mā**) in the results (**phalēṣu**) thereof (**kadācana**). Do not think (**mā bhūḥ**) you are the author of the results of action (**karmaphalahetuḥ**). Let your *(te)* attachment (**saṅgaḥ**) not be (**mā astu**) to inaction (**akarmaṇi**) [Sankya Yoga: 2.47]

At a Glance: Capturing the Spirit of the Shloka

You control your actions but not the outcomes. External factors often influence results beyond your control. Not becoming anxious about the results does not mean avoiding action altogether. Instead, focus on performing your duties expertly and release the worry about the outcomes.

Commentary

In this oft-quoted but often misunderstood Shloka, Krishna introduces the fundamental principles of Karma Yoga, which holds immense significance throughout the Bhagavad Gita. A proper understanding of this Shloka is crucial for grasping the essence of the Bhagavad Gita.

While the concept of Karma Yoga exists in Vedic thought, it is Krishna who brings remarkable clarity and expands its scope to encompass every aspect of our lives. His teachings on Karma Yoga are among the most transformative contributions to humanity, offering a practical path that blends worldly pursuits with spiritual growth. For anyone on a spiritual journey, Karma Yoga serves as the starting point. The beauty of this path lies in its ability to help us achieve worldly success while simultaneously advancing spiritually, making it a game-changer in both material and spiritual dimensions of life.

In this Shloka, Krishna presents four foundational principles of Karma Yoga. These principles help us understand our role in performing actions and teach us the art of balancing effort and acceptance.

Principle 1: Your Control in Karma- The Choice of Action and Attitude

The first principle Krishna highlights in this Shloka is *'karmaṇi evā adhikāra te'*—meaning we have the power or choice regarding our actions. The word '*adhikāra*' emphasizes that we have control over the actions we choose and how we perform them.

We might face a difficult decision at work or need to decide how to handle a challenging family situation. In every situation, Krishna reminds us that we can choose which action to take: *Karthum* (to act), *Na Karthum* (not to act), or *Anyathā Karthum* (to act differently).

Apart from deciding to act, this choice comprises how we approach and execute our actions. We can perform our work with total commitment and put in our best effort or go at it with a lackadaisical approach and do it half-heartedly. For instance, you could complete a task at work with a sense of honor and responsibility or rush through it, feeling detached and indifferent. In the end, the attitude you execute it with will make all the difference.

We also have a choice of attitude while performing our actions. Some people go about their duties burdened with negativity - complaining and cursing. Some might perform their tasks indifferently, with minimal engagement or anxiety and fear about the outcome. Others may approach their work with inspiration, doing their best and letting go of unnecessary worry about the results. Consider how much more fulfilling cooking a meal with love and care is than cooking out of obligation and frustration. The same meal can taste tremendously different when prepared with the right attitude.

The first principle of Karma Yoga teaches us that we have control over our actions and the attitude we bring to them. But this is where our control ends.

Principle 2: You Have no Control over the Results, Only the Effort

Krishna explains that the second principle of Karma Yoga is that while we have control over our actions, we have no control over *karma-*

phalam—the outcome. The results of our actions are influenced by many factors beyond our efforts alone. *Mā phaleṣu kadācana states* that we do not have choice or complete control over the outcomes because they are not entirely in our hands.

Outcomes are determined by innumerable unseen, incomprehensible variables in nature. For instance, a farmer can choose when to plow, what crops to plant, what fertilizers to use, and how to care for the field. However, the crop's final yield is not within the farmer's control. Factors the farmer has no control over, such as rainfall, temperature, and other environmental conditions, play a significant role in determining the final harvest.

Similarly, consider someone investing money in the stock market today. They may conduct thorough research and decide to invest $1,000 with the expectation of a 10% return. However, stock market fluctuations lie beyond their jurisdiction. While the investor can control their decision to invest and pick the best possible method, the actual return could be higher, lower, or even a loss, depending on market conditions.

Outcomes are shaped by more than just our effort. Understanding this fact helps us focus on doing our best in the areas where we have influence and leaving the outcomes to cosmic laws that justifiably fashion all our ends.

Principle 3: You Alone Do Not Determine the Result:

In the third principle of Karma Yoga, Krishna cautions – *Mā karmaphalahetuḥ bhūḥ*—"Do not think you alone are the cause of the outcome." This principle explains that while we initiate action (*karma-hetu*), the result (*karma-phala*) is shaped by numerous factors beyond our individual efforts.

An athlete training for the Olympics is singularly focused on their training schedules, diet, and sleep routines. Still, a gold, silver, bronze, or nothing at the end of the competition depends on variables like other competitors' performance, weather conditions, or even chance. Similarly, our actions are critical in any endeavor, but other visible and invisible forces define the final result.

Krishna advises us to approach the results with a balanced attitude-*samatva*. Understanding that success or failure is not entirely in our hands, we must go easy on ourselves in the face of unexpected outcomes. A person working hard for a promotion may not receive it due to office politics or timing. Acknowledging these factors keeps us from succumbing to self-doubt and incapacitating frustration. Instead, we can choose to learn and grow from the experience. This balance between effort and acceptance is a critical lesson in Karma Yoga.

Principle 4: Don't Slip into Half-Hearted Action or Inaction:

Krishna highlights the final principle of avoiding slipping into inaction or performing actions half-heartedly. Understanding that we do not have complete control over results and that our efforts alone do not determine the outcome inadvertently brings into play the human frailty of adopting a fatalistic mindset, believing our efforts are utterly useless. Krishna insists that our actions still carry extraordinary value. Think. Can there be any outcome without initiating action and putting in the necessary effort?

Even though the outcome is influenced by various factors, putting forth our best effort is the only way to create the possibility of success. Inaction, out of hopelessness or fear, guarantees failure. If someone avoids working hard for a promotion because they are convinced that office politics will play against their favor, they have already set themselves up for failure by simply not even trying. The intelligent approach is to put in your best effort in areas of your control and accept whatever result follows.

As Chris Bradford, English author and black belt martial artist best known for his children's fictional series, says, *"There is no failure except in no longer trying."*

Having no control over how things eventually turn out does not make your actions worthless. If you fail to act or act with a lackadaisical attitude, you have lost even before starting. On the other hand, acting with total dedication and not obsessing over outcomes beyond your control opens every possibility of success. Even if the results are contrary to your expectations, the right attitude will give you critical experience for future endeavors and strengthen your character. American inventor Thomas Edison concludes, *"I have not failed; I've just found 10,000 ways that won't work."*

Fig: 4 Principles of Karma Yoga

In this pivotal Shloka of the Bhagavad Gita, Krishna emphasizes the amalgamation of dedicated effort and acceptance of the result. This approach toward all our actions- putting in our best effort and accepting the results with equanimity - is the crux of Karma Yoga.

The bottom line is to Focus on what you can control—your actions. This incorporates selecting the most appropriate action from the possibilities before you and executing those actions to the best of your ability. Once you have done your part, accept the outcome wholeheartedly. Even when the result differs from what you expected, recognize that factors are at play beyond your understanding.

This approach allows us to perform optimally in the world while making the best out of every situation. By cultivating the right mindset, we prevent mental exhaustion and can choose appropriate actions and execute them efficiently. Krishna points out that true success lies not in achieving the desired outcome but in performing actions with excellence and an equanimous attitude. A Karma Yogi needs to master these two skills: **Samatvam**—maintaining balance and calm in success or failure—and **Kushalata**—the skill of wisely choosing and executing the right actions. These points are further elaborated upon in Shlokas 48 and 50. Understanding these concepts is key to grasping the true essence of Karma Yoga.

Principle	Description	Key Takeaway	Example: Cricket Team Member
Control Over Your Actions (*Karmaṇy-eva-adhikāras-te*)	You have control and responsibility over your preparation and effort, but not the outcome.	Focus on your actions and give your best effort with dedication.	A cricket team member can control their practice, fitness, and preparation to perform at their best during the game.
No Complete Control Over Results (*Mā Phaleṣu Kadācana*)	The results of your actions are not completely in your control. They depend on multiple factors.	Let go of attachment to the results and focus on your effort.	The match outcome depends on various factors: the opponent's performance, weather conditions, umpiring decisions, etc.

You Alone Do Not Determine the Results (*Mā Karma-phala-hetur-bhūḥ*)	You alone do not determine the outcome; results are shaped by collective effort and external factors.	Recognize that success or failure depends on teamwork, external conditions, and shared efforts.	A player's performance contributes, but the result depends on the team's collective effort and external conditions like the pitch.
Avoid Inaction or Complacency (*Mā Saṅgaḥ-stv-akarmaṇi*)	Avoid inaction or complacency just because results are uncertain. Act wholeheartedly and responsibly.	Do your role to the best of your ability, irrespective of the result.	A player must still play their role with full effort, such as bowling, batting, or fielding, regardless of whether the team wins.

Table: Four Principles of Karma Yoga

Karma Yoga and Flow for Optimal Living

Karma Yoga, which emphasizes focusing on actions without worrying about results, aligns closely with the modern psychological concept of "flow," described in Mihaly Csikszentmihalyi's book *Flow: The Optimal Experience*.

In both approaches, the key is total immersion in the present task, leading to optimal performance. In flow, individuals are intensely focused and engaged, free from worry about what will be.

According to Neuroscience, flow states occur when the brain's prefrontal cortex activity is reduced, allowing for less self-consciousness and heightened focus. This aligns with Karma Yoga's principle of not being overwhelmed by worries or anxieties about outcomes. Focusing entirely on the present action, without attachment to future results, we can engage deeply in the task, leading to inner satisfaction and optimal performance.

Furthermore, both emphasize emotional resilience - Individuals who can accept results, whether favorable or unfavorable, with a balanced mind, experience less stress, and maintain mental clarity—traits essential for achieving flow and living in alignment with Karma Yoga principles.

Ultimately, Karma Yoga and the state of flow share a common goal: to help individuals reach their highest potential by engaging fully in the present moment, staying attentively with the process, and maintaining equanimity.

Karma Yoga is a combination of two Sanskrit words: *Karma* and *Yoga*. In this context, *Karma* refers to "proper action," while *Yoga* signifies "a proper attitude of the mind." As we go along in our exposition of the subject, we will explain in greater detail what it means to choose the right action and infuse it with the right attitude.

In conclusion, this shloka defines Karma Yoga as performing appropriate actions with a stable, focused, and balanced attitude without obsessing over the outcome.

Reflective Prompt

Think back to an episode in your life where excessive worry over the outcome marred your efforts in the action. In hindsight, did your anxiety influence the outcome in any positive way? What memories do you have about the process itself? How would the action and the outcome have been different if you knew and applied the four principles of Karma Yoga expounded in this shloka?

Master your action, let the result unfold; freedom lies in a steady mind

SHLOKA 48: YOGA DEFINED: *SAMATVAM*

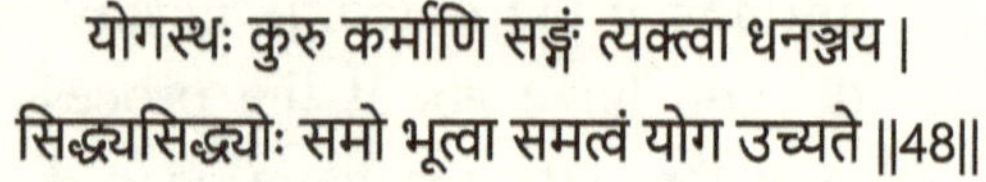

योगस्थः कुरु कर्माणि सङ्गं त्यक्त्वा धनञ्जय ।
सिद्ध्यसिद्ध्योः समो भूत्वा समत्वं योग उच्यते ॥48॥

yōgasthaḥ kuru karmāṇi saṅgaṁ tyaktvā dhanañjaya |
siddhyasiddhyōḥ samō bhūtvā samatvaṁ yōga ucyatē ||48||

Translation:

O Dhananjaya (**Arjuna**), remaining steadfast in yoga (**yogasthaḥ**), perform your actions (**kuru karmāṇi**) by giving up attachment (**saṅgaṁ tyaktvā**) and maintaining an evenness of mind (**samatvam**) in success and failure (**siddhi-asiddhyoḥ**). Equanimity (**samatvam**) of the mind is Yoga (**yoga ucyate**) [Sankya Yoga: 2.48]

At a Glance: Capturing the Spirit of the Shloka

Perform all actions with the right attitude (*Yoga Buddhi*), doing your best while letting go of binding attachment to the results. Cultivating evenness of mind (*samatvam*) in both success and failure converts every action and its consequent result into an opportunity for inner growth. A fundamental aspect of Karma Yoga is maintaining equanimity of mind.

Commentary:

In this Shloka, Krishna's definition of yoga is simple yet profound: An ability to maintain an even state of mind (*samatvam*) through life's ups and downs-success or failures is yoga.

Krishna instructs all of us through Arjuna to perform our actions while being established in yoga (*yogasthah kuru karmāṇi*). This means approaching every action with '*Yoga Buddhi*'—a mindset rooted in balance and detachment. '*Yogastha*' implies cultivating an attitude of even-mindedness (*samatvam*) toward both success (*siddhi*) and failure (*asiddhi*), which is what distinguishes a yogi from ordinary people.

A Karma Yogi's success is measured by their mental balance through all situations rather than visible material achievements. Krishna sums this up beautifully: '*Samatvam yogaḥ ucyate*'—Yoga is the evenness of mind.

The Power of Attitude: Transforming Ordinary Actions into Karma Yoga

Krishna's instruction in this Shloka, '*Yogasthaḥ kuru karmāṇi*' (perform your actions established in Yoga), elucidates that *attitude* is the key to turning ordinary activities, whether cooking, walking, or working, into Karma Yoga. We cannot "do" Karma Yoga physically; we perform *Karma* (action), and the mental approach—our attitude— elevates the Karma into Karma Yoga.

In the West today, there is a strong focus on elevating our mental states and understanding how attitude impacts the quality of our actions. A criminal's actions erupt from one state of mind, while a sage's blossom from another. The mental state from which actions originate determines their impact on us and society.

Yoga-buddhi (yogic intellect) operates from a vantage point where actions are not dictated by likes, dislikes, or personal gain but are guided by *duty* and righteousness. It is an effortless response to do what needs to be done rather than what we desire.

Modern discoveries in neurology validate Krishna's teaching of *yoga-buddhi*. Just as the human body maintains its internal equilibrium (homeostasis), our minds must achieve a similar balance—an "inner homeostasis"—to function optimally. This mental equilibrium allows us to perform actions calmly and effectively [1].

The famous French physiologist **Claude Bernard** emphasized the necessity of a "fixed interior milieu" for freedom. Similarly, **Gray Walter**, a pioneering British neurophysiologist, uses the metaphor of ripples on a calm lake to conclude, "High intellectual development can only occur in a mind that has achieved stabilization [1]."

This state of mental balance—***samatvam***—is crucial for intellectual and spiritual growth. Without it, our mind is like a hurricane, powerful but unharnessed, unable to create anything of lasting value. In spiritual practice, this balance is achieved through *śama* (calming the mind) and ***dama*** (control of the senses). Through constant practice, the mind and senses learn to remain calm and balanced, allowing for a steady focus on actions without being affected by external occurrences.

Swami Vivekananda reminds us that the calm and steady individual produces the most significant amount of work, not the restless and agitated person. When our actions are driven by a stable mind, they are more effective and purposeful, leading to extraordinary personal accomplishments and contributions to society. This calm, focused state of mind, or buddhi established in yoga, is the ideal foundation for all actions and what Krishna encourages us to cultivate.

From Anxiety to Serenity: Embracing Ishvara for Mental Equanimity

While putting our best into every action, detaching from outcomes (*sangam tyaktvā*), and maintaining even-mindedness (*samatvam*) sound simple, they are far from easy to practice in real life. Human nature is deeply conditioned with emotional attachments and helplessly prone to obsessing over results.

The Bhagavad Gita offers a profound solution that can ease us into the state of *samatvam*: incorporating *Ishvara,* the intelligent order of the universe, into our daily actions.

As elaborated upon in our book *First Step Into Bhagavad Gita*, *Ishvara* represents the intelligent order that governs and sustains the universe. Everything follows a natural order, from the movement of stars and planets in the macro-universe to the intricate workings of our own physiology and psychology.

The same intelligent order of the universe that dictates the laws of gravity and the workings of our body extends to the outcomes of our actions. Knowing that forces beyond our control are at play despite our best efforts eases us into accepting consequences that do not align with our expectations. We trust that every outcome has a reason, even if it is unknown to us. We can then detach from the anxiety over the outcomes (*sangam tyaktvā*).

Ishvarapana Bhavana: Offering Actions as Worship

How can we continue to give our best to every action while remaining detached from the outcome? The Bhagavad Gita introduces us to the concept of '*Ishvarapana Bhavana*,' where '*Arpana*' means offering and '*Bhavana*' refers to the mindset or attitude behind it. As in prayer, we make various offerings at our altars; throughout the day, we can transform all our actions—whether cooking, writing, or programming—into a sacred offering to *Ishvara*.

In ritualistic worship we take great care to offer only the choicest fruit or flower to *Ishvara*. Similarly, if we consider all our actions as worshipful offerings, we will naturally strive to offer our absolute best. Our actions effortlessly align with *Dharma* and are performed with the highest care and attention.

Acceptance of Results: Prasada Bhavana

Once we adopt the attitude of offering our actions to *Ishvara*, the next step is to develop the proper attitude toward the results of those actions. This is where *Prasada Bhavana* comes in -accepting the results as *Ishvara's Prasada* or blessing. In Hindu temples, sanctified *Prasada* is distributed amongst the devotees, to acknowledge, as it were, their prayer offerings. They give something – they receive something in return. Just as the temple *Prasada* is accepted gratefully and without judgment, the results of our actions offered to *Ishvara* should be received with the same gratitude.

When we realize that the outcome of any action is determined by *Ishvara*- the natural order of the Cosmos, the result transforms into something sacred. Whether the outcome is less, more than, or precisely what we desired, we accept it with serenity, knowing it has been ordered by divine intelligence. This attitude helps us develop *samatva*—mental equanimity—in all situations.

It is interesting to note that a person who avoids eating nuts in general would never reject nuts given as *Prasada*, knowing they carry the blessings of *Ishvara*. Similarly, when we receive the result of any action with the understanding *Ishvara* is the *karma-phala-dātā* (the giver of the results of actions), we do not criticize or reject it. We accept it with gratitude, knowing it has been ordained by the divine—

this attitude of accepting results as *Prasada* fosters *samatvam*-a calm and balanced mind. When every outcome is seen as *Prasada*, we have nothing to complain about—only lessons to learn and wisdom to gain.

The *Mundaka Upanishad* emphasizes the importance of aligning with the universal order: *"Lose thyself in Him, even as the arrow is lost in the target" (2.2.4)*. This profound teaching reminds us that true peace comes from dissolving our ego-driven desires and resting in the larger framework of divine will. The Bible, too, highlights the great solace found in surrender, "Thy will be done."

Modern scientific research also supports the practice of mindfulness and surrender. Studies in psychology and neuroscience have shown that mindfulness practices—such as meditation and reframing thoughts—can significantly reduce stress and increase emotional resilience. Research in neuroplasticity has demonstrated that the brain can be rewired to cultivate calmness and equanimity through consistent practice. This aligns with the idea of maintaining *samatvam* as the brain learns to disengage from habitual patterns of anxiety and attachment, developing a more balanced and centered approach to life.

Incorporating the understanding of *Ishvara* into our daily lives allows us to align our minds with a broader, cosmic perspective. Over time, this helps reduce worry, anxiety, and emotional turbulence, allowing us to perform actions with clarity and focus, a sense of inner peace, and joyful acceptance of the result.

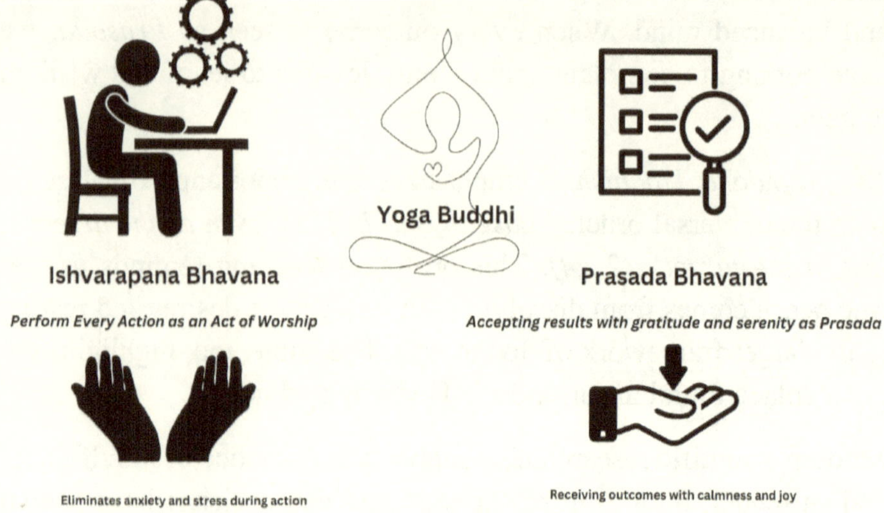

Fig: Yoga Buddhi

Samatvam: A Universal Truth Across Cultures and Scriptures

The principle of *samatvam*—equanimity, or the evenness of mind—has been emphasized as a vital virtue for inner peace and spiritual growth across cultures, religions, and philosophies. From the teachings of ancient Indian texts like the Mahābhārata, Ramayana, and Thirukkural to the insights of Buddhism, Christianity, Islam, Stoicism, and even modern thought, the message remains consistent: true strength lies in the ability to remain tranquil amidst life's challenges.

In the **Mahābhārata**, a poignant story highlights the value of equanimity. A young prince named Sañjaya from the northern Sindh region was defeated in battle and sank into a deep depression, unable to cope with failure. His mother, Vidula, offered him powerful advice: "Don't stay dejected. Success and failure are like waves in the ocean, rising and falling. You must stay above them." She encouraged him to rise with strength and determination, emphasizing the need for mental balance. Her famous words, '*muhūrtam jvalito śreyo na tu* *dhūmāyitam ciram'*—"It is better to burn brightly for a moment than to smolder in the smoke for ages"—remind us that it is better to live with intensity and focus, rather than to be consumed by the ups and downs of life - to maintain balance and resilience in adversity.

In one episode in the Valmiki Ramayana, Lord Rama enters his father, King Dasharatha's chambers before his intended coronation ceremony and is told about his exile instead. Remarkably, he comes out having received that shocking news, adorning the same smiling countenance with which he entered. Rama's unwavering poise in fortune and misfortune reflects the essence of *samatvam*—mental balance and detachment from the fluctuating circumstances of life.

In the following verse from the Ramayana, Lord Rama is seen advising his brother Lakshmana to cultivate equanimity:

'Sarvatra samabuddhiryo lakṣmaṇaḥ sa sukhī naraḥ'
(Ramayana, Ayodhya Kanda 30.7)
"He who remains even minded in all situations, O Lakshmana,
is truly happy."

Kural 629 in the *Thirukkural*, authored by Sage Thiruvalluvar, offers profound insights into the essence of *samatvam*: *"Sorrow and joy, the wise hold alike, neither swayed by delight nor cast down by grief."* The Kural encourages us to maintain emotional balance, treating success and failure as transient experiences. Similarly, *"Bear with all that fate may bring, but never fail in virtue's way,"* found in Kural 621, echoes the principle of *Prasada Bhavana*—to accept outcomes as part of the universal order without getting perturbed.

Verse 83 of the *Dhammapada*, one of the most revered texts in Buddhism, also emphasizes *samatvam*—equanimity—as a vital spiritual virtue: *"The wise remain calm, unshaken by praise or blame. Like a rock, they stand firm in the face of criticism."* It reiterates the even-mindedness needed to navigate success and failure without getting attached to the outcomes.

In Philippians 4:11-13 of the Holy Bible, the Apostle Paul writes, *"I have learned in whatever situation I am to be content. I know how to be brought low, and I know how to abound. In any and every circumstance, I have learned the secret of facing plenty and hunger, abundance and need."* This passage, too, reflects the same spirit of *samatvam* that Krishna speaks of—finding peace and balance in every circumstance without being swayed by external success or failure.

The Quran emphasizes equanimity through the concept of *sabr* (patience and perseverance). Surah Al-Baqarah *2:286* states, *"Allah does not burden a soul beyond that it can bear."* This encourages us to remain steadfast and balanced in all situations, trusting that challenges are a part of divine will and that nothing we cannot handle comes into our lives. These words remind us to maintain mental poise and patience, accepting life's outcomes as part of a larger divine plan.

In his famous work, Meditations, the Roman emperor Marcus Aurelius, a key figure in Stoic philosophy, writes, *"You have power over your mind—not outside events. Realize this, and you will find strength."* a resounding call for mental control and detachment from the oscillating outcomes of success and failure.

The ability to remain mentally balanced in both success and failure, fortune and adversity, reflects the highest form of inner mastery and is taught in one form or another through stories or direct instruction across all spiritual and philosophical traditions. The widely accepted and preached idea of *samatvam* reveals that Yoga is not restricted to any singular scripture or culture but is a timeless and universal approach to living with wisdom, resilience, and peace. By imbibing this quintessential virtue, anyone can transcend the otherwise binding disappointments of life and experience true freedom.

Reflective Prompt

Reflect on a time when, despite your best efforts, you were met with failure. Did it shock and knock you down? Were you able to bounce back soon after for your next task, or did you waste a lot of precious time moaning about the loss? Knowing what you know now, how will you meet the outcomes of your forthcoming actions?

Steady the mind, rise above gain and loss—this is true yoga

SHLOKA 49: WORK WISELY, LIVE FREELY

दूरेण ह्यवरं कर्म बुद्धियोगाद्धनञ्जय ।

बुद्धौ शरणमन्विच्छ कृपणाः फलहेतवः ॥49॥

dūrēṇa hyavaraṁ karma buddhiyōgāddhananñjaya |
buddhau śaraṇamanviccha kṛpaṇāḥ phalahētavaḥ ||49||

Translation:

Actions (***karma***) performed without the attitude of Yoga are far inferior
(***dūrēṇa hy avaraṁ***) to those performed with the mindset of Karma
Yoga (***buddhi-yoga***), O Dhananjaya [Arjuna]. Seek refuge (***śaraṇam
anviccha***) in this buddhi-yoga [yoga of right attitude]. Those who act
solely for the results (***phala-hetavaḥ***), without the wisdom of Yoga
Buddhi, are indeed misers (***kṛpaṇāḥ***) [Sankya Yoga: 2.49]

At a Glance: Capturing the Spirit of the Shloka

Karmas performed with the right attitude (*Yoga Buddhi*) are far superior and beneficial than those performed without it. Karma Yoga accrues material rewards and frees the performer from worries and anxieties over the outcomes. It enhances work efficiency and fosters spiritual growth. Those who perform actions devoid of the spirit of Karma Yoga lose the valuable opportunity for deeper fulfillment and personal transformation.

Commentary

In this Shloka, Krishna addresses Arjuna as *'Dhananjaya'* to highlight that true wealth is not measured by material pursuits in the world but by inner spiritual growth that is required to transform ordinary karma into Karma Yoga. Krishna contrasts the mindset of a materialist (*karmi*) with that of a *Karma Yogi*. A materialist, or *karmi*, focuses solely on material gains, success, and recognition—without valuing inner growth or spiritual progress. For such a person, success brings fleeting elation, while failure can lead to deep frustration or even despair. Such dependency on the results is detrimental, as it leads to a persistent state of anxiety, stress, and emotional turmoil.

Here, *'buddhi-yoga'* refers to Karma Yoga, where the critical difference lies in the mental attitude (*buddhi*) with which the action is carried out. Karma Yoga involves equanimity and surrender, naturally ensuring external results and inner growth. Without this understanding, actions done purely for material gain are considered inferior and limiting.

Not furnishing actions with *Buddhi-Yoga* or the right attitude makes individuals *'kripanāḥ'*- overly attached to results. These misers focus singularly on the material outcomes of their actions. Such a narrow focus deprives them of the inner contentment and mental peace that come from adopting the broader perspective of Karma Yoga.

Furthermore, when actions are performed solely for material results (*phala-hetavah*), the performer becomes trapped in a constant loop of anxiety and dissatisfaction. This is because they measure their success by external outcomes- subject to continuous change and beyond their control. In contrast, led by *Ishvararpana Buddhi*, focusing on the action and accepting the outcome as *Prasada* (grace), the Karma Yogi experiences greater mental clarity and inner peace, regardless of resulting success or failure.

Karma Yoga is superior to ordinary actions because it effortlessly ensures better outcomes and facilitates spiritual growth. By approaching all outcomes with detachment and equanimity, the Karma Yogi reduces anxiety, improves the quality of their work, and fosters personal growth.

Example: A Corporate Professional Seeking Promotion (Expanded)

Picture this scenario: A Director in Corporate America is striving for a promotion to a Vice President (VP) role. How would the mindset and consequent approach of a *Karmi* (materialist) and a Karma Yogi differ in pursuing the same goal?

1. Karmi's Approach: A *Karmi*, or materialist, would focus heavily on the outcome—the VP title, the pay hike, and the associated prestige. They would be overly anxious, work long hours, and find themselves in unhealthy competition with their peers, riddled with envy and fear of failure. Every missed opportunity or negative feedback would create inconsolable disappointment and frustration. For the *Karmi*, because success is defined entirely by getting a promotion, they are on a constant rollercoaster of fiercely oscillating emotions. And if they do not get the promotion - they are devastated and bitter.

2. Karma Yogi's Approach: In contrast, a Karma Yogi works hard for promotion with dedication, integrity, and a focus on giving their best effort (*Yoga Buddhi*). They understand that a promotion is not the sole determinant of their success or worth. They perform their duties diligently, but instead of being consumed by the outcome, they see the promotion as a result that lies beyond their control—one that depends on many factors, including their own eligibility compared to others, the organization's needs, and timing. They accept that if they get the promotion, it is a blessing (*Prasada Bhavana*). They remain calm, readying themselves for the next opportunity if they do not. They recognize that the experience itself contributed to their personal and professional growth.

Because the Karma Yogi is free of the emotional turmoil and distractions of excessive attachment to the result, they can think more clearly, make better decisions, and work more efficiently. Ironically, their detachment enables them to fully engage in the present moment and give their best effort without fearing failure. This makes their overall performance more consistent and improves their chances of getting a promotion in the future.

Aspect	*Karmi* (Materialist)	Karma Yogi
Focus	Solely on external achievements, material gains, and success.	On internal spiritual growth along with external outcomes
Emotional Response	Highly reactive to success and failure, often experiencing anxiety, elation, or despair.	Maintains equanimity (*samatvam*) in success and failure, staying calm and composed.
Mental State	Prone to stress, anxiety, and emotional turmoil due to attachment to outcomes.	Free from worry and anxiety, focused on performing actions with clarity and peace.
Primary Goal	Achieve material success, recognition, and satisfaction.	Achieve inner growth, spiritual progress, and mental peace along with material success.
Result Orientation	Measures success only by external outcomes, such as wealth or status.	Measures success by the effort and the spiritual growth achieved, regardless of external results.

Impact of Failure	Failure can lead to deep frustration, emotional breakdown, or despair.	Views failure as a learning opportunity, accepting outcomes as part of a higher order (*Prasada*).
Motivation	Driven by personal desires, ego, and fear of failure.	Driven by *dharma*, a growth mindset, and a sense of surrender to the universal order (*Ishvara*).
Efficiency	Efficiency is often compromised by worry, stress, and attachment to outcomes.	Higher efficiency due to calm, focused action, free from anxiety and distractions.
Overall Growth	Limited to material success, often missing opportunities for personal or spiritual growth.	Facilitates both external success and internal spiritual development, leading to holistic growth.

Reflective Prompt

Take a closer look at your current pursuits? Are they very materialistically driven with set outcomes in mind? How does this approach affect your overall well-being? Would you consider incorporating the idea of spiritual growth into your goals? What change would this bring to your physical and emotional health?

Effort is yours, the outcome divine; efficiency and peace flow when you align.

Shloka 50: Yoga as Skill in Action

बुद्धियुक्तो जहातीह उभे सुकृतदुष्कृते ।
तस्माद्योगाय युज्यस्व योगः कर्मसु कौशलम् ॥50॥

buddhiyuktō jahātīha ubhē sukṛtaduṣkṛtē |
tasmādyōgāya yujyasva yōgaḥ karmasu kauśalam ||50||

Translation:

A person endowed with wisdom and equanimity (***buddhi-yukta***) transcends both good and bad deeds (***sukṛta and duṣkṛta***). Therefore, commit yourself to Karma Yoga (***tasmādyōgāya yujyasva)***. Yoga is the art of skillful and efficient action (***yōgaḥ karmasu kauśalam***)
[Sankya Yoga: 2.50]

At a Glance: Capturing the Spirit of the Shloka

Ordinary actions (*karma*) create *punya* (merit) and *papa* (demerit). The Karma Yogi transcends these karmic bonds because, through the diligent practice of Karma Yoga, they gradually qualify for *Atma Jnanam* (Self-knowledge). Realization of *Atma* as their true nature culminates in *Moksha* (liberation). Therefore, perform your actions (*karma*) led by *Yoga Buddhi*. Another definition of Yoga is the skill of selecting appropriate actions and executing them efficiently.

Commentary

This shloka underscores the profound outcome of Karma Yoga and contrasts it with desire-prompted actions (*Karma*). The *Karma Yogi* is '*buddhiyuktaḥ*'—endowed with '*Yoga Buddhi*'—the correct understanding. He performs all actions and lives his life with a higher perspective. The *Karma Yogi's* unclouded vision prioritizes spiritual growth over personal preferences and material accomplishments.

Transcending Karma Through the Practice of Karma Yoga

Karma Yoga sets the seeker on the right spiritual path with absolute clarity on life's ultimate goal. They understand that true happiness does not come from finite external achievements but lies within. As a result, they prioritize the spiritual goal of realizing their identity as *Atma* while keeping worldly goals secondary and aligned with this higher pursuit. Through sincere practice, Karma Yoga gradually qualifies the seeker (*Adhikaritvam*) for *Jnana Yoga* to internalize this transcendental knowledge and realize the infinite nature of the Self (*Atma*).

Endowed with *Jnana* (knowledge of the *Atma*), a Karma Yogi realizes that their identity is not tied to the physical or subtle body but is *Atma*—the unchanging Consciousness. This realization frees them from all effects of *karma*, as *karma* and its consequences return to the body, mind, and intellect. As long as one's identity is tied to the body, mind, and intellect, one remains bound by the laws of cause and effect, eternally relegated to the cycles of birth and death. Krishna iterates 'Sukṛta-duṣkṛta jahāti' - the Karma Yogi, identified with the Self, is freed from both merits (*punya*) and demerits (*papa*) because they realize their true nature as *Atma*, beyond all dualities- never the actor, feeler, thinker, or the receiver of any action, feeling, or thought.

Yoga Defined: The Art of Skillful Action

Every action (*karma*) performed without *yoga buddhi* creates karmic impressions (*samskaras*), which shape our future thoughts, desires, and behaviors, compelling us to act similarly again. We find ourselves entrapped in a never-ending cycle of action and reaction, which keeps us bound to the laws of karma- viciously reinforcing desires and attachments and obstructing spiritual liberation.

Karma Yoga slowly shifts our identification from the body, mind, and intellect to the *Atma* (Self). This shift helps cultivate detachment from the ephemeral aspects of our being that act and accrue consequences. We begin to disentangle ourselves from the chains of karmic impressions. Krishna urges us through Arjuna, '*tasmādyōgāya yujyasva*' - commit yourself to Yoga, emphasizing that actions performed in the spirit of Karma Yoga free us of all bondage.

This shloka offers another revolutionary definition of Yoga: '*yōgaḥ karmasu kauśalam*'— Yoga is skill in action. But what does this skill (*kauśalam*) mean? It is often misunderstood as mere technical efficiency in completing tasks. Think. Someone performing harmful actions (e.g., a cyber hacker) is also technically efficient. Does that make this hacker a Karma Yogi? No.

Action is the insignia of life. No one can live without action; everyone is already trying to act as skillfully as possible to achieve success. Shankaracharya explains that the actual *skill* in Karma Yoga lies in transforming binding actions into liberating actions – ordinary everyday karma into *Kama Yoga*. Karma Yoga has never advocated changing any particular actions but changing the attitude with which they are performed.

Just as cobra venom can either kill or heal depending on its usage, action can either bind or liberate. Without the proper intent and attitude, action can lead to stress, anxiety, and endless entanglement in binding desires. But by practicing Karma Yoga—the same actions purify the mind (*chitta-shuddhi*) and lead to *Moksha* – freedom from all sufferings.

Thus, the skill in action (*karmasu kaushalam*) emphasized in this shloka is the ability to convert ordinary actions that would otherwise bind us into a force for liberation. This transformation happens through an ever-evolving ability to choose proper actions (aligned with *Dharma) and* execute them with *Yoga Buddhi (Ishvararpana Bhavana* – every action an offering and *Prasada Bhavana* – every result a rightly-deserved blessing).

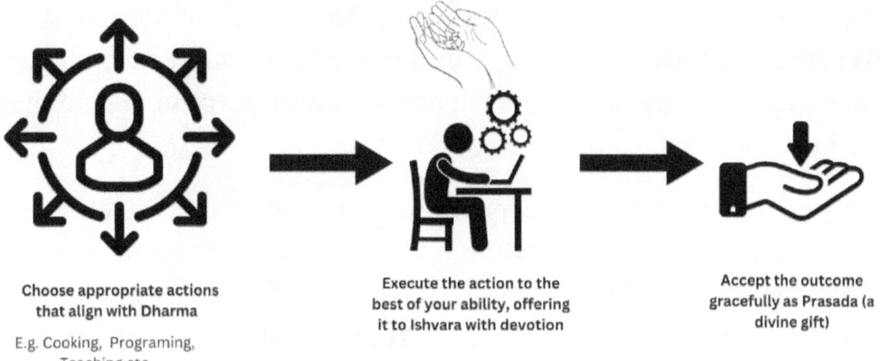

Fig: Skill in Action

Skill in Action: The Dual Efficiency of Outer Success and Inner Peace

'Yōgaḥ karmasu kauśalam' - or understanding Yoga as a skill in action is revolutionary because it allows us to recognize divinity in every area of our lives, not just in places of worship. Most people associate spirituality with certain rituals or religious activities, believing that the path to spiritual growth lies only in prayer, meditation, or visits to holy places. However, Krishna shatters this conventional view by bringing spirituality into the kitchen, the workplace, and every aspect of life. True spirituality is not limited to specific actions or spaces—it is about the attitude with which we approach everything we do.

Let us take the example of a homemaker often engaged in what society might consider routine or mundane tasks, such as cooking, cleaning, and caring for the household. Traditionally, these activities may not be seen as having any spiritual significance. However, in the light of Karma Yoga, these very tasks can become a powerful means of spiritual progress. The homemaker going about their day with *Yoga Buddhi* (the wisdom of Yoga) transforms even the simplest action—like preparing a meal—into a spiritual practice. By performing their duties with care, attention, and an attitude of offering (*Ishvararpana Bhavana*), they free themselves from attachment to the outcome. Whether the meal is praised or criticized, their inner peace remains unaffected because they understand the deeper purpose behind their actions.

This approach not only fosters equanimity of mind and greater peace in and through very demanding household tasks - but also converts every mundane activity into an opportunity for inner growth. The homemaker who practices Karma Yoga is not just preparing food or organizing the home; they are purifying their mind, refining their thoughts, and growing spiritually with each action. This is the dual benefit of Karma Yoga—outer efficiency and inner transformation.

The *Grahasta Ashrama* (life of a householder) is saluted in *Sanatana Dharma* as the most direct pathway to liberation when lived in the spirit of *yōgaḥ karmasu kauśalam*— wherein perfect skill elevates even the most mundane tasks into opportunities for inner growth.

A Timeless Teaching for Modern Life

Modern life exclusively focuses on the endless acquisition and enjoyment of material goals. These shlokas, however, emphasize the importance of inner peace and fulfillment regardless of external circumstances. Karma Yoga's dual approach, covering worldly success and spiritual development, is particularly relevant in today's fast-paced world, where stress and burnout are rampant.

In our book, ***First Step Into Bhagavad Gita,*** we elaborately discuss the role of Bhagavad Gita's teachings in helping us cultivate inner peace and outer success. Is this really a possibility? No. Being endowed with *Buddhi* (intellect) - it becomes our human birthright.

In conclusion, shloka 48 defined yoga as equanimity (*samatvam*) and showed us the path to inner peace. This shloka defined yoga as skill in action (*karmasu kaushalam*), illuminating the path to skillful action. Together these two crucial shlokas of Chapter II give us the template to act dynamically in the world while maintaining perfect inner peace.

Reflective Prompt

Do routine day-to-day activities exasperate you? After studying these revolutionary definitions of Karma Yoga, can you view them as opportunities for cheerful engagement and spiritual growth?

Action with wisdom turns bondage into liberation, turning the ordinary into divine

SHLOKA 51: STAGES OF SPIRITUAL GROWTH

कर्मजं बुद्धियुक्ता हि फलं त्यक्त्वा मनीषिणः |
जन्मबन्धविनिर्मुक्ताः पदं गच्छन्त्यनामयम् ||51||

karmajaṁ buddhiyuktā hi phalaṁ tyaktvā manīṣiṇaḥ |
janmabandhavinirmuktāḥ padaṁ gacchantyanāmayam ||51||

Translation:

The wise, equipped with the right attitude of karma yoga
(**buddhi-yukta**), renouncing attachment to the fruits of actions
(**phalaṁ tyaktvā**), are freed from the bondage of birth (**janma-bandha
vinirmuktāḥ**) and attain (**gacchanti**) the state of liberation (**padaṁ**) free
from all suffering (**anāmayam**)
[Sankya Yoga: 2.51]

At a Glance: Capturing the Spirit of the Shloka

The wise individuals perform their actions with the attitude of Karma Yoga (*Ishvara Arpana Bhava*), offering all actions to the divine and letting go of anxiety or attachment to outcomes (*Prasada Bhava*). They maintain an evenness of mind in success and failure. Over time, the practice of Karma Yoga qualifies them for the highest knowledge (*Jnana*) to realize their identity as the *Atma* (Consciousness), which is beyond the body, mind, and intellect. This realization liberates them from the cycle of *karma* and associated suffering.

Commentary

This shloka outlines the four stages of spiritual growth that a practitioner (*sadhaka*) undergoes before achieving *Moksha* (liberation).

Stage 1: *Buddhi-Yuktaḥ* – Cultivating the Right Attitude

The first stage is to become '*buddhi-yuktaḥ*'—endowed with the right attitude (*yoga buddhi*). Those alien to the path of Karma Yoga often prioritize *artha* (wealth) and *kama* (pleasure) as their primary goals. Affirms Austrian philosopher Viktor Frankl - *"When a man can't find a deep sense of meaning, they distract themselves with pleasure."*

However, as people mature spiritually, they realize *Dharma* (doing what is right) and *Moksha* (liberation) are what human life is about. The Karma Yogi develops discernment (*viveka*) to understand that spiritual progress holds more value than material accomplishments. They know wealth and pleasure are fleeting. Hence, without rejecting material pursuits, they focus primarily on spiritual growth. A Karma Yogi masterfully aligns both material success and spiritual development - keeping an ever-focused eye on the latter.

Stage 2: *Karmajaṁ Phalaṁ Tyaktvā* – Giving Up Attachment to Results

Having imbibed the right attitude, the Karma Yogi progresses to the next stage—performing actions without being overly anxious about the material results (*karmajaṁ phalaṁ tyaktvā*). Krishna reiterates the importance of releasing the binding attachments to the outcomes of one's actions. Please note this does not mean abandoning action or neglecting results but instead adopting an attitude of *Prasada Bhavana*—accepting all results as a *prasada* from Ishvara (the universal order).

Because the Karma Yogi focuses primarily on cultivating equanimity and inner peace, material achievements like wealth, fame, or recognition are seen as secondary. Hence, there is naturally no hankering after any specific results, as every outcome is viewed as an opportunity to learn and grow.

Stage 3: *Manīṣiṇaḥ* – Transition to Jnana Yoga

The active practice of Karma Yoga qualifies the seeker for *Jnana Yoga*, the path of knowledge. Having cultivated the right attitude and relinquished attachment to results, the Karma Yogi becomes a *manīṣiṇaḥ*—a wise person or seeker of higher learning. At this stage, the seeker begins to inquire into the fundamental questions of life: "Who am I? What is this world? What is the ultimate reality?"

The Karma Yogi turns inward, seeking to understand their true nature beyond the body, mind, and intellect -marking the beginning of *Jnana Yoga*, where the focus shifts from material pursuits to the realization of the Self (*Atma*). The intellectual and spiritual growth in this stage helps the practitioner (*sadhaka*) transcend the limitations of worldly life and move closer to Self-realization.

Stage 4: *Anāmayam Padam* – Attaining the Ultimate State of Peace

In the final stage, the practitioner (*sadhaka*) attains ultimate freedom from the bondage of karma (*janma-bandha-vinir-muktāḥ*). As long as one identifies with the body, mind, and intellect, one is driven by karmic impressions (*samskaras*) that shape one's actions and desires. However, once the seeker realizes their true nature as *Atma*—the pure, unchanging Consciousness—they are no longer subjected to the cycle of rebirth.

Through Self-knowledge, the *sadhaka* goes beyond *punya* (merits) and *papa* (demerits), as these dualities only apply to those still caught in the cycle of *karma*. By realizing one's identity as *Atma*, the seeker becomes free from all suffering and the endless loop of death and rebirth. This state is *Anāmayam Padam*—free from all afflictions. In this stage, the individual attains *jivanmukti*—freedom while still alive. Life on earth takes an all-different hue, filled with inner joy and contentment, free from all worries and anxieties.

The seeker discovers happiness within and is no longer affected by the ups and downs of life. They experience a state of unbroken peace that is independent of external circumstances.

Fig: Stages of Spiritual Evolution

In this shloka, Krishna provides a detailed roadmap of spiritual evolution, guiding us from the practice of Karma Yoga to the ultimate realization of the Self. The stages of this journey are transformative, beginning with the development of the right attitude toward life, moving toward relinquishing attachment to the results of actions, and culminating in Self-realization through Jnana Yoga.

The practitioner transcends all forms of bondage, including the cycle of birth and death, and attains liberation (*Moksha*). Through this process, one attains inner joy and peace independent of external circumstances and experiences freedom from all mortal suffering.

Reflective Prompt

Pause to reflect upon how many objects and beings of the world you have chased in the pursuit of happiness. Through your own experiences you realized those pursuits were in vain but did not know where else to look. Knowing what you know now, are you ready to commit to the teachings of the Bhagavad Gita to help you make the U-turn inward?

Karma Yoga purifies, wisdom illuminates, and peace eternally bloom

SHLOKAS 52 & 53: PURIFICATION AND SELF-REALIZATION

यदा ते मोहकलिलं बुद्धिर्व्यतितरिष्यति ।

तदा गन्तासि निर्वेदं श्रोतव्यस्य श्रुतस्य च ॥52॥

श्रुतिविप्रतिपन्ना ते यदा स्थास्यति निश्चला ।

समाधावचला बुद्धिः तदा योगमवाप्स्यसि ॥53॥

yadā tē mōhakalilaṁ buddhirvyatitariṣyati |
tadā gantā'si nirvēdaṁ śrōtavyasya śrutasya ca ||52||
śrutivipratipannā tē yadā sthāsyati niścalā |
samādhāvacalā buddhiḥ tadā yōgamavāpsyasi ||53||

Translation:

When your intellect *(buddhi)* crosses beyond the dense forest of delusion *(mohakalila)*, you will develop dispassion *(nirveda)* toward both what you have heard *(shrutasya)* and what is yet to be heard *(shrotavyasya)* [Sankya Yoga: 2.52]

When your mind/ intellect, which is currently unsettled by conflicting teachings *(śruti-vipratipannā)*, becomes steady *(niścalā)* and firmly established in the Self *(ātma)*, without wavering *(samādhā)* or doubt, then you will attain true Yoga *(yōga)*. [Sankya Yoga: 2.53]

At a Glance: Capturing the Spirit of the Shloka

Karma Yoga purifies the mind by removing confusion and infusing clarity. It enables the practitioner to look beyond temporary material ideals and realize that the ultimate goal of spiritual liberation (*moksha*) offers far greater fulfillment than any short-lived worldly achievements. This shift in understanding shifts one focus from material desires to a more profound sense of peace.

When the mind is distracted by material attractions, it struggles to remain steady or focused on the Self (*Atma*). However, through Karma Yoga, the mind overcomes these distractions, making the intellect steady and resolute. The unobstructed path of *Jnana Yoga* (Self-knowledge) then reveals one's true identity as the *Atma*, leading one from all suffering into the abode of ultimate peace.

Commentary

Shlokas 52 and 53 compress the spiritual path into two essential leaps of spiritual evolution. In Shloka 52, the first significant leap entails the purification of the mind, which leads to a natural state of withdrawal from worldly distractions (*nirveda*) and qualifies the practitioner for *Jnana Yoga*, the path of knowledge. In Shloka 53, Krishna elaborates *that Jnana Yoga* fixes a steadfast intellect in the Self, culminating the seeker's journey in *Moksha* (liberation).

Step 1: Karma Yoga – Purifying the Mind and Preparing for Knowledge

In Shloka 52, Krishna emphasizes the transformative power of Karma Yoga by saying, *'buddhir vyatitariṣyati mōha-kalilam,'* meaning that through the consistent practice of Karma Yoga, with the mind purified and quietened, the intellect crosses over the confusion of delusion (*mōha*).

Mental delusions often stem from misunderstandings about what is truly valuable in life. Before being initiated onto the spiritual path, we mistakenly believe that material success (*Artha*) and sensory pleasures (*Kama*) are the highest goals, while *Moksha* (liberation) seems like a distant or irrelevant concept meant only for renunciates.

Krishna clarifies that *Moksha* is not exclusively reserved for monks or the last option for those who have failed in worldly life. There is no mention of escaping to a forest, wearing special robes, or withdrawing from society. Instead, *Moksha* is about attaining spiritual maturity—an internal state of freedom and peace that anyone can achieve, regardless of their external circumstances. It represents the ultimate goal of Self-realization, where we transcend the limitations and sufferings of worldly life.

As the practitioner (*sadhaka*) progresses in Karma Yoga, they develop *viveka*—discernment or clarity about what truly matters. This understanding begins to clear the *mōha-kalilam*—the "fog" of mental confusion. The practitioner realizes that while material well-being is essential, it is fleeting and cannot provide lasting fulfillment. *Dharma* (doing what is right) and *Moksha* (liberation) become the primary focus, while wealth and pleasure are viewed as secondary pursuits.

Through this shift in thinking, Karma Yoga gradually brings the practitioner to a state of *Prasada Bhavana*—the ability to accept the results of one's actions as gifts from *Ishvara* (the universal order) without being attached to specific outcomes. With this new-found freedom, the practitioner can now clearly distinguish between actions that lead to inner growth and those that provide only temporary satisfaction.

The practitioner then begins confronting their *vasanas*—deep-rooted mental impressions and tendencies. These *vasanas* often create solid likes and dislikes that can influence behavior, sometimes in ways that go against one's better judgment. For example, a diabetic knows that consuming sugar is unhealthy, yet due to an intense craving, they might indulge in sweets, even when it is detrimental to their health. Similarly, greed, anger, or fear may overpower a person's ability to act by *dharma* (righteousness).

Through Karma Yoga, the practitioner gradually overcomes these tendencies by learning to focus on actions without being swayed by emotional impulses. With a clearer mind, they can act aligned with their higher purpose rather than driven by fleeting desires.

With a purified mind, the practitioner naturally develops *nirveda*—dispassion toward material objects and achievements. This does not mean abandoning the world but recognizing the risks of placing too much dependence on external sources of security and happiness. As the practitioner grows in wisdom, they understand that everything in life is impermanent—jobs, wealth, relationships, and even the body. Placing one's sense of fulfillment in these transient things leads to anxiety and fear of loss.

Krishna encourages practitioners to shift their dependence from external sources to *Ishvara* (the divine order) and ultimately to their inner Self. By doing this, they become free from psychological reliance on material objects and the fear accompanying such dependence. This *nirveda* is not about rejecting the world but about finding freedom within it—acting without attachment to outcomes and without relying on external circumstances for peace.

For example, consider a professional striving for promotions, recognition, or financial success. Initially, they may believe that climbing the corporate ladder is the ultimate goal. However, through Karma Yoga—working without attachment to results—they begin to see that no matter how many promotions or raises they receive, true fulfillment does not come from external achievements. They develop a broader perspective, realizing that inner peace and spiritual growth are far more enduring than any material reward. Eventually, they find joy in their work itself, free from anxiety about outcomes.

Step 2: Jnana Yoga – Establishing the Self-Identity with *Atma*

In Shloka 53, Krishna introduces the second leap in spiritual evolution, transitioning from Karma Yoga to Jnana Yoga, which culminates in realizing the *Atma* (Consciousness) as one's identity.

This realization is the ultimate goal for all human beings, as it grants complete freedom from suffering. After the practitioner (*sadhaka*) purifies the mind and overcomes mental delusions through Karma Yoga, they are ready to experience the union with *Atma* through *Jnana Yoga*. In this second step, the mind becomes free from external distractions, making way for the intellect (*Buddhi*) to firmly take root in the awareness of *Atma*.

Krishna explains this transition using the phrase '*śruti-vipratipannā buddhi*'—referring to a mind confused and distracted by the conflicting teachings of scriptures and material desires. We are constantly bombarded with various teachings and promises of happiness from external sources—wealth, status, material comforts, or even the ritualistic portions of the Vedas that offer specific results through religious practices. These conflicting messages confuse us about what is truly valuable, leading to dissatisfaction and inner turmoil.

Krishna urges that the intellect (*buddhi*) overcomes this confusion (*vyatitariṣyati*) to find clarity and focus on the higher purpose of life—Self-realization. The key idea here is that while external objects and material success have their place in life, they cannot provide lasting fulfillment. True happiness within can be experienced only through discovering the *Atma*—an eternal source of joy and peace. The mind, having been purified through Karma Yoga, the practitioner's intellect becomes steady (*sthāsyati niścalā*) and firmly established in the pursuit of Self-knowledge (*Jnana Yoga*).

'*Samādhi,*' which traditionally refers to a state of deep meditative absorption, in this context, signifies something far more profound—

the mind becoming fully absorbed in the realization of the *Atma* (Consciousness), free from distractions, doubts, and confusion.

Shankaracharya, in his commentary, defines '*samādhi*' as "*samyag ādhīyate cittam asmin iti samādhiḥ*" meaning that a state in which the mind is entirely (*samyag*) absorbed and firmly established (*ādhīyate*) in the *Atma*, free from all disturbances. This absorption is not merely a meditative trance but an unwavering state where the intellect (*buddhi*) is firmly rooted in the truth of the *Atma* (Consciousness) as one's identity.

In this state, the practitioner's mind is no longer shaken by external attractions, swayed by the various conflicting teachings of the scriptures or worldly pursuits (*śruti vipratipanna*)- but remains steady (*niścalā*) and resolute (*acalā*), entirely focused on the *Atma*. This is the state of inner clarity and stability, where the mind has withdrawn from all distractions and dissolves into the knowledge of one's true Self.

At this stage, Jnana Yoga goes beyond intellectual understanding to provide a direct experience of one's identity as the *Atma*. The practitioner realizes they are not the body, mind, intellect, or ego but the pure, unchanging Consciousness that pervades all existence. This Self-knowledge leads to liberation (*moksha*), freeing the practitioner from the suffering caused by attachment to the material world and the cycle of birth and death.

Krishna beautifully explains that once the intellect (*Buddhi*) becomes steady and fully established in the knowledge of the *Atma*, the practitioner attains *Yoga*—union with the Self—and experiences freedom from all suffering and lasting peace. This is the final goal of every spiritual practice: freedom from all forms of bondage and realizing one's eternal, peaceful nature.

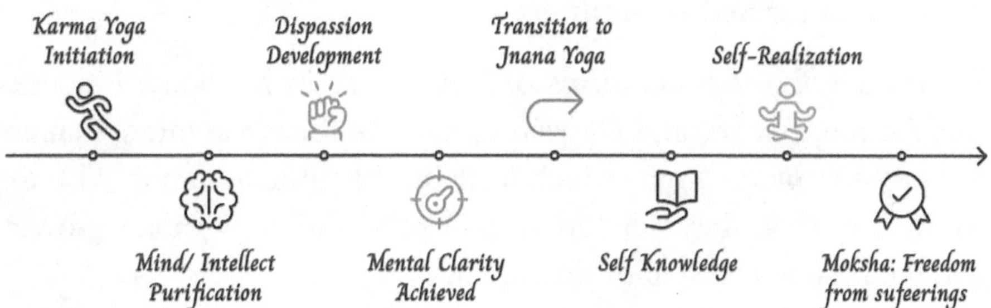

Fig: Journey to Liberation

Yoga Explained: Paths to Mental Equanimity and Spiritual Union

The teachings of the Bhagavad Gita revolve around this central discipline of Yoga in various forms. '*Yoga*' comes from the Sanskrit root '*Yuj,*' which holds different meanings depending on its context. The following two definitions of Yoga help us understand its broader significance:

'***Yujir Yogane***' defines yoga as "union" or "joining." This refers to the union of the individual self, often identified with the body, mind, and intellect, with the *Atma* (pure Consciousness). This form of Yoga focuses on realizing our true identity beyond the physical, mental, and intellectual realms through *Jnana Yoga* (the path of knowledge), wherein the practitioner gains direct Self-knowledge, leading to liberation (*moksha*).

'***Yuj Samadhau***' defines yoga as mental stability or a focused state of mind. This interpretation emphasizes calmness, clarity, and control over the mind. In the Bhagavad Gita, different forms of Yoga—such as

Karma Yoga (the yoga of action), *Bhakti Yoga* (the yoga of devotion), and *Dhyana Yoga* (the yoga of meditation)—serve to cultivate this well-placed, disciplined mental state. While these practices differ in their approaches, their purpose is to purify and stabilize the mind, preparing it for Self-realization.

In essence, the various forms of Yoga work in harmony. Practices like *Karma*, *Bhakti*, and *Dhyana* purify and focus the mind, making it ready for *Jnana Yoga*, which leads to the ultimate union with the *Atma*. Together, they support mental purification, spiritual growth, and the final attainment of liberation.

Three Definitions of Yoga in Chapter 2 (Sankhya Yoga)

In the second chapter of the Bhagavad Gita, Krishna presents three definitions of Yoga, each revealing a different aspect of spiritual practice.

***Samatvam Yoga Uchyate* (2.48):** Yoga is **equanimity**—the balance of mind in success and failure. It emphasizes cultivating an attitude of mental stability and calmness, regardless of external circumstances.

***Yogaḥ Karmasu Kauśalam* (2.50):** defines Yoga as **skill in action**, referring to the ability to perform one's duties with focus and the right attitude.

Both definitions align with the broader definition of Yoga—***Yuj Samadhau*** - a steady and controlled mind as they all point toward the same goal of stabilizing the mind.

Samādhau acalā buddhiḥ* (2.53):** defines Yoga as establishing the intellect in the unwavering realization of the Self (*Atma*). This definition aligns with ***Yujir Yogane - the union of the individual identity with the *Atma*.

These three definitions demonstrate the broader scope of Yoga in the Bhagavad Gita and the need to align each practice with its specific purpose— cultivating mental stability, skillful action, or realizing one's true nature as the *Atma*.

Three Definitions of Yoga in the Second Chapter
of Bhagavad Gita

Maintaining mental equanimity
(*Samatvam Yoga Uchyate [2.48]*)

Skill in Action
(*Yogaḥ Karmasu Kauśalam [2.50]*)

Realizing one's true nature
(*Samādhau acalā buddhiḥ [2.53]*)

Fig: Definition of Yoga

With this shloka, Krishna concludes his brief introduction to Karma Yoga, which began in Shloka 38. Karma Yoga, a critical and central teaching of the Bhagavad Gita, is one that any sincere practitioner can immediately apply in their life. It offers a practical approach to spiritual growth through the purification of the mind and selfless action. While this section lays the foundation for understanding Karma Yoga, Bhagavan Krishna will further elaborate on this concept in the chapters to come.

Chapter III delves deeply into the nature of karma, offering detailed explanations on how actions can be transformed into a spiritual practice. Chapters IV and V continue to clarify the relationship between karma and knowledge, integrating the teachings of Karma Yoga with Jnana Yoga. References to karma appear throughout Chapters VI to XVII, reinforcing its importance, and Krishna revisits

Karma Yoga again in Chapter XVIII, emphasizing its role in the path to liberation. This progression highlights the enduring relevance and importance of Karma Yoga as a key component of spiritual evolution in the Bhagavad Gita.

Students and seekers are encouraged to revisit this core section often, as a solid understanding of these verses is essential to fully grasp the vision and purpose of the revered Bhagavad Gita.

Reflective Prompt

Do you find your mind bombarded with innumerable distractions and conflicting information? Do you find it hard to sit down, close your eyes, breathe, and focus on the transcendental, even for a few moments? Try to pick any one activity that will help draw your attention away from the world and ground it into thoughts of the Divine. A walk in nature, listening to Vedic chants, mindfulness practice, or a hatha yoga session?

Project Self, United Consciousness, and the Gita Odyssey Series offer a range of guided practices to help you with this. Visit our social media platforms to take your first steps toward quietude and reflection.

When the mind is pure and the intellect still, the Atma's light shines with quiet thrill

SHLOKA 54: THE STEADY WISDOM OF THE ENLIGHTENED

अर्जुन उवाच -

स्थितप्रज्ञस्य का भाषा समाधिस्थस्य केशव |

स्थितधी: किं प्रभाषेत किमासीत व्रजेत किम् ||54||

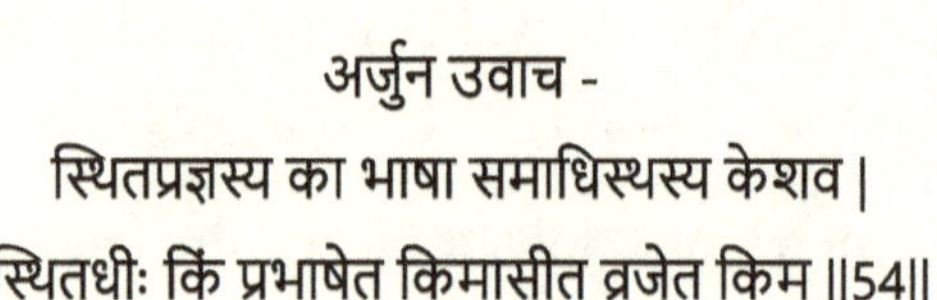

arjuna uvāca -
sthitaprajñasya kā bhāṣā samādhisthasya kēśava |
sthitadhīḥ kiṁ prabhāṣēta kimāsīta vrajēta kim ||54||

Translation:

O Krishna (**Kēśava**), what are the characteristics of a person with firm wisdom (**sthitaprajña**), one who is deeply absorbed in the *Atma* (**samādhistha**)? How (**kim**) does such a person speak (**prabhāṣeta**), sit (**āsīta**), and walk (**vrajeta**)? [**Sankya Yoga: 2.54**]

At a Glance: Capturing the Spirit of the Shloka

Having heard all about his true identity, *Atma*, and being given a path to realize it firsthand, Arjuna now probes into the qualities of a person (*sthitaprajña*) who has fully realized their identity as the *Atma* (Self) and consistently lives with this deep awareness. Arjuna seeks to understand both the internal state and outward expressions of one rooted in wisdom, unaffected by external circumstances, and living in a state of unbroken peace.

Commentary

In Vedic culture, spirituality is not based solely on theory, mysticism, or blind faith. It encourages seekers to understand the tangible benefits of spiritual practices (*sadhana*) and promotes experiential learning. Like any sincere seeker, Arjuna is not interested in the teachings of the Bhagavad Gita just to garner knowledge or for intellectual satisfaction. He wants to know how these teachings will directly influence his life. This desire for immediate impact is especially relevant today, as people view time as a valuable resource and want to know, "What benefit will I gain here and now?"

After hearing about the great and grand qualities of a spiritually evolved human being, Arjuna seeks to know how a person who has successfully completed both stages of spiritual practice—first, preparing his mind through Karma Yoga and then progressing to Self-realization through Jnana Yoga—would experience everyday life. He is trying to understand the qualities of a person who lives in the world with a steady awareness of their true Self. By posing this question directly to Krishna, he is exercising the freedom to question and understand, a hallmark of *Sanatana Dharma,* which boasts a faith rooted in comprehension and personal transformation, not blind acceptance.

This revered and most widely discoursed upon **Sthitaprajna Lakshana** portion of the Bhagavad Gita introduces us to the qualities of an individual who, having realized their true nature as the *Atma,* lives in steadfast awareness. This concluding section of Chapter II, from Shloka 54 to 72, **paints a living portrait of inner strength and spiritual freedom for every sincere seeker**.

Mahatma Gandhi recited these verses daily, regarding the *Sthitaprajna* as the ideal of moral and spiritual stability—a life anchored in truth, self-restraint, and selfless service. Eknath Easwaran, a modern spiritual teacher, described it as *"a profound and practical guide for anyone seeking inner peace and strength, one of the highest ideals in world spirituality—a roadmap to freedom from the storms of daily life."* Paramahansa Yogananda speaks of a peace "beyond understanding" attained by the *Sthitaprajna*. Swami Ranganathananda calls it a *"manual for conquering oneself and the world,"* and Swami Chinmayananda likens it to a "treasure map," guiding us to inner calm, clarity, and unshakable strength.

These reflections inspire every seeker to explore the qualities of this ideal human being of steady wisdom. This section of the Gita perseveres as a timeless guide, lighting the path to wisdom, resilience, peace, and true self-mastery.

Arjuna's Description of the Enlightened

Arjuna refers to a person of steady wisdom using three specific terms—***sthita-prajña***, ***samādhisthaḥ***, and ***sthita-dhīḥ***. Each of these terms captures a unique aspect of the realized state, helping us understand the depth of such a person's knowledge and inner stability.

In his first reference, '*sthita-prajña*'- '*prajña*' means wisdom. Thus, *sthita-prajña* refers to one whose wisdom is unwavering and firmly established. Unlike fleeting or superficial knowledge, this wisdom about the nature of the *Atma* (who am I) is free from doubt, error, or vagueness. For this person, the knowledge of the *Atma* is no longer a theoretical concept; it is a living reality. Being established in steady wisdom implies that such a person does not waver in their awareness of the *Atma,* even in challenging circumstances, which often jostle the unsteady mind. *Sthita-prajña* thus highlights the quality of unshakeable wisdom that remains constant through the ups and downs of life.

In Arjuna's second reference, *samādhisthaḥ* -*samādhi* goes beyond its usual meaning of meditative absorption in this context to imply a state of complete absorption in the knowledge of the *Atma. Samādhisthaḥ* means one who is ever anchored in the *Atma,* or *ātmaniṣṭā*—deeply established in their true nature. Unlike the fleeting peace one might feel during quiet meditation, the *samādhisthaḥ* retains this awareness throughout their daily activities. This person's connection to the *Atma* is never broken or forgotten, even amid life's demands. They have internalized this knowledge so thoroughly that it remains accessible every moment. It keeps them calm and balanced through all interactions. This constant awareness of their true identity enables them to move through life with deep inner peace and self-assurance.

In Arjuna's final reference, *sthita-dhīḥ*, like *sthita-prajña*, emphasizes clarity and conviction in one's knowledge. Here, *dhīḥ* refers to the intellect, and *sthita-dhīḥ* describes a person whose intellect is firm and free of doubt regarding their true identity. For the *sthita-dhīḥ*, the understanding "I am the *Ātma*, not the body-mind-intellect complex" is as clear and indisputable as I am alive. This knowledge is not a belief; it is as clear as holding an object in one's hand (*hasta āmalakavat*) beyond every shadow of a doubt. This person's wisdom is not borrowed from scriptures but is a direct firsthand realization.

Term	Meaning	Explanation
Sthita-prajña	Steady wisdom	Describes one whose wisdom is unwavering and firmly established in the knowledge of the Self.
Samādhisthaḥ	Anchored in the Self	Refers to a person absorbed in the awareness of their true identity as *Atma* in all situations.
Sthita-dhīḥ	Steadfast intellect	Highlights a clear, doubt-free understanding of one's identity as pure Consciousness (*Atma*).

Table: Key Terms in Arjuna's Inquiry

Together, these three terms—*sthita-prajña*, *samādhisthaḥ*, and *sthita-dhīḥ*—paint a comprehensive picture of an enlightened person's state of mind. **This person's wisdom is unwavering (*sthita-prajña*), their awareness is ever-anchored in the *Atma* (*samādhisthaḥ*), and their conviction is unshakeable (*sthita-dhīḥ*).** Arjuna seeks to understand the qualities and behavior of such a person of steady wisdom.

Arjuna's Inquiry into the Inner and Outer Life of the Enlightened

Arjuna's question in this shloka is twofold. It reflects his curiosity about the inner state of the enlightened and how it impacts their behavior in the world. First, he seeks a description of the state of mind of a person of steady wisdom. He seeks an understanding of the inner transformation that defines a truly enlightened being.

In this context, *bhāṣā* means "description," not merely the language spoken. Arjuna wants to know how a person who has attained inner steadiness experiences himself within. Outwardly, the wise may look like anyone else, but inwardly, they are vastly different. Sri Ramakrishna's comparison of people to sweets with varied fillings captures this idea: while appearances may seem similar, the inner essence of each person differs, shaped by wisdom or ignorance.

By seeking this understanding, Arjuna wants to learn how a *sthita-prajna* maintains an unwavering connection to the Self (*Atma*), undisturbed by ego or external distractions. His question seeks a practical glimpse into the clarity, strength, and peace that accompany wisdom.

The second part of Arjuna's question dives into the practical side of enlightenment: how does a realized person interact with the world? For any seeker, the question goes beyond intellectual curiosity—it is a question of lifestyle and perception. How should an enlightened person act? Would they retreat from worldly life or interact with others just like anyone else? These questions cover every aspect of daily living: does enlightenment mean abandoning a regular job, leaving family, or renouncing enjoyment? Will the enlightened laugh at a joke, find joy in a baby's smile, or grieve at a loved one's passing? Are they bereft of human emotions and indifferent to life?

Many expect a *jnani* (enlightened person) to appear and act quite differently from ordinary people. There is a notion that such a person must be serious, somber, and detached to the point of indifference. Some might expect them to speak only of religious matters, never joke, or avoid typical social situations. Others envision a *jnani* as someone who withdraws entirely, even giving up speech and going silent (a *mouni*) -completely disengaged from life.

Like any of us, Arjuna wonders if there will be visible changes in how an enlightened person sits, walks, speaks, or interacts. This line of questioning—*kim prabhāṣeta? kimāsīta? vrajeta kim?*—touches on the visible, outward expression of a jnani's inner peace and understanding. Is there a difference in their interactions with the world? Are their actions noticeably different from everyone else's?

As we will see, Krishna's answer masterfully dismantles these stereotypical images of enlightenment.

Qualities of the Enlightened: A Guide for Seekers

Many may wonder about the value of studying these characteristics of a *sthita-prajna* -an enlightened person, mainly because these qualities seem so surreal - almost impossible to inculcate into our limited mortal selves. Besides, what does an ordinary human so far from Self-realization have to do with the qualities of a realized being? But, these qualities, as you will see, provide incalculable practical guidance for seekers on the spiritual path:

1. Clear Vision of the Goal

Understanding the qualities of an enlightened being offers seekers a clear picture of the goal they are striving toward. Knowing that enlightenment grants profound inner freedom and peace to navigate all aspects of life helps practitioners see that Self-realization is not an abstract or remote ideal for the afterlife but a tangible transformation that impacts daily living. This vision of the end goal reinforces a seeker's commitment to their path, encouraging them to deepen their dedication and appreciate the real-world value of inner growth.

2. Dismantling Misconceptions

Many mistake enlightenment as a state requiring complete withdrawal from the world or a drastic change in outward behavior. Such beliefs presume that a *jnani* (enlightened one) must avoid worldly joys, speak only of scriptures, or remain isolated. When we study the qualities of a man of steady wisdom in this revolutionary text, we will be amazed at how much enlightenment is needed to live and thrive optimally in the world rather than withdraw from it. This knowledge helps dismantle misconceptions and makes pursuing enlightenment more relatable and appealing.

3. A Practical Guide for Self-Reflection

Adi Shankaracharya highlights the practical value of these characteristics for seekers, saying, '*yanani kr̥tārtha-lakṣaṇāni tānyeva sādhanāni upadiśyante yatna-sādhyatvāt'*—**The natural qualities of an enlightened person are the very practices prescribed for seekers, as they require dedicated effort**. The calm stability that comes effortlessly to an enlightened person is the same quality a seeker needs to cultivate through practice. As one progresses on the spiritual path, these characteristics serve as checkpoints, helping the seeker gauge their inner transformation.

Spiritual progress is very subtle; outwardly, a seeker may appear the same, but inwardly, they grow in equanimity, clarity, and compassion. Reflecting on the qualities of a *sthita-prajna* provides seekers with a mirror to assess their own development, guiding them to cultivate those traits until they become second nature.

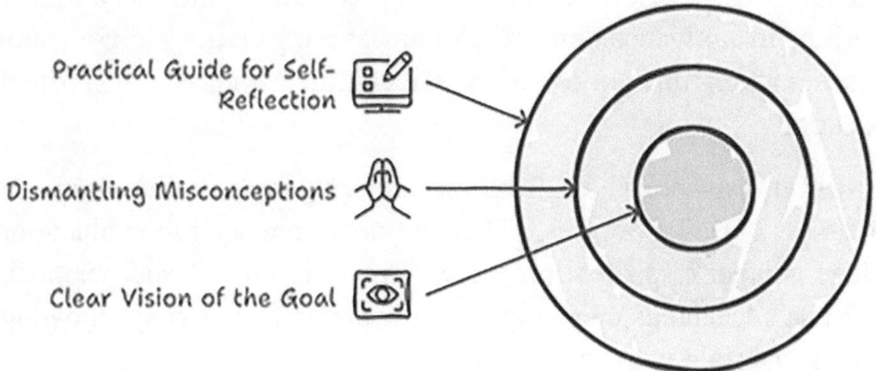

Fig: Qualities of the enlightened: A guiding light for seekers on the path

Insights from Christian Mysticism: Imitation of Christ

The *Imitation of Christ*, a beloved book of Swami Vivekananda, presents profound guidance for seekers aspiring to embody the virtues demonstrated by Jesus. Vivekananda admired this work for its ability to guide individuals in internalizing Christ-like qualities, emphasizing humility, compassion, and unwavering devotion to truth. Much like the Bhagavad Gita, which describes the steady wisdom and inner stability of the enlightened, *The Imitation of*

Christ encourages readers to cultivate these qualities naturally as a way of life. By aligning one's outward actions with inner spiritual virtues, both texts inspire a path where spiritual growth transforms minds and intellects, making these ideals aspirational and lived realities.

Conclusion

Arjuna's question in this shloka opens the way for one of the most profound teachings in any scriptural literature. In the following 18 shlokas, Krishna will describe the qualities of a *sthitaprajna*—one who has attained steady wisdom and lives anchored in the awareness of the Self. These qualities are not exclusive to sages or mystics but can be embodied by anyone who pursues them with sincere effort and practice. These life-transforming teachings guide any seeker aspiring to cultivate an inner life of unwavering clarity, strength, and peace, making this portion of the Gita a timeless classic in spiritual wisdom.

However, a sincere word of caution: exploring these qualities is meant to assess our own progress. They are never intended to evaluate or judge another's spiritual progress. Growth is inward and personal. Krishna's teachings encourage us to focus on our journey, allowing others to unfold in their own time and way.

Reflective Prompt

What are your ideas of enlightenment? Have you ever considered spiritual evolution to be an aid to living a whole and flourishing life? Or did you steer clear, thinking it is a lack of luster life enforcing complete withdrawal?

The enlightened walk a path where truth steadies every step

Shloka 55: Inner Completeness

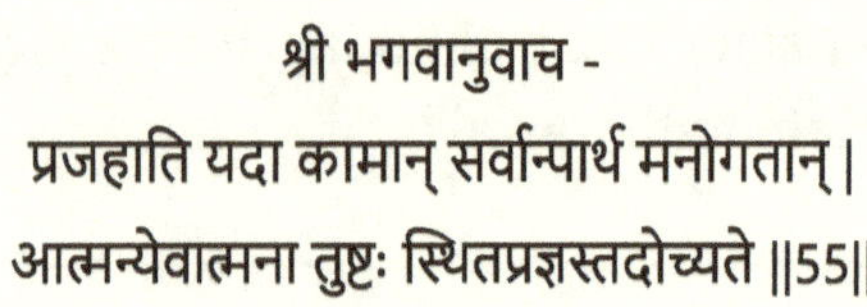

श्री भगवानुवाच -
प्रजहाति यदा कामान् सर्वान्पार्थ मनोगतान् ।
आत्मन्येवात्मना तुष्टः स्थितप्रज्ञस्तदोच्यते ॥55॥

śrī bhagavān uvāca -
prajahāti yadā kāmān sarvānpārtha manōgatān |
ātmanyēvātmanā tuṣṭaḥ sthitaprajñastadōcyatē ||55||

Translation:

Shree Bhagavan Said:

When a person transcends (**prajahāti**) all desires (**sarvān kāmān**) arising
in the mind (**manogatān**) and is fully content within (**ātmanā tuṣṭaḥ**),
by the Self alone (**ātmani eva**), Arjuna (**Pārtha**), that person is said to
(**ucyate**) be one of steady wisdom (**sthitaprajña**). [Sankya Yoga: 2.55]

At a Glance: Capturing the Spirit of the Shloka

An enlightened person finds complete contentment within themselves. Perpetually anchored in profound inner joy and peace, they need nothing outside themselves to be content. This state does not allude to an absence of preferences or natural inclinations but is a liberating experience of a life that is not bound or dependent on external sources of happiness. This self-sufficiency is a hallmark of true freedom.

Commentary

In this shloka, Krishna begins by defining the essence of a *sthita-prajna*, or person of steady wisdom, as **one who finds complete fulfillment within themselves** *(ātmanyevātmanā tuṣṭaḥ)*. Such a person is self-sufficient, drawing their satisfaction from the boundless nature of *Atma*, the true Self. This inner contentment is not due to any possession or circumstance but arises from a deep, unshakeable awareness of one's intrinsic completeness. The phrase *ātmanyevātmanā tuṣṭaḥ* highlights the joy and wholeness that come from one's own essence, independent of external conditions or achievements. Even Jesus Christ describes this freedom reflecting profound spiritual stability as the "peace that surpasses all understanding"—a peace unruffled by worldly upheaval or temporary gain.

In defining the nature of a *sthita-prajna*, Krishna emphasizes that this state of fulfillment does not require physical withdrawal from the world but implies spiritual independence within it. A *sthita-prajna* moves through life with a sense of emotional freedom, liberated from attachment to changing, transient sources of happiness. With inner joy and security as their firm foundation, they experience a self-sustained and unbroken contentment.

Krishna highlights another key trait of the *sthita-prajna*—their **transcendence of desires** *(prajahāti sarvān kāmān)*, signifying that an enlightened person rises above conventional desires. Yet this transcendence is not a suppression of desires or a forced renunciation but a natural transformation in how desires are experienced. Desire is often defined as a strong inclination toward achieving or acquiring something, whether it be material possessions, success, or even emotional fulfillment like love and approval. No matter what we have, that nagging feeling of something missing persists. We rush into the world trying to fill this unfillable void. We do not understand that no amount of outer gratification can appease this unquenchable thirst for wholeness. Besides, desires are binding because we equate happiness and self-worth with their fulfillment. When desires are left unmet, it results in disappointment or even distress

In contrast, a *jñāni* (enlightened person) possesses an inner contentment rooted in the *Paripurnata* or completeness of their union with *Atma*. They are not tormented by the same feeling of insufficiency that we are. They need to chase nothing in the world to feel whole or complete, freeing them entirely from dependency on external acquisitions or enjoyments. For them, inner joy shines like sunlight, while the fleeting satisfaction derived from external achievements appears as insignificant as the glow of an artificial flashlight.

External Fulfillment

Leads to temporary satisfaction and emotional dependence

Inner Fulfillment

Provides lasting peace and emotional freedom

Fig: External Fulfillment Vs Inner Fulfillment

This self-sufficiency allows them to experience life in a non-binding way. They may be engaged in pursuits such as personal well-being, career, family, or social welfare, but their happiness remains independent of whether these pursuits reach their logical ends. *Sarvān manogathān kāmān* clarifies that, although a *sthita-prajna* may still express desires, they are free from emotional dependence on the outcomes. For example, they may prefer peace and wellness, aspire to uplift others, or share knowledge; yet, whether these desires are realized or not, they remain undisturbed. Such *śuddha-kāmāḥ*, or pure desires, reflect an engagement with life that is untainted by attachment.

Adi Shankaracharya further illuminates this by explaining that even divine beings have non-binding desires. *So'kāmayata*—"He desired to become many," in the *Taittiriya Upanishad* describes divine creation as an act of joyous expression, not a necessity. Thus, a *jñāni* acts purposefully but is unaffected by outcomes, maintaining a steady peace regardless of success or failure.

In a parable in the New Testament, Jesus speaks of building one's house on solid rock rather than on shifting sands. "A foolish man built his house on sand, and the rains descended, and the floods came, and the winds blew, and beat upon that house, and it fell, and great was its fall. But a wise man built his house on rock, and the rains descended, and the floods came, and the winds blew, and beat upon that house, and it fell not, because it was founded on a rock."

Similarly, where ordinary humans build their lives upon the sands of fleeting worldly acquisitions and enjoyments only to be repeatedly ripped apart by every passing breeze or tornado, the *sthita-prajna* builds the foundation of their life on the rock of the *Atman*, the eternal Self. They remain unscathed by the inevitable storms of life because their peace is independent of their surroundings.

In Shloka 543 of his scriptural gem *Viveka Chudamani*, Adi Shankaracharya captures this self-sufficiency beautifully:

'Nirdhano'pi sadā tuṣṭo'pyasahāyo mahābalaḥ;
Nityatṛpto'pyabhuñjāno'pyasamaḥ samadarśanaḥ'

"Even if they lack wealth, they are ever joyful; though without support, they are immensely strong; ever content without sensory pleasures, incomparable in inner peace, yet viewing all beings with equal regard."

This shloka entreats that true contentment is not dependent on wealth, status, or material comfort. Such a person's joy springs from within and remains steady, unshaken by external conditions.

Bertrand Russell, a British philosopher and logician, observes, "We are in the middle of a race between human knowledge as to means and human folly as to ends. Unless men increase in wisdom as much as in knowledge, increase of knowledge will be increase of sorrow." We all *know* the ephemeral nature of possessions and circumstances - but it amounts to superficial knowledge that waxes and wanes beyond our control and proves useless when needed most. On the other hand, experiential *wisdom* is the hallmark of the *sthita-prajna*, who remain unbound by anything the world has to offer owing to their total identification with *Atma*.

Modern psychology affirms that true contentment rests within. Martin Seligman, founder of positive psychology, describes *Authentic Happiness* as a state that transcends the pursuit of external pleasures. Seligman argues that true happiness emerges when individuals align with their inner values, live by their strengths, and engage in meaningful pursuits. Similar to the *sthita-prajna* or person of steady wisdom in the Bhagavad Gita, in Seligman's view, authentic happiness is not bound to external accomplishments or material rewards but reflects an inner source of fulfillment. For an enlightened individual, this inner satisfaction, or *tuṣṭi*, is natural and self-sustained, independent of outcomes.

Additionally, Self-Determination Theory (SDT), proposed by psychologists Edward Deci and Richard Ryan, underscores that lasting well-being derives from fulfilling core psychological needs: autonomy, competence, and relatedness. According to SDT, individuals flourish when they align with their true Self, without dependence on external rewards or conditions. This mirrors the concept of non-binding desires in the *sthita-prajna*, where one's actions and preferences are fulfilled from a place of inner freedom, unconditioned by attachment to outcomes.

Krishna's definition of the *sthita-prajna* in this shloka calls us to recognize the true source of our joy and fulfillment. It reveals that ultimate human maturity comes not from clinging to or the fulfilment of fleeting desires but from the steady awareness of our infinite, divine nature.

Reflective Prompt

Is your peace and happiness hugely dependent on external sources—like achievements, relationships, or possessions? How much of an emotional roller coaster does this put you on? Would you like to tune out of this dependency and approach life from a place of fulfillment within yourself rather than the hapless need for validation?

Fulfillment blooms not from the fleeting, but from the infinite within

SHLOKA 56: EMOTIONAL MASTERY

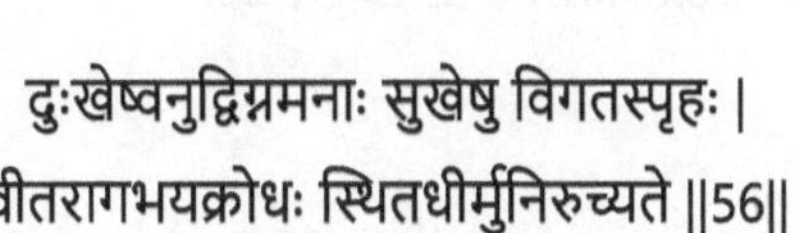

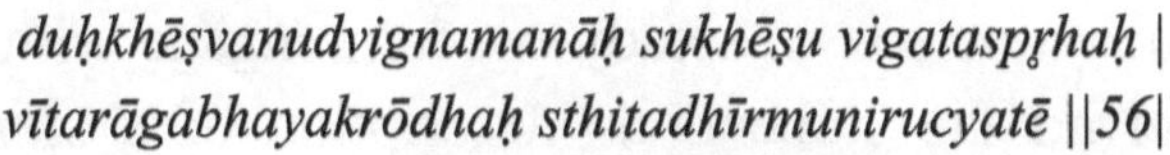

duḥkhēṣvanudvignamanāḥ sukhēṣu vigataspṛhaḥ |
vītarāgabhayakrōdhaḥ sthitadhīrmunirucyatē ||56||

Translation:

One whose mind remains unshaken amidst sorrow (***duḥkheṣu anudvigna-manāḥ***), who is free from longing in times of joy (***sukheṣu vigata-spṛhaḥ***), and who is beyond attachment, fear, and rage (***vīta-rāga-bhaya-krodhaḥ***) is called a sage of firm wisdom (***sthitadhīḥ muniḥ ucyate***) [Sankya Yoga: 2.56]

At a Glance: Capturing the Spirit of the Shloka

A *sthita-prajna,* or person of steady wisdom, embodies proper emotional intelligence and exemplifies self-mastery. They are neither overwhelmed by adversity nor swept away in euphoric joy by success. Common human emotions like attachment, fear, and anger—do not disrupt their mental state or force them into impulsive actions. They remain anchored in a calm and balanced awareness, navigating life's highs and lows with resilience and grace.

Commentary

In this shloka, Krishna answers the second part of Arjuna's question: how does such a person of steady wisdom engage with the world? Having received the stupendous description of a *sthita-prajna's* inner state, understanding how this established wisdom impacts their daily behavior is equally essential for a seeker aspiring to embody these qualities.

In the following verses, Krishna describes how a person of steady wisdom navigates the inevitable vicissitudes of life. A wise person's reactions to pleasure and pain and the texture of their expression of attachment, fear, and anger unerringly reflect their inner state. This exploration is not meant to evaluate or judge others but is a valuable mirror for personal reflection. By understanding the elevated quality of expressions of the wise, a seeker gains insight into the traits to cultivate on their spiritual journey. Krishna's teachings remind us that the characteristics of a *sthita-prajna* are not only the product of wisdom but also the practices that lead one toward it. The dual role of this analysis—as both goal and means—makes these insights invaluable for anyone committed to inner growth and lasting peace.

Pain Without Suffering: Enlightened Person's Response to *duḥkha*

In this shloka, Krishna affirms a basic fact of mortal life: even an enlightened person, a *sthita-prajna*, faces the same unfavorable situations and challenges as anyone else. Enlightenment does not make difficulty and pain disappear from one's life. Contrary to popular belief, attaining wisdom does not turn life into an uninterrupted stream of bliss. The very context of the Bhagavad Gita rests on this premise. Think. Arjuna had Bhagavan Narayana beside him, guiding him – but that did not make his war-bound dilemma disappear. Arjuna still had to face his battle and fight. What made the difference was with Krishna by his side – he fought it with wisdom and fortitude. A glimpse into the lives of saints and sages like Sri Ramakrishna, Ramana Maharishi, or even Sai Baba of Shirdi shows that their paths were often fraught with hardship. Even Divine incarnations like Krishna, Rama, Buddha, Jesus were struck with unthinkable mortal calamity – right through their earthly sojourn, yet their responses set them apart from the ordinary and gave us the blueprint to transcendence.

As explained earlier, the sources of pain and difficulty are threefold (*tapatrya*): *ādhyātmika*, *ādhibhautika*, and *ādhidaivika*. *Ādhyātmika* refers to suffering from one's own body and mind, such as illness or mental anguish. *Ādhibhautika* is the pain caused by the external world—difficult people, challenging circumstances, and even everyday annoyances like bugs and insects. Finally, *ādhidaivika* represents the suffering imposed by natural forces beyond human control, such as earthquakes, floods, or other calamities. '*Duḥkheṣu,*' mentioned in the plural, indicates the persistent and manifold nature of these sources of pain.

An ordinary person becomes overwhelmed when pain is experienced from any of these sources. Physical or emotional discomfort leads to restlessness and frustration. A simple headache can knock someone down for a whole day, adversely impacting everyone around them. Due to preexisting mental disturbances, their mind quite easily becomes *udvigna-manāḥ*—shaken or distressed.

In contrast, Krishna describes the enlightened person as '*anudvigna-manāḥ*' - their mind remains unshaken even amidst sorrow. Like the rest of us, they, too, experience pain, but they do not succumb to suffering. The inner stability of the enlightened acts like a shock absorber that prevents the knocks and shocks of life from disturbing their inner peace. When unfavorable situations arise, they acknowledge the pain and feel it as any human would but do not let it grow into a source of ongoing anxiety or distress. Unlike Arjuna, who collapsed and froze in the face of conflict in the first chapter, a *sthita-prajna* stands firm, anchored in wisdom.

A previously elaborated upon quote attributed to the Buddha, *"Pain is inevitable, suffering is optional,"* perfectly fits this context too. The wise may be hit by all three sources of *duḥkha* (sorrow), but they do not let it disrupt their emotional equilibrium. Their steady awareness and self-mastery transform the pain into an experience - acknowledged but not internalized, keeping their mind clear and composed even amid challenges.

The Parable of the Two Arrows: Wisdom in Action

The Buddha explained: When an individual is struck by an arrow—representing life's unavoidable pains, such as illness, loss, or adversity—there is an immediate physical or emotional impact. This first arrow is an inescapable aspect of human existence that spares neither the sage nor the commoner.

However, the second arrow, symbolizing the suffering we create through our emotional responses to pain, differentiates one person from another. Our responses are directly proportionate to our mental state. Responding from a place of attachment, resistance, anger, or fear magnifies the initial pain tenfold. Krishna's description of a *stitha-pragna* who remains *anudvigna-manāḥ* (unperturbed) illustrates their hold over the second arrow. They cannot dodge the first arrow. However, because they are disidentified with the body-mind-intellect complex and identified with the *Atma* (Self), they are not tormented by suffering.

The Bhagavad Gita provides a step-by-step guide to embodying this enlightened state, where, despite the sting of the first arrow, we, too, know how not to inflict the second arrow upon ourselves. Slowly but surely, we learn how to transform our responses from reactive suffering to peaceful acceptance. We begin to master the art of living without multiplying life's inevitable pains into paralyzing agony.

Neuroscience and Psychology: Insights into Pain and Suffering

Insights from modern neuroscience and psychology align closely with these ancient teachings. Neuropsychology research has revealed that our brain's initial response to pain is automatic and unstoppable. This is the "first arrow" that the Buddha described—our brain signals physical or emotional distress when faced with adversity. However, our subsequent thoughts and interpretations, the "second arrow," convert this pain into prolonged suffering.

Cognitive Behavioral Therapy (CBT) highlights the role of cognitive distortions—negative patterns of thought that contribute to increased emotional distress. For example, when faced with an unfavorable situation, our mind can spiral into catastrophizing—"This is the worst thing ever," or personalizing—"This is all my fault." These self-defeating thought patterns turn momentary pain into ongoing misery, reminding us of the second arrow of the parable.

Neuroscientific studies also show that mindfulness and meditation practices, which cultivate present-moment awareness and non-reactivity, can significantly alter how we process pain. By training the mind to observe discomfort without attachment or judgment, individuals can reduce the activation of brain regions associated with suffering, such as the amygdala, and increase the engagement of the prefrontal cortex, which is responsible for higher-order thinking and emotional regulation. These findings align perfectly with Krishna's description of the *sthita-prajna*—a person who, through Self-knowledge, develops inner strength to remain unshaken by pain and is free from suffering.

The Art of Inner Equanimity: Enlightened Person's Response to Sukha

Just as the wise remain composed amid *'dukha'* (life's challenges), Krishna also describes their poised engagement with *'sukha'* (moments of joy). Most people respond to joy completely uninhibited. The joy of a person receiving much-awaited good news may find them jumping up and down in unbridled excitement. The nature of one's reaction to situations reveals one's dependency on external triggers- makes it extremely easy to distinguish the wise from the 'otherwise.'

'Sukheṣu Vigata-Spṛhaḥ' describes the enlightened one's response to pleasure. Joy could be triggered by various sources- a delicious meal, a hugely successful event, or the hope of a future promotion at work. However, unlike the typical human response driven by longing—"Encore, once more!"—the *stitha-pragna* experiences *sukha* without craving its repetition.

An enlightened person does not suppress joy or deny its experience. They engage wholly with all the delightful experiences that come their way. But, like most of us, they are not tormented by the nagging inner whispers, "When can I experience this again?" They end perception with perception and prevent longing memories of the experience from tormenting the moments that follow. They partake in the fullness of the encounter without permanently hooking their understanding of contentment to it.

Adi Śaṅkara's commentary on this shloka illustrates this dynamic of mind and desires beautifully through the metaphor of fire: A fire blazes more fiercely when twigs are thrown into it. When teased with gasoline, a single spark can erupt into a wild inferno. And so, it is with the mind's longing when fueled by an onslaught of desires. The more one craves and clings to moments of *sukha*, the more the mind becomes consumed by its hunger for pleasure, spiraling into a state of perpetual longing - never satisfied, forever restless.

In contrast, when *sukha* is experienced by the *stitha-pragna*, it dissolves into the fullness of their being, not needing more fuel to sustain itself. Their inner contentment does not rely on any external stimuli. They enjoy pleasure as and when it comes and do not flinch when it departs. Their joy is authentic and not possessive.

For most of us, pleasure is inextricably intertwined with dependence. The excitement of planning a vacation, watching the latest movie, or achieving a career milestone brings happiness, but it frequently comes with an unwritten clause: *"I need more of this to feel fulfilled."* We chase this idea of *sukha* endlessly and in vain. We flit and float from one object, being, place, or circumstance to another, hoping our next find will satiate us. But alas! Bereft of that inner fullness enjoyed by the *stitha-prajna*, our quest has no end. We journey from womb to tomb with this sense of lack.

The wise understand that true contentment lies beyond these temporary states. They, too, enjoy a movie, appreciate the beauty of a landscape, or cherish time with loved ones. Yet, their inner peace does not hinge on these experiences. This self-sufficiency is not a form of detachment that diminishes life's joy but deepens it. They remain fully present at every moment, savoring experiences without needing them to last or repeat.

In his poem *Eternity*, William Blake echoes Krishna's description of the enlightened person's response to *Sukha*:

"He who binds to himself a joy
Does the winged life destroy
He who kisses the joy as it flies
Lives in eternity's sunrise."

Have you ever tried to catch a butterfly? The more you try to get close to it - the more it eludes you. And if you forcefully catch it - you damage its wings and paralyze its flight. Stand still, and it alights upon you. Blake's words remind us that holding on to moments of joy with desperation suffocates their true nature.

Similarly, a *stitha-prajna* does not long for or cling to pleasure. When delight appears, an enlightened one "kisses the joy as it flies," savoring the moment fully and letting it pass naturally, free from the anxiety of wanting it to stay. This act of non-attachment allows them to dwell in a state that Blake beautifully describes as "eternity's sunrise"—a metaphor for abiding in a continuous state of inner peace and contentment that is not dependent on external circumstances.

The Neuroscience of Joyful Detachment

Scientific research on happiness and non-attachment aligns closely with the teachings of the Bhagavad Gita. Modern studies in psychology and neuroscience have explored how non-attachment contributes to greater well-being. Positive psychology research reveals that individuals who practice non-attachment report higher levels of life satisfaction and emotional stability. A 2015 study published in the *Journal of Happiness Studies* found that people who enjoy positive experiences without becoming overly attached to or dependent on them exhibit greater emotional resilience and long-term happiness.

Emotional Intelligence of the Enlightened: Freedom from Attachment, Fear, and Anger

Krishna describes this enlightened being as free from *vīta-rāga-bhaya-krodhaḥ*. They are void of binding attachment (*rāga*), fear (*bhaya*), and anger (*krodha*). These three emotions are powerful enough to disrupt inner peace and societal harmony when left unchecked. Understanding how a *stitha-prajna* processes these emotions can guide seekers on the spiritual path.

Freedom from Attachment (*Rāga*) Freedom from *rāga* (attachment) is an inherent quality of a *stitha-prajna*. Their personal preferences or inclinations do not control or bind them. Unlike an ordinary individual, whose happiness is often tethered to fulfilling desires, the enlightened, already reveling in the wholeness of their true identity - *Atma*, are free from this dependency. Their actions align naturally with *Dharma* (what is right) rather than personal likes or dislikes - always keeping their inner contentment unscathed and intact.

For a *sadhaka* (practitioner), overcoming attachment requires dedicated practice. Most of our actions are driven by personal likes and dislikes, leading to emotional disturbances when outcomes contradict our expectations. However, by aligning actions with *Dharma* and practicing *Karma Yoga,* we can gradually weaken the hold of *rāga*. Another way to overcome *raga* is to develop non-binding desires—preferences that, when fulfilled, bring joy but, when unmet, do not disturb our inner peace. This approach addresses the human frailty of getting inextricably attached to what we like.

For the enlightened, the otherwise overwhelming emotions of *rāga-dveṣa* (attachment and aversion) are "toothless" - holding no power to disturb them. Because they have no inherent need for or dependency on the world, these mortal vices bear no sting, are harmless, and are non-intrusive. The *stitha-prajna* observes and releases them without reaction.

Freedom from Fear (*Bhaya*)

An enlightened person, fully aware of their true nature as eternal Consciousness beyond body, mind, and intellect, is not troubled by fear. An experiential understanding of their immutable, indestructible, and infinite nature as *Atma* armors them with an unshakeable sense of security and fearlessness. They remain calm and composed even in their last moments in the body, knowing that the *Atma* is beyond death.

Vedanta spurns fear as an impediment to moral and spiritual development. Swami Vivekananda famously declared, "Fear is a sin." Children raised with fear as a motivator often grow into adults controlled by it, whether fear of failure, social judgment, or punishment. Vedanta, however, advocates for raising individuals in an environment of fearlessness, nurturing a mindset where truth and integrity flourish without the shadow of fear.

Instinctual fear—like the caution needed to avoid danger—is natural and protective. However, irrational fears stemming from attachment or insecurity can paralyze the mind and inhibit growth. These fears find their roots in sheer ignorance. We often fear what we do not understand. Our best defense is knowledge. We can loosen the grip of fear on our lives by increasing our knowledge base and cultivating trust in the higher Self.

As John Paul Jones, often referred to as the Father of the American Navy, says, *"If fear is cultivated, it will become stronger. If faith is cultivated, it will achieve mastery. We have the right to believe that faith is the stronger emotion because it is positive, whereas fear is negative."*

Mastery Over Anger (*Krodha*)

This shloka finally describes the *stitha-prajna* as free from *krodha* (anger).

At the onset, it is essential to note that anger is not inherently negative in its controlled form. Constructive anger, or righteous indignation, can drive one to address injustice and effect change. However, uncontrolled anger, known as rage, where one loses mastery over one's emotions and actions, is destructive.

For the enlightened, freedom from anger is a natural outcome of being free from attachment and fear. Anger often arises when desires are obstructed or when fear triggers defensive reactions. Because the *sthita-prajna* is not driven by preferential likes and dislikes, anger does not take root in their minds or drive them to impulsive behavior. Instead, they channel intense emotion into positive, conscious responses.

Practitioners seeking mastery over anger must trace its origins back to unfulfilled desire. Anger is a great tool to help us understand where we are attached and weak in life. What in our environment has the power to destabilize us into rash actions. Even if anger does arise, it need not be suppressed but educated and channeled for constructive purposes. Swami Vivekananda described character as "emotion controlled and directed to work." In his book *Character and the Conduct of Life*, Harvard psychologist William McDougall echoes the same thought, advocating for the disciplined management of emotions to build strong character. This means reflecting on episodes of anger, understanding their triggers, and developing the willpower to respond with calmness and clarity.

Muni: The Art of Living with Steady Thoughtfulness

Krishna concludes this shloka with the declaration that a person whose mind is firmly anchored in the awareness of his true identity is a *muni* (sage). The word muni comes from the Sanskrit root "'*mann*'- to think" or to contemplate, putting strong emphasis on deep introspection and contemplation as defining qualities. Thereby, the *muni* is much more than one who practices outer silence; he is representative of deep thoughtfulness and Self-inquiry. The word '*muni*' is elaborated upon in *mananaśīlo muniḥ*, meaning "one who is deeply thoughtful." His knowledge is steady; he is not disturbed by ups and downs- a quality crucial not only for his own spiritual growth but also as an ideal for stability and thoughtful behavior in society.

The *muni* is a beacon of reflective wisdom and balance for humanity, often drowned in unbridled emotions and led to impulsive actions.

Fig: A man of wisdom amidst life's storms, untouched by waves of joy or sorrow, radiating balance and clarity—a timeless portrait of inner mastery.

Practical Insights for the Seeker: Applying the FIR Technique

Developing emotional resilience is crucial for any seeker on the spiritual path. Swami Paramarthananda, an authentic teacher of Advaita Vedanta in Chennai and a disciple of Swami Chinmayananda and Swami Dayananda Saraswati, offers the FIR technique as a structured approach to cultivating this resilience. FIR stands for Frequency, Intensity, and Recovery—three essential markers that help assess and improve emotional responses to life's challenges.

1. **Frequency** refers to how often we become emotionally disturbed by various situations, whether minor inconveniences or significant challenges. The practice involves increasing self-awareness to notice and gradually reduce the occurrences of these emotional upheavals over time.

2. **Intensity** measures how strong or severe the emotional reaction is when it occurs. Initially, even minor issues may trigger intense anger or anxiety. The goal is to practice techniques like deep breathing or pausing before responding to lessen the emotional surge and render reactions more controlled.

3. **Recovery** is the time it takes to return to a state of calm after an emotional disturbance. While an ordinary person might remain upset for days after a negative experience, a *sthita-prajna* recovers almost immediately. One can engage in reflective activities like meditation, journaling, or gratitude practices to shorten the recovery period and restore emotional balance more quickly.

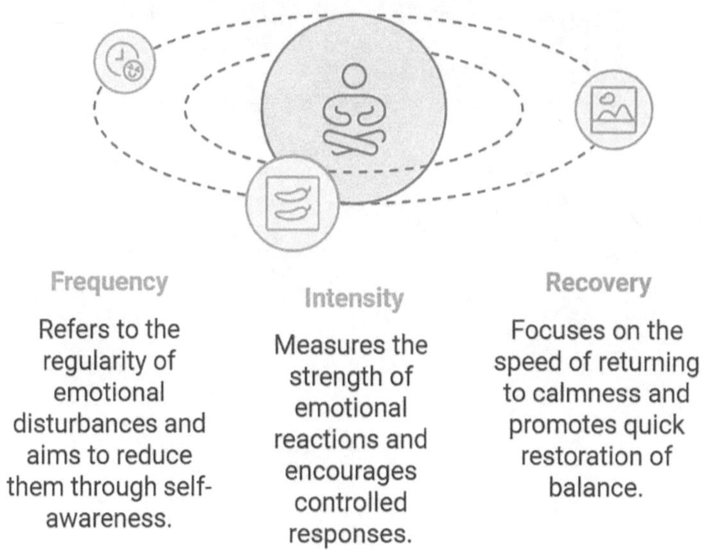

Fig: Tame frequency, soften intensity, and embrace swift recovery

An integrated approach of Karma Yoga and the FIR technique proves very handy for a seeker trying to emulate the qualities of a *stitha-prajna*. This very pragmatic combination fosters gradual transformation, turning emotional reactions into measured, thoughtful responses.

This shloka highlights the power of emotional regulation, and the profound peace experienced from mastering one's inner world. Krishna describes the person of steady wisdom as one who remains unshaken by pleasure (*sukha*) and sorrow (*duḥkha*) - mastering one's emotional landscape through non-attachment, not suppression. The *sthita-prajna* is free from attachment, fear, and anger. And, anchored in the Higher Self, such a person - a *muni* (sage) stands as a beacon of light exemplifying the pinnacle of introspection and contemplation - an eternal guide for all who seek inner mastery.

Reflective Prompt:

How often did you have an emotional outburst in the last 12 months? How intense were your reactions? Did that intensity significantly disrupt your life or the lives of others? How quickly were you able to achieve homeostasis after each episode? Can you commit to working with the FIR technique for 12 months alongside studying the *Stitha-Prajna* section of the Bhagavad Gita?

Emotions ripple, but wisdom remains still—this is the calm of the steady mind.

SHLOKA 57: UNSHAKEN AMID LIFE'S DUALITIES

यः सर्वत्रानभिस्नेहः तत्तत्प्राप्य शुभाशुभम् ।
नाभिनन्दति न द्वेष्टि तस्य प्रज्ञा प्रतिष्ठिता ॥57॥

yaḥ sarvatrānabhisnēhaḥ tattatprāpya śubhāśubham |
nābhinandati na dvēṣṭi tasya prajñā pratiṣṭhitā ||57||

Translation:

One who remains unattached (**anabhisnehaḥ**) to everything everywhere (**sarvatra**), and upon encountering both favorable (**śubha**) and unfavorable (**aśubha**) outcomes, neither rejoices excessively (**na abhinandati)** nor reacts with hatred (**dveṣṭi**)—such a person's wisdom (**prajñā**) is firmly established (**pratiṣṭhitā**). [Sankya Yoga: 2.57]

At a Glance: Capturing the Spirit of the Shloka

A person of true wisdom is free from binding attachment to people, possessions, or situations. This profound state of detachment enables them to approach every praise or criticism, success or setback, with a composed and balanced mind. Such a person neither jumps too high with joy nor shrinks away from aversion. This equanimity - their proportional response to life's highs and lows demonstrates their established wisdom.

Commentary

In this shloka, Krishna describes how a person of steady wisdom engages with the world and people around them. *"Sarvatra Anabhisnehah'* reveals a crucial aspect of enlightened living—being free from binding attachments. *Sneha* in Sanskrit means affection or a sticky substance like oil, symbolizing how attachments can cling to and bind the mind. While affection itself is natural and healthy, when it putrefies itself into *'abhisneha'*—intense, binding attachment—it becomes problematic, leading to emotional dependence and control.

A *sthita-prajna* embodies *'sarvatra anabhisnehah'* by steering relationships with conscious detachment. Unlike the ordinary person, who might cling to loved ones or material possessions as sources of happiness, the *sthita-prajna* loves freely and deeply but remains unattached. This detachment does not imply apathy; rather, it signifies emotional freedom—a state where one enjoys interactions and relationships thoroughly but is not bound by them.

The difference between *sneha* (affection) and *abhisneha* (binding attachment) is subtle but significant. Affection, as seen in a mother's love for her child, is nurturing and essential. However, when this same affection turns into possessiveness and control, it becomes binding. Look around, Investigate. In our world today, so many children that have drifted away from their parents in adulthood are victims of this unfortunate metamorphosis of love into obsessive attachment. This is where most people struggle—letting affection morph into an attachment that hampers their emotional well-being. Krishna highlights that an enlightened person with a heart full of love avoids this pitfall. Their love is whole and undivided, not fragmented across possessions or relationships. They experience love as a generous, non-binding force while remaining ever centered within themselves.

This emotional freedom is vital because wherever the heart is, the mind follows. For most people, the mind chases after numerous attachments scattered across relationships, material objects, or even ambitions. This dispersal leads to anxiety and emotional turmoil. A *sthita-prajna*, however, retains their heart within themselves, ensuring that their mind remains focused and composed. Their love and involvement in life are sincere, yet they are never consumed by longing or dependency.

Krishna continues to delve into the characteristics of the *sthita-prajna* by explaining how they interact with the dualities of life—both the favorable (*subha)* and the unfavorable (*asubha*). He underscores that while an enlightened person encounters praise and criticism, health and illness, or success and failure, their response remains equipoised.

With all its unpredictability, life presents a mix of auspicious and inauspicious events to one and all, sparing none. *"Tattat prāpya subhāsubham'* clarifies what we explained earlier that a *sthita-prajna* does not live in a bubble of perpetual comfort or immunity from hardship. What sets the wise apart is *'nābhinandati na dveṣṭi'*—they neither over-celebrate in moments of joy nor are overly disturbed in times of distress. This equanimity reflects *samatvam*, the inner poise Krishna has consistently emphasized. It is not that the wise are indifferent or emotionless; they do not become captive to emotional highs and lows. While most people feverishly cling to joy and resist pain, a *sthita-prajna* approaches both with equanimity, recognizing that both *subha* and *asubha* are transient.

Fig: Equanimity of Sthitaprajna

For an ordinary person, moments of success and praise can inflate the ego, leading to a temporary sense of joy quickly followed by the fear of losing that high. Similarly, setbacks and criticism can trigger a spiral of distress and resentment. This constant oscillation between elation and depression mirrors the volatile nature of the stock market, where highs are celebrated, and lows cause panic. In contrast, the *sthita-prajna* is grounded and composed because their inner well-being is not tied to external events. They possess what Śaṅkara refers to as *ātma-anātma-viveka*—the discernment between the real and the unreal. This knowledge enables them to remain calm amidst life's ephemeral uncertainties

This unwavering peace may seem like an unattainable ideal, but our commitment to this study will posit these surreal qualities as a goal and a practice. For those on the path, this equanimity is cultivated through the practice of *Karma Yoga* infused with *Prasada Bhavana*-accepting all outcomes as sacred blessings for our actions performed as divine offerings.

Intelligent Response Over Reaction: The Balance of Wisdom

This shloka highlights the balanced response of a *sthita-prajna* through all of life's glaring vicissitudes. A common misconception is that maintaining equanimity means passively accepting everything, leading to being perceived as weak or a "doormat." Vedanta clarifies that this is not the case.

A *sthita-prajna* avoids two extremes: impulsive reaction and passive inaction. Impulsive reactions may seem effective in the immediate moment but lead to long-term emotional and physical strain, like taking a powerful drug with severe side effects. On the other hand, passive surrender, born of weakness, allows injustice to continue unchecked and breeds helplessness.

Vedanta advocates for thoughtful, intelligent action. This involves pausing to assess whether a situation is choiceless (beyond change) or can be influenced. In choiceless situations, the wise focus on strengthening their mind and acceptance. When change is possible, they respond with discernment, using strategies such as persuasion (*sāma*), negotiation (*dāna*), strategic intervention (*bhēda*), or decisive action (*daṇḍa*).

This balanced approach distinguishes the enlightened from ordinary people: they act not on impulse but with clarity, knowing when to retreat and when to take firm, conscious action. Krishna's guidance to the *Pandavas* during the Mahabharata war embodies this wisdom, showing that true strength lies in deliberate, mindful responses.

Grace Under Praise and Persecution: Lessons from Christ

Two moments from Jesus Christ's life vividly illustrate the essence of Shloka 57: *nābhinandati na dveṣṭi*—the ability to remain steadfast in praise and suffering:

One notable instance was His triumphant entry into Jerusalem, where crowds gathered to chant "Hosanna" and praise Him, laying down palm leaves as He passed through the streets. It was a grand celebration, with people treating Him like a king. Yet, despite this overwhelming adulation, Jesus remained composed, accepting the honors without letting them inflate His sense of Self.

Contrasting this scene is the account of Christ's arrest and suffering. Jesus was dragged through the streets, mocked, and treated as a common criminal, facing intense humiliation and physical torment. Despite the stark change in circumstances—from exaltation to condemnation—He exuded the same unwavering calm and control. He did not succumb to anger, resentment, or despair but maintained His grace and compassion, even forgiving those who persecuted Him, saying, *"Father, forgive them, for they do not know what they are doing."*

Jesus demonstrated that true wisdom and spiritual maturity are marked by inner stability transcending external circumstances. He exemplified how a *stitha-prajna* interacts with the world without being swayed by the dualities of life. His equanimous response to adoration and unjust blame displays the natural expression of an enlightened being.

Reflective Prompt

How do you react to praise and criticism? Is your sense of self dependent on and impacted by positive validation or negative feedback from those around you? How can you cultivate inner stability and confidence that will hold you unaffected by these external factors?

Rooted in wisdom, free from extremes, life's waves touch not the steady mind

SHLOKA 58: THE WISDOM OF WITHDRAWAL

यदा संहरते चायं कूर्मोऽङ्गानीव सर्वशः |
इन्द्रियाणीन्द्रियार्थेभ्यः तस्य प्रज्ञा प्रतिष्ठिता ||58||

yadā saṁharatē cāyaṁ kūrmō'ṅgānīva sarvaśaḥ |
indriyāṇīndriyārthēbhyaḥ tasya prajñā pratiṣṭhitā ||58||

Translation:

When a person can withdraw his/her senses (***indriyāṇi***) from the objects of the senses (***indriyārthēbhyaḥ***), just as a tortoise (***kūrmaḥ***) withdraws its limbs (***aṅgāni***) completely, then that person's wisdom (***prajñā***) is firmly established (***pratiṣṭhitā***) [Sankya Yoga: 2.58]

At a Glance: Capturing the Spirit of the Shloka

A wise person demonstrates complete mastery over their senses and mind. Just as a tortoise instinctively withdraws its limbs for protection, a person with steady wisdom can fully retract their attention and engagement from the sensory world when needed. This does not mean detachment from life but signifies the freedom to act with discernment, participating in the world without being dominated by external influences. Such self-regulation is a mark of true inner strength and control, allowing one to remain unshaken and deeply anchored in wisdom regardless of external circumstances.

Commentary

In this shloka, Krishna answers Arjuna's question on how a person of steady wisdom interacts with the world around them. Krishna uses the brilliant metaphor of a tortoise to highlight the *sthita-prajna's* control over the senses. This shloka offers a practical insight into stable wisdom's ability to withdraw senses at will and keep the *muni* (sage) wholly centered amid life's myriad pulls.

Have you watched a tortoise leave the water and walk around on the ground? It is a fascinating remarkable sight. It flaunts a slow but sure-footed stride but instinctively retracts its limbs—head, legs, and tail—into its impenetrable shell at the slightest sign of danger, ensuring total retraction and protection from all sides (*'sarvaśaḥ'*). Similarly, the wise person (*'sthita-prajna'*) interacts freely and confidently with the world but demonstrates the ability to pull their senses (sight, hearing, smell, taste, and touch) and mind (sixth sense) away from external objects at will (*'indriyāṇīndriyārthēbhyaḥ'*).

This does not imply a physical withdrawal, such as closing one's eyes or shutting one's ears. It symbolizes a mental equilibrium that is not open to affectation by external objects and experiences. Most people are so heavily dependent on possessions, relationships, and achievements that the slightest upheaval in these areas disturbs their sense of self. This leads to emotional highs and lows, leaving them unguarded and vulnerable to the ever-changing nature of life.

In contrast, the wise person's withdrawal signifies a state of inner contentment independent of external circumstances. They do not need constant pleasure or validation from the outside world to feel fulfilled. Their intellect, always rooted in the Reality of *Atma*, is agile enough to sense areas of weakness and withdraw engagement at will to not get carried away by the *dvandvas* (opposites) that incapacitate most.

While the tortoise withdraws for physical safety, the wise person's withdrawal is an intellectual and spiritual act. It portrays the ability to engage with the world while remaining unattached. This detachment does not imply indifference; instead, it means participating in life without being controlled by desires or external influences. The enlightened individual continues to love, interact with others, and engage in worldly activities but from a place of inner freedom and self-mastery.

The metaphor of the tortoise finding safety within its shell illustrates retreat into the protection of the knowledge of Self. The wise person, rooted in the awareness of the *Atma* (Self), does not succumb to outer disturbances. This self-awareness ensures they do not need to disengage from the world to evade trial and temptation; they can effortlessly pull back their senses and mind into their reigning identity with *Atma* when danger lurks. For the enlightened, external events do not pose a threat. Whether faced with praise or criticism, gain or loss, they remain composed. Their sense of joy and peace comes from within, making them immune to life's external tumult.

Krishna's metaphor underscores that true wisdom (*'prajna'*) is measured by one's non-reliance on the external world for emotional or psychological fulfillment. Just as the tortoise withdraws for protection, when necessary, the wise person draws inward to maintain inner stability without physically isolating themselves. This mastery indicates that their wisdom is firm and established (*'pratiṣṭhitā'*) -

stable and unshaken. It enables them to face life with joy, freedom, and unwavering equanimity.

Applying Krishna's Wisdom in day-to-day life

The control of the senses and mind comes naturally to the *stitha-prajna*. However, as discussed earlier, the description of their qualities can be used as a practical guide by seekers. Understanding how to "practice" these qualities can make the goal more tangible and the journey to it more feasible.

Consider the example of a student aspiring to ace a critical exam. To succeed, they must commit to a clearly mapped-out study plan. But as often happens, they are bombarded with distractions from all sides—friends invite them to social gatherings, a new Netflix series with a raving review tugs at their heart, late nights from endless online scrolling followed by groggy mornings leave them fatigued, and unmotivated - the list goes on. These external temptations serenade their mind to the point of completely disrupting their commitment and focus. How do you think this saga ends? Most certainly in abject disappointment over abysmal performance on what was meant to be a life-defining exam.

Fig: Mastery over sense organs

Just as the tortoise withdraws its limbs, tail, and head into its shell at the threat of danger, the student must learn to withdraw their senses and mind from these distractions and redirect their energy inward to stay centered on their goal. This does not mean isolating themselves completely or avoiding all interactions, but it signifies having the inner strength to prioritize their purpose over fleeting pleasures.

Withdrawal of the senses is a slow and steady conscious practice of self-control that can be mastered over time. What facilitates the process is fixing a solid ideal for oneself - material or spiritual. Uptake of the proper knowledge helps fortify the resolve to stay fixated on that ideal. In the case of the student, clearly understanding the benefits of taking the exam and the sorry repercussions of not studying well will keep them on track. Like-minded people (*satsangha*) who are headed in the same direction play a massive role in developing self-mastery. Over time, this ability to withdraw the senses and mind at will and focus on the task becomes an ingrained quality, enabling them to combat the din of distractions with calm determination.

Practicing this withdrawal of the senses and mind is an absolute prerequisite for someone on the spiritual path. If the mind gets sucked into every temptation that comes up - it is impossible to progress on the inward journey to Self. Every distraction you succumb to only entraps you further into the world and away from *Atma*. "Live, Love, Laugh," as they say, yes, but never let the impermanent objects and beings of the world distract you from the permanent abode of *Atma* - the bliss of the eternal Self. The more you practice, the more centered you learn to remain, and that centeredness is what makes all the difference in your ability to enjoy your life and eventually transcend it.

Reflective Prompt

Think back to a time when silly distractions got the better of you and took you away from a crucial goal you had set for yourself. How did it make you feel in hindsight? How would you tackle similar distractions in the future?

Play in the world but learn to withdraw inward at will. The vagaries of the world cannot touch the one who rests within.

SHLOKA 59: FROM SUPPRESSION TO LIBERATION

विषया विनिवर्तन्ते निराहारस्य देहिनः |
रसवर्जं रसोऽप्यस्य परं दृष्ट्वा निवर्तते ||59||

viṣayā vinivartantē nirāhārasya dēhinaḥ |
rasavarjaṁ rasō'pyasya paraṁ dṛṣṭvā nivartatē ||59||

Translation:

The sense objects fall away for one who abstains from them (***nirāhārasya dēhinaḥ***), yet the taste or subtle attachment (***rasa***) to them remains. However, even this attachment fades when one experiences the supreme (***paraṁ dṛṣṭvā***) [Sankya Yoga: 2.59]

At a Glance: Capturing the Spirit of the Shloka

One may physically remove themselves from the lure of sense objects, but the underlying desire or subtle craving for them often remains. Cravings are dismantled only when one becomes intensely aware of the Self (*Atma*) within. Experiencing the profound joy of Self-realization dissolves the pull of external pleasures, as the greater satisfaction within surpasses all external attractions.

"I once had a thousand desires. But in my one desire to know You, all else melted away." - Rumi

Commentary

"Is the mere capacity to withdraw the senses and mind from external objects, like a tortoise withdraws its limbs, enough to establish one in true wisdom (*jñāna-niṣṭhā*)?" is a common question that arises in the seeker's mind.

This understanding is crucial for all seekers: physically restraining the senses from sense objects is not enough. And in fact, it can prove detrimental eventually. People may forcefully distance themselves from sense objects but will be highly frustrated and agitated if the inner craving remains. Imagine someone who abstains from indulgences externally yet internally yearns for them—this is akin to suppression, a temporary hold that can eventually lead to frustration or even emotional outbursts. Such suppression, Krishna warns, only aggravates the problem, as the cravings still reside within. And anything forced is not sustainable. At the most inopportune moment, faced with the objects of their desire, there is a strong possibility of unbridled re-engagement due to severe repression.

The term *rasa* conveys the subtle allure or "taste" for sense objects that often lingers even after one has renounced their outward pursuit. It goes beyond physical craving; it signifies the subtle, lingering attachment we develop toward sensory experiences and emotional dependencies. Krishna warns that for those merely practicing withdrawal, the taste for these objects remains intact, keeping them tied to a cycle of longing and dissatisfaction. True inner peace remains elusive as long as the underlying emotional value—*rasa*—is present. The problem is that these residual attachments reign powerfully, constantly drawing the mind outward and away from inner fulfillment.

So, what can free us from these cravings? Krishna declares that only the realization of the Self (*Atma*) can dissolve all longings. Only by experiencing a more profound, enduring joy within, one that is infinitely more fulfilling than transient pleasures, can desires for sense objects naturally fade away. This profound joy, born from the knowledge of the Self, eclipses any pleasure derived from external objects. When one experiences the divine (*param dṛṣṭvā*), the *rasa* or taste for lesser, worldly joys simply loses its grip.

Adi Shankaracharya, in his commentary, elaborates that *param dṛṣṭvā* refers to the realization of the Self - the seeker's understanding that their true nature is not separate from the infinite Consciousness. This knowledge fills them with a joy so complete that it renders all other pursuits insignificant. The craving for sense pleasures dissipates not through suppression but through inner fulfillment. Just as one with access to a limitless reservoir of water no longer worries about water shortages in their vicinity, the enlightened person, experiencing the boundless joy of their own nature, is no longer bound by desires for fleeting worldly pleasures.

Krishna does not imply that the enlightened person shuns all worldly enjoyments. Instead, they experience these pleasures as a "bonus" without leaning on them for happiness. A *sthita-prajna* enjoys the world without becoming enslaved by it.

When the mind chases sense objects, cravings persist; but when anchored in the Self, contentment flows unbound

Fig: freedom from cravings

This shloka conveys that while the withdrawal of senses is valuable, liberation from mentally obsessing over various objects of desire is achieved only when one's awareness shifts to a higher plane. Knowledge of the Self, alone, frees the individual from lingering cravings, allowing them to live fully yet remain unshaken by life's passing pleasures. The wise, having tasted the bliss of their true nature, are naturally bereft of cravings for sense objects.

Beyond Suppression: Finding True Freedom from Cravings

Consider a seasoned alcoholic aspiring to quit. They may avoid places where alcohol is served, distance themselves from friends who drink, and remove all reminders of alcohol from their lives. Externally, they appear to have given up drinking. However, if the deep-seated craving—the internal "taste" or *rasa* for alcohol remains—it lingers beneath the surface, waiting for the right situation to reemerge. This unresolved attachment can lead to intense internal struggle through the abstinence period, and, in many cases, at the slightest opportunity, the person irrevocably relapses, succumbing to the craving they never indeed addressed.

True freedom from such vices cannot be experienced through suppression alone. Only when one connects with a far more significant and lasting sense of joy and peace can cravings like the venomous pleasure of alcohol naturally dissolve. This is the inner transformation Krishna speaks of, where the "taste" for sense pleasures fades because a person has found something infinitely more satisfying within.

The Strength of Inner Realization: Insights from Kalidasa's Kumara Sambhavam

Kalidasa's celebrated Sanskrit poem, *Kumāra Sambhavam,* complements this shloka beautifully:

Pratyartha bhūtām api tām samādheḥ
suśrūṣamāṇām giriśo anumene;
Vikārahetau sati vikriyante
yeṣām na cetāmsi ta eva dhīrāḥ

"Even though Parvati's presence could potentially be a distraction to his meditation, Shiva, known as Girisha (Lord of the Mountains), granted her permission to serve him. Those alone are truly wise (*dhīrāḥ*) whose minds remain unperturbed even in agitating circumstances." **(Kumāra Sambhavam, Canto 1, Verse 58)**

Parvati yearns to serve and marry Shiva, who is immersed in intense ascetic practices. Although he knows that Parvati's service could be a source of distraction (*vikārahetau*), Shiva is unperturbed. Kalidasa praises those who remain undisturbed even in agitating circumstances, describing them as the truly wise, or *dhīrāḥ*. In this scene, Shiva embodies the essence of inner mastery—his Self-knowledge and supreme awareness give him the strength to transcend all temptations and desires. His heart is rooted in the infinite, where worldly cravings hold no sway.

Absolute freedom from desire for sense objects comes not from avoiding temptations but from realizing the higher Self (*Atman*). This realization uproots desires entirely, making them powerless before the profound joy that arises from knowing one's infinite nature.

Neuroscientific Insights on Rewiring Desires and Habits

Research on neuroplasticity reveals that the brain is constantly reshaping itself in response to experiences and focus. Studies, such as those by Andreas Fink and colleagues on Creative Thinking and Heather A. Berlin on the "Neural Basis of the Dynamic Unconscious," indicate that focusing on new, positive experiences while diminishing attention to old habits can lead to the gradual "pruning" of neural pathways associated with outdated or undesired behaviors. This principle aligns with Krishna's guidance to seek fulfillment within, naturally reducing the lure of sense objects over time.

Attempting to forcefully eradicate cravings often has the opposite effect, as struggling against deeply cherished desires not only causes frustration and agitation but can inadvertently reinforce them. However, by focusing on higher pursuits and shifting one's attention toward inner satisfaction and Self-discovery, the brain's circuitry can gradually rewire, allowing the old attractions to lose their hold as they are no longer fed by conscious attention.

Seeking Higher Fulfillment: Biblical Parallels to Krishna's Teaching

The glory of transcending cravings through higher knowledge is affirmed by Biblical teaching, "But seek ye first the kingdom of God, and his righteousness; and all these things shall be added unto you" (Matthew 6:33, also Luke 12:31). Just as Krishna encourages the seeker to look beyond fleeting pleasures and find lasting contentment through Self-realization, the Bible advises prioritizing "the kingdom of God within you" over worldly desires.

Both teachings highlight that when one's priorities align with a more profound spiritual truth, the usual cravings for worldly pleasures gradually lose intensity. The fulfillment derived from spiritual insight replaces the need for external validations, leading to an abundant life enriched by a sense of purpose. Just as Krishna promises that the wholeness of inner transformation diminishes worldly desires, the Bible assures that everything else follows when one is firmly established in higher wisdom. Nothing needs to be chased in the world - everything comes to you of its own accord.

In this shloka, Krishna offers a profound insight into true freedom from desires. Self-discipline and sensory restraint, though vital, are insufficient to eliminate deeper cravings. Only through realizing one's true nature, *Atma,* which holds an unparalleled, lasting joy, does lingering *rasa* or subtle attachment to sense objects dissolve entirely. Discovery of the Self replaces the need for external validation with a steady contentment that flows from within.

Reflective Prompt

Have you tried forcefully giving up a detrimental habit or craving in the past? Were you able to get rid of it in this manner? How will you approach it now with what you have just studied?

Seek the infinite within, and the fleeting will lose its hold

SHLOKA 60: A CALL FOR VIGILANCE

यततो ह्यपि कौन्तेय पुरुषस्य विपश्चितः |
इन्द्रियाणि प्रमाथीनि हरन्ति प्रसभं मनः ||60||

yatatō hyapi kauntēya puruṣasya vipaścitaḥ |
indriyāṇi pramāthīni haranti prasabhaṁ manaḥ ||60||

Translation:

O Kaunteya [Arjuna], even for a wise person (***vipaścitaḥ***) who is earnestly striving (***yatatō***) for self-mastery, the turbulent senses (***indriyāṇi pramāthīni***) can forcefully (***prasabham***) carry away the mind (***manaḥ***). **[Sankya Yoga: 2.60]**

At a Glance: Capturing the Spirit of the Shloka

Regulating sensory engagement is essential but challenging for a seeker aspiring to attain steady wisdom. The senses are powerful enough to lead the minds of even those with clear goals and sincere effort astray. This shloka is not meant to discourage earnest aspirants but serves as a reminder of the inherent challenges on this path and the importance of constant vigilance and perseverance.

Commentary

In this shloka, Krishna deepens his exploration of sense mastery by alerting seekers to the challenges of this inner journey. While preceding verses focused on the necessity of regulating sensory engagement, Krishna now acknowledges the inherent difficulty of this task. The force of the senses can unsettle the minds of even those who possess knowledge and are disciplined.

'Indriyāṇi pramāthīni' describes the senses as powerful churning rods, highlighting their ability to create internal turbulence. Just as a churning rod stirs up the contents of a vessel, the senses can agitate the mind. The eyes and ears are potent channels through which sensory impressions enter, often triggering memories, thoughts, and emotions that disrupt inner calm. One harsh word or a disturbing image can linger, pulling the mind away from the wisdom it seeks to cultivate. Krishna explains how a moment of sensory disturbance can undo hours of focused contemplation, leaving the mind in turmoil and disconnecting it from higher knowledge.

'Manaḥ haranti' (carries away the mind) explains how the senses can overpower the mind, especially if not kept in check. A person might spend time in meditation or study Vedantic teachings, only to find themselves losing their equilibrium when faced with a sudden provocation. In such moments, even someone knowledgeable may feel their hard-won peace slip away as their mind is pulled into restlessness and reaction. Hence, Vedanta's call for continuous

vigilance; without it, an otherwise sound and focused mind can be led astray by fleeting sensory experiences.

"Yatataḥ api" affirms that the senses can be difficult to control even by one who understands the importance of restraint and earnestly strives on the spiritual path. The senses are *'pramāthīni,'* inherently disruptive, requiring significant effort and mindfulness to maintain balance. Sita's devastating attraction to the golden deer in the Ramayana is a powerful reminder that even a brief lapse in vigilance can lead us away from our inner peace. Though Sita was with Rama, who represents the all-joyful Self (Consciousness), her momentary fascination with the golden deer—symbolizing sensory allure—led her away from her trustworthy source of happiness.

"Vipaścitaḥ" means wise and learned. Even those who have studied the scriptures and are intellectually aware of the pitfalls of sensory attachment are vulnerable. Knowledge is not power. The application of knowledge is power. To master the otherwise indomitable senses, a seeker must exercise vigilance and practice the gathered knowledge daily to avoid falling into the traps set by sensory allurements.

The sensorial aspect of our being is primal and intrinsic. It is bound by its very nature to fleeting attractions. Vedanta exalts human life as a conscious journey to spiritual freedom—freedom from the dictates of the senses. Swami Vivekananda often implored, *"Work like a master, not like a slave."* He urged seekers to maintain control over the senses, ensuring they serve rather than enslave.

A Hindi proverb, *"Kambal choḍtā nahī"* (the blanket does not let go), speaks of a man who clings to what he believes is a floating blanket in a flood, only to discover it is a bear holding him tight. Like this "blanket," the sense objects appear desirable, but if not approached with caution, they can grip us tightly, turning a source of comfort into a source of danger.

Knowledge about how our senses work, backed up by self-discipline to keep them in check, is essential for inner mastery. Otherwise, life becomes a series of reactions to sensory demands with unfavorable consequences that are hard to deal with rather than a journey of purposeful action.

This shloka reminds us that the path to the state of a *'sthita-prajna'* -where one's wisdom remains unshaken amidst life's sensory pulls demands constant self-awareness and alertness. The senses are powerful forces, and only through sustained effort and a commitment to inner discipline can a seeker hope to transcend their influence.

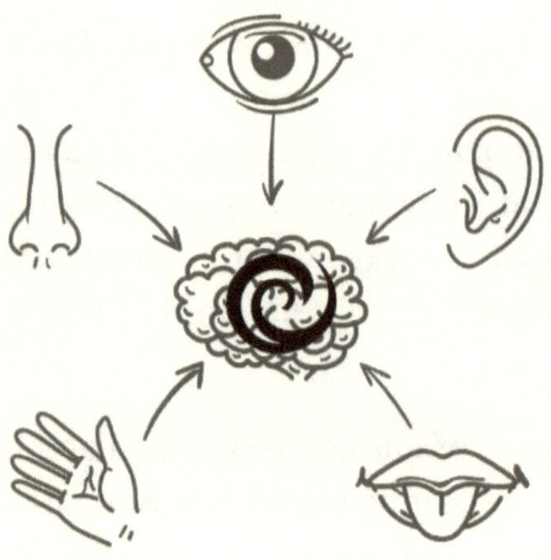

Unbridled senses churn the mind, stirring chaos, leaving peace behind

Fig: Impact of sense organs on mind

A Caution on the Mind's Fickleness: Insights from Srimad Bhagavatam

Srimad Bhagavatam also warns against the mind's unpredictability and emphasizes the need for constant vigilance: *"The mind, even when seemingly controlled, is not to be fully trusted, as it can mislead a person at any time."*

Verses 5.6.2-5.6.5 of the Srimad Bhagavatam compare the mind to an unfaithful partner or a captured animal that, if given freedom, will easily escape or turn on its captor.

The Bhagavatam advises, "Do not compromise with the fickle mind, for even the powerful can be betrayed by their own thoughts." It reiterates Krishna's caution to remain ever-alert. True mastery over the mind requires ongoing vigilance, as its disruptive tendencies linger even in the advanced aspirant.

Illustrative Examples: The Consequence of a Single Lapse in Vigilance

Ramakrishna Paramahamsa often shared the parable of the rice field to convey the importance of guarding one's efforts with complete vigilance:

A farmer, after toiling for hours to bring water into his field, found that his field was still dry. Upon investigation, he discovered a single hole through which all the water had escaped. Despite his hard work, that one small oversight ruined the result. Similarly, the concerted effort of even the wise can be wasted if they lose even momentary control over their senses.

Adi Shankaracharya emphasizes the same caution in *Vivekachudamani* with the example of five different creatures who succumb to the lure of just one sense each. A moth whose weakness lies in the sight of the flame rushes into it and perishes. A fish has a weakness for taste – it bites right into the delicious bait hanging off the end of a fishing rod and is caught. A deer has a weakness for sound and following the drumbeats of a hunter, gets easily hunted. An elephant has a weakness for touch and during the mating season rushing haywire for contact falls into the hunter's pit. Finally, a bee with its weakness for smell dives right into the folds of flowers or fruit where it gets trapped. Think. Each of these creatures lose themselves in the lure of just one sense. And we have a weakness for all five senses. What are our chances without due vigilance?

Returning to our previous example of a student, imagine they spend months preparing for the exam. But the night before, they are lured into a party, drink heavily, and wake up late, missing the exam altogether. In a single night, all those months of arduous work are compromised due to one lapse in judgment. The bottom line is no matter how knowledgeable or committed one is, sustained vigilance is essential to prevent the senses from undoing one's progress.

Reflective Prompt

Has a momentary lapse in judgment brought about by sensory distraction caused a severe misstep in your life? Was it revocable? If not, what did you learn from it? How would you apply this shloka's learnings to potential future distractions?

Even the wise must guard the mind, for the senses drag with the force of a frenzied tide.

Shloka 61: Mastery of Senses

तानि सर्वाणि संयम्य युक्त आसीत मत्परः |
वशे हि यस्येन्द्रियाणि तस्य प्रज्ञा प्रतिष्ठिता ||61||

tāni sarvāṇi saṁyamya yukta āsīta matparaḥ |
vaśē hi yasyēndriyāṇi tasya prajñā pratiṣṭhitā ||61||

Translation:

Having restrained all the sense organs (***tāni sarvāṇi saṁyamya***), the self-controlled person (***yukta āsīta***) should remain committed to My pursuit(***mat-paraḥ***). For the one whose sense organs are under control (***vaśe hi yasya indriyāṇi***), knowledge becomes firm and steady (***tasya prajñā pratiṣṭhitā***). [Sankya Yoga: 2.61]

At a Glance: Capturing the Spirit of the Shloka

Mastery of the senses is essential for a seeker to advance on the path of Self-discovery. Through the diligent practice of Karma Yoga, one gains purity of mind and inner control, creating the conditions for knowledge acquired through Jnana Yoga to become firm and experiential. This inner mastery establishes a steady and unwavering understanding of one's true identity (*Atma*), sustained at all times.

Commentary

In this shloka, Krishna brings together his teachings on mastering the senses for anyone on the spiritual path. He begins with '*tāni sarvāṇi saṁyamya*' (having restrained all the sense organs), emphasizing the need for total control over the sense organs. This by no means implies suppression but an intelligent channeling to serve the higher purpose of spiritual growth. Here, Krishna stresses that even one uncontrolled sense organ can be enough to destabilize the mind and derail a person from their goal. Just as a driver needs all the wheels of a car under control to reach their destination safely, a seeker requires all senses to be aligned and purposefully directed.

'*Saṁyamya*' means discipline, not suppression—allowing the senses to serve their purpose without dominating the mind. Suppression often results from external imposition and can backfire, creating internal tension. For example, a student who abstains from movies purely due to family pressure might appear focused but feel deprived and harbor resentment. This is suppression, where restraint lacks understanding or personal commitment. Conversely, true mastery ensues when the student voluntarily limits distractions out of a personal desire for success.

The senses should function as instruments under our guidance, not as forces that pull us in various directions. A question every seeker must consistently sit with is - who is leading whom? Consider the example of walking a dog: while ideally, the owner leads the dog, sometimes the dog takes the lead, dragging the owner in all directions. In the same way, the senses often act independently, pulling the mind toward sensory attractions. The Bhagavad Gita encourages us to lead the senses, not be led by them.

Fig: Let the mind steer the sense organs

Although foundational, controlling all the senses alone is insufficient for cultivating inner stability. It must be accompanied by a focused dedication to the Divine or *Atma* (Self). '*Mat-parah*' has layers of meaning. At one level, it invites a seeker to dwell upon Him as the divine ideal or '*saguṇa Īśvara*'—the personal deity who embodies divine qualities. For practitioners who connect with a form, '*mat-parah*' suggests focusing on Krishna or a beloved deity such as Rama, Jesus, or any divine figure their heart resonates with. This focus helps channel the mind toward spiritual ideals, especially when the senses and external influences threaten to disrupt inner calm.

From the Advaita Vedanta standpoint, '*mat-parah*' means meditating on the Self (*Atma*), the universal Consciousness residing within everyone- the ultimate Reality beyond personal identity. Krishna no longer stands apart as a distant deity but reveals Himself as the core of one's own being.

The Gopis, devotees of Krishna, express this beautifully in the Srimad Bhagavatam: *'Na kalu gōpikām Nandanō bhavān, akila dēhinām antharātma dṛk'*—O Krishna, you are not merely the son of Nanda; you are the inner Self of all beings." This non-dualistic meaning of *'mat-paraḥ'* inspires seekers to see Krishna as their own inner Self and contemplate that divinity within.

'Mat-paraḥ' does not mean lackadaisical imagination but a focused, disciplined practice- *'yuktaḥ.'* Combining the two steps of contemplation *(mananam)* and experiential wisdom (*nididhyāsanam*), it involves a regular and dedicated focus on the nature of the Self or the divine presence within.

In the concluding line, Krishna glorifies the outcome of these disciplines: *'Vaśe hi yasyendriyāṇi'* -for the one whose senses are under control, *'tasya prajñā pratiṣṭhitā'* -wisdom becomes steady and unwavering. When the senses are disciplined, and the mind remains focused on the Self (*Atma*), one's wisdom becomes unshakable. Krishna assures us that this steadfast focus shields wisdom from wavering in the throes of sensory impulses.

Human beings possess a unique capacity for restraint—distinguishing us from other living beings, often led solely by sensory impulses. The dignity and grace of being human lies in our ability to choose responses, to control impulses, and to focus on a higher purpose. From childhood, we receive training on what to pursue and avoid; this foundation sets the stage for a disciplined, purpose-driven life. As we mature into adulthood, we must extend this foundational training to mastering the senses and focusing on the divine to fulfill the singular goal of human existence - Self-realization.

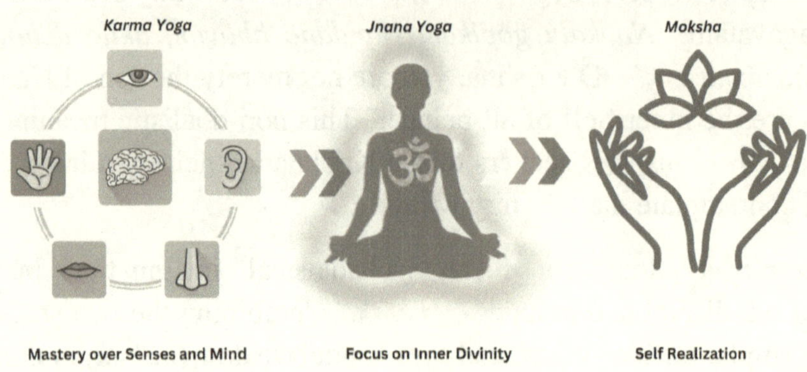

Fig: Spritual path

This shloka professes control over the senses through Karma Yoga and dedication to a higher ideal through Jnana Yoga. When cultivated together, these two practices establish the seeker in steady wisdom that can withstand the challenges of worldly distractions. Such an individual is firmly established in their Identity as *Atma*.

Reflective Prompt

Reflect on a habit that regularly distracts you from your life goals. What steps can you take to replace or transform it into a supportive force on your journey?

With senses tamed and mind on the divine, steady wisdom becomes thine

Shlokas 62 & 63: The 8 Stages of Downfall

ध्यायतो विषयान्पुंसः सङ्गस्तेषूपजायते ।
सङ्गात्सञ्जायते कामः कामात्क्रोधोऽभिजायते ॥62॥

क्रोधाद्भवति सम्मोहः सम्मोहात्स्मृतिविभ्रमः ।
स्मृतिभ्रंशात् बुद्धिनाशः बुद्धिनाशात्प्रणश्यति ॥63॥

dhyāyatō viṣayānpumsaḥ saṅgastēṣūpajāyatē |
saṅgātsañjāyatē kāmaḥ kāmātkrōdhō 'bhijāyatē ||62||

krōdhādbhavati sammōhaḥ sammōhātsmṛtivibhramaḥ |
smṛtibhramśāt buddhināśaḥ buddhināśātpraṇaśyati ||63||

Translation:

For the person who dwells on sense objects (***viṣayān***), binding attachment (***saṅga***) to them develops. From attachment arises obsessive desire (***kāma***), and from unfulfilled desire, anger (***krōdha***) is born. From anger comes delusion (***sammōha***), and from delusion arises the loss of wisdom (***smṛti vibhrama***). When wisdom is lost, discernment (***buddhi***) is destroyed, and with the destruction of discernment, the person is ruined (***praṇaśyati***) [Sankya Yoga: 2.62 & 63]

At a Glance: Capturing the Spirit of the Shloka

Famously known as the "ladder of fall," these oft-quoted shlokas highlight in eight vividly described stages how a person quickly progresses from innocent thought indulgence to complete destruction. They illustrate how the mind merely musing on sensory objects can set off a chain reaction that gradually erodes one's stability and wisdom—and, in worst-case scenarios, leads to total annihilation.

Commentary

In these two shlokas, Krishna describes step-by-step how humans fall prey to their unrecognized pondering over sense objects and spiral down to their destruction. These shlokas are not meant to discourage but alert us to stay vigilant to avoid this self-inflicted ruin.

The Eight Stages of The Ladder of Fall.

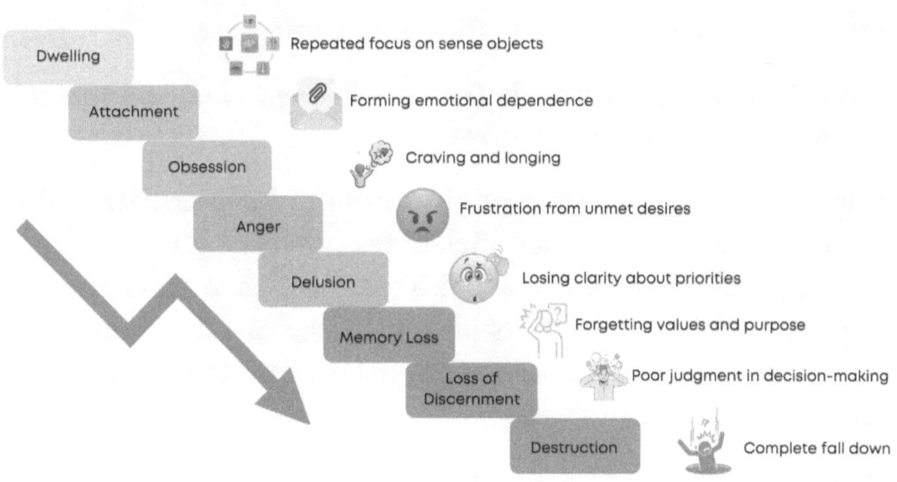

Fig: Ladder of Downfall

Stage 1: The Seed of Indulgence – *"Dhyāyatō viṣayānpuṁsaḥ"* (When a person dwells on sense objects)

Krishna begins by pointing out our innocuous habit of dwelling on sensory pleasures. A person might think of a pleasurable object, and initially, it might not seem problematic. However, as one's thoughts keep returning to this object, the mind begins to build a pattern around it, giving it undue importance. This "dwelling" is not merely noticing; it is an investment of mental energy that can become the root cause of the ensuing attachment.

Stage 2: Formation of Attachment – *"Saṅgastēṣūpajāyatē"* (Attachment is born)

As the mind repeatedly dwells on an object, a subtle attachment, or *saṅga*, forms. This attachment grows over time, creating a sense of dependency. The mind starts to feel incomplete without the object, being, or experience. What began as an innocent mental indulgence slowly takes the shape of a need, where the individual craves the object, being, or experience. The thoughts of the object consume the mind, making it unavailable to focus on anything else.

Stage 3: Attachment Breeds Desire – *"Saṅgātsañjāyatē kāmaḥ"* (From attachment arises desire)

This all-consuming attachment gives birth to *kāma* or desire. This is not a simple wish but an often-obsessive longing to possess or experience the object or being. It drives the person to act to get what they crave. Krishna highlights how this stage can cloud judgment, as powerful desires often push us beyond our ethical boundaries and distract us from higher goals.

Stage 4: Desire Leads to Frustration and Anger – *"Kāmātkrōdhō'bhijāyatē"* (From desire arises anger)

When desires are thwarted—when we cannot obtain what we crave or when obstacles arise—*krōdha* (anger) emerges. This anger is a natural response to frustrated desire. It can lead to irritability, frustration, and even aggression. At this stage, the mind is no longer calm or rational; it becomes reactive. Krishna warns that this anger can easily overpower reason and self-control, disrupting the mind's balance and pushing the individual further from wisdom.

Stage 5: Anger Clouds Perception – *"Krōdhādbhavati sammōhaḥ"* (From anger comes delusion)

Krōdha, or anger, creates *sammōha*-delusion or mental fog. A person's perception is clouded, and they lose sight of reality. Delusion distorts one's understanding, leading to misinterpretations of situations and people. Anger-driven delusion can cause us to act irrationally, often regretting our actions once the anger subsides. At this point, the connection to higher wisdom is grossly weakened, and we are more likely to act against our values.

Stage 6: Delusion Leads to Loss of Memory – *"Sammōhātsmṛtivibhramaḥ"* (From delusion arises loss of memory)

This delusion further leads to *smṛtivibhramah* - loss of memory. Here, memory refers to one's ability to recall goals, principles, and spiritual teachings. So deluded, a person forgets their purpose, values, and, in most cases, even who they are. This loss of memory severs the individual's connection to wisdom entirely, leading them to act on impulses rather than on mindful intentions.

Stage 7: Loss of Memory Destroys Discernment – *"Smṛtibhraṁśāt buddhināśaḥ"* (Loss of memory leads to loss of discernment)

With the memory of one's values and purpose lost, *buddhināśaḥ*, or the destruction of wisdom and discernment, follows. The intellect, which is supposed to guide us and make thoughtful decisions, loses its clarity and decisiveness. At this stage, the person's judgment is severely compromised. They cannot distinguish between beneficial and harmful, short-term gratification and long-term growth. The loss of discernment leaves the mind vulnerable and directionless.

Stage 8: Downfall of the self – *"Buddhināśātpraṇaśyati"* (When wisdom is lost, the person is destroyed)

The final consequence is *praṇaśyati*— self-annihilation. This does not necessarily mean physical death but rather the loss of the self in terms of integrity, purpose, and peace. With wisdom eroded and discernment no longer functioning as a guide, one's life loses direction, and actions become impulsive, chaotic, and harmful. At this stage, one may think, feel, speak, or act in ways contrary to their values, defying their own principles or culture. This decline affects not only one's personal well-being but also disrupts relationships.

Stage	Description	Example
Dwelling	Repeated focus on sense objects	Constantly checking social media posts
Attachment	Forming emotional dependence	Feeling incomplete without certain luxuries
Desire	Craving and longing	Obsessing over buying a luxury car
Anger	Frustration from unmet desires	Getting irritated when promotion is delayed
Delusion	Losing clarity about priorities	Believing material success equals happiness
Memory Loss	Forgetting values and purpose	Ignoring family or spiritual goals
Loss of Discernment	Poor judgment in decision-making	Reckless spending, unethical choices
Destruction	Self-inflicted suffering	Financial ruin, strained relationships

The Importance of Vigilance and Awareness

Through these two shlokas, Krishna paints a powerful image of the swift decline of the unvigilant mind. It is not a pessimistic prophecy of inevitable failure but an encouragement for continuous awareness and discipline. By understanding this progression, a seeker can be mindful of their thoughts and desires before they spiral into attachment, leading to negative consequences.

Awareness and intervention, particularly in the first three stages, can prevent this otherwise unstoppable downfall. Imagine standing at the top of a long stairwell with a ball in your hand. If the ball slips out of your palm, you can catch it maximum on the first two or three stairs, depending on your agility. If you do not, the momentum of its roll increases, and you will just have to stand witness to its arrest at the bottom of the stairwell.

Similarly, we can intervene in the first three stages of this downward spiral to stop our own downfall by empowering our understanding to reveal the futility of our desire and even project the untoward consequences. Once anger sets in, the remaining stages occur in quick succession, and the fall becomes unstoppable.

The mind is naturally drawn to sensory objects, but one can redirect this energy towards higher goals with consistent practice of Karma Yoga (*Ishavararpanana Bhavana and Parsada Bhavana*). This shloka alerts us to cultivate awareness so that wisdom remains steadfast and undisturbed by fleeting desires and the scintillating lure of the external world.

The Spiral of Attachment: A Modern Tale of Downfall

Meet Rahul, a bright and ambitious young professional who recently started working at a prestigious company. He is disciplined, driven, and has clear goals for his future. But like many, he is also largely influenced by social media hounding him with the temptations of luxury and success.

1. Dwelling on Sense Objects

One evening, Rahul stumbles upon the profile of a famous influencer flaunting an extravagant lifestyle with designer clothes, luxury cars, and exotic vacations. Initially, he thinks it harmless to check in on these posts now and then, just for fun.

2. Attachment Begins

Gradually, what started as casual browsing becomes a daily ritual. Rahul eagerly awaits updates and new posts, feeling a subtle pull toward that lifestyle. The luxurious world he sees online takes up more of his mental space.

3. Desire Takes Root

Over time, this attachment grows into an intense desire. Rahul starts wanting that life for himself—a bigger paycheck, flashier possessions, and the envy of his peers. This desire becomes his motivation and obsession, and he begins measuring his worth by these external standards.

4. Unfulfilled Desire Leads to Anger

Despite working harder and even taking on extra projects, Rahul finds that the rewards and recognition are not coming fast enough. The weight of his unfulfilled desires bogs him down. The resentment grows, and he starts feeling anger not just toward his own situation but even toward those who already have the life he desires.

5. Anger Breeds Delusion

Rahul's frustration clouds his understanding. He convinces himself that success is solely about wealth and possessions. Lost in this delusion, he dismisses values he once held dear—authenticity, purpose, and relationships. He begins to believe that only luxury and fame can bring him happiness.

6. Delusion Leads to Memory Loss

In his obsession, Rahul forgets why he embarked on his career in the first place. His initial goal of positively impacting his company, family, and society and growing as a person fades into the background. His mind is focused on his lack. He disregards the values he once cherished and the consequent success he has enjoyed thus far.

7. Loss of Discernment

With his true purpose forgotten, Rahul's judgment becomes impaired. He begins making impulsive decisions—spending recklessly on things he cannot afford, bending the truth to impress others, and distancing himself from friends who do not align with his new aspirations. His actions, once guided by principles, become increasingly reckless.

8. Self-Destruction

Rahul's life spirals out of control. His finances are in disarray, his relationships are strained, and his peace of mind is shattered. He feels hollow, constantly anxious, and deeply unsatisfied despite his material possessions. He is disconnected from himself, lost in a cycle of desire and frustration, far removed from the peace and fulfillment he once experienced.

The Science of Self-Control and Krishna's Teachings

Krishna's portrayal of the "ladder of fall" in these shlokas finds strong parallels in modern psychology and neuroscience. In his descriptive progression to destruction lies a profound understanding of human behavior. Psychology reveals how a repetitive focus on an object or goal creates habits in the brain, strengthening neural pathways associated with that desire. Over time, these attachments can dominate, often leading to frustration and impulsive decisions if desires go unfulfilled.

Neuroscience attributes this to our brain's "reward system," where dopamine release in anticipation of a reward drives repetitive pursuit.

Left unchecked, this can trigger what scientists call the "emotional hijack," where the brain's rational center loses control. This mirrors Krishna's warning of how anger and delusion lead to memory loss (*smṛtivibhramaḥ*), impaired judgment (*buddhināśaḥ*), and ultimately, self-destruction (*praṇaśyati*).

Krishna's call for vigilant awareness of inner impulses and self-discipline resonates with the modern understanding of self-control to align with one's values. Like the "reward cycle" in neuropsychology, attachment can steer behavior away from reason, leading to impulsive actions and suffering. Krishna's teaching encourages cultivating a balanced mind, where the senses are disciplined but not suppressed, enabling a life rooted in clarity and self-mastery.

In these shlokas, Krishna warns us against enslaving the mind to fleeting desires. This advice holds even greater relevance in the virtual world we inhabit today, where everything is accessed at our fingertips. He guides us to employ our inner resources to avoid the destructive patterns of unrestrained desire and attachment.

The Source of Downfall: Contrasting Eastern and Western Spiritual Approaches

Swami Nirmalananda Giri (also known as Abbot George Burke) is a Western scholar of Eastern spirituality who has deeply explored the spiritual traditions of both the East and the West. In his work *The Bhagavad Gita for Awakening: A Practical Commentary for Leading a Successful Spiritual Life*, he highlights a fascinating difference between these two approaches to spirituality. He observes that Western ascetic traditions often blame negative thoughts and impulses on external demons or evil spirits. On the other hand, eastern traditions like Hinduism, Buddhism, and Taoism see these tendencies as arising within the individual. According to Eastern wisdom, our ignorance and unregulated desires—the very forces Krishna discusses in these shlokas— lead us to fall away from our true nature and bring about our downfall. Rather than seeing harm as something inflicted by outside forces, the Bhagavad Gita teaches that the root of all collapse lies within—an internal misalignment of thoughts and desires that clouds wisdom. This self-inflicted damage can be avoided through awareness, self-discipline, and inner mastery without externalizing the cause.

Swami Nirmalananda also points out that the Western tradition's focus on external demons and sin often leads to a fixation on wrongdoing and guilt, detracting from personal growth. He notes that *"obsession with sin is an attraction to sin."* Eastern spirituality focuses on one's innate piety and ability to uncover and exude it externally. The Bhagavad Gita, he affirms, offers a clear roadmap for understanding and overcoming inner delusions and attachments, providing the seeker with a means of genuine self-mastery.

This observation powerfully reminds us to take responsibility for our inner state. It echoes Krishna's teaching that the true enemy lies not in external forces but in our own unmanaged impulses. Swami Nirmalananda suggests that by mastering these impulses, we align ourselves with the Bhagavad Gita's path to Self-realization—a path that, unlike fear-based obedience, fosters true wisdom and spiritual liberation.

Reflective Prompt

Have you personally experienced the ladder of fall elaborated upon in these shlokas? Or have you seen someone close be destroyed by it? At what stage would a powerful intervention have saved the day?

You build your life. You alone break it down. It all depends on whether you succumb to the mind's slipshod meanderings or consciously lead it home.

SHLOKA 64: INNER PEACE AMIDST OUTER ENGAGEMENT

राग‍द्वेषवियुक्तैस्तु विषयानिन्द्रियैश्चरन् |
आत्मवश्यैर्विधेयात्मा प्रसादमधिगच्छति ||64||

rāgadvēṣaviyuktaistu viṣayānindriyaiścaran |
ātmavaśyairvidhēyātmā prasādamadhigacchati ||64||

Translation:

By moving among sense objects (*viṣayān*) with the sense organs (*indriyāni*) that are disciplined and free from attachment and aversion (*rāga-dvēṣa*), the self-controlled person (*vidhēya-ātmā*) attains a state of tranquility (*prasāda*) [Sankya Yoga: 2.64]

At a Glance: Capturing the Spirit of the Shloka

A person who has mastered their mind and senses engages freely with the world. Free from the lure of likes and dislikes, such a self-controlled individual remains unperturbed through all interactions. Experiencing Peace does not require withdrawal from the world; it is the natural state of one who has gained self-mastery amidst the inescapable noise and din of mortal existence.

Commentary

Contrary to the idea that spiritual Peace requires withdrawal from the world, Krishna teaches that true Peace comes from self-control, not isolation. A *sthita-prajna* need not abandon society to attain tranquility. They move freely among the sense objects yet remain undisturbed, with their mind firmly anchored in wisdom.

'Indriyaiḥ viṣayān caran' affirms that engaging in the world brings no harm. It is natural for the senses to perceive and interact with sense objects. It is impossible and impractical to avoid sensory input entirely. Self-mastery boils down to how one engages.

Freedom from Attachment and Aversion: *rāgadvēṣaviyuktaiḥ*

Rāga refers to an attachment or intense liking toward an object, experience, or outcome, while *dveṣa* signifies an extreme aversion or repulsion. These two—attachment and aversion—are conditioned responses that easily hijack our ability to think clearly and act wisely. A *sthita-prajna* may nurture personal preferences. However, they do not allow *rāga* and *dveṣa* to interfere with what needs to be done.

Consider a person invited to a buffet boasting a wide variety of junk and nutritious food options. They may feel drawn to junk food (an expression of *rāga*) but recognize that choosing healthy food aligns with their goal of health and well-being. The wise person's decision will reflect this commitment, selecting food that nourishes rather than indulging a fleeting craving. This ability to choose what aligns with one's personal values and goals in life over momentary impulses is what Krishna refers to as being free from *rāga* and *dveṣa*.

Mastery Over the Senses: *ātmavaśyaiḥ rāga-dveṣa-viyuktaiḥ indriyaiḥ*

Krishna describes a person with disciplined senses as *ātmavaśyaiḥ*—one who has mastery over their sensory system. This mastery ensures one's decisions are based on discernment rather than likes or dislikes. The senses do not dictate the *sthita-prajna's* choices; instead, established in wisdom and having mastered control, they direct the senses towards all things conducive.

Attaining Peace: *prasādam adhigacchati*

Krishna concludes by explaining that this state of self-mastery and freedom from the lure of the senses leads to *Prasāda-* inner tranquility and contentment. *Prasāda* is a Sanskrit word that means calmness, clarity, and serene joy. It reflects a mind that is no longer agitated by desires or attachments and is free from emotional upheaval. In this state, one remains unshaken by the ups and downs of life, able to engage fully with the world without losing inner equilibrium.

Again, *Prasāda* does not imply apathy or detachment from the world. It signifies a mind that, while interacting with the world, remains undisturbed by it. The *sthita-prajna* moves through life with even-mindedness and experiences Peace in every moment, regardless of external circumstances. The achievement of *prasāda* makes one's engagement with life a source of fulfillment rather than frustration.

Stillness Amid Chaos, Action with Clarity

Fig: Inner Tranquility

Practical Implications for Seekers

Self-possession is second nature for a *sthita-prajna*. However, for seekers still on the path, this inner balance can be cultivated through the disciplined practice of *Karma Yoga* - engaging in actions with dedication and non-attachment. Consistent practice teaches one to keep sensory desires in check, act with awareness and intentionality, and align with what needs to be done rather than personal likes or dislikes. Over time, this practice brings one closer to the state of *prasāda*, laying a foundation for steady wisdom.

This shloka assures us that we do not need to flee from the sensory world to find peace. True peace lies within. Once discovered, we gain the freedom to move freely through life with equanimity. The spiritual path does not advocate withdrawal from life but empowered engagement. It enables us to conceive and experience the absolute viability of a harmonious co-existence of inner peace and outer success.

Reflective Prompt

In a world that constantly bombards you with sensory distractions — notifications, advertisements, and social media — how do you ensure your mind stays calm and focused?"

A tranquil mind dances with life, untouched by its fleeting highs and lows

Shloka 65: The Dual Blessings of a Tranquil Mind

प्रसादे सर्वदुःखानां हानिरस्योपजायते |
प्रसन्नचेतसो ह्याशु बुद्धिः पर्यवतिष्ठते ||65||

prasādē sarvaduḥkhānāṁ hānirasyōpajāyatē |
prasannacētasō hyāśu buddhiḥ paryavatiṣṭhatē ||65||

Translation:

When one attains inner tranquility (***prasāda***), all sorrows (***sarva-duḥkhānām***) come to an end. In a calm mind (***prasanna-cetasaḥ***), wisdom (***buddhi***) becomes firmly established (***paryavatiṣṭhate***)
[Sankya Yoga: 2.65]

At a Glance: Capturing the Spirit of the Shloka

A person of inner mastery is free of obsessive likes and dislikes. They direct their mind toward constructive ideals and align their actions accordingly. They experience life as a cheerful adventure graced by inner peace. This perpetual state of tranquility has two profound effects:

1. **Freedom from Misery:** A calm mind remains unperturbed through sorrows and challenges.
2. **Established Wisdom:** Within this peaceful, centered state, the Knowledge of the Self (*Atma*) takes firm roots - having transformed from intellectual understanding into a lasting, experiential truth.

Tranquility fosters both freedom from suffering and a secure habitat for wisdom.

Commentary

This shloka describes the profound benefits of achieving a tranquil and balanced mind. Krishna calls this state *prasāda* —an inner calm, clarity, and contentment immune to external disturbances.

This peace—*prasāda*—has two-fold benefits, which sustain and transform a seeker on the spiritual path:

1. Freedom from Misery (*Sarva-Duḥkhānām Hāniḥ*)

Krishna declares, '*Prasāde sarva-duḥkhānām hāniḥ bhavathi* '- when one attains tranquility, all sorrows are destroyed. The state of inner tranquility dissolves suffering, not by eliminating external difficulties but by changing our mental state.

Vedanta explains that joy or contentment is not something to be acquired from the world; it is already inherent within us. The external world seems to be its source only because it can occasionally shift our minds into a temporary state of satisfaction. Even the happiness felt from something outside of us stems only from a quietened mind and balanced emotions.

Krishna emphasizes that, in *prasāda*, the mind achieves a serene state independent of external sources. This tranquility makes the mind less reactive to external stimuli, meaning life's inevitable ups and downs do not disturb its balance. Even amidst life's challenges, the calm mind remains unaffected, experiencing an underlying sense of contentment.

2. Strengthened Wisdom (*Prasanna-Cetasaḥ Buddhiḥ Paryavatiṣṭhate*)

Krishna goes on to explain the second benefit as *'prasanna-cetasaḥ buddhiḥ paryavatiṣṭhate'*—when the mind is serene and cheerful, wisdom becomes well-established. Here, *'buddhi '*refers to discernment and wisdom that leads to Self-knowledge (*jñānam*), which becomes firmly rooted when the mind is calm.

Good digestion strengthens the body by assimilating nutrients from food. Similarly, a tranquil mind allows the intellect to assimilate and integrate Self-knowledge. As seen earlier, knowledge alone is not power; well-integrated and applied knowledge empowers one's actions. Mental quiet and peace allow knowledge to transform into *'sthira-prajña'* (steady wisdom), never wavering when tested by life's challenges and always available as an inner compass to guide the way.

Fig: Dual benefits of Tranquil mind (Prasada)

Rising from Sensory Pleasure to Inner Fulfillment

These shlokas offer a more profound perspective on a seeker's journey from sensory indulgence to inner mastery. It begs reiteration that true freedom and peace do not come from suppressing desires but transcending them. Rather than abandoning the sensory world by adorning the robes of an ascetic, one learns to live in the world with an unshaken mind, free from the pull of fleeting pleasures. This freedom and mastery over the mind are accessible to anyone seeking to rise above sensory cravings and find fulfillment in the only place it can be found - within.

The distinction between *bhoga* (enjoyment) and *yoga* (discipline) describes the path from external pleasure to inner contentment. When we remain in a state of *bhoga*, attached to sensory objects, we may enjoy temporary satisfaction, but this often leads to dependency, discontent, and even mental or emotional imbalances. Rising from *bhoga* to *yoga* requires redirecting energy toward deeper, lasting fulfillment. This flight does not leave pleasure behind but amplifies it to a much more profound level.

As we mature on the spiritual path, we discover two distinct levels of joy: '*Viṣayānanda*' is the joy derived from sensory pleasures. While comforting, it is transient and often leaves a sense of incompleteness in its wake. The second, '*Atmananda*,' is the boundless joy of realizing one's true Self—the *Atman*. Moving from the bind of the senses to the freedom of *Atma* grants the seeker enduring contentment independent of external conditions.

By controlling our impulses and being mindful of our sensory interactions, we foster inner balance and become better contributors to society. The Bhagavad Gita advocates not for an ascetic denial of sensory stimuli but for a recognition of the infinite potential within that is bursting with perpetual joy and surpasses any worldly pleasure. The *Taittiriya Upanishad* assures all spiritual enthusiasts that the highest contentment found in the nature of *Atma* transcends all sensory joys combined.

Ultimately, these teachings offer the wisdom to live fully in the world, work meaningfully, and experience joy consciously at all levels—all while remaining firmly rooted in tranquility and wisdom.

This shloka assures seekers that by achieving *prasāda*—a calm and contented mind, the seeker transcends suffering and makes way for the intellect to ground the knowledge of the Self. *Prasāda* is a self-evident state where '*ashoka*' (no sorrow) and *sthira-prajna* (enduring wisdom) coexist harmoniously, enabling seekers to experience life's fullness without losing inner balance.

Reflective Prompt

Think about your sources of joy—are they rooted in fleeting external pleasures or a stable sense of inner peace? How can you shift towards the latter?

In the stillness of a tranquil mind, wisdom takes root and sorrows fade away

SHLOKA 66: THE LADDER TO INNER PEACE AND HAPPINESS

नाऽस्ति बुद्धिरयुक्तस्य न चायुक्तस्य भावना ।
न चाभावयतः शान्तिः अशान्तस्य कुतः सुखम् ॥66॥

nā 'sti buddhirayuktasya na cāyuktasya bhāvanā |
na cābhāvayataḥ śāntiḥ aśāntasya kutaḥ sukham ||66||

Translation:

For the undisciplined (**ayuktaḥ**), there is no wisdom (**buddhi**); for the undisciplined, there is no contemplation (**bhāvanā**). Without contemplation, there is no peace (**śānti**), and without peace, how can there be happiness (**sukham**)? [Sankya Yoga: 2.66]

At a Glance: Capturing the Spirit of the Shloka

In our journey to find true peace and happiness, discipline over the senses and mind is essential. Without this inner control, we struggle to focus and reflect on our identity as *Atma* (the Self). This contemplation is the foundation for inner peace, and without peace, lasting happiness remains elusive. Thus, mastering our senses and mind is fundamental for genuine peace and joy.

Commentary

This shloka underscores the crucial role that sense-control and tranquility of mind play in attaining true peace and happiness. Krishna lays down a step-by-step path, where each stage of self-discipline builds upon the previous one to bring about lasting tranquility and fulfillment.

The Role of Discipline in Attaining Wisdom

Krishna begins by saying, '*nāsti buddhir ayuktasya*'—the undisciplined person cannot attain wisdom (*buddhi*). This wisdom is not merely intellectual understanding, but the insight and clarity needed to pursue higher life goals. A mind without control over its senses will be constantly pulled in various directions, unable to focus or establish clear priorities. How can '*buddhi*' take root in such a cluttered mind?

Imagine a student with no discipline or focus. Though fully aware of the importance of education, such a student will struggle to prioritize studies over distractions. Similarly, someone lacking '*śama*' (mind control) and '*dama*' (sense control) will be forever distracted by the allure of temporary pleasures and bereft of '*buddhi*' to connect with the more profound values of life.

The Necessity of Focus and Contemplation (*Bhavana*)

Krishna continues to say, '*na ca ayuktasya bhāvanā*'—the undisciplined mind cannot develop *bhavana*, or the ability to focus and contemplate. Here, *bhavana* has two implications depending on one's goal: for material pursuits, it translates as focused attention; for spiritual pursuits, it is the power of contemplation on the nature of the Self (*Atma*). A mind scattered by sensory distractions lacks the stability needed for deep contemplation, essential for turning intellectual knowledge into experiential realization.

For instance, even if one theoretically understands the nature of the *Atma-* without contemplation (*nidhidhyāsana*), this knowledge serves no practical purpose. Only through disciplined contemplation does the knowledge of the Self (*Atma*) become an experienced reality, bringing about clarity, inner transformation, and peace.

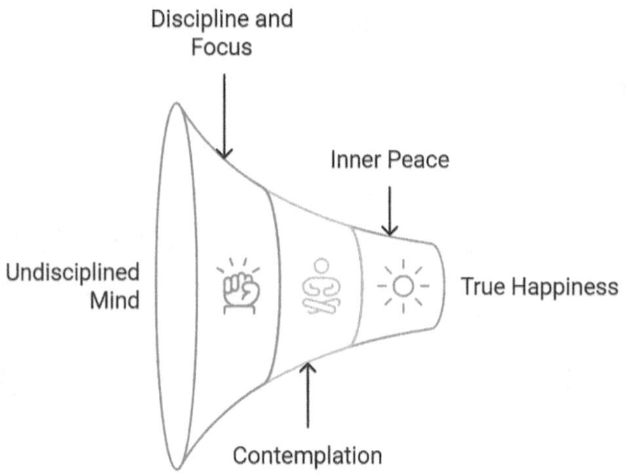

Fig: Discipline: The Gateway to Happiness

The Link Between Contemplation and Inner Peace (*Shanti*)

Krishna then explains the direct connection between contemplation and inner peace: '*na ca abhāvayatah śāntih*'—without contemplation, there is no peace. Shanti refers to a profound peace that arises from a mind no longer agitated by desires or external disturbances. This peace comes from the quietude of mind achieved through understanding one's identity beyond the ego and sensory impulses.

This state of *shanti* grants freedom from the threefold miseries (*tapatraya*) studied earlier:

1. ***Adhibhautika*** (sufferings from external factors like people or events),
2. ***Adhidaivika*** (suffering from natural forces or accidents) and
3. ***Adhyatmika*** (sufferings originating from one's own mind and body).

True peace arises from a mind anchored in Self-knowledge, remaining undisturbed by temporary experiences or external pressures. Without direct, experiential knowledge of the Self (*Atma*), achieving this deep *shanti* (inner peace) is impossible. And this experiential knowledge can only be reached through focused contemplation (*nidhidhyāsana*).

Without Peace, Happiness Remains Elusive

Finally, Krishna logically concludes that true happiness (*sukham*) is unattainable without peace. A restless mind that lacks discipline and is burdened by desires cannot experience the deep contentment that comes from inner peace. When the mind is free from agitation, it experiences a natural state of joy and fulfillment independent of external circumstances.

The Missing Link: Why Inner Peace Eludes Many on the Spiritual Path

While the idea that 'happiness lies within' is widely accepted and propagated, many people on the spiritual path struggle to experience it. Why? According to Krishna, the cause rests within the seeker's lopsided effort. Without sense control and mental focus, external distractions easily sway the mind, keeping it from experiencing inner tranquility. Thus, only through disciplined control of the senses and mind can one shift from knowing peace intellectually to living it as an experiential reality.

Discipline as the Key to Happiness

Achieving true happiness requires mastery over the mind, which begins with control over the sensory system. A spiritually disciplined approach to life is a universally recognized principle for a fulfilled existence. Even modern thinkers like Bertrand Russell, in *The Conquest of Happiness*, suggest that genuine happiness arises with three essential integrations: harmony with society, nature, and within one's mind. Despite his agnostic perspective, Russell recognizes that happiness is rooted in the unity of mind and Self, which aligns closely with the wisdom Krishna imparts here.

Without self-control and inner harmony, the mind becomes vulnerable to external forces, leading to inner turmoil. As Krishna warns, this lack of discipline is the source of life's catastrophes. Greek tragedies, Shakespearean dramas, and epics like the Mahabharata consistently illustrate human lives ensnared in turmoil due to the failure of self-restraint. From the ancient stage to contemporary life, the absence of self-discipline often leads to sorrow and destruction.

Krishna explains that discipline over the senses and mind is the cornerstone of inner peace and true happiness. Without control, one cannot achieve wisdom. Without wisdom, contemplation is not possible. Without contemplation, peace remains elusive. And, without peace, lasting happiness is unattainable.

This shloka lays out a clear progression that powerfully reminds us that if happiness and fulfillment are the goals, self-discipline is the first step. Only with this foundation can we experience the inner harmony and peace that sustain enduring joy.

Reflective Prompt

Can you identify the distractions that consistently divert you from your life goals? How can you introduce focused discipline into your routine to align your thoughts, feelings, words, and actions with your goals?

Master your senses, calm your mind—only then will joy be yours to find

SHLOKA 67: THE DRIFTING MIND

इन्द्रियाणां हि चरतां यन्मनोऽनुविधीयते ।
तदस्य हरति प्रज्ञां वायुर्नावमिवाम्भसि ॥67॥

indriyāṇāṁ hi caratāṁ yanmanō 'nuvidhīyatē |
tadasya harati prajñāṁ vāyurnāvamivāmbhasi ||67||

Translation:

When the mind (***manas***) follows the wandering senses (***indriyāṇām caratām***), it indeed carries away one's wisdom (***prajñā***), just as the wind sweeps away a boat on the water. [**Sankya Yoga: 2.67**]

At a Glance: Capturing the Spirit of the Shloka

Just as the wind carries an untethered boat off course, a mind drawn to sensory distractions is pulled away from life's higher goals and true purpose. This shloka is a powerful reminder of mastering one's senses to stay anchored in wisdom and focused on meaningful pursuits.

Commentary

Krishna presents a vivid analogy in this shloka to illustrate how a person's wisdom is undermined when the unbridled mind chases sensory pleasures. When the senses heedlessly hanker after sense objects, the mind tends to follow, consequently rendering wisdom dysfunctional. Lack of discipline weakens the mind's clarity and stability, leading one astray from life's goals and purpose.

Krishna begins with *'indriyāṇām hi caratām yanmano'nuvidhīyate'* - the mind that follows the wandering senses. This line captures a fundamental truth about the mind's susceptibility to sensory influences. By their very nature, the senses are naturally drawn to sense objects—and the mind, if untrained, loses itself entirely in that attraction. In other words, without discipline and vigilance, the mind loses focus and direction and succumbs to whatever sensory desire presents itself.

Krishna explains that this complete surrender of the mind to the pull of the senses, *'harati prajñām'*—robs the person of their wisdom. Wisdom here refers to the capacity for deeper understanding and discernment, the ability to see beyond the immediate and transient to what is truly valuable. When the mind follows the senses, wisdom is overshadowed, and clarity of purpose is lost in the pursuit of momentary pleasures.

Fig: When senses steer the mind, wisdom is lost in the storm of desire

A Striking Analogy: The Boat and the Wind

To illustrate the impact of an uncontrolled mind, Krishna offers the analogy *'vāyur nāvam iva ambhasi'*—like the wind carries away a boat on the waters. Imagine an unanchored little boat adrift on the vast expanse of the sea. Just as an untethered boat is at the mercy of every gust of wind, a mind without control is easily swept away by the currents of sensory desire. This powerful imagery conveys how a lack of mastery over the senses can lead a person into confusion and, ultimately, a sense of inner shipwreck.

History and literature down the ages recount innumerable tragedies of individuals who, like the boat on the waters, were driven off course by unchecked desires. Think of Goethe's *Faust*, in which the central character Faust laments the human tendency to *"stumble from desire to possession, and in possession languish from desire."* This cycle of longing, attaining, and finding no absolute satisfaction mirrors the mind's fruitless expedition when it is ruled by the senses. It is a tragic cycle, repeated throughout history, of people searching for fulfillment externally and losing sight of their inner peace.

Self-Discipline as the Key to Liberation

Individuals are vulnerable to external forces without this discipline, just as a boat is vulnerable to shifting winds. This state of susceptibility can lead to inner turmoil, as desires and sensory temptations constantly push and pull the mind in multiple directions. The shloka is a call to take responsibility for our mental discipline, realizing that one can attain true freedom and joy only through control of the mind and senses.

Vedanta reinforces that this arduous inward pilgrimage requires personal effort. No one else can travel the distance for us, just as no one else can experience the moon's beauty on our behalf. In *Vivekachudamani*, Shankaracharya echoes this point: while others may help with worldly burdens, spiritual liberation is a personal journey only we can undertake. One must cultivate '*sphuṭabodha cakṣuṣā*' - the eye of understanding to recognize and grasp the true nature of existence.

Krishna's message here is self-mastery and freedom. Rather than being driven by external stimuli, he encourages us to cultivate inner discipline and clarity, guiding us toward a life aligned with higher purpose and inner peace. The Bhagavad Gita's primary goal is transforming us from creatures governed by impulses to individuals empowered by wisdom.

> ## Reflective Prompt
>
> Do you remember any instance in your life where, despite seeing the pitfall, your mind haplessly gave in to a sensory impulse? Did the regret make you more mindful going forward? How will you approach a similar episode in the future?
>
> ---
>
> ---
>
> ---

*Wisdom fades when the senses lead and the mind
follows blindly*

SHLOKA 68: MASTERING THE SENSES, ANCHORING THE MIND

तस्माद्यस्य महाबाहो निगृहीतानि सर्वशः |
इन्द्रियाणीन्द्रियार्थेभ्यः तस्य प्रज्ञा प्रतिष्ठिता ||68||

tasmādyasya mahābāhō nigṛhītāni sarvaśaḥ |
indriyāṇīndriyārthēbhyaḥ tasya prajñā pratiṣṭhitā ||68||

Translation:

Therefore, O mighty-armed (***mahā-bāho***), the wisdom of one whose senses (***indriyāṇi***) are fully restrained (***nigṛhītāni***) from their objects (***indriya-arthēbhyaḥ***) is steady and well-established
[Sankya Yoga: 2.68]

At a Glance: Capturing the Spirit of the Shloka

Discipline over the senses and mind is essential for personal growth and spiritual evolution. A person who practices this self-mastery gains steadiness in wisdom, ultimately leading to inner clarity and Self-realization.

Commentary

In this shloka, Krishna concludes his advice on achieving steadiness of wisdom (*sthira-prajña*) by emphasizing the crucial role of discipline over the senses. In addressing Arjuna as *'mahābāho'* (mighty-armed), Krishna acknowledges Arjuna's physical strength and valor but gently alludes to the higher challenge: the need for inner strength to master the mind and senses. Krishna encourages Arjuna to direct the might of his physical prowess inward and conquer the senses that drag the mind into all untoward directions.

'Tasmāt' (therefore) marks the logical summation of Krishna's discourse on self-control and steadiness of mind in this chapter. He emphasizes that self-mastery is consciously restraining the senses from their respective sense objects—just as a tortoise withdraws its limbs at will. The capacity to engage or withdraw one's senses as needed indicates actual control, where the senses do not dictate one's actions but serve the higher goals of one's intellect (*buddhi*).

Discipline, Not Suppression

We need to reiterate here that sense control does not mean suppression. A common misconception, especially among those studying Eastern spirituality, prevails that controlling the senses means repressing them. Suppression can be harmful, leading to inner conflicts or unintended expressions of desire at inopportune moments. The Bhagavad Gita does not advocate stifling one's desires or senses. Instead, it prescribes intelligent regulation- a balanced approach that neither suppresses nor indulges but channels sensory energy effectively. This approach ensures that desires do not disturb our peace of mind or hinder our spiritual progress.

Let us take the analogy of a river. Abruptly stopping its gush would create a flood. At the same time, letting it flow unbridled to ultimately empty itself into the ocean would waste its potential to nourish life around its banks. Instead, building a dam would channel the river's usefulness purposefully. Likewise, Krishna proposes a disciplined approach where one's sensory energy is directed deliberately toward constructive ends.

Channeling Energy for Higher Goals

Modern science also supports the idea that we have a vast reservoir of mental and intellectual energy, which often goes untapped due to lack of focus. By consciously directing sensory impulses toward meaningful goals, we harness this energy and prevent it from dissipating through distractions. *'Nigraha,'* or restraint, thus becomes a means of channeling mental resources toward achieving exponential outer success, inner peace, and wisdom rather than denying or suppressing natural tendencies.

Wisdom Anchored in Self-Control

Krishna explains, *'yasya indriyāṇi indriyārthebhyaḥ nigṛhītāni'*— wisdom becomes steady only for those who have gained control over their senses. Attraction toward sense objects is natural; fatal attraction is not. We must perceive sense objects for what they are and willfully direct our senses to align with our highest values and goals.

Only human beings are given the freedom to choose their actions. All other beings function within the confines of a set template nature provides. However, the freedom to choose our actions can be exercised only by mastering our impulses rather than being at their mercy. Only then can we rest assured that our decisions and actions come from our highest wisdom.

Path to Steady Wisdom

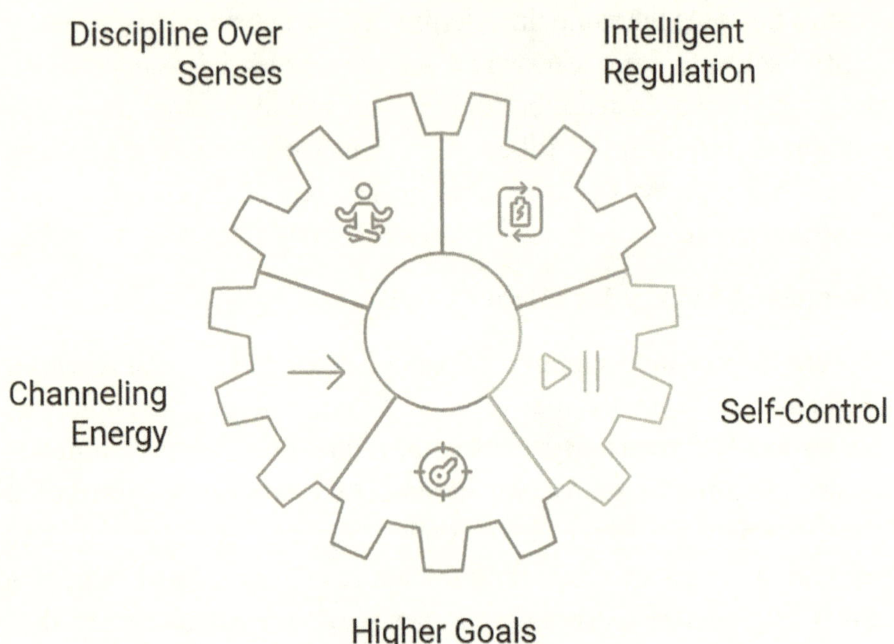

Fig: Path to steady wisdom

This shloka provides guidance for anyone seeking lasting peace and wisdom. It reiterates that sense control is the foundation for inner stability. By disciplining sensory energy, we align our actions with wisdom, allowing us to productively engage with the world while maintaining peace and clarity. This approach ensures that our choices consistently align with our highest aspirations.

Reflective Prompt

In any decision-making process, are your choices dictated by your senses, or do they emerge from clarity and wisdom? What steps can you take to ensure the latter?

Like a river guided by its banks, wisdom flows when the senses are tamed

SHLOKA 69: DAY AND NIGHT OF AWARENESS

या निशा सर्वभूतानां तस्यां जागर्ति संयमी |
यस्यां जाग्रति भूतानि सा निशा पश्यतो मुनेः ||69||

yā niśā sarvabhūtānāṁ tasyāṁ jāgarti saṁyamī |
yasyāṁ jāgrati bhūtāni sā niśā paśyatō munēḥ ||69||

Translation:

That which is night for all beings (*yā niśā sarva-bhūtānām*), the one
with mastery over oneself (*saṁyamī*) is awake (*jāgarti*). What is
wakefulness for beings (*yasyāṁ jāgrati bhūtāni*) is like night (*sā niśā*)
for the discerning sage (*paśyataḥ muneḥ*) who truly sees.
[Sankya Yoga: 2.69]

At a Glance: Capturing the Spirit of the Shloka

The wise and the materialistic inhabit the same world and encounter similar challenges along their path, yet their perspectives are vastly different. The wise, identified with the eternal, all-pervading *Atma*, recognize the underlying unity in all things—a Reality imperceptible to the unwise. Conversely, the separateness and binding attachments perceived by the materialists go unnoticed before the wise.

Commentary

Over the following two verses, Krishna presents profound and poetic metaphors to illuminate the contrasting perspectives of the wise (*jñāni*) and the ignorant (*ajñāni*). He highlights the transformative shift in perception that comes with spiritual wisdom. Using the analogy of day and night, Krishna illustrates the fundamental difference between how someone established in Self-knowledge views Reality and how an uninitiated person does.

Two Perspectives, One World

The wise and the ignorant live in the same world, operating with nature-endowed senses, mind, and intellect, and experience similar sense objects, beings, and circumstances. The difference between them lies not in what they experience but in their internal perceptions. While the world unapologetically remains what it is - dynamic, challenging, and impermanent, the perspective of the wise is lifted by their identification with a more profound, unchanging truth beyond these surface realities.

The Bhagavad Gita offers no magic formula to change other people's behavior or the world. Instead, it calls for a transformation within oneself—to develop a different way of looking at the world. Thus, the same world that can be a source of attachment, grief, and fear for an ordinary person can be experienced with immense peace, joy, and contentment by the wise. It is beautifully put forward by American writer and teacher of courses in self-improvement Dale Carnegie: "Two men look out from prison bars; One saw the mud, the other saw stars."

The Metaphor of Night and Day

Krishna uses very relatable imagery of night and day to expound on the glaring difference in perspectives of the wise and 'otherwise':

1. Night for the World, Day for the Wise: Krishna begins by saying, *'yā niśā sarvabhūtānām'*—that which is night for all beings (where "night" represents ignorance or darkness). For those bereft of the wisdom of the more profound, non-dual truth of existence—their true identity as the *Atma* (Consciousness) that is beyond the body, mind, and intellect, and the oneness underlying all things—appears as "night," something obscure and hidden.

However, *'tasyāṁ jāgarti saṁyamī'*—the wise are awake to this eternal truth. The *jñāni* (wise person) transcends the confines of the body, mind, and intellect, wholly identified with their true identity as *Atma*, the fundamental reality of the universe, and sees this one reality in every name and form.

2. Day for the World, Night for the Wise: Conversely, Krishna explains, *'yasyām jāgrati bhūtāni sā niśā paśyatō muneḥ'* - what is day for the world" is "night for the wise." In other words, the limited identification with the body, mind, and intellect along with desires, attachments, and diversions that occupy most people, are viewed as "night" or insignificant by the wise. While others remain absorbed in these fleeting realities, the sage remains detached, fully aware that these temporary experiences cannot provide lasting fulfillment. For the wise, true peace and contentment lie beyond these superficial pursuits in recognizing the true Self (*Atma*) that transcends the changing world.

The Example of the Ocean and Waves

To understand this metaphor better, imagine a group of people observing large and small waves rising and falling across the vast expanse of the ocean. However, some understand that irrespective of their size or fervor, all waves are ultimately just forms of water—expressions of the underlying reality, the ocean. Amazed, though undisturbed, they remain focused on the constancy and eternal nature of the ocean behind the continual crest and trough of the waves.

In contrast, others get carried away in the dynamic roll of the waves, perceiving each one as an independent, distinct phenomenon. They celebrate every rise and lament every fall, failing to perceive the truth that, ultimately, it is all just water temporarily rising from the ever-constant ocean beneath and disappearing back into it.

Similarly, the wise person (*jñāni)* perceives and remains singularly focused on the unity (a*dvaita*) of the *Atma* beneath life's changing appearances. The ignorant person (*ajñāni*), oblivious to the immutable, indestructible, and immutable substratum of existence, is fixated on the surface realities, experiencing elation and despair in response to life's inevitable fluctuations.

The Human and the Owl: Different States of Awareness

Krishna's metaphor compares the *jñāni* (the wise) to a human being awake during the day, while the *ajñāni* (the ignorant) is likened to an owl, a creature awake at night but asleep during the day. Here:

- **Day** represents the awareness of one's identity as *Atma* (Consciousness) and the oneness underlying all things.
- **Night** symbolizes ignorance, seeing oneself only as the body, mind, and intellect, which perceive plurality and division.

The *jñāni*, like a human awake in daylight, clearly perceives their true identity as *Atma*, recognizing the non-dual Reality and resting peacefully in its truth. The *ajñāni*, like an owl, is oblivious to this light, perceiving only in the "night" of ignorance, grossly inhibited by separateness and impermanence that dominate their view.

Aspect	*Jnani* (The Wise)	*Ajnani* (The Ignorant)
Perception of Reality	Sees the eternal, unchanging *Atma* (Self) as the ultimate truth.	Focuses on fleeting, external appearances and temporary realities.
Response to Life	Remains calm and unshaken amidst dualities of success and failure, joy and sorrow.	Gets easily disturbed by external events and fluctuates with circumstances.
Attachment to Sense Objects	Detached from sensory pleasures; uses senses with awareness and discipline.	Enslaved by sensory desires; driven by impulses.
State of Mind	Serene, content, and undisturbed.	Restless, discontent, and easily agitated.

Applying the Teaching to Life

Krishna's metaphor carries profound practical implications. For those living solely in the material realm, life is but a series of births, deaths, unions, and separations—each event bringing its own share of joy and sorrow. Unbridled mental and intellectual involvement in these transient experiences creates inconsolable grief and fear. The wise, who are grounded in the awareness of their true identity as *Atma* (Consciousness), view life's impermanence for what it is, as it is. Blessed with this higher perspective, they remain undisturbed through the dualities of pleasure and pain, loss and gain.

The Bhagavad Gita does not advocate avoiding or escaping life but rather transforming one's inner perspective. By anchoring awareness in the *Atma*—the eternal truth of oneness—a person becomes free from the constant emotional turmoil tied to external situations.

The Qualities of the Wise: *Saṁyamī* and *Muni*

Krishna describes the wise as *'saṁyamī* 'and *'muni.'* These terms emphasize the inner mastery and clarity of perception gained through focused discipline, which enables the wise to experience life's higher truths distinct from ordinary perceptions.

'Saṁyamī 'comes from the root *'yama,'* which means self-mastery or control over the mind and senses. A *saṁyamī* is someone who has disciplined the mind, directing it away from fleeting desires and toward enduring truths. And *'Muni, 'refers* to one with an unobstructed vision, often achieved through deep contemplation (*mananaśīla*).

For such a wise person, the usual worldly pursuits of sensory attachments and transient goals appear like "night," holding no real value. Instead, they remain "awake " to the deeper Reality of *Atma.* These terms, *'saṁyamī'* and *'muni,'* spotlight the discipline and clarity that enable the wise to experience life's higher truths, distinct from ordinary perceptions.

Reflections Across Spiritual Traditions

The *Bible, Sufi teachings*, and the *Guru Granth Sahib* each affirm the same truth that the wise perceive the world differently - awake to a more profound Reality unknown to the ordinary.

Jesus Christ says in the Bible, *"The eye is the lamp of the body. If your eyes are healthy, your whole body will be full of light" (Matthew 6:22).* Here, a "healthy eye" symbolizes spiritual awareness and wisdom. The wise have an inner clarity, enabling them to perceive a truth beyond transient material concerns. In this state, they remain "awake" to spiritual Reality while others may be asleep, entangled in worldly pursuits.

"The wound is the place where the Light enters you"—the oft-quoted words of Sufi poet Rumi, imply that wisdom, born from life's challenges, opens one's awareness to a profound inner truth. For

the Sufi, ordinary reality may feel like "night," but through inner awakening, they experience a "daylight" that reveals the eternal and boundless.

The *Guru Granth Sahib* speaks of those whose consciousness is centered in the divine Name (Naam), perceiving the world as a fleeting dream while remaining steady in the unchanging Reality. While others remain entangled in the illusions of Maya, these individuals live fully awake to the divine truth.

Echoes of Goethe: Awakening to Truth Beyond Illusion

The German polymath Goethe, known for his profound reflections on human nature and the quest for truth, offers insights in *Maxims and Reflections* that resonate closely with the message of this shloka. Goethe suggests that *"error stands in the same relation to truth as sleeping to waking,"* reiterating the contrast between ignorance and wisdom that Krishna highlights. He implies that ignorance, like sleep, veils the clarity of truth. Yet, just as waking brings a sense of renewal, moving from ignorance to awareness offers a revitalizing return to truth. For the wise person, the "waking" state of spiritual knowledge is a natural state of alertness to the enduring Reality, while for the ordinary person, this awareness remains hidden, like a truth missed during sleep. This migration from error and illusion to clarity and wisdom illustrates the inner transformation Krishna speaks of, where one awakens to one's true identity and finds lasting peace.

Progressing Beyond Immediate Pleasures

Throughout life, we progress from one level of pleasure to another. Just as a child finds complete joy in simple toys, adults seek joy in more complex quests. Each pursuit attained offers a different kind of fulfillment. Yet, no matter how grand each conquest is, an unbroken experience of peace and happiness remains elusive to most. Vedanta encourages us not to get enmeshed and entangled in any particular phase but to keep progressing toward attaining the Self.

Adi Shankaracharya in his famous Bhaja Govindam laments:

bāla stāvat krīḍāsaktaḥ
taruṇa stāvat taruṇīsaktaḥ |
vṛddha stāvat-chintāmagnaḥ
parame brahmaṇi koapi na lagnaḥ ‖ 7 ‖

Childhood is lost in attachment to games. Youth is lost in attachment to passion. Old age is lost in attachment to regret and worry. But hardly anyone wants to be lost (attached) in Para-Brahman, the Supreme Spirit.

Each phase of life no doubt holds its charm and must be enjoyed thoroughly. But one must not get lost in any of them. Sri Ramakrishna's parable of the woodcutter describes the ideal spiritual journey perfectly:

Initially, the woodcutter only gathers simple wood for his livelihood. But after hearing the words "march on" (*egiye jāo*), he ventures further, discovering increasingly valuable resources—better wood, copper, gold, and even diamonds. Just as the woodcutter finds more incredible treasures as he progresses, the spiritual seeker who moves beyond sensory attachments toward inner mastery and wisdom finds more profound and enduring joy.

For spiritual growth, it is essential to "march on." Instead of stagnating at the level of fleeting pleasures and surface realities, we are encouraged to seek limitless joy beyond material or sensory indulgences. The human journey is meant to be one of ever-evolving understanding, where we progressively discover the deeper layers of fulfillment available to us. All concerted efforts finally culminate in the realization of *Atma*, the eternal Self, and the unchanging truth that underlies all existence.

This shloka hails the wise who see beyond surface appearances, recognizing their true identity as *Atma* and the unity underlying all existence. This understanding allows them to attain a peace unruffled by the ephemeral. Such a vision transforms life into an experience of lasting joy and contentment—not by altering the world but changing how one perceives it. Awakening to this truth enables one to rise above the dualities of ordinary experience and enjoy life from the highest spiritual vantage point.

Reflective Prompt

Having embarked on the spiritual journey, do you find your perspective on little and significant happenings in life becoming increasingly different from those around you? Knowing what you now know, how will you respond to these differing standpoints?

The wise are awake to the timeless - as the world continues to sleep in the lull of fleeting dreams

SHLOKA 70: THE INNER WHOLENESS OF THE WISE

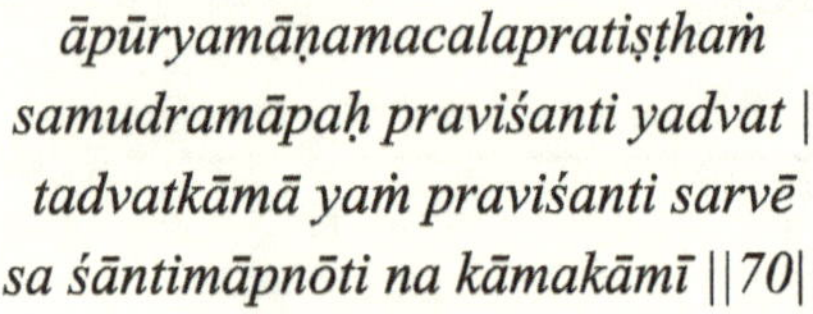

आपूर्यमाणमचलप्रतिष्ठं
समुद्रमापः प्रविशन्ति यद्वत् ।
तद्वत्कामा यं प्रविशन्ति सर्वे
स शान्तिमाप्नोति न कामकामी ॥70॥

āpūryamāṇamacalapratiṣṭham
samudramāpaḥ praviśanti yadvat |
tadvatkāmā yaṁ praviśanti sarvē
sa śāntimāpnōti na kāmakāmī ||70||

Translation:

Just as waters flow into the vast ocean, constantly filled from all sides
yet remaining steady and full (***ācala-pratiṣṭham***), so too do all desires
enter the wise person (***yaṁ praviśanti sarve***) without disturbing their
inner peace. Only such a person attains true peace (***śāntim āpnōti***),
unlike one who is constantly driven by cravings (***kāma-kāmī***)
[Sankya Yoga: 2.70]

At a Glance: Capturing the Spirit of the Shloka

A wise person, firmly rooted in the awareness of their true identity as *Atma* (Consciousness), lives in the world *Paripūrṇam* - wholly content. Unlike others who seek fulfillment from external sources and feel inadequate without them, the wise engage in life without needing anything from the world and feel no loss if anything is taken from them. Krishna likens this state to an ocean, full and undisturbed, into which rivers flow continuously without altering its depth. Similarly, innumerable sense stimuli come before the wise but do not disturb their peace. In contrast, like a small pond, an unwise person floods with every downpour and dries up in scorching heat, unable to maintain inner stability.

Commentary

In this shloka, Krishna uses a beautiful simile from the *Mundaka Upanishad* to illustrate the difference between the wise *(jñāni)* and the unwise *(ajñāni)*. He portrays the image of an ocean that so powerfully contrasts the calm, fullness, and independence of the Self-realized sage with the restlessness and dependency of the unwise.

The Ocean as a Symbol of Fullness and Stability

Krishna compares the *Jnani* to an ocean. The ocean, vast and complete, is unaffected by the rivers that flow into it. Though countless rivers pour their waters into it from all directions, it remains full *(pūrṇam)* and steady *(acalapratiṣṭham)*, never overflowing or disturbed. This fullness symbolizes independence—the ocean is not dependent on the rivers to maintain its wholeness. If the rivers flow in, the ocean accepts them; if they do not, it remains unaltered.

Similarly, the sage's mind is like this ever-full, self-sufficient ocean. Such a person remains unscathed by the fluctuating world of desires and external validation. Their sense of wholeness is independent and unwavering. Just as the ocean remains undisturbed by the gushing in or not of rivers, the wise person remains undisturbed by the presence or absence of sensory experiences or the opinions of others.

Fig: Like the vast ocean, the wise remain unshaken by the rivers of desires—full, calm, and infinite within

The Unwise and the Dependence on External objects and situations

In contrast to the wise, the mind of the unwise (*ajñāni*) depends on external inputs to feel complete. If something positive happens, they are elated; if something negative occurs, they are distressed. Their peace and happiness lie at the mercy of external circumstances—fulfillment of desires, people's approval, or favorable situations.

This dependency makes the *ajñāni* very vulnerable. They depend on others for validation and are easily impacted by praise and criticism. The mind becomes a slave to external factors and is constantly disturbed, like a little pond flooding with each heavy downpour and becoming parched in drought.

The Wise and Inner Peace

Krishna states that the wise, whose minds are like the ocean, remain unaffected regardless of what comes their way. Just as the ocean's depth is unfathomable and unconquerable, the inner fullness of the wise person makes them content and resilient. Even as sensory experiences enter their mind from all directions, their wholeness is steady. They do not depend on these external inputs for happiness. Only a person with this steady equipoise, Krishna declares, '*sa śāntimāpnōti*' - attains peace.

On the other hand, the desires of the unwise are never-ending, and their minds are constantly perturbed. Krishna calls such individuals *kāmakāmī*—those continually seeking the fulfillment of desires. They are like a bucket with a hole in it; no matter how much water you pour into it; you cannot fill it. Such a person can never find true peace because they always clutch at something outside themselves to feel complete.

Inner Fullness

The wise person has cultivated a mind that is so satiated, so complete, that external circumstances neither add to nor subtract from it. They have achieved what the ocean symbolizes: self-sufficiency and remain unchanged by the flow of life around them.

The wise person does not suppress or reject desires but transcends the need to depend on them for happiness. Just as the ocean remains unaffected by all the rivers that flow into it, the wise person remains steady and content in all situations, neither rising with praise nor retreating with criticism.

The Litmus Test for Wisdom

This metaphor is a valuable guide for self-reflection. We can measure our progress on the path of wisdom by observing how we respond to situations. If our equilibrium is easily disturbed by others' opinions or the ups and downs of life, it is a sign that the mind is still dependent on external factors. If we can remain centered and undisturbed, we can rest assured that we are steadily moving toward the wisdom Krishna describes as ocean-like.

Spiritual Parallels of a Steady Mind

An undisturbed, ocean-like mind is a universal vision across most spiritual traditions, iterating its timeless value for human fulfillment. In Buddhism, the term *bodhicitta*, or the awakened mind, represents a state where desires and attachments no longer cause disturbance. This stable and expansive mind allows all thoughts and emotions to flow, like rivers entering the ocean, without causing turbulence. It reflects the peace of an enlightened being who has transcended worldly cravings.

Similarly, the Bible's "And the peace of God, which passeth all understanding, shall keep your hearts and minds through Christ Jesus" (Philippians 4:7), echoes the idea of an inner peace that guards the heart and mind, unaffected by the external world. This peace, rooted in divine presence, offers stability beyond ordinary comprehension, akin to the fullness of the ocean that Krishna describes.

The Guru Granth Sahib declares, *"He who meditates on the Lord and is intoxicated with His Love is satisfied and contented; sorrows and sufferings do not afflict him."* This peace, found in divine connection, releases one from worldly disturbances, like the steady and undisturbed mind focused on the *Atma* (Self) described in the Bhagavad Gita.

Walt Whitman's Vision of Inner Completeness

Walt Whitman, one of America's most celebrated poets, is best known for his expansive, inclusive verse and celebration of the human spirit. In *"Song of "Myself,"* from his larger collection *Leaves of Grass*, Whitman poeticizes: "I am large, I contain multitudes."

These words laud the essence of an undisturbed, expansive self-awareness that transcends the fluctuations of life, just as Krishna describes the wise person who is like an ocean—complete and full, unaffected by the rivers (sense stimuli or desires) that flow into it. Whitman's self-proclaimed "multitudes" suggest a vast, accommodating Consciousness that encounters life's diversity and experiences without becoming overwhelmed. For Whitman, true contentment comes not from external sources but from within, where fullness remains intact amidst change. His verse reflects an understanding that lasting peace is found through recognizing one's true, infinite nature.

Through this beautiful simile of the ocean from the *Mundaka Upanishad*, Krishna offers a timeless lesson: true peace and contentment come not from external achievements or validation but from cultivating inner completeness. By becoming like the ocean—whole and unaffected by the flow of desires—the wise person revels in a state of enduring peace that the unwise, outwardly craving and searching can never attain. This state of independence and self-mastery is the foundation of a life of true freedom and joy.

> **Reflective Prompt**
>
> Does your peace and joy depend on what you receive from the world or what is taken from you? How do others' opinions and outcomes of your efforts affect your inner equilibrium? Is it ok to put the key to your happiness in another's pocket? And for how long? Think.
>
> --
>
> --
>
> --

---

*Desires come, desires go, but on the whole and steady minds
of the wise, they have no hold*

SHLOKA 71: THE INNER FULFILLMENT OF THE WISE

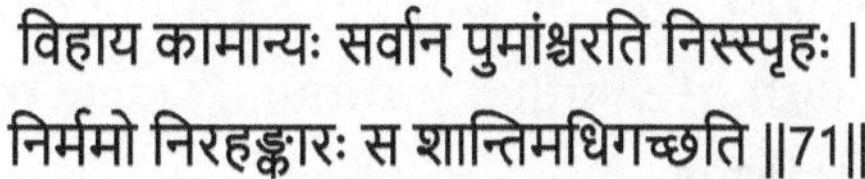

विहाय कामान्यः सर्वान् पुमांश्चरति निस्स्पृहः ।
निर्ममो निरहङ्कारः स शान्तिमधिगच्छति ॥71॥

vihāya kāmānyaḥ sarvān pumāṃścarati nissprṛhaḥ |
nirmamō nirahaṅkāraḥ sa śāntimadhigacchati ||71||

Translation:

Having given up all binding desires *(kāmān)*, the person who moves around, devoid of longing *(niḥsprṛhaḥ)*, without the sense of limited 'I' *(nirahaṅkāraḥ)* and 'mine' *(nirmamaḥ)*, gains peace *(śāntiḥ)*
[Sankya Yoga: 2.71]

At a Glance: Capturing the Spirit of the Shloka

The *sthitaprajñā* (wise) moves freely in the world, independent of external validation or possessions. Wholly identified with the immutable, indestructible, and eternal Self (*Atma*), they disentangle from the narrow confines of 'I' and 'mine.' They experience boundless joy and unbroken peace through all the vicissitudes of life.

Commentary

In the following two shlokas, Krishna concludes his description of the *sthitaprajñā* (wise). In this shloka, Krishna explains that a wise person moves through life with a profound sense of non-attachment, inner freedom, and peace.

A Life Beyond Longing and Dependency

Krishna describes the wise person as *'kāmān sarvān vihāya'* - one who has transcended all binding desires and moves freely in the world *'pumāṁścarati nisspṛhaḥ,'* independent and self-sufficient.

The Bhagavad Gita repeatedly clarifies that true freedom cannot be experienced by withdrawing from the world or avoiding relationships but by releasing attachments to them. The inner equilibrium of the wise is not destabilized by the outcomes of events or the opinions of others. Whether they be a king, like Janaka, a renunciant, like Adi Śaṅkara, a software engineer on Wall Street, or a homemaker caring for family- the *sthitaprajñā* (wise) navigates this world with absolute sovereignty.

Identified with Self (*Atma*), the wise enjoy an inner completeness independent of what the world offers. They remain internally detached while engaging with relationships, responsibilities, and the ever-changing circumstances of life, irrespective of what life brings to their table or takes away.

British poet William Ernest Henley's poem Invictus reveals this state of Inner Freedom like no other words in English literature ever have:

"Out of the night that covers me,
Black as the pit from pole to pole,
I thank whatever gods may be
For my unconquerable soul.

In the fell clutch of circumstance
I have not winced nor cried aloud.
Under the bludgeonings of chance
My head is bloody, but unbowed.

Beyond this place of wrath and tears
Looms but the Horror of the shade,
And yet the menace of the years
Finds and shall find me unafraid.

It matters not how strait the gate,
How charged with punishments the scroll,
I am the master of my fate,
I am the captain of my soul."

Apart from the scriptures, leaders of thought have sought inspiration and solace from poetry throughout the ages. Nelson Mandela, the anti-apartheid leader, is known to have recited this poem repeatedly during his harrowing 27-year imprisonment.

Transcending 'I' and 'Mine'

The *sthitaprajñā* is *'nirmama'* -free from possessiveness and *'nirahaṅkāraḥ'* - free from ego or self-importance. Disidentified with the body, mind, and intellect, they possess nothing as 'mine.' This detachment does not imply neglect or indifference but an understanding that all things are temporary. The wise identify themselves with the larger whole, free from attachments to things, people, and even the body. Their perspective shifts from a narrow sense of 'I' and 'mine' to an expansive identification with the *Atma* (true Self), which is universal and eternal.

Seeing Beyond the Illusion of Ownership

To understand the evolutionary process of one's attachment, think of children who perceive their toys as the center of their world. They would not trade them for anything you believe is more valuable. But they are no longer obsessed with those toys as they mature. They do not struggle to throw the toys away but simply lose interest in them. As adults, those "silly" toys are replaced with more complex attachments of wealth, status, family, and the like. But the sting of attachment persists right through life, as seen in Adi Śaṅkara's Bhaja Govindam, highlighted in the exposition of the previous shloka.

The wise, however, perceive all material things as leased, recognizing that nothing truly belongs to them—not even their physical body, which is eventually returned to the elements. This understanding dissolves the ego, leaving no room for possessiveness or pride.

Relationships Without Attachment

The Bhagavad Gita advocates for conscious engagement in relationships and activities while being internally independent of them. The wise love profoundly but do not hinge their happiness on the response or behavior of others. If a relationship is harmonious, they enjoy it; if it changes, they remain at peace. Their sense of self is not tied to the affection, actions, or approval of others, which shields them from the emotional turmoil often associated with dependency.

Such freedom enables them to enjoy life thoroughly and tackle its inevitable changes with resilience. They live in the world to give rather than to receive, showering the gifts of love and understanding on one and all without needing reciprocation. They view life as an opportunity for sharing and expressing compassion rather than fulfilling personal desires.

Experiencing Life with True Freedom and Joy

Krishna concludes by stating, '*Sa śāntimadhigacchati*'—*such* a person gains peace. The *sthitaprajñā's* approach *to* life and living produces a profound sense of inner peace (*śānti*). Free from desires, ego, and possessiveness, the wise engage joyfully with every moment. Their inner peace, independent of all external phenomena, is firmly established in the unchanging Self.

The Wisdom Beyond 'I' and 'Mine'

This shloka shows us how attachment to 'I' and 'mine' generates endless cravings and self-centeredness. On the other hand, when a person feels oneness with others, their personal cravings diminish. They celebrate the joys of others and share in their sorrows without envy or pride. Think. If your little toe hurts, are *you* not affected? Of course, you are because, although small and perhaps insignificant, it is an integral part of your body. Expand this thought outward from the body to all of humanity.

In a healthy society, this identification with the whole as one's own Self (*Atma*) nurtures a disciplined mind that prioritizes the well-being of all, establishing the basis for genuine ethics and morality. Such a society values shared fulfillment over selfish gain, reflecting Krishna's statement, "*sa śāntim adhigacchati*"—such a person attains peace. This thought is beautifully articulated by African American revolutionary and human rights activist Malcolm X through an interesting wordplay, " When "I" is replaced by "we" even illness becomes wellness."

As narrated in the *Śrīmad Bhāgavatam* (11.7.29), King Yadu meets a young ascetic who was calm and peaceful even in his youth. When Yadu inquires how the ascetic found this inner peace in a world driven by desire, his answer re-establishes the same truth: true peace is a lived experience, not just a theoretical ideal. It is attained by letting go of personal craving and finding contentment within and in harmony with others.

This shloka offers us a timeless lesson: lasting peace and contentment are born not from amassing possessions or fulfilling desires but from letting go of binding attachments and embracing a broader sense of identity. By transcending the narrow confines of 'I' and 'mine,' one can live with the boundless joy and peace emanating from a state of inner freedom.

Reflective Prompt

Reflect on a recent situation that disrupted your peace. What does this episode reveal about your attachments to the world? What steps can you take to begin to rise above these dependencies?

The wise are like the sky—holding everything, yet bound by nothing

SHLOKA 72: ONENESS WITH BRAHMAN

एषा ब्राह्मी स्थितिः पार्थ नैनां प्राप्य विमुह्यति ।
स्थित्वाऽस्यामन्तकालेऽपि ब्रह्मनिर्वाणमृच्छति ॥72॥

ēṣā brāhmī sthitiḥ pārtha naināṁ prāpya vimuhyati |
sthitvā'syāmantakālē'pi brahmanirvāṇamṛcchati ||72|

Translation:

Arjuna (***Pārtha***)! This is the state of being established in Brahman
(***brāhmī sthitiḥ***). Attaining this state, one is never again deluded
(***na vimuhyati***). Even at the final moment of life (***antakāle***),
remaining established in this state, one attains liberation in Brahman
(***brahmanirvāṇam***) [Sankya Yoga: 2.72]

At a Glance: Capturing the Spirit of the Shloka

Sthitaprajñā represents an unbroken awareness of oneself as *Brahman* (Consciousness)—the foundational Reality of the universe, beyond the physical body, mind, and intellect. It is a transformative understanding of one's inherent and inextricable connection with the Creator and the created. The knowledge of the Self (*Atma Jnana*) is accessible to all seekers and, once realized, is lasting and irreversible. Having attained this state, at the end of one's physical incarnation, one is freed from the karmically binding repetitive cycle of birth and death, merging fully with the divine Reality. This awareness is the ultimate purpose of human existence and the validation of the timeless Upanishadic truth, *"Tat Tvam Asi"*—Thou art That.

Commentary

In this concluding shloka of Chapter II, Krishna wraps up the discourse on the nature of the *sthitaprajñā* or one of steady wisdom, by explaining that this enlightened state is truly a state of being established in *Brahman*, the ultimate Reality.

The State of Brahman: *Brāhmī Sthitiḥ*

This shloka begins by affirming that this *'stithi'*—the steadiness of the wisdom of knowing oneself as Atman (Consciousness)—is none other than being established in *Brahman* (the foundational Reality of the universe), or *brāhmī sthitiḥ*.

Brāhmī sthitiḥ portrays a continuous awareness of oneself as Brahman. It is not a transient experience or state of mind like those in meditation (*samādhi*), which can be gained and lost.

Tat Tvam Asi—"Thou art That"—is the highest truth about ourselves and the ultimate goal of all human beings. It is the destination that evolution is guiding us toward. The Bhagavad Gita unravels this timeless truth step-by-step and encourages us to recognize and embrace it.

Fig: Know Thyself – The Atma is Brahman, the Absolute Truth.

No Fall Down: *Nainām Prāpya Vimuhyati*

Krishna assures Arjuna that there is no falling back into ignorance or regressing once this awareness is established. When we hear of individuals losing their way on the spiritual path, we must understand that they have not yet reached this depth of realization. For one established in *brāhmī sthitiḥ*, the wisdom remains intact, steady, and available through any temporary setbacks or external challenges.

When one attains *brāhmī sthitiḥ*, all delusion (*moha*) disappears—doubts, insecurities, and existential conflicts like the ones that plagued Arjuna on the battlefield are annihilated. Unlike the unwise, constantly torn between conflicting desires and fears, the *sthitaprajñā* engages with life with profound clarity, rooted in a deep understanding of their eternal nature.

The Transformative Power of *Atma Jnana*: *Antakāle Api Brahmanirvāṇam ṛcchati*

The transformative power of Self-knowledge (*Atma Jnana*) lies in its capacity to free the seeker from all forms of suffering. Krishna emphasizes that this freedom is attainable in life itself (*Jivanmukti*), whether one gains it in youth or later in life. It releases the seeker from the psychological and emotional pain rooted in desires, attachment, and ego-centric thinking. Once firmly established in *jivanmukti*, the seeker gains *videhamukti* (freedom from the body) when the physical body dies and merges back into *Brahman*.

Krishna reassures Arjuna that even if this wisdom is attained only at the end of life (*antakāle*), it leads to *brahmanirvāṇam*—"nirvana in Brahman"- final freedom from the cycle of birth and death, uniting the individual with the Absolute Reality.

Adi Śaṅkarācārya implores that while attaining a state of *brāhmī sthitiḥ* at the end of life leads to ultimate *nirvana* (liberation), gaining Self-knowledge at any stage of life enables one to live the human experience with clarity and inner peace. Thus, the Bhagavad Gita is best studied and internalized at an early age when the mind is still relatively unclogged and malleable.

This wisdom illuminates every choice, interaction, and action, empowering one to live steadfastly and joyfully amid life's changes. Harmonizing one's understanding of life with the truth of one's own Self as Brahman transforms each experience into an expression of this ultimate insight.

Brahma-Nirvāṇa and the Buddhist Vision of Liberation

The term *Brahma-Nirvāṇa* is notably used as a compound in the Bhagavad Gita, differentiating it from the Buddhist use of *nirvāṇa*. In Buddhist philosophy, *nirvāṇa* represents enlightenment and is considered the state of ultimate freedom from suffering. The *Dhammapada* describes *nirvāṇa* as the "highest happiness," a state free from desires and attachments. In this light, the Gita and Buddhist teachings share a common goal of ending suffering. However, the Bhagavad Gita offers a nuanced perspective by combining *Brahman* (the Absolute Reality) with *Nirvāṇa* (liberation), expressing liberation not as emptiness (*śūnya*) but as a positive realization of one's oneness with Brahman, the eternal foundation of all existence.

As we continue to study the Gita, the nature of Brahman and *Brahma-Nirvāṇa* will reveal itself in greater depth, enriching our understanding of the enlightened state Krishna invites us to pursue.

With this shloka, Krishna concludes his teaching on the *sthitaprajñā*— the one whose wisdom is unshakeable and whose peace is eternal. The final message of this chapter is timeless and universal: The state of *brāhmī sthitiḥ* is a rational, practical, and accessible goal for anyone willing to pursue self-knowledge. It invites us to explore and establish ourselves in this freedom, finding peace and wholeness in this very life.

By declaring that knowledge alone is the means to liberation, Krishna invites us to begin or deepen our own journey toward this inner freedom. The wisdom of the Bhagavad Gita is not merely to be studied but to be lived through every moment of our life. It inspires us to look beyond the ephemeral obvious and embrace the unchanging truth of who we are. If only we realized that ultimate freedom lies within our reach, patiently awaiting our discovery.

Reflective Prompt

How do you now view your current engagement with life, having completed Chapter II of the Bhagavad Gita? Are you fired up to deepen your understanding of the rest of what Krishna has to say?

Know thyself, for in the Self lies the infinite Brahman

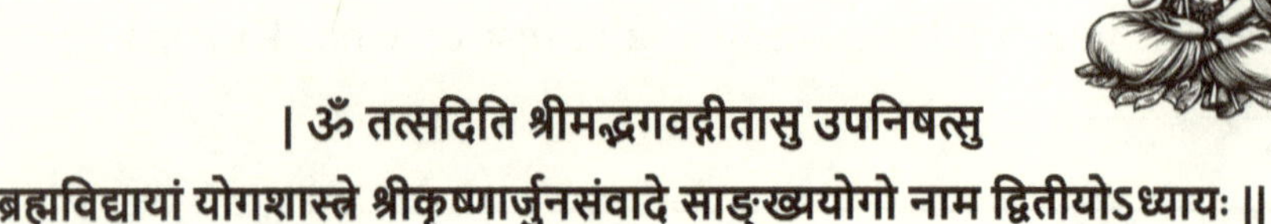

| ॐ तत्सदिति श्रीमद्भगवद्गीतासु उपनिषत्सु
ब्रह्मविद्यायां योगशास्त्रे श्रीकृष्णार्जुनसंवादे साङ्ख्ययोगो नाम द्वितीयोऽध्यायः ||

|| *ōṁ tatsaditi śrīmadbhagavadgītāsu upaniṣatsu
brahmavidyāyāṁ yōgaśāstrē śrīkṛṣṇārjunasaṁvādē sāṅkhyayōgō
nāma dvitīyō'dhyāyaḥ* ||

Translation:

Om, Brahman is the only Reality. Thus ends the second chapter, called 'Sankhya Yoga,' - the Yoga of Knowledge, in the Bhagavad Gita. A scared dialogue between Śrī Kṛṣṇa and Arjuna, rooted in the essence of the Upaniṣads, which imparts both *Brahmavidyā* (knowledge of Brahman) and *Yoga Śāstra* (the practices to attain it).

Shri Krishna Arpanam Astu

-Our humble offering at the altar of the Self-

Section III

Recap and Key Takeaways

KEY TEACHINGS AND LESSONS FROM CHAPTER II

In Chapter II of the Bhagavad Gita, Krishna takes Arjuna—and through him, all of humanity—on a profound inner pilgrimage toward Self-knowledge and purposeful action. Across 72 transformative shlokas, Krishna not only diagnoses the root of human suffering but also provides a comprehensive roadmap to transcend it. This chapter serves as a microcosm of the entire Gita, unveiling the highest goal of human life (*Moksha*) and equipping us with the practical tools to reach it.

With poetic brilliance, Krishna paints a vivid portrait of the *sthita-prajna*—the person of steady wisdom—offering both an inspiring ideal and a practical blueprint for living with clarity, resilience, and inner freedom. As we step into this *Recap and Key Takeaways* section, we aim to distill the timeless teachings of Chapter II, summarizing its profound wisdom and providing a clear guide for navigating the complexities of life with unwavering purpose.

The following table presents a structured overview of the chapter's key themes, offering a snapshot of its most essential lessons.

#	Topic	Shlokas	Focus
1	The Fundamental Human Problem	1–10	Arjuna's emotional turmoil and surrender to Krishna
2	Self-Knowledge (*Atma Jnana*)	11–25	Discovering 'Who Am I' (Jnana Yoga)
3	A Practical Approach to Life's Challenges	26–29	Accepting the inevitable while focusing on action

4	The Importance of *Svadharma*	30–33	Aligning actions with one's unique role (*Svadharma*)
5	Worldly Reasons for Performing Duty	34–37	The material and societal consequences of inaction
6	Karma Yoga: How to Act Wisely and Efficiently	38–53	The art of proper action with the right attitude
7	The Characteristics of the Wise (*Sthitha Prajna Lakshana*)	54–72	The qualities of a person of steady wisdom

Topic 1: The Fundamental Human Problem

The first ten shlokas of Chapter II use Arjuna's crisis on the battlefield as a powerful example of universal ineptitude to face life challenges with intellectual clarity and inner mastery. When advising others through their problems, we have all the knowledge handy. But in personal crises, our fears, attachments, and riotous emotions entirely overwhelm and incapacitate us.

In Chapter I, we resonate deeply with a common human frailty pictorially portrayed in Arjuna, who faces the daunting task of battling against his own family and mentors. While most of us are not caught in a literal war zone, we each have battles to fight—professional challenges, financial struggles, health issues, or relationships. On confronting the reality of fighting those he holds dear, the indomitable Arjuna is sabotaged by an intense inner conflict that brings him down to his knees in despondency.

His collapse highlights three core elements of the human dilemma, often referred to as *saṁsāra*: binding attachment (*rāgaḥ*), emotional overwhelm (*śōkaḥ*), and delusion (*mōhaḥ*).

Aspect of *Saṁsāra*	Definition	Arjuna's Experience	Modern Life Example
Binding Attachment *(Rāgaḥ)*	Clinging to people, situations, or outcomes, leading to dependency and vulnerability to suffering.	Arjuna's attachment to family and loved ones prevents him from fulfilling his duty.	Attachment to a career, relationship, or health outcome, leading to fear of loss and dependency.
Emotional Overwhelm *(Śōkaḥ)*	Intense fear or grief over the potential loss of what we hold dear.	Fear of the death of his loved ones paralyzes Arjuna.	Anxiety and stress when facing job insecurity, financial loss, or personal setbacks.
Delusion *(Mōhaḥ)*	Clouded judgment that makes it difficult to distinguish right from wrong.	Arjuna is confused about his duty as a warrior, caught between personal desires and moral responsibilities.	Struggling to make decisions or act properly under pressure, unsure of the best course of action.

Binding attachment to objects, beings, situations, or outcomes entangles us in a loop of dependency and expectation in a dynamic world constantly shifting and changing. This attachment triggers emotional overwhelm, as we fear the loss of what we hold dear, paralyzing our ability to think clearly and act effectively. Finally, delusion clouds our judgment, making it difficult to distinguish between right and wrong or balance personal desires with broader responsibilities. These forces create confusion and indecision, preventing us from facing life's challenges with inner strength and clarity. Arjuna's predicament is universal, reflecting our struggles to live a practical and efficient life.

At first, we watch Arjuna trying to resolve his inner turmoil himself. He expresses his reluctance to fight by belting out numerous rationales for why engaging in this battle would be wrong. Yet, instead of finding a resolution within his uninterrupted monologue of unending justifications, his conflict only intensifies, leaving him even more distressed. Krishna stands apart, silently witnessing Arjuna's struggle, patiently waiting for him to reach a crucial realization of his own helplessness—known as *kārpaṇya* - the sense of inadequacy.

In Shloka 2.7, Arjuna finally admits his inability to solve the problem and turns to Krishna for guidance. Recognizing that his mind, clouded by attachment and sorrow, cannot find a resolution, he surrenders. He says, "I am your disciple; please instruct me" (*śiṣyaste'ham śādhi mām tvām prapannam*), fully opening himself to Krishna's wisdom. This surrender is pivotal as Arjuna shifts from irrational self-reliance to a willingness to seek help and learn.

Centuries later, the same scenario persists. We often attempt to solve impossible problems ourselves, rarely acknowledging the deep-rooted attachments and fears that impede our ability to find a solution. We seldom seek wisdom or help outside of ourselves. Arjuna's shift in stance reminds us that meaningful transformation begins only when we become humble enough to ask for help, whether reaching out to a counselor, mentor, or trusted guide.

With Arjuna's surrender, Krishna, who was previously just his charioteer, now assumes the role of his teacher and guide. This transformation marks a profound shift—*Pārthasārathy*, the charioteer of Arjuna, becomes *Jagadguru*, the teacher of the world. Krishna's approach is calm and compassionate, symbolized by his demeanor as *prahasanniva*, "as though smiling." This expression reflects Krishna's mastery over the situation, his clarity, and his unwavering sense of inner peace. As the Gita unfolds, Krishna's teachings to Arjuna will resonate as timeless wisdom, offering guidance to all who seek peace and clarity amidst life's challenge

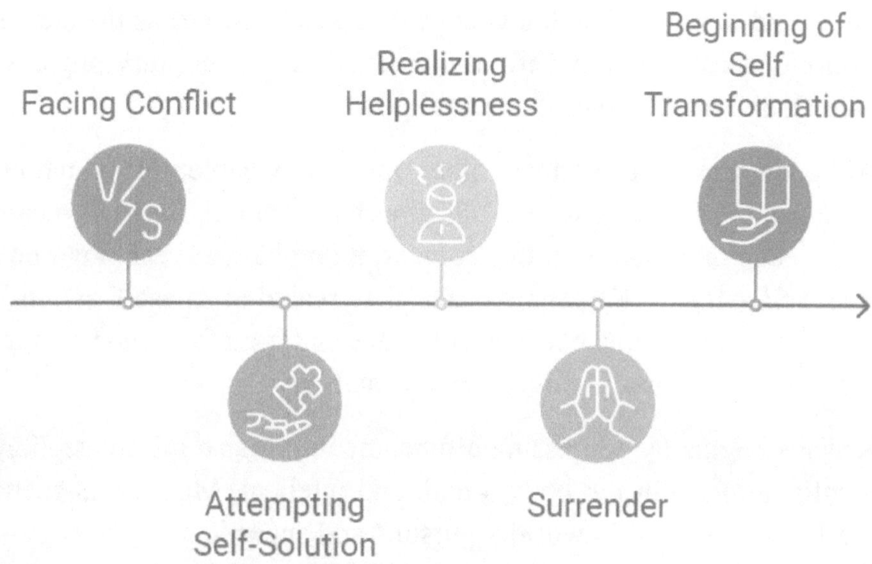

Fig: Arjuna's journey from conflict to surrender

In this way, the first ten shlokas use Arjuna's journey from conflict to surrender to illuminate the struggles of human life and the beginnings of a way out of them. This introductory session invites us to recognize our binding attachments, dependencies, and conflicts and exhorts us to surrender to higher wisdom, which is the fundamental step to overcoming them.

Topic 2: Discovering 'Who Am I' (*Jnana Yoga*)

The second topic of Chapter II (Shlokas 11–25) is one of the most challenging portions of the Bhagavad Gita to interpret and comprehend, especially for new students of the text. Many commentators and teachers worldwide take this as the actual starting point of the Gita. Interestingly, *Shankara Bhashya* - Adi Shankaracharya's commentary on the Bhagavad Gita also begins here. These foundational 13 shlokas introduce us to the profound knowledge of the Self (*Atma Jnana*), the cornerstone of the Bhagavad Gita. They unveil the ultimate truth of our existence, asserting that our true identity is beyond the body, mind, and intellect. The knowledge of the Self (*Atma*) as the eternal Consciousness is distinct from and beyond the temporary physical, mental, and intellectual constructs known to us.

Although covering various other themes, Chapter II is named *Sankhya Yoga*, owing to this all-important section. *Sankhya* means knowledge or wisdom; in this context, it emphasizes realizing one's true Self (*Atma*). Krishna assures that realizing oneself as *Atma* resolves all existential conflicts, liberates one from fear, and provides the foundation for a life of clarity and stability.

Krishna begins by addressing a fundamental human misconception: identification with the body, mind, and intellect. Most of us spend our lives immersed in worldly pursuits and superficial knowledge—studying everything but ourselves. This inextricable identification with the physical body leads to fears, particularly the fear of death and attachment to fleeting pleasures and possessions. Krishna dismantles these misunderstandings, teaching Arjuna to look beyond the temporary and recognize his eternal, unchanging Self (Consciousness).

- **The Body, Mind, and Intellect Are Instruments**: Krishna explains that the body, mind, and intellect are merely tools for interaction with the world, akin to temporary garments we wear and discard. Death is simply the shedding of one "garment," and birth is taking on another.
- **The Consciousness Beyond**: The true Self (*Atma*) is Consciousness (*Chit*), an awareness infusing but distinct from the body, mind, and intellect. This Consciousness is eternal, unchanging, and independent, untouched by the cycles of birth and death.

Essential Insights into Consciousness

Krishna systematically unveils four profound truths about *Atma* **(Consciousness)** in this section. These insights redefine how we view ourselves, providing a clear understanding of our eternal nature [3]:

1. Not a Part, Product, or Property of the Body

Consciousness is not a byproduct of the physical body or the brain. Modern science often suggests that consciousness arises from neurological processes, but Krishna declares this as a misconception. Consciousness is an independent entity—it is neither a part of the body, like an organ, nor a product of the body, like thoughts, nor a property of the body, like height or weight.

Example: A light bulb glows because of electricity, but the electricity itself is not part of the bulb or produced by the bulb. But, without it, the bulb cannot shine. Similarly, Consciousness enlivens the body but exists independently of it.

2. Enlivens the Body

Consciousness is the life-giving force that animates the body. Without it, the body is inert, like a lifeless machine without electricity. Consciousness pervades every body part, enabling perception, movement, and interaction with the world.

Example: When a light bulb is powered by electricity, it illuminates. In the same way, consciousness powers the body, making it functional and alive.

This insight helps us see that the body is merely a medium for Consciousness to express itself, not the source of life.

3. Not limited by the boundaries of the Body

Consciousness is not confined to the physical boundaries of the body. While it manifests through the body, it is universal and all-pervading.

Outside the body, Consciousness exists but is unmanifest—like light that is visible only when it strikes a surface.

Example: The sunlight falling on your hand is visible, but the same light between your hand and the sun is invisible to the eye. Similarly, Consciousness is evident in the living body but remains unmanifest outside it. This understanding reveals the all-pervasiveness of Consciousness, emphasizing that it transcends the limitations or the boundaries of the body.

4. Eternal and Unchanging

Consciousness is not affected by the body's birth, growth, change, decay, disease, or death. It remains constant and unchanging, existing before the body comes into being and continuing after it perishes. Unlike the body, mind, and intellect, which undergo all these inevitable modifications, Consciousness is immutable, indestructible, and eternal.

Example: Just as electricity exists independently of a light bulb—existing before the bulb was plugged into it, while the bulb was shining, and continuing after the bulb fuses—Consciousness endures before, through, and beyond the physical body. The bulb merely provides a temporary medium for electricity to manifest as light, much like the body is a temporary medium for Consciousness to express itself.

Understanding this truth dismantles the fear of death, revealing to us our identity as *Atma*—immortal and beyond the reach of time.

Insight	Explanation
Independent Existence	Consciousness is not a part, product, or property of the body or mind. It exists independently.
Source of Life	Consciousness pervades and animates the body, enabling it to function, much like electricity powers a machine.
Boundless and Universal	Consciousness is not confined to the boundaries of the body; it is infinite and all-pervading.

Timeless and Changeless	Consciousness remains constant and unaffected through all changes, existing before the body and continuing after its dissolution.

Table: Key Insights about Atma

The Six Indicators of the Nature of *Atma* (Consciousness)

One cannot know *Atma*—one can only become it. It goes beyond articulation and conception. Self-realized Masters down the ages used various pointers to enable seekers to meditate on its profundity. Knowledge moves from the known to the unknown. Therefore, words known to us were used to describe *Atma* to get us as close to its peripheries as possible.

Krishna provides six key pointers to familiarize us with the immensity of our true nature:

1. ***Atma* is Eternal (*Nityaḥ*):**

   Unlike the transient body, mind, and intellect - *Atma* is eternal. It neither comes into existence nor ceases to exist. It always is (Shloka 12).

2. ***Atma* is the Ultimate Reality (*Satyaḥ*):**

   The *Atma* is the foundational reality upon which everything else depends. While the body, mind, and intellect are temporary and dependent, the *Atma* exists independently (Shloka 16).

3. ***Atma* is All-Pervading (*Sarvagataḥ*):**

   Consciousness (*Atma*) is all-pervading, though it manifests through the body. Just as light exists beyond the object it illuminates, Consciousness exists beyond the body (Shloka 17).

4. ***Atma* is the Ever-Experiencer (*Apraméyaḥ*):**

The *Atma* is the eternal subject, never an object of experience. It cannot be perceived, measured, or objectified, as it is the one witnessing all experiences. Like a camera that captures everything but cannot photograph itself, the *Atma* illuminates all but cannot be illuminated by anything else (Shloka 18).

5. ***Atma* is Neither Doer nor Enjoyer (*Akartā-Abhōktā*):**

The *Atma* performs no actions and experiences no results. While actions and consequences belong to the body, mind, and intellect - the *Atma* remains unscathed, free from *karma* and its fruits (Shloka 19).

6. ***Atma* is Free from Modifications (*Nirvikāraḥ*):**

The *Atma* undergoes no changes or transformations. It is free from the six modifications of existence: potential existence, birth, growth, transformation, decay, and destruction (Shloka 20).

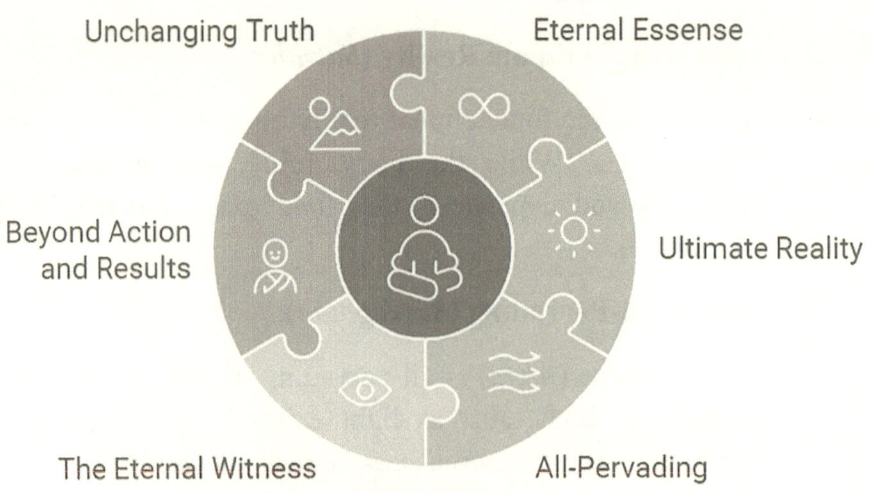

Fig: Six pointers revealing the nature of Atma

These insights, backed by consistent contemplation, slowly shift our perception from being finite, vulnerable beings to recognizing our boundless, eternal nature. Krishna urges us to move beyond the transient identity of the body, mind, and intellect and embrace our essence as the *Atma*—the eternal, unchanging witness of all experiences.

This realization forms the core of Self-Knowledge (*Atma Jnana*), liberating us from attachment, delusion, and fear. Krishna declares *Atma Jnana* the ultimate solution to the human condition—a permanent state of inner peace and freedom from the cycles of birth and death. Says Adi Shankaracharya in his Bhaja Govindam - '*nityanitya vivekavicaram*' - seeking this liberation through the discernment and contemplation of what is real (*nitya*) and unreal (*anitya*) and identifying with the real (*nitya*)- the Self (*Atma*) - is what is referred to as *Jnana Yoga* in the scriptures.

This transformative teaching lays the foundation for the rest of the Bhagavad Gita. It empowers us to navigate life's challenges with a deep awareness of our true identity and oneness with *Brahman*, the ultimate Reality. Krishna urges us to claim this truth and experience liberation—a state of eternal peace and freedom from the bondage of ignorance.

Topic 3: A Practical Approach to Life's Challenges

In the previous topic, Krishna provided profound insights into the true nature of the Self (*Atma*), revealing it as eternal, unchanging, and beyond the limitations of the body, mind, and intellect. This knowledge is the ultimate antidote to the fear of death, as it reveals that death is not the end of existence but merely a transition. However, Krishna recognizes that everyone cannot grasp the profundity of Self-knowledge at once. For those beginning their spiritual journey internalizing these truths may be challenging. Thus, Krishna employs a more practical approach, addressing Arjuna's emotional overwhelm with a logical, more relatable perspective.

The Central Teaching: Focus on What You Can Control

Krishna explains that life unfolds in two ways with:

1. **Things we can control** (our choices, actions, and attitudes).
2. **Things we cannot control** (birth, death, and life's inevitable changes).

He emphasizes that sorrow and worry over what is inevitable and beyond our control are futile. Instead, we must focus on what lies within our control and accept the rest with grace and equanimity.

"tasmādaparihāryē'rthē na tvam śōcitumarhasi" – "Therefore, for that which is unavoidable, you should not grieve." 2.27

Practical Lessons with Everyday Applications

1. Inevitability of Birth and Death

Krishna reminds Arjuna that just as birth is a certainty for the living, death is inevitable for the dying. This cycle is beyond human control, and grieving over it is as illogical as lamenting the setting sun when by the laws of nature it will rise again.

Example: Consider aging. Worrying about growing older or resisting the passage of time does not stop it from happening. A wise person focuses instead on living well in the present moment, making meaningful contributions, and accepting the natural flow of life.

2. Channeling Effort Where It Matters

Worrying about the uncontrollable diverts energy from what can be done. Krishna advises focusing on action and duty, aligning efforts with one's responsibilities rather than being paralyzed by anxiety over outcomes beyond control.

Example: We may encounter layoffs or market downturns in a professional setting. While we cannot change external economic conditions, we can channel our energy constructively by developing our skills further, networking, or seeking new opportunities.

How to effectively manage life's challenges?

Fig: Practical approach to life challenges

In this topic, Krishna reminds us of an understanding we already have through observation but cannot accept or employ when a crisis hits: the body and its experiences are transient. Resurrecting and firmly rooting ourselves in this understanding assures us that emotional overwhelm serves no purpose. The attitude of accepting change and impermanence with courage and composure becomes the rational and effective response - and our second nature.

This topic of Chapter II is a practical guide to navigating life's challenges. Krishna's argument encourages us to focus on what lies within our control—our choices, attitudes, and actions—while letting go of anxiety over the inevitable and unchangeable. By internalizing this teaching, we can approach life's uncertainties with peace, clarity, and resilience, transforming even the most difficult circumstances into opportunities for learning and growth.

Through these powerful shlokas, Krishna provides a timeless framework for living a balanced, purposeful life rooted in acceptance and mindful action.

Topic 4: The Importance of Svadharma

In the previous topics, Krishna clearly explained an individual's true identity as *Atma*—eternal and unchanging—while highlighting the futility of worrying over inevitable aspects of life, such as the mortality of the body. He urged Arjuna to focus on what can be controlled while gracefully accepting what cannot. Building on this foundation, Krishna now shifts to the practical application of this wisdom: the importance of performing our *Svadharma*—aligning our intrinsic qualities with our responsibilities.

Krishna underscores actions disconnected from intrinsic qualities lead to dissatisfaction, inner turmoil, and unproductive outcomes. Conversely, employing our natural strengths to fulfill our responsibilities is to live by *Svadharma* - empowering ourselves to thrive and contribute meaningfully to society.

This lesson extends far beyond Arjuna's battlefield. In modern life, Krishna's insights invite us to reflect on our true nature and inner calling, ensuring our actions are in harmony with who we are at our core. Whether in personal relationships, professional endeavors, or societal roles, living in alignment with *Svadharma* brings a sense of clarity, purpose, and resilience in the face of challenges.

Krishna's message is clear: embracing *Svadharma* is not merely a duty but a path to unleashing one's inner potential, fostering authentic self-expression, and achieving inner peace and material fulfillment.

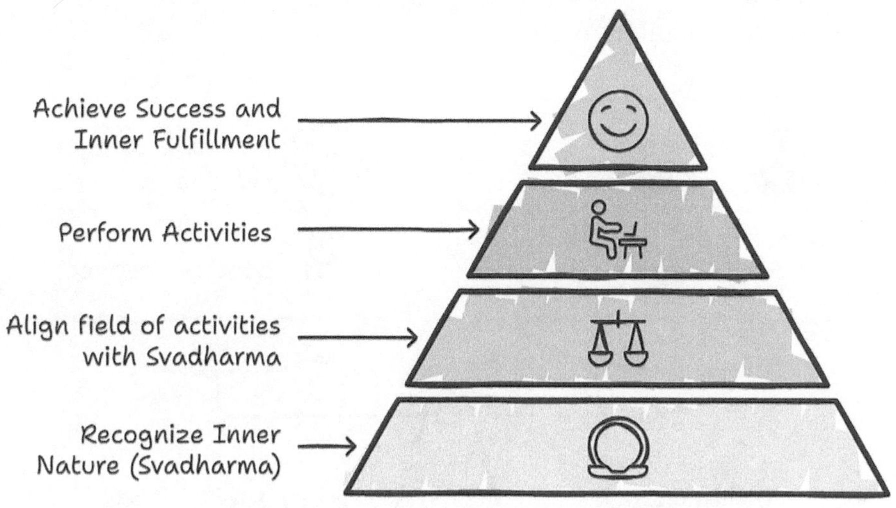

Fig: Importance of aligning with Svadharma

Topic 5: Worldly Reasons for Performing Duty

After emphasizing the importance of fulfilling one's duty for inner harmony and aligning with *Svadharma* (shlokas 31–33), Krishna shifts to a more worldly perspective in Shlokas 34–37. He underscores the significant impact of one's actions—or inactions—on reputation, social standing, and personal dignity. For Arjuna, a revered warrior, abandoning the righteous battle would not only bring dishonor but tarnish his legacy and invite ridicule from peers and enemies alike. Krishna reminds Arjuna that disgrace is often more unbearable than death for someone honored throughout their life. This teaching crosses the boundaries of the battlefield to become wholly applicable to the challenges of modern life. Whether in professional, personal, or social settings, neglecting one's responsibilities can lead to a loss of trust, credibility, and respect, which are far more painful than the difficulties of fulfilling one's duties. "The guilty conscience," as is often said, pricks to no end creating a life of enduring misery. By rising to meet our challenges, we uphold our integrity and maintain the confidence of those around us, paving the way for personal growth and societal harmony.

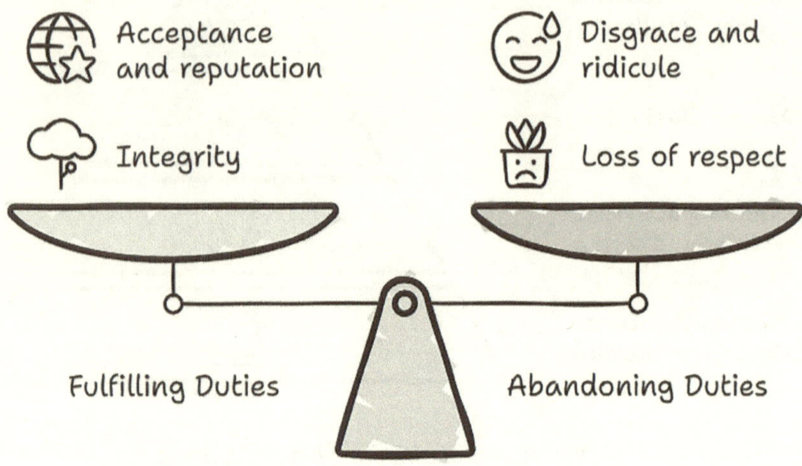

Fig: Importance of performing duties

Topic 6: Karma Yoga: How to Act Wisely and Efficiently

In this section, Krishna introduces the revolutionary vision of Karma Yoga, a groundbreaking approach to life that elevates ordinary actions into profound spiritual practices. Karma Yoga teaches us *what* to do and *how* to do it, ensuring that our actions are both efficient and spiritually meaningful. The art of performing "proper work" with "the proper attitude" enables us to choose actions wisely, execute them skillfully, and manage the stress and mental strain associated with them effectively. Through Karma Yoga, Krishna provides a practical framework for living purposefully while cultivating inner growth and harmony.

Proper Action: Guided by *Dharma*

The first step of Karma Yoga is selecting appropriate actions, known as *proper work*. These actions must align with *Dharma*—

universal ethical principles—and should not harm others. Krishna emphasizes that our actions should not only serve personal goals but also contribute to the well-being of others. This balance between self-interest and collective good ensures that our work is meaningful and beneficial. In Shloka 50, Krishna refers to the ability to choose such actions as the true skill of Yoga. By aligning our work with *Dharma*, we transform mundane tasks into purposeful endeavors, laying the groundwork for a life of fulfillment and contribution.

Proper Attitude: The Heart of Karma Yoga

Equally important is the *proper attitude* with which actions are performed. Krishna encourages approaching every grand or menial task with love, sincerity, and wholeheartedness. When we learn to enjoy what we do, even the most routine actions become opportunities for learning and growth. This transformation is achieved by adopting two essential attitudes:

1. ***Ishvara Arpanam*** (*offering to the Ishvara or Higher Purpose*): Viewing every action as an offering to a higher power /purpose imbues it with a sense of sacredness.

2. ***Prasada Bhavana*** (*accepting the result as divine grace*): Receiving the outcomes of our actions, whether favorable or not, with equanimity and gratitude.

These attitudes help us stay focused on the quality of our effort rather than being consumed by attachment to results. As Krishna highlights in Shloka 48, *Yoga is Samatvam*—a state of even-mindedness that transforms ordinary karma into Karma Yoga.

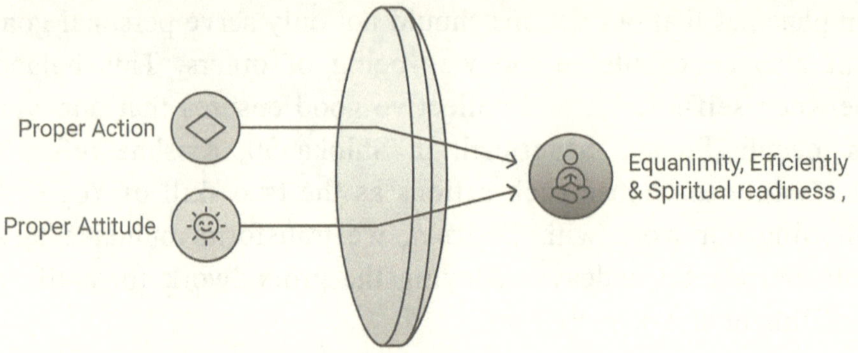

Fig: Karma Yoga: Transforming Action into Spiritual Practice

The Transformative Power of Karma Yoga

Karma Yoga is not a direct path to liberation (*moksha*) but prepares the practitioner for higher spiritual pursuits. By cultivating discipline, clarity, and focus, it enables one to develop the mental composure and focus necessary for Jnana Yoga—the quest for Self-knowledge. Through Karma Yoga, we refine our ability to navigate life's challenges with grace and efficiency, achieving not only worldly success but also spiritual readiness.

In essence, Karma Yoga is a practical approach that bridges the gap between spiritual ideals and everyday life. It teaches us to act with purpose, integrity, and devotion, turning every encountered moment into an opportunity for growth. By following this path, we align our actions with our inner nature and the universal order, creating a life of meaning, fulfillment, and inner peace.

Topic 7: The Characteristics of the Wise (*Sthitha Prajna Lakshana*)

In the concluding section of Chapter II, Krishna describes the characteristics of a *Sthitha Prajna*, a person of steady wisdom who has fully assimilated the knowledge of the *Atma* (the true Self) and transformed intellectual understanding into an unshakable emotional strength. A *Sthitha Prajna* is not merely knowledgeable but unwaveringly lives this wisdom amidst life's challenges. This section explores both the disciplines required to cultivate this state and the profound transformation it brings.

Cultivating Steady Wisdom: Path to Becoming a *Sthitha Prajna*

Krishna outlines three essential disciplines (*sādhanā*) to convert intellectual knowledge into practical, emotional strength:

1. **Sense Mastery (*Indriya Nigrahaḥ*):**

   - The mind is constantly influenced by what enters through the senses. Without regulation, the senses allow distractions and negativity to overwhelm us.
   - Sense mastery is not about suppression but about channeling and regulating sensory inputs. This discipline enables a calm and focused mind, which is critical for absorbing and living Vedantic teachings.

2. **Mind Mastery (*Mano Nigrahaḥ*):**

   - While we cannot control the speed or nature of thought flow, we can decide which thoughts to entertain and perpetuate. Krishna emphasizes letting go of harmful or unnecessary thoughts and nurturing those conducive to inner peace and wisdom.
   - Practical tip: Do not feel guilty about intrusive thoughts; focus instead on consciously redirecting your attention to constructive ideas.

3. **Contemplation on Teachings (*Nidhidhyāsanam*):**

   - Regularly dwelling on the teachings of the Bhagavad Gita reinforces wisdom. This can involve reading a few shlokas daily or regularly listening to discourses, reflecting on insights, or sharing knowledge with others – best through your own example of living the wisdom.

- Repeated engagement ensures deep assimilation and integration of teachings into daily life.

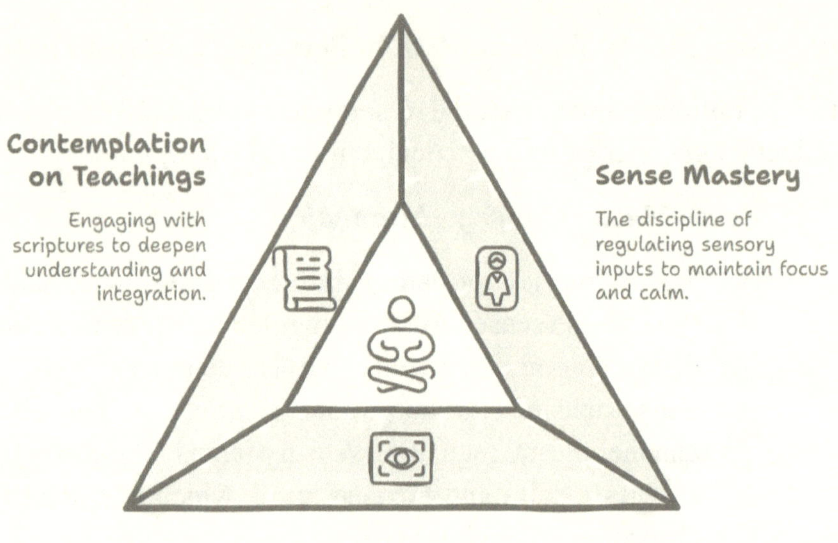

Fig: Path to Becoming a Sthitha Prajna

Transformation of a *Sthitha Prajna*:

Two key markers that render the assimilated wisdom of the *Sthitha Prajna* self-evident are:

4. **Freedom from Binding Desires (*Pūrṇatvam*):**

A *Sthitha Prajna* experiences self-sufficiency and inner completeness. This fulfillment annihilates all *binding desires* that create dependency and emotional turmoil. Non-binding desires, if any, are harmless preferences that do not disturb their equanimity, regardless of whether they are fulfilled.

5. **Equanimity (*Samatvam*):**

The steady wisdom of a *Sthitha Prajna* brings unwavering mental tranquility. They remain undisturbed by the highs and lows of life, free from emotions such as fear, anger, and jealousy. Krishna compares this equanimity to the ocean, which remains full and steady regardless of whether rivers flow into it or not.

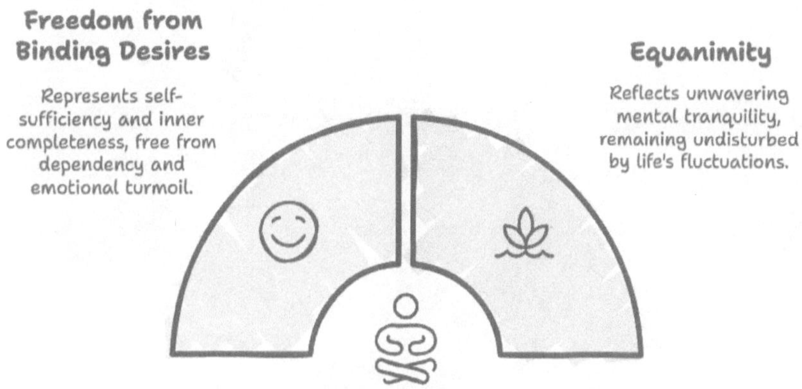

Fig: Two defining traits of Sthitha Prajna

Krishna concludes this section by describing the ultimate freedom a *Sthitha Prajna enjoys*. Such a person experiences liberation (*jivanmuktiḥ*) while living and remains free (*videhamuktiḥ*) after the body perishes. Their established wisdom enables them to navigate life without conflict and embrace the ultimate peace of liberation in life and beyond.

Modern Relevance

The vision of a *Sthitha Prajna* is not just a philosophical concept but a practical guide for modern living. It represents a state of unshakable inner stability and emotional resilience that can help individuals manage stress, uncertainty, and challenges in a balanced way. By cultivating sense mastery, regulating thoughts, and consistently reflecting on higher truths, we, too, can aspire to embody the steady wisdom that leads to material fulfillment and inner peace. This section offers timeless guidance on living a meaningful and harmonious life rooted in Self-awareness and firm resolve.

Key Shlokas for Reflection

With its timeless wisdom, the Bhagavad Gita is a step-by-step manual for personal evolution and a source of solace, inspiration, and motivation amidst life's complexities. Many towering personalities down the centuries have sought comfort and guidance in its teachings during times of need. We have quoted some of their thoughts about the grandeur of this life-transforming text in our book *First Step Into Bhagavad Gita*.

Although all 701 verses of this scripture carry crucial life lessons, certain key shlokas from each chapter stand apart more strongly to instantaneously rein in overwhelming moments of joy and despair. Even if you take up a daily study practice of the Bhagavad Gita, particularly pausing to reflect upon the profound teachings within these highlighted shlokas and attempting to weave them into your everyday experiences will infuse your spiritual quest with tremendous clarity and strength. This continues to be the author trio's personal experience.

The most impactful shlokas from Chapter II - *Sankhya Yoga* - to contemplate and cherish:

1. Shloka 7: Recognition of Helplessness and Surrender

kārpaṇyadōṣōpahatasvabhāvaḥ
pṛcchāmi tvāṁ dharmasammūḍhacētāḥ |
yacchrēyaḥ syānniścitaṁ brūhi tanmē
śiṣyastē'haṁ śādhi māṁ tvāṁ prapannam || 7||

This shloka marks Arjuna's moment of surrender as he acknowledges his helplessness and seeks Krishna's guidance, opening the door to transformative wisdom. It reminds us of the indispensable value of seeking guidance during moments of confusion, paving the way for clarity and growth.

2. Shloka 11: Life's Challenges Don't Demand Endless Worry

śrī bhagavān uvāca -
asōcyānanvaśōcastvaṁ prajñāvādāṁśca bhāṣasē |
gatāsūnagatāsūṁśca nānuśōcanti paṇḍitāḥ ||11||

This shloka marks the beginning of Krishna's life-transforming discourse. It emphasizes that enduring grief is unnecessary, as life's progression is inevitable, irreversible, and unstoppable. The wise travel this passage with a higher spiritual perspective and composure.

3. Shloka 12: We transcend birth and death; our essence is eternal

na tvēvāhaṁ jātu nāsaṁ na tvaṁ nēmē janādhipāḥ |
na caiva na bhaviṣyāmaḥ sarvē vayamataḥ param ||12||

This shloka reveals that our true identity is the *Atma*, an eternal Consciousness that exists beyond the confines of the body, mind, and intellect, unbound by birth or death. Recognizing this eternal truth frees us from fear of mortality and binding attachment to the physical world and fosters a more profound sense of purpose and peace.

4. Shloka 14: Mastering Life's Waves

mātrāsparśāstu kauntēya śītōṣṇasukhaduḥkhadāḥ |
āgamāpāyinō 'nityāḥ tāṁstitikṣasva bhārata ||14||

Our interactions with the world bring varied experiences - pleasant and unpleasant. Learning to endure these calmly is the hallmark of intelligent living. It helps us maintain the necessary balance and resilience to navigate life's highs and lows with fortitude and grace.

This shloka concludes with one of the most uplifting lines of the Bhagavad Gita: '*tāṁstitikṣasva bhārata.*' It has been the author trio's experience that repeating this phrase with devotion in troubled times injects the frail human spirit with renewal and strength to face squarely whatever challenge it confronts.

5. Shloka 16: Infinite Within: Unlocking Your True Potential

nāsatō vidyatē bhāvaḥ nābhāvō vidyatē sataḥ |
ubhayōrapi dṛṣṭō'ntaḥ tvanayōstattvadarśibhiḥ ||16||

Atma, our true identity, is the foundational Reality of the universe (*Brahman*), all-pervading and eternal. Recognizing this truth unerringly points us toward the Upanishadic fact, *Tat Tvam Asi*—Thou art That, as we, too, are a part of the universe. It directly aligns us with the Infinite. A clear understanding of our oneness with the universal Reality frees us from the limitations of the body, mind, and intellect - unleashing a life of fearlessness, peace, and success.

6. Shloka 27: Control What You Can, Accept What You Can't

jātasya hi dhruvō mṛtyuḥ dhruvaṁ janma mṛtasya ca |
tasmādaparihāryē'rthē na tvaṁ śōcitumarhasi ||27||

What is born must die, and what dies will be born again—accepting this inevitable fact of life's cyclical nature frees us from unnecessary worry and redirects our focus to what we can control. This acceptance fosters the necessary clarity and inner peace to shift our focus from resisting the inevitable to living a life of purpose.

7. Shloka 31: Living Your True Nature

svadharmamapi cāvēkṣya na vikampitumarhasi |
dharmyāddhi yuddhācchrēyō'nyat kṣatriyasya na vidyatē ||31||

We each possess an intrinsic nature and unique tendencies, known as *Svadharma*, which reflect our core competencies and personality. Living in alignment with *Svadharma* ensures mental peace and peak performance, but ignoring it can lead to inner conflict and inefficiency. Aligning our choices and actions with our *Svadharma* empowers us to effortlessly fulfill our unique purpose with great finesse in ways that contribute to the collective good.

8. Shloka 47: Mastery in Action

karmaṇyēvādhikārastē mā phalēṣu kadācana |
mā karmaphalahēturbhūḥ mā tē saṅgō 'stvakarmaṇi ||47||

We have control only over our actions—to choose them with diligence and execute them to the best of our ability—but not over their results. This does not mean we resort to inaction, either. Act we must. But, by focusing on effort rather than outcomes, we free ourselves from anxiety and perform our best in the present.

9. Shloka 48: Graceful Balance is Yoga

yōgasthaḥ kuru karmāṇi saṅgaṁ tyaktvā dhanañjaya |
siddhyasiddhyōḥ samō bhūtvā samatvaṁ yōga ucyatē ||48||

In this shloka, yoga is defined as equanimity, maintaining a balanced mindset toward the results of actions and life situations. This perspective fosters inner stability, enabling us to navigate successes and challenges with clarity, peace, and resilience.

This shloka, too, concludes with another uplifting phrase that can be pinned on the wall for instant pacification: *samatvaṁ yōga ucyatē.* If you ever feel overwhelmed by any situation, repeated recitation of this one line with devotion begins to slowly but surely rebalance the emotions. Try it.

10. Shloka 50: Yoga is the art of skillful action

buddhiyuktō jahātīha ubhē sukṛtaduṣkṛtē |
tasmādyōgāya yujyasva yōgaḥ karmasu kauśalam ||50||

In this shloka, yoga is defined as the art of skillful action—choosing the right action from various possibilities and executing it with focus and excellence. This mastery transforms ordinary tasks into opportunities for learning, growth, and success.

11. Shloka 55: Happiness Within

prajahāti yadā kāmān sarvānpārtha manōgatān |
ātmanyēvātmanā tuṣṭaḥ sthitaprajñastadōcyatē ||55||

A person of steady wisdom (*Sthitha Prajna*) derives happiness and contentment from within, independent of external circumstances. This inner connection to an infinite source of joy ensures lasting fulfillment. This absolute self-sufficiency empowers us to remain unshaken and peaceful through incessant onslaughts of changes and uncertainties.

12. Shloka 55: Liberation Through Self-Knowledge

ēṣā brāhmī sthitiḥ pārtha naināṁ prāpya vimuhyati |
sthitvā'syāmantakālē'pi brahmanirvāṇamṛcchati ||72||

The ultimate purpose of human life is realizing and experiencing our true identity as *Atma* (Consciousness). Once achieved, one does not regress into ignorance again. Mastering this knowledge of Self while alive grants inner peace, clarity, and a deep sense of purpose that transcends worldly challenges. Being established in the knowledge of Self, even in the last moments of one's life, assures liberation from the cycles of birth and death.

Although these are the more widely quoted shlokas from Chapter II, we encourage you to pick the shlokas that resonate with you the most from the 72 we have studied together. The journey through the Gita is very personal, and its teachings unfold differently for each seeker. While a particular shloka might be the need of the hour for one – it may not be for another. Rest assured there is something of transformative value for everyone who approaches the Bhagavad Gita with reverence and devotion.

Universal Relevance of Chapter II

Chapter II of the Bhagavad Gita endures as a timeless guide for navigating the complexities of human life, transcending cultural, temporal, and geographical boundaries. Its teachings are not confined to the battlefield of Kurukshetra or limited to a particular era—they resonate universally with every seeker striving for clarity, purpose, and inner peace in an ever-changing world.

At its core, Chapter II addresses a fundamental human question: *Why do we suffer despite having skills, knowledge, and resources?* Through Arjuna's emotional turmoil, Krishna unveils the root cause of human distress—*misidentification with the temporary and attachment to fleeting outcomes.* This insight remains profoundly relevant today, where anxiety, burnout, and dissatisfaction persist despite material abundance and technological advancements.

By distinguishing between the eternal and transient, Krishna urges us *not to settle for transient pleasures or material gains but to strive for Moksha—the ultimate goal of life.* This higher goal does not reject worldly pursuits but integrates them into a larger, more meaningful purpose. **Why settle for less when we are capable of so much more?** This question serves as the foundation of Krishna's teaching.

To initiate our journey toward attaining this goal, Krishna introduces two transformative paths: **Karma Yoga** (the art of acting with detachment and dedication) and **Jnana Yoga** (the wisdom of realizing one's true identity as *Atma*). These two paths are not separate but complementary forming a masterful template for a holistic life marked by clarity, inner stability, and purpose. *Karma Yoga* teaches us to act efficiently, with focus and without attachment, while *Jnana Yoga* reveals our true, unchanging identity as the eternal Self.

The teachings of Chapter II are universally applicable. Whether one is a *leader making impactful decisions, a student shaping their future, or an individual balancing family and career responsibilities.* The message is clear: ***Engage dynamically in the world with focus and resilience but remain inwardly anchored in peace and wisdom.***

Ultimately, *Chapter II is not merely a spiritual doctrine—it is a life manual.* It urges us to rise above reactive living and move toward *conscious, responsible, and purposeful action.* It teaches us to embrace our responsibilities without being consumed by outcomes and to discover an enduring sense of completeness within ourselves.

The chapter serves as both a *mirror reflecting our current state of being* and a *map guiding us toward our highest potential.* Its wisdom assures us an abundant life blessed with material success, *contentment, and a more enduring inner peace.*

Key Takeaways in Bite-Size

#	Takeaway	Description
1	Understanding the Human Problem	Arjuna's emotional turmoil reflects the universal human struggle—attachment, emotional overwhelm, and confusion—that prevents clarity and purposeful action. Transformation begins with humility and surrender to higher wisdom.
2	The Power of Self-Knowledge (*Atma Jnana*)	True identity lies beyond the body and mind. *Atma* (Consciousness) is eternal, unchanging, and limitless. Realizing this truth brings freedom from fear, sorrow, and existential anxiety.
3	Focus on What You Can Control	Worrying about the inevitable wastes energy. Wisdom lies in focusing on what we can control—our actions, choices, and attitudes—and accepting the rest with grace.
4	Embracing *Svadharma* (One's Unique Duty)	Living in alignment with one's intrinsic nature (*Svadharma*) ensures clarity, fulfillment, and resilience in the face of challenges. It's about performing our role with dedication and integrity.
5	The Importance of Responsibility and Reputation	Neglecting responsibilities leads to long-term consequences, including loss of credibility and inner regret. Fulfilling duties preserves dignity and societal trust.

6	The Art of Work	Karma Yoga teaches us to act with dedication, detachment, and equanimity. Offering our actions to a higher purpose transforms work into a path of inner growth.
7	Proper Action and Attitude in Karma Yoga	Actions aligned with dharma (righteousness) and performed with the attitudes of *Ishvara Arpanam* (offering to the divine) and *Prasada Bhavana* (accepting results gracefully) create harmony and peace.
8	Wisdom and Steady Mind (*Sthitha Prajna*)	A person of steady wisdom remains unshaken by life's highs and lows, free from emotional turbulence and firmly anchored in self-awareness.
9	The Ocean Analogy: Inner Fullness	Like the ocean remains full despite rivers flowing in, a wise person remains content and steady, unaffected by desires and external outcomes.
10	Freedom from 'I' and 'Mine'	True peace arises when we transcend ego and possessiveness, recognizing the transient nature of ownership and finding fulfillment within.
11	Integration of Karma Yoga and Jnana Yoga	Karma Yoga (skillful action) and Jnana Yoga (self-knowledge) complement each other, creating a holistic path to material success and spiritual freedom.
12	Living with Purpose and Inner Stability	The wisdom of Chapter II is not abstract philosophy but a practical guide to living a meaningful, resilient, and fulfilling life in today's world.

Conclusion

The second chapter of the Bhagavad Gita offers a profound and holistic vision of life, seamlessly integrating the ultimate goal of

Self-realization through *Jnana Yoga* with the practical discipline of *Karma Yoga* as its preparatory foundation. *Karma Yoga* equips us to act with purpose, dedication, and detachment, laying the groundwork for inner clarity and emotional resilience. *Jnana Yoga*, in turn, reveals our true identity as *Atma*—the eternal, unchanging Consciousness—liberating us from fear, sorrow, and existential conflict.

As we journey further in the *Gita Odyssey* series, each subsequent chapter will serve as a deeper exploration of the timeless insights introduced here. Together, we will continue to unravel Krishna's teachings, illuminating their relevance to our modern lives and offering a roadmap for inner peace, purposeful action, and lasting fulfillment

Closing Remarks

REFLECTING THE JOURNEY

As we pause to reflect on this transformative journey through *Chapter II* of the *Bhagavad Gita*, we are filled with a deep sense of reverence, humility, and joy. What began as an earnest effort to share insights from this sacred text became, for us, an intense personal expedition—one that deepened our understanding far beyond our expectations.

Over the course of this year-long endeavor, we have learned more about the *Gita* and ourselves than in the past two decades of study. Every verse we explored, every commentary we contemplated, revealed new layers of meaning, offering us moments of quiet introspection and profound clarity. Yet, we remain aware that the journey is far from complete. The wisdom of the *Gita* is an infinite ocean, and we are but humble seekers, drawing what little we can from its boundless depths.

We extend our heartfelt thanks to Poojya Swami Swaroopananda, Global Head of Chinmaya Mission, for graciously penning the foreword to this book. His inspiring words and guidance have added immense value to our endeavor and serve as a source of inspiration for all seekers journeying through the Gita

This book is not merely an academic or philosophical presentation but a heartfelt attempt to guide fellow seekers in logically approaching the *Gita's* teachings while staying rooted in the wisdom of traditional commentaries. We sought to blend reason with reverence, analysis with surrender, and scholarship with experiential insight.

We bow in gratitude to *Bhagavan Krishna*, whose timeless wisdom continues to illuminate countless lives, including ours. This opportunity to reflect, study, and share His teachings has been an immense privilege—one for which we are eternally thankful.

May this our humble offering guide every reader toward clarity, purpose, and inner peace.

DEDICATIONS FROM ATHOR TRIO

ॐ

Tvam-Eva Maata Ca Pita Tvam-Eva |
Tvam-Eva Bandhush-Ca Sakha Tvam-Eva |
Tvam-Eva Vidya Dravinnam Tvam-Eva |
Tvam-Eva Sarvam Mama Deva Deva ||
O' Krishna!
Right through this mammoth endeavor (and through my entire life)
In the guise of Srimad Bhagavad Gita
You have been the purity of my intent and the strength behind my effort
You have been my confidante and motivation
You have been the well-spring of my wisdom and creativity
You have been the uninterrupted Grace
Providing all necessary physical, emotional, and Spiritual sustenance
You have, indeed, been my every-all.

I am deeply grateful to Dr. Vikrant Singh Tomar, whose serendipitous appearance in my life, right after my life-changing *JYOTIRLINGA MAHAKAAL* darshan in the ancient *Avanti Nagari* (City of Ujjain) India, led me to Project Self. His support in this work has been immense.

And an outpouring of gratitude to Rajesh Rabindranath, whose lifelong study of various scriptural texts, a solid grounding in the original commentary of Adi Shankaracharya's *Shankara Bhashya,* and brilliant hold of the Sanskrit language was not just a foundation but the very bedrock of the otherwise impossible task of commentating in any right on Chapter II of the Bhagavad Gita. His contributions have been invaluable, and his influence, immeasurable.

My heartfelt prayer at the altar of the Self: May the transformative wisdom of the Bhagavad Gita illuminate, inspire, and empower every seeker's material and spiritual journey as it has mine.

Avanti Kundalia

Namaste,

As I stand at the completion of this second book in the *Gita Odyssey* series, my heart overflows with gratitude and reverence. The opportunity to immerse myself in the timeless wisdom of the *Bhagavad Gita* and share its transformative teachings has been one of the greatest blessings of my life. This journey is not just an intellectual pursuit but a deeply spiritual experience—one that has shaped me in ways beyond words. At the heart of this offering lies my dedication to *Ishvara*, the Supreme Reality, and the luminous lineage of teachers who have preserved and shared this wisdom across generations.

My gratitude to ***Adi Shankaracharya*** and ***Shri Narayana Guru*** for providing us with an unshakable foundation and teaching framework in *Advaita Vedanta*, which has profoundly helped me understand the message of the *Gita*.

My deepest reverence also goes to ***Swami Chinmayananda***, ***Swami Dayananda***, ***Swami Ranganathananda***, ***Swami Tadatmananda***, ***Swami Paramarthananda***, and ***Swami Sarvapriyananda***—each of whom has illuminated my understanding and deepened my connection with the *Gita*. I also extend my gratitude to ***Acharya Vivek*** for being a guiding light, offering inspiration, and reminding us of the practical relevance of this timeless wisdom in our daily lives.

I extend my heartfelt thanks to my ***Project Self*** **family**, whose unwavering support and tireless contributions have made this endeavor possible. To ***Avanti Kundalia,*** your dedication, hard work, and passion have been instrumental in bringing this book to life, and I am deeply grateful for your commitment to this vision. A special note of gratitude to ***Dr. Vijay Reddy, Sanjay Rajput, Vinod Varapravan*** **and** ***Jeena Suresh*** for being a constant support system throughout the creation of this book—your encouragement and presence have been invaluable. To all my mentors, friends, supporters, and well-wishers, thank you for walking alongside me on this sacred journey.

A special note of gratitude to our generous sponsors—*Ratnakar Reddy* for sponsoring all upcoming books in the *Gita Odyssey* series, ***Satyapal*** and ***Kavitha Reddy*** for sponsoring the *Ramayana* book series, and ***Rohit Mehta*** and ***Kiran K. Nair*** for sponsoring recordings and a set of books to be gifted and shared with seekers far and wide. Your contributions are deeply appreciated and ensure that this timeless wisdom reaches many more hearts and minds.

I extend my sincere gratitude to **Shri Dutta Peetham** for graciously allowing us to use the **Sanskrit version of the shlokas**, adding authenticity and depth to this offering. My heartfelt thanks to ***Shri Kavalam Srikumar*** ji for soulfully chanting the verses, creating a divine auditory experience that beautifully complements this book. A special thank you to my dear friend ***K.I. Alexander*** for composing and singing inspiring songs that enrich the essence of this work. Lastly, my deep appreciation goes to ***Sreya Sajan*** for her creative brilliance in **designing the cover** of this book, capturing its spirit with elegance and thoughtfulness

Finally, to my family—***Deepthy*** and ***Daksha***. You are the light and love of my life. ***Deepthy*, every moment of my existence is shaped by your boundless love, strength, and support**. You are the foundation of all that I do, and every word I write carries your imprint. ***Daksha*, you are God's most precious gift to me—a radiant source of joy and inspiration**. I am immensely proud of your growing interest in *Gita* and *Vedanta*, and it fills my heart with gratitude to see these timeless teachings taking root in your life. **This book is lovingly dedicated to you, *my dearest girl*.**

To my ***parents***, thank you for raising me with deep cultural values and a connection to our spiritual heritage. Your support have shaped the person I am today. To my *sister, uncles, aunties,* and *cousins*, thank you for being there for me with your unwavering love, encouragement, and warmth, creating a foundation of belonging and support.

My heartfelt gratitude also goes to my God-given siblings, **Dr. Vikrant Singh Tomar** and **Avneet Baid**, whose love, kindness, and encouragement continue to enrich my life and deepen my resolve. Together, all of you are my sanctuary, my strength, and my greatest blessing

May this offering serve as a humble contribution to the timeless wisdom of the Bhagavad Gita and inspire all seekers to walk this sacred path with courage, clarity, and love.

Blessings and gratitude,

Rajesh

I dedicate this book to my wife, ***Dr. Shweta Tomar***, whose unwavering commitment to managing our home single-handedly allowed me to focus on social and spiritual endeavors. **Her silent sacrifices and boundless support have been my greatest inspiration**.

With deepest gratitude, I honor the Guru Parampara, through which this ancient wisdom has descended to us. I also extend heartfelt thanks to the seen and unseen forces that made this work possible.

I acknowledge my brother, Shri ***Rajesh Rabindranath*** Ji, for being the guiding light and foundation of this endeavor, and Ms. ***Avanti Kundalia***, for her invaluable contribution as a co-author throughout this journey.

I humbly bow before all the known and unknown divine forces that have facilitated our journey in bringing this work to fruition.

With you in Consciousness,

Dr. Vikrant Singh Tomar

CONTINUING THE ODYSSEY

This in-depth exploration of *Chapter II* of the *Bhagavad Gita* was intended to lay a solid foundation, by introducing some profound insights into Self-knowledge (*Jnana Yoga*) and the art of wise action (*Karma Yoga*). As we travel further in the **Gita Odyssey** series, *Chapter III* will dive deeper into the transformative teachings of *Karma Yoga*—the path of selfless action performed with wisdom, detachment, and dedication.

In *Chapter III*, Krishna elaborates on *how* our ordinary daily actions transform into the means and methods of worldly fulfillment and spiritual evolution when infused with the right attitude. This chapter addresses one of life's greatest dilemmas: How can one live fully engaged in the world without getting entangled in it? Krishna's timeless wisdom shows us how to act for a higher purpose with clarity and efficiency.

Our next offering wading through Chapter III of the Bhagavad Gita will reveal how the principles of *Karma Yoga* can be seamlessly integrated into personal relationships, professional goals, or the spiritual quest. Our tried-and-tested insights into these revolutionary teachings promise to illuminate a path of resilience, balance, and fulfillment as they have ours.

Stay with us as we journey on through this transformative **Gita Odyssey** where the wisdom of *Karma Yoga* awaits to inspire, empower, and uplift every seeker.

|| Om Shanti Shanti Shanti ||

Author Bios

Avanti Kundalia

 Avanti Kundalia is a Vedanta teacher based in Singapore. Through ongoing intensive research and rigorous experimentation, she has dedicated her life to validating the efficacy of Vedantic teachings in daily life. A mother of two, Avanti currently runs several Bhagavad Gita classes globally with a keen focus on one-on-one Spiritual coaching that guarantees dramatic inner transformations. Her insightful writings on Vedanta and beautiful translations of spiritual texts in English are well-loved by seekers of Truth. A true patriot of Bharat, Avanti has been championing the cause of Sanatan Dharma traditions across the globe, especially with householders. She presented her thoughts on the practicality of the Bhagavad Gita at the 2023 *Vasudhaiva Kutumbakam* C-20 Summit in Chennai, India; and was also a panelist speaking on Hindu Vision of Womanhood at the World Hindu Congress 2023 in Bangkok, Thailand. As Coordinator for International Events for The English-Speaking Union India, she has represented India to promote the vision of international peace and understanding through the medium of English language in St Petersburg -Russia, Paris, UK, And Cleveland -USA. Amongst other books, Avanti has co-authored the introductory book of the Gita Odyssey Series – *First Step Into Bhagavad Gita.*

Rajesh Rabindranath

Rajesh Rabindranath is a multifaceted technology and management professional who seamlessly integrates his expertise in modern innovations, especially Artificial Intelligence, with a deep passion for Vedantic teachings. Residing in New Jersey, USA, Rajesh actively shares the timeless wisdom of the Bhagavad Gita through regular classes and diverse forums, including corporate settings and interfaith gatherings. As a co-founder and dedicated volunteer of the nonprofit organization Project Self, he is committed to fostering spiritual awareness. Rajesh is also the co-author of the first book in the Gita Odyssey series, 'The First Step into Bhagavad Gita,' which has been well-received for its insightful approach to this ancient text. In his personal life, Rajesh embodies the balance between worldly responsibilities and spiritual pursuits, cherishing time spent with his wife, Deepthy, and daughter, Daksha

Dr. Vikrant Singh Tomar

 Dr. Vikrant Singh Tomar is an internationally recognized scholar, writer, and management consultant. He has been nominated by Civil 20 (under G-20) as the 'International Coordinator' for the "Vasudhaiva Kutumbakam" initiative, aiming to propagate this philosophy among G-20 nations. His contributions have been acknowledged globally, including an address at the United Nations Headquarters in Geneva on the International Day of Conscience. In June 2023, Dr. Tomar served as the Global Convener for the World Yoga Summit in Germany. He is also the 'International Coordinator' for the Global Conference on "The Holistic Yoga Beyond Physiology-2023" in Germany, as nominated by the Indian Council of Cultural Relations (MEA,Government of India). His work has impacted over 300,000 beneficiaries across 120 countries, including cabinet ministers, bureaucrats, defense and paramilitary personnel, corporate professionals, and prison inmates.

APPENDIX

<u>Supporting Team</u>

Project Self Team

Avneet Baid, Deepthy Nair, Gokul Kallambunathil, Jeena Suresh, Karthik Palamalai, Madhurika Arvind, Muthuvelan Swaminathan, Dr. Prasad Akavoor, Rajesh Menon, Sanjay Rajput, Sunil Veettil, Suresh Kadavath and Dr. Vijay Reddy

Gita Insight Squad

Bhuvana Iyer (Guidance), Ramurti Shrivastava (Poetry), Kavalam Srikumar (Chanting), K.I Alexander (Music), Muktha Sathe (Music), Sreya Sajan (Painting) and Pradeep Krishnan (Malayalam Translation)

Supporters

Ratnakar Reddy, Satyapal Reddy, Kavitha Reddy, Rohit & Bharati Metha, Kiran Kumar Nair, United Consciousness, Avadhoota Datta Peetham, Bhakti Manjari Group, and Sadhaka Music Foundation

<u>Contact Information</u>

Project Self: https://pself.org: Contact: Info@pself.org

Gita Odyssey: https:Gitaodyssey.org: Contact: Info@pself.org

United Consciousness: https://unitedconsciousness.in/, Contact: info@ unitedconsciousness.in

REFERENCES

Ranganathananda, Swami. (2023). The Universal Message of the Bhagavad Gita: An Exposition. Bharatiya Vidya Bhavan.

Saraswati, Swami Dayananda. Bhagavad Gita - Volume 2 (Bhagavad Gita Series (English)) Arsha Vidya Research and Publication Trust. Kindle Edition.

Saraswati, Swami Paramarthananda. Bhagavad Gita Lecture Series. Audio recording. Sastraparakashika Trust, 2002

Chinmayananda, Swami. The Holy Geeta). Central Chinmaya Mission Trust. Kindle Edition

Saraswati, Swami Dayananda. Introduction to Vedanta. Vision Books Pvt. Ltd., New Delhi, India, 2014. ISBN 81-7094-289-6.

Swami Abhedananda. (2023). The Gospel of Ramakrishna. Abhedananda Publishing House

Yogananda, Paramahamsa. (2021). God Talks with Arjuna: The Bhagavad Gita [Ebook]. Self-Realization Fellowship

Nataraja Guru, S. (2022). The Bhagavad Gita: Sublime Dialectics. Orient Blackswan Private Limited

Arsha Bodha Center. (2011). Gita 2011. Retrieved from https://arshabodha.org/teachings/gita-2011/

Vedanta USA Podcast of Swami Sarvapriyananda. (n.d.). Retrieved from Spoitify

Arsha Bodha Center. (n.d.). Teachings. Retrieved from https://arshabodha.org/teachings/

Parthasarathy, R. (2023). The Bhagavad Gita [Ebook]. Penguin Books India.

Burke, A. G. (Swami Nirmalananda Giri). (2018, November 27). The Bhagavad Gita for awakening: A practical commentary for leading a successful spiritual life (Dharma for Awakening Collection). Kindle Edition

Easwaran, E. (2008). Bhagavad Gita for daily living (12th printing, 3 vols.). Blue Mountain Center of Meditation

Pillai, C. K. S. (n.d.). Srimad Bhagavad Gita: The Quintessential essence of the Upanishads- A modern vision (Vol. 1) (p. 507). Kindle Edition

Teachings of Swami Dayananda. (2023). [Mobile app]. Apple App Store. https://apps.apple.com/us/app/teachings-of-swami-dayananda/id807400667

Atmopadesa satakam". advaita-vedanta.co.uk. Archived from the original on 14 August 2014

Seligman, M. E. P. (2002). *Authentic Happiness: Using the New Positive Psychology to Realize Your Potential for Lasting Fulfillment*. New York: Free Press.

Csikszentmihalyi, M. (1990). *Flow: The Psychology of Optimal Experience*. New York: Harper & Row.

Clear, J. (2018). *Atomic Habits: An Easy & Proven Way to Build Good Habits & Break Bad Ones*. New York: Aver

Goleman, D. (1995). *Emotional Intelligence: Why It Can Matter More Than IQ*. New York: Bantam Books.

Goleman, D. (2013). *Focus: The Hidden Driver of Excellence*. New York: HarperCollins.